*To Martin Menez, Michael Menez, Mary Menez Kearns,
and her husband Michael Kearns*

Summaries of
Leading Cases
on the
Constitution

Summaries of
Leading Cases
on the
Constitution

Paul C. Bartholomew
Professor of Government
University of Notre Dame

Joseph F. Menez
Professor Emeritus of Political Science
Ball State Universtiy

Thirteenth Edition

Littlefield Adams Quality Paperbacks

LITTLEFIELD, ADAMS QUALITY PAPERBACKS

a division of Rowman & Littlefield Publishers, Inc.
8705 Bollman Place, Savage, Maryland 20763

Copyright © 1990 by Rowman & Littlefield Publishers, Inc.

British Cataloging in Publication Information Available

Thirteenth edition. Previous editions were
published as a Littlefield, Adams Quality Paperback.

Library of Congress Cataloging-in-Publication Data

Menez, Joseph Francis, 1917–
Summaries of leading cases on the Constitution / Joseph F. Menez.
— 13th ed.
p.   cm.
Rev. ed. of: Summaries of leading cases on the Constitution / by
Paul C. Bartholomew and Joseph F. Menez. 12th ed. 1983.
1. United States—Constitutional law—Digests.   I. Bartholomew,
Paul Charles, 1907– Summaries of leading cases on the
Constitution.   II. Title.
KF4547.8.B3   1990   342.73'00264—dc20
[347.3020264]   90–35358 CIP

ISBN 0–8226–3008–7

5   4   3   2   1

Printed in the United States of America

CONTENTS

Contracts *102*

The Presidency *112*

War and the Military *131*

**Religion   *341*

**Taxing/Spending Regulatory Powers   *364*

PREFACE

The purpose of this volume makes readily available in convenient form the gist of the major decisions of the United States Supreme Court since its establishment. No previous book has done just that. The briefs are complete for the student, teacher, or casual reader who wishes to know only the basic points of a case. For the person who wishes to go beyond that, a listing of leading correlative cases has been appended to each case covered.

This thirteenth edition of the *Summaries* covers the Supreme Court through the 1988–1989 term and differs from its predecessor in that some twenty-five cases have been dropped and some twenty-five new ones added. The corollary cases have been updated and expanded. In addition, the cases have been grouped in chapter headings so as to be easily adaptable to current constitutional texts. One can immediately see from the full table of contents under what topic a leading case is to be found. The table of contents together with the alphabetized listing of cases should make it easy for the reader to find the material sought. Material found in the "Note" has been reviewed and in some instances expanded. Much of Paul Bartholomew's style and thinking remains in *Leading Cases* and will continue to do so.

As in the previous edition a number of persons were most helpful with time, knowledge, and encouragement. Herbert Hamilton, Professor Emeritus of Constitutional Law, Ball State University and a member of the Delaware County Bar, Muncie, Indiana, prepared the legal glossary and foreign phrases. A keen student of constitutional law, he often stimulated me to see *Leading Cases* in a new and fresh light. Richard A. Matre, professor of History and provost for the Medical Center, Loyola University, Chicago, a knowledgeable student of constitutional history and a long-time Court watcher, was gracious with his time. Several former students familiar with the previous edition helped immeasurably and focused my attention on ways to improve the text. Jim Crody, a former student assistant and also a former "con law" student was helpful with suggestions. Kimberly Achleman unscrambled handwriting and transformed it into readable type. She was always gracious despite the work load. Terence Laux, an outstanding student in constitutional law was meticulous in reading cases and in making suggestions. He was most helpful in assembling the entire manuscript. He plans to go to law school and, I am sure, will make a fine lawyer.

I especially want to thank Mr. Roger F. Jacobs of the library of the Supreme Court of the United States for his generous information on the work of the Court. On the one hand, he helped me to no end with precise information and, on the other, saved me from one or two inaccuracies.

Dr. Sally Jo Vasicko, chair of the Department of Political Science, extended me numerous courtesies. I want to thank her not only for these "helps" but for always being ready and generous in putting at my disposal her wide knowledge of constitutional law. Sharon Hinkley, secretary of the political science office and the office assistant, Stephanie Thomas, were always obliging and willing to help in the smallest matter so that this revision could continue uninterrupted. I sincerely thank them both for their kindnesses.

I want to thank Mr. and Mrs. Robert Knoerzer, friends of Supreme Court Justice and Mrs. Paul Stevens, for acquiring from the justice an autographed copy of the twelfth edition.

An expert of the political branches of the government, Dr. John Cranor, Department of Political Science of Ball State University, was of considerable help. More than once, he cleared a point involving the political branches that saved me from error. I want to thank Helen Hudson of Lanham, Maryland, for her generous advice and counsel. Mary Simmons, my editor at Rowman and Littlefield, improved the manuscript with criticisms and suggestions.

My wife, Charlene Knoerzer Menez helped me in a number of ways during this recasting. Notwithstanding an adequately furnished study, she generously allowed me to utilize the dining room table with "important" papers.

First as a reader-advisor in the early editions of *Leading Cases* and then following Dr. Bartholomew's death in 1975, the twelfth edition carried our joint names although I was its sole author. Within the last fifteen years, however, *Leading Cases* became a new book. This thirteenth edition is considerably larger than its predecessors, dozens and dozens of old cases have been replaced by more current ones, the numerous "notes" have been updated, expanded, and linked to cases and other notes, and new sections added that have made *Leading Cases* a worthy successor to the previous editions.

Needless to say, not all my colleagues or readers agree with my selection of cases, my notes or my essay, This Is Your Supreme Court. However, they all had valuable comments to make. I am, of course, solely responsible for errors and mistakes.

THIS IS YOUR SUPREME COURT

"We are under the Constitution," said Chief Justice Charles E. Hughes "but the Constitution is what the judges say it is." The chief justice was stretching a point, of course, because as Alexander Hamilton noted in The Federalist, the Court has neither the purse nor the sword but only judgment. A good deal of its power depends on congressional grants, it must convince the executive to enforce its decisions, and when it lags or outstrips public opinion it finds little support. The people have demonstrated with whom ultimate power rests for on four separate occasions the Constitution has been amended to "recall" a previous Supreme Court opinion! Judicial activists would like to push the Court forward in an ever widening circle of cases but as Justice John Marshall Harlan wrote: "The Constitution is not a panacea for every blot upon the public welfare."

Of the three branches, the Court is easily the most prestigious and most traditional. Alexis de Tocqueville, the very perceptive Frenchman who came to this country and in 1835 published his magisterial, *Democracy in America* noted:

> If I were asked where I place the American aristocracy, I should reply without hesitation . . . that it occupies the judicial bench and bar. . . . Scarcely any political question arises in the United States that is not resolved, sooner or later, into a judicial question.

Unlike the presidency and Congress, the "political branches," the Supreme Court is barely visible. Its proceedings are not televised, the justices do not hold press conferences or appear on television, they avoid the Washington social scene, and rarely, no matter how unpopular their decisions, do they engage in public debate. And yet, this does not mean that the Supreme Court is not in the center of issues. The reverse is true. As Justice Oliver Wendell Holmes once wrote: "We are very quiet there, but it is the quiet of a storm center."

1

Created under Article Three of the Constitution, the Supreme Court is co-equal to and independent of the "political branches." There are nine members of the Court, a number set by statute in 1869. All the members are male and white except Thurgood Marshall who is black and Sandra Day O'Connor who is female. Although the members are lawyers and several formerly were judges, the Constitution, unlike in the case for the presidency and the Congress, lays down no qualifications. Without exception, however, the justices have been active in public life. "This is a select company," said Chief Justice Warren Burger, "not because we are all-knowing, but because we were selected and we are here." It was the belief of Justice Louis D. Brandeis that "the reason the public thinks so much of the justices is that they are the only people who do their own work." Chief Justice Earl Warren typified that hard work. "I thought my attendance record was pretty good," he said, "because I missed only one day in sixteen years. . . ."

There is a good deal of journalistic scorekeeping and the justices are often defined as "liberal," "conservative," or "centrist," or as belonging to this or that "bloc" or "camp." But neither the justices themselves nor careful Court watchers see the membership so neatly categorized. There is a certain amount of unconscious yielding on lesser matters but no real sacrifice of principle. There are no "blocs" in the sense of a number of persons who act in concert or as a unit. Even when one may guess how a justice might vote on the closest issues, said Justice Lewis F. Powell, "advance predictions are hazardous, even for those who serve together. Still should a vacancy occur on the Court or a resignation appear imminent—as with the resignations of Chief Justice Burger (1986) or Justice Lewis Powell (1987), then there is indeed much talk of "qualifications."

For the term ending July 1988, the Court handed down 175 cases of which 164 were decided by signed opinions and ten decided by percuriam opinions—opinions by the Court which expresses its decision in the case but whose author is not identified. This, of course, is the public work of the Court. In its private work, it disposed over 5,268 cases! Since the Constitution provides for only one Supreme Court and precludes the Court from separating into panels, chambers, or sections, moreover, every justice passes on each case. The Court neither contains nor encourages the specialist; what the Court seeks and gets is the generalist. But justices are fiercely individualist and independent and thus individualist opinions now predominate over institutional opinions for the Court. During all the years Chief Justice Warren was on the Court, he tried hard to see that everyone had an equal load and "that we weren't all writing in one field where one person would be considered the expert." At an average each justice writes about fourteen to eighteen decisions yearly.

Completed in 1935, the four story Supreme Court building, measuring nearly 400 by 300 feet, is located east of the Capitol which it faces across a wide plaza. The doors to the main entrance are sliding leaves of bronze, each weighing six and one-half tons. Eight relief panels trace the growth of law from ancient Greece and Rome to the young United States. Finished at a cost of $9,000,000, it is an imposing marble edifice dedicated to preserving the union as one of laws and not of men. Exhibiting twenty-four massive columns and containing marble from Spain, the courtroom was deliberately made small— it measures 82 by 91 feet with a coffered ceiling 44 feet high— so that the audience would not have an impact upon the judicial proceedings. Chief Justice William Rehnquist, once asked if justices were able to insulate themselves from public opinion replied: "No, and it would probably be unwise to try. We read newspapers and magazines, we watch news and television, we talk to our friends about current events. No judge worthy of his salt would even cast his vote in a particular case simply because he thought the majority of the public wanted him to vote that way."

In addition to the section set off for the bar and the raised area where the nine justices sit, are the benches made available for the general public. Of the 300 seats, 112 are allotted to the press, the justices' families, and members of the bar. The remaining 188 seats are available to the public on a first-come-first-serve basis. On days in which very important cases are being argued, some seats in the public area are rotated every three minutes to accommodate the tourists. Close to the Court benches, there are special areas: the press are seated in red benches on the left side of the courtroom, the red benches on the right are for guests, the black chairs in front of the benches are for officers of the Court, or distinguished dignitaries. There is even a seat for the president if he desires to visit the Court. It might be mentioned that the Court does not permit any writing, whispering, sketching, taping, or photographing. By statute a "term" begins in October and by custom ends the following July for "vacation." When not in Washington, petitions follow the justices even in diplomatic pouches. On very rare occasions there is a special sitting of the Court, when it can extend its term, as in the Pentagon Papers case (1971) and the Nixon Tapes ruling (1974), and reassembles, as in the case of the Nazi saboteurs (1942) and the Rosenberg treason trial of 1953. In all, there have been only four such instances in this century. The Court is in session two weeks and in recess for two weeks. When the Court is "on" it hears oral arguments; when it is "off" it is deciding petitions, researching cases, and writing opinions. Six justices must participate in each decision and cases are decided by a majority. In the event of a tie vote, the decision of the lower court is sustained although the case may be reargued.

Exactly at 10:00 A.M. Monday through Wednesday, the Court pages part the beautiful drapes allowing the justices, who have previously met and shaken hands all around, to enter the courtroom. In speaking to or about one another the justices use "Brother" or "My Brother." The clerk cries out:

> Oyez, oyez, oyez! All persons having business before the honorable, the Supreme Court of the United States, are admonished to draw near and give their attention, for the Court is now sitting. God save the United States and this honorable Court.

The Court hears two cases before noon and, following an hour's recess, it hears two cases until it adjourns at three. Punctuality is the rule for the Court and for its litigants. The advocate's time—one half hour—is monitored by the Court Marshal. When the white light flashes at the advocate's lectern, there are five minutes left. On the red light the chief justice, promptly but firmly, says "Thank you, ... The case is submitted." Once when Ex-President Grover Cleveland addressed the Court, he looked up at the clock and remarked that, despite the closing time, he would take only a couple of minutes to complete his argument. Melville Fuller, who had been appointed chief justice by Cleveland, remarked with great courtesy: "Mr. Cleveland, we will hear you tomorrow." On another occasion, Chief Justice Charles E. Hughes when asked how much time was left, responded: "14 seconds." Solicitor Stanley Reed who subsequently became a justice once fainted before the Court.

Unlike the days of the Court "Greats,"—Webster, Clay, and Calhoun—when arguing a case before the Supreme Court was a "happening" that brought out in attendance Washington's social set, what counts today is merit, not reputation. In case of great public import, the one-hour-per case limit has been increased as in the three hours for *United States versus Nixon* (1974) and two hours for *Bowsher versus Synar* (1986). The scant one-half hour provided the advocate is frequently dissipated by questions from the bench. The "Felix Problem"—called after Justice Felix Frankfurter who consumed a good deal of an advocate's allotted time—treated counsels as students taking an examination. The Court looks with disfavor on any oral argument that is read from a prepared text and requires an advocate to answer any question that is asked. Once when a lawyer said he was coming to a point, Justice James McReynolds snapped: "You're there already!" Recently, Justice Thurgood Marshall told a lawyer who did return to his question to forget it, he was not interested anymore.

The most frequent lawyer before the Court is the solicitor general of the United States. His principal function is to decide what cases the government will or will not appeal. He is often called the ninth-and-a-half member because he has an advantage that an attorney appearing less often does not possess. He not only argues on behalf of the government, he also decides which cases to bring to the Court, and which to appeal. The solicitor general, to illustrate the extent of his visibility, participates in about half of the Court's entire docket and perhaps two-thirds of all argued cases. Robert Jackson, a former solicitor general, relates that he made three arguments in every case:

> First came the one that I planned—as I thought, logical, coherent, complete. Second was the one actually presented—interrupted, incoherent, disjointed, disappointing. The third was the utterly devastating argument that I thought of after going to bed that night.

However hazardous and traumatic the exchange between the justices and the advocate, it can be significant as Chief Justice

Charles E. Hughes once commented: "I suppose . . . that the impressions that a judge has at the close of a full oral argument accords with the convictions which control his final vote."

When the Court is in recess studying appeals, petitions, and writing opinions, conferences are held on Wednesday afternoons and all day Friday. The justices are called to conference by a buzzer that rings in the several chambers five minutes before the hour. The oak-paneled conference room is lined with books containing lower and Supreme Court opinions. There is a portrait of the fourth and greatest chief justice, John Marshall. Each justice's chair is different and bears a name plate. Justices are seated according to seniority. The main law library of some 300,000 books and a staff of twenty serve the justices. Each justice has an agenda of the cases to be discussed and, in addition, a movable cart containing all the materials he might need in discussion.

There are no clerks, stenographers, pages, or even a tape recorder visible. There is absolute secrecy and confidentiality. If it is necessary to get material outside the conference chamber or answer the door, the most recently appointed justice acts as a "doorkeeper." Justice Kennedy will be the "doorkeeper" until a new justice is appointed.

Justice Tom Clark was the junior justice for five years and he was fond of relating that he "was the highest paid doorkeeper in the world." So rarely is the conference disturbed that Chief Justice Earl Warren reports that during the sixteen years he was chief justice the conference telephone never rang once!

Chief Justice William H. Rehnquist opens a session by giving the judicial history of the case and putting the precise question before the justices. Beginning with the most senior, William Brennan, down to the most junior justice, Anthony M. Kennedy, the justices "report." There is no time limitation, the order is never altered, nor is the speaker interrupted. When all the justices have been heard there is more informal and sometimes heated discussion as to points raised and positions taken. If the chief justice perceives that nothing more can be said on the issue, he will call for a vote. Thus, although the chief justice's office carries scant inherent power, he does have tactical advantages: he opens the issue and in so doing sets the tone of the discussion and the direction and he casts a "swing vote" that could determine the result in case of a tie.

If the chief justice votes with the majority, he has still another advantage. He can write the opinion himself or assign it to someone else. This gives him a special opportunity for leadership. Assignments are not made at the conference but formally in writing several days later. If the decision is considered a "landmark" one, the chief justice is expected to write it himself and thus throw the weight of the Court behind it. He might assign the opinion to the justice whose position is closest to his own on the issue. Or the chief justice might recognize the "realities of external politics" and select a justice whose views will carry more weight.

Almost every chief justice has assigned a "conservative" opinion to a "liberal" judge, as when Justice Hugo Black wrote the opinion for the famous Japanese internment case, *Korematsu v. United States,* and a "liberal" opinion to a "conservative" judge, as when Justice Tom Clark was assigned *Abington School District v. Schempp,* which dealt with the separation of church and state.

Writing an opinion is laborious as well as artful, Rufus Choat once observed: "You cannot drop the Greek alphabet and pick up the Iliad." At this point a legal battle is likely to occur all over again if one or more of the majority justices disputes the terminology, the content, the style or the structure of the decision. It occasionally happens that the judge who wrote the opinion will not backtrack on his style or statements—what Justice Holmes called "pulling out all the plums and leaving all the dough"—and thus makes it necessary for his supporters to write concurring opinions, that is, opinions that agree with the result but not with the reasoning of a holding. In a memo to Justice Felix Frankfurter, Justice Harlan Stone wrote: "If you wish to write, placing the case on the ground which I think tenable and desirable, I shall cheerfully join you. If not, I will add a few observations myself."

The political effect of concurring opinions, however, is to weaken the majority opinion. Not only is the force and singleness of the majority opinion lost, but its message can be scattered by dicta, that is, interesting but extraneous material. The use of individual opinions now predominates over institutional opinions for the Court.

It is not unknown for a justice, moreover, to write a dozen drafts of an opinion, circulate them for approval and then see them disintegrate.

As Justice Lewis Powell put it: "The drafting of an opinion is a process, not an event. . . . What really dismays a justice is to circulate a draft opinion, and receive no word at all except perhaps a cryptic note or two saying: 'I will wait circulation of the dissent.' " There are a few cases, moreover, in which the majority opinion was changed into a minority opinion as a consequence of a powerful dissent. On the basis of such a dissent, Chief Justice William H. Taft wrote his colleagues: "I think we made a mistake in this case," and wrote a new and contrary opinion which carried the Court.

Although the dissent is an appeal to what Chief Justice Charles E. Hughes called "the brooding spirit of the law, to the intelligence of a future day," still, it is not the controlling law. It attempts to undermine the Court's reasoning and discredit its results. Justice Robert Jackson noted that a dissent was a confession of a "failure to convince the writer's colleagues, and the true test of a judge is his influence in leading, not in opposing, his court."

When the majority and minority opinions are ready, they are printed in the Supreme Court's special, high-security printing room. Copies for distribution by the Public Information Office are made available to the public. Camera ready copies of the "Bench Opinions" are sent to the Government Printing Office (GPO).

In the city where even serious leaks are almost a daily occurrence, it is the glory of the Court's personnel that advance knowledge of an opinion is rarely known. The final opinions, being public knowledge, go across town to the Government Printing Office and are first issued as "advance sheets" (small-size paperbacks) and later as bound volumes.

There is no particular pattern for delivering oral opinions. At one time—from 1867 to 1965—opinions were always "reserved" for Monday, jocularly called judgment day. Chief Justice Warren Burger altered this practice largely to avoid or reduce weekend pressures and high overtime payments to the Court's printers.

The reading of opinions can take different forms depending upon the length, the number of concurring and dissenting opinions, or the importance of a case. There is no prior announcement as to when the cases will be handed down. Each justice selects the style he likes. Some justices read the Court's prepared "syllabus" or digest that precedes the full opinion, some outline the decision themselves sticking close to the text, and still others might simply indicate their vote and refer the listener to the text.

As the justices read the opinions, the ever present pages circulate printed copies to distinguished visitors in the foreground of the Court. Meanwhile, a phone rings in the Information Office and printed copies are released to newspaper reporters gathered there. The case is finished. The justices have judged. New constitutional issues will absorb their energies for as the great Chief Justice John Marshall declared: "We must never forget that it is a Constitution we are expounding."

LEADING CASES OF THE COURT

DUE PROCESS

Calder v. Bull, 3 Dallas 386; 1 L. Ed. 648 (1798)

A dispute arose between Calder and his wife on one side and Bull and his wife on the other side concerning a right to property left by N. Morrison, a physician, in his will of March 1793. The said will was rejected by the Probate Court of Hartford, and the decision was given in favor of Calder and his wife. As a result of a law enacted in 1795 by the state legislature, a new hearing of the case (which was not allowed according to the old law) took place, and the will involved in this case was approved, thus transferring the right of the property from Calder to Bull.

OPINION BY MR. JUSTICE CHASE
(No evidence from the report that the decision was not unanimous.)

Question—Was this statute of Connecticut an ex post facto law?

Decision—No.

Reason—Mr. Justice Chase defined ex post facto laws as contained in the prohibition of the Constitution as:

1. Every law that makes criminal an action done before the passing of the law and which was innocent when done, and punishes such an action.

2. Every law that aggravates a crime, or makes it greater than it was, when committed.

3. Every law that changes punishment, and inflicts a greater punishment, than the law annexed to the crime when committed.

4. Every law that alters the legal rules of evidence, and receives less or different testimony than the law required at

11

the time of the commission of the offense, in order to convict the offender.

Thus a distinction must be made between retrospective laws and ex post facto laws. Likewise, ex post facto laws do not affect contracts, but only criminal or penal statutes.

Corollary cases

Thompson v. Utah, 170 U.S. 343 (1898)
Malloy v. South Carolina, 237 U.S. 180 (1915)
Thompson v. Missouri, 171 U.S. 380 (1898)
Cummings v. Missouri, 4 Wallace 277 (1867)
Ross v. Oregon, 227 U.S. 150 (1913)
Weaver v. Graham, 76 L. Ed. 2d 17 (1981)
Dobert v. Florida, 53 L. Ed. 2d 344 (1977)

*Quotations from the "Reason" in the following cases are taken from the Holding of each case cited.

Davidson v. New Orleans, 96 U.S. 97, 24 L. Ed. 616 (1878)

The city of New Orleans sought to make an assessment on certain real estate within the parishes of Carroll and Orleans for the purpose of draining the swamp lands there. Included in the assessment was part of the estate of John Davidson, which was assessed for $50,000. The city brought suit to collect.

OPINION BY MR. JUSTICE MILLER
(No evidence from the report that the decision was not unanimous.)

Question—Is Mrs. Davidson being deprived of her property without due process of law?

Decision—No.

Reason—"Due process of the law" according to unanimous interpretation of the Court does not necessarily imply a regular proceeding in a court of justice, or after the manner of such courts. The "due process" clause is not to be looked upon as giving a blanket protection for anyone wishing to test the decision of a state court of justice against him. "That whenever by the laws of a State, or by state authority, a tax assessment, servitude, or other burden is imposed upon property for the public use, whether it be for the whole state or of some more limited portion of the community, and those laws provide for a mode of confirming or contesting the charge thus imposed, in the ordinary courts of justice, with such notice to the person, or such proceeding in regard to the property as is appropriate to the nature of the case, the judgment in such proceedings cannot be said to deprive the owner of his property without due process of law, however obnoxious it may be to other objections.''

Whenever a state takes property for public use, and state laws provide a mode for contesting the charge in the ordinary courts, and if due notice is given to the person, and if there is a full and fair hearing, there is no cause for a suit charging lack of "due process" of the law.

Corollary cases

Murray's Lessee v. Hoboken Land & Improvement Company, 18 Howard 272 (1856)
Citizens Savings and Loan Association v. Topeka, 20 Wallace 655 (1875)

Note—The *Munn* principle—*Munn* v. *Illinois,* 94 U.S. 113 (1877)—is applied here. A business subject to the control of rates was not under the "due process" clause entitled to a court review of just compensation. Moreover, the "due process" clause of the Fourteenth Amendment is subject to "the gradual process of inclusion and exclusion."

Buck v. Bell, 274 U.S. 200, 47 S. Ct. 584, 71 L. Ed. 1000 (1927)

The superintendent of the State Colony for Epileptics and Feeble Minded in the state of Virginia ordered an operation upon Carrie Buck, the plaintiff in error, for the purpose of making her sterile. She contended that the Virginia statute authorizing the operation was void under the Fourteenth Amendment as denying to her due process of law and the equal protection of the laws. The evidence in this case showed that Carrie Buck's mother was feeble-minded, that Carrie Buck was feeble-minded, and that she had a child that was feeble-minded. All of them were committed to the State Colony. Under the procedure of the law, the rights of the patient were most carefully considered, and every step, as in this case, was taken in scrupulous compliance with the statute and after months of observation.

OPINION BY MR. JUSTICE HOLMES
(Vote: 8-1)

Question—Can this law under any circumstances be justified?

Decision—Yes.

Reason—The Court reasoned that more than once the public welfare may call upon the best citizens for their lives. The Court said that it would be strange if it could not call upon those who already sap the strength of the state for these lesser sacrifices, in order to prevent our being swamped with incompetence. "But, it is said, however it might be if this reasoning were applied generally, it fails when it is confined to the small number who are in the institutions named and is not applied to the multitudes outside. It is the usual last resort of constitutional arguments to point out shortcomings of the sort." The Court answered that "the law does all that is needed when it does all that it can, indicates a policy, applies it to all within the lines, and seeks to bring within the lines all similarly situated so far and so fast as its means allow." So far as the operations enable those who otherwise must be kept confined to be returned to the world, and thus open the asylum to others, the equality aimed at will be more nearly reached.

Corollary cases

Jacobson v. Massachusetts, 197 U.S. 11 (1905)
Skinner v. Oklahoma, 36 U.S. 535 (1942)
Griswold v. Connecticut, 381 U.S. 479 (1965)
Roe v. Wade, 410 U.S. 113 (1973)

Note—*Buck* was questionable doctrine even for that time. *Skinner* v. *Oklahoma* (1942) deprives *Buck* of any constitutional strength.

INCORPORATION

Barron v. Baltimore, 7 Peters 243; 8 L. Ed. 672 (1833)

The city of Baltimore in paving its streets diverted several streams from their natural course, with the result that they made deposits of sand and gravel near Barron's Wharf, which rendered the water shallow and prevented the approach of vessels. The wharf was rendered practically useless. Barron alleged that this action upon the part of the city was a violation of the clause in the Fifth Amendment that forbids taking private property for public use without just compensation. His contention was that this amendment, being a guarantee of individual liberty, ought to restrain the states, as well as the national government.

OPINION BY MR. CHIEF JUSTICE MARSHALL

(No evidence from the report that the decision was not unanimous.)

Question—Does the Fifth Amendment restrain the states as well as the national government?

Decision—No.

Reason—The Constitution was established by the people of the United States for their own government, not for the government of the individual states. The powers they conferred on that government were to be exercised by that government. Likewise, the limitations on that power, if expressed in general terms, are necessarily applicable only to that government.

The Fifth Amendment contains certain restrictions obviously restraining the exercise of power by the federal government. Since the Constitution is a document framed for the government of all, it does not pertain to the states unless directly mentioned.

Corollary cases

Gitlow v. New York, 268 U.S. 652 (1925)
Palko v. Connecticut, 302 U.S. 319 (1937)
Wolf v. Colorado, 338 U.S. 25 (1949)

Note—Since *Gitlow* v. *New York,* 268 U.S. 652 (1925), the seminal case of selective incorporation of the Bill of Rights

15

under the Fourteenth Amendment, the impact of *Barron* has been diminished.

Gitlow v. State of New York, 268 U.S. 652; 45 S. Ct. 625; 69 L. Ed. 1138 (1925)

Benjamin Gitlow was convicted in the Supreme Court of New York for having published and circulated, unlawfully, pamphlets and leaflets detrimental to the government. These advocated overthrowing organized government by violent and other unlawful means. Gitlow appealed the case through the Appellate Division and Court of Appeals of the New York system.

OPINION BY MR. JUSTICE SANFORD
(Vote: 7-2)

Question—Does the New York State Criminal Anarchy statute contravene the due process clause of the Fourteenth Amendment?

Decision—No.

Reason—There is no absolute right to speak or publish, without responsibility, whatever one may choose. A state in the exercise of its police power may punish those who abuse this freedom by utterances inimical to the public welfare. Utterances such as the statute prohibited, by their very nature, involve danger to the public peace and to the security of the state. The statute was not arbitrary or unreasonable.

This case has long been regarded as a "landmark" decision because here for the first time the Court held portions of the "Bill of Rights" applicable to the states by means of the Fourteenth Amendment. The Court said, "For present purposes we may and do assume that freedom of speech and the press—which are protected by the First Amendment from abridgment by Congress—are among the fundamental personal rights and 'liberties' protected by the due process clause of the Fourteenth Amendment from impairment by the states."

Corollary cases

Schenck v. United States, 249 U.S. 47 (1919)
Abrams v. United States, 250 U.S. 616 (1919)

Schaefer v. United States, 251 U.S. 466 (1920)
Toledo Newspaper Co. v. United States, 247 U.S. 402 (1918)
Debs v. United States, 249 U.S. 211 (1919)
Cantwell v. Connecticut, 310 U.S. 296 (1940)

Note—*Gitlow* is where incorporation began in earnest. The principle but not the application of *Barron* v. *Baltimore,* 7 Peters 243 (1833) took hold. For an early listing of incorporation cases see *Palko* v. *Connecticut,* 302 U.S. 319 (1937).

Palko v. State of Connecticut, 302 U.S. 319; 58 S. Ct. 149; 82 L. Ed. 288 (1937)

Palko was indicted in Connecticut for murder in the first degree. A jury found him guilty of murder in the second degree and sentenced him to life imprisonment. The state appealed this verdict and the Supreme Court of Errors for Connecticut ordered a new trial. The basis for this order was the discovery that there had been error of law to the prejudice of the state in the lower court. At the second trial additional evidence was admitted and additional instructions given to the jury. A verdict of first degree murder was returned and Palko was sentenced to death. He appealed the legality of this procedure under the due process clause of the Fourteenth Amendment, claiming double jeopardy.

OPINION BY MR. JUSTICE CARDOZO
(Vote: 8-1)

Question—Is the appellant, by the new trial and subsequent sentence to death, deprived of due process under the Fourteenth Amendment?

Decision—No.

Reason—The due process clause of the Fourteenth Amendment applies to the states only those provisions of the Bill of Rights (Amendments 1 to 8) that are of the very essence of a scheme of ordered liberty. These provisions are those that involve principles of justice "so rooted in the traditions and conscience of our people as to be ranked as fundamental." The Court noted that to date only the guarantees of the First Amendment and the right to benefit of counsel have been found to fit this test.

The Court noted further that there could be no valid charge of double jeopardy and no deprivation of due process unless the first trial had been without error. Since there was error in the conduct of the first trial and the second trial was requested by the state to rectify the errors of the first trial, and to further the purposes of justice, there was no deprivation of due process involved.

Corollary cases

Hurtado v. California, 110 U.S. 516 (1884)
Twining v. New Jersey, 211 U.S. 78 (1908)
Near v. Minnesota, 283 U.S. 697 (1931)
Adamson v. California, 332 U.S. 46 (1947)
De Jonge v. Oregon, 299 U.S. 353 (1937)
Herndon v. Lowry, 301 U.S. 242 (1937)
Grosjean v. American Press Co., 297 U.S. 233 (1936)
Cantwell v. Connecticut, 310 U.S. 296 (1940)
United States v. Wheeler, 254 U.S. 281 (1920)
Powell v. Alabama, 287 U.S. 45 (1932)
Hamilton v. University of California, 293 U.S. 245 (1934)
Pierce v. Society of Sisters, 268 U.S. 510 (1925)
Walker v. Sauvinet, 92 U.S. 90 (1876)
Maxwell v. Dow, 176 U.S. 581 (1900)
Weeks v. United States, 232 U.S. 383 (1914)
Wolf v. Colorado, 388 U.S. 25 (1949)
North Carolina v. Pearce, 395 U.S. 711 (1969)

COURT JURISDICTION

Marbury v. Madison, 1 Cranch 137; 2 L. Ed. 60 (1803)

In compliance with the Act of Congress of February 1801, an act revising the judicial system, a commission for William Marbury, as a justice of the peace for the county of Washington, D.C., was signed by John Adams, then president of the United States, after which the seal of the United States was affixed to it, but the commission never reached Marbury. It was held back by James Madison, secretary of state under Jefferson. Marbury, desirous of the commission, filed an affidavit on which basis a rule was granted requiring the secretary of state, Madison, to show cause why a mandamus should not be issued directing him to deliver to Marbury his commission. The Judiciary Act of 1789 in Section 13 had provided that the Supreme Court could issue writs of mandamus.

OPINION BY MR. CHIEF JUSTICE MARSHALL
(No evidence from the report that the decision was not unanimous.)

Questions—1. Has the applicant a right to the commission he demands?

2. If that right has been violated, do the laws of the United States afford him a remedy?

3. Is this remedy a mandamus issuing from the Supreme Court?

Decisions—1. Yes.
2. Yes.
3. No.

Reasons—1. By signing the commission of Mr. Marbury, John Adams, president, appointed him a justice of the peace, and the seal of the United States affixed thereto by the secretary of state was conclusive testimony of the legitimacy of the signature, and of the completion of the appointment. That appointment, under its terms, conferred on Marbury a legal right to the office for the space of five years. Thus, Marbury had a right to the commission he demanded.

2. In all cases, it is a general and indisputable rule, that

19

where there is a legal right, there is also a legal remedy by suit, or action at law, whenever that right is invaded. Marbury had a legal right, as shown above, and this right was obviously violated by the refusal of Madison to deliver to him the commission. Thus a remedy under United States laws was due Marbury.

3. The Supreme Court of the United States had no power to issue a mandamus to the secretary of state since this would have been an exercise of original jurisdiction not warranted by the Constitution. Congress had no power to give the Supreme Court original jurisdiction in other cases than those described in the Constitution. The Constitution says that the Supreme Court will have appellate jurisdiction except in the cases in which it has original jurisdiction. The original jurisdiction of the Supreme Court is specifically stated by the Constitution, and Congress cannot enlarge or decrease this jurisdiction. "The particular phraseology of the Constitution of the United States confirms and strengthens the principle, supposed to be essential to all written constitutions, that a law repugnant to the Constitution is void, and that courts, as well as other departments, are bound by that instrument."

Corollary cases

United States v. Ravara, 2 Dallas 297 (1793)
Hylton v. United States, 3 Dallas 171 (1796)
Fletcher v. Peck, 6 Cranch 87 (1810)
United States v. Butler, 297 U.S. 1 (1936)
Massachusetts v. Mellon, 262 U.S. (1923)
Norton v. Shelby County, 118 U.S. 425 (1886)
United States v. Nixon, 418 U.S. 683 (1974)

Note—This is the first time the Court declared an act of Congress unconstitutional, and thus established the doctrine of judicial review. It was not until a half century later in *Dred Scott* v. *Sandford,* 19 Howard 393 (1857) that the Court was to do it again. As of 1979 the Supreme Court has held 105 acts of Congress unconstitutional in whole or in part. Cited countless times, *Marbury* was again cited by the Court against President Nixon holding he had to make subpoenaed tapes available to the Court.

Martin v. Hunter's Lessee, 1 Wheaton 304; 4 L. Ed. 97 (1816)

In the case of Fairfax's *Devisee* v. *Hunter's Lessee,* 7 Cranch 603, the Court reversed the decision of the state court and sustained title to certain Virginia land previously held by Lord Fairfax, a citizen and inhabitant of Virginia until his death in 1781. He devised the land to Denny Fairfax (previously Denny Martin), a native-born British subject who resided in England until his death. The Court held that Denny Fairfax, although an alien enemy, whose property might have been confiscated, was in complete possession of the land at the time of the commencement of the suit in 1791 and up to the treaty of 1794. It was said to be clear "that the treaty of 1794 completely protects and confirms the title of Denny Fairfax, even admitting that the treaty of peace left him wholly unprovided for." Denny Fairfax died while the suit was still pending, and the Supreme Court vested title in his heirs. Hunter's lessee claimed title under the Commonwealth of Virginia.

OPINION BY MR. JUSTICE STORY

(No evidence from the report that the decision was not unanimous.)

Question—Does the appellate power of the United States extend to cases pending in the state courts?

Decision—Yes.

Reason—Appellate jurisdiction has been given by the Constitution to this Court in all cases under the Constitution where it has no original jurisdiction, subject, however, to such regulations and exceptions as Congress may prescribe. State judges in their official capacities are called on to decide cases, not according to the laws and constitution of their own state, but according to "the supreme law of the land"—the Constitution, laws, and treaties of the United States. Yet to all these cases, the judicial power of this Court is to extend, according to the Constitution. It cannot extend by original jurisdiction, so it must extend to them by appellate jurisdiction or not at all.

A final motive, for the appellate power over the state tribunals, is the importance and necessity of uniformity of decisions throughout the United States. Different interpretations would result, and the laws, treaties, and the Constitution of the

United States would never have the same construction or efficiency in any two states. For such an evil, the only remedy is the appellate jurisdiction of this Court.

Corollary cases

New Orleans Water Works Co. v. Louisiana Sugar Refining Co., 125 U.S. 18 (1888)
Cohens v. Virginia, 6 Wheaton 264 (1821)
Kendall v. United States, 12 Peters 524 (1838)

Note—The Court strongly reaffirmed its right to review state decisions and, according to Charles Warren, the historian of the Court, made this view the keystone of the federal judicial power.

Cohens v. Virginia, 6 Wheaton 264; 5 L. Ed. 257 (1821)

To effect improvements in the city of Washington, Congress passed a law in 1802 authorizing the District of Columbia to conduct lotteries. Acting under this authority, the city passed an ordinance creating a lottery. The state of Virginia had a law forbidding lotteries except as established by that state. P. J. and M. J. Cohen were arrested in Norfolk, Va., charged with selling tickets for the Washington lottery. They were found guilty and fined $100. Then they appealed to the Supreme Court, to which Virginia did not object since the states were desirous of forcing the issue of the Supreme Court's authority over state actions.

OPINION BY MR. CHIEF JUSTICE MARSHALL
(No evidence from the report that the decision was not unanimous.)

Question—Is the jurisdiction of the court excluded by the character of the parties, one of them a state and the other a citizen of that state?

Decision—No.

Reason—"Where, then, a state obtains a judgment against an individual, and the court, rendering such judgment, overrules a defense set up under the Constitutions or laws of the United States, the transfer of this record into the Supreme Court, for the sole purpose of inquiring whether the judgment violates the Constitution or laws of the United States, can, with no propriety, we think, be denominated by a suit commenced or prosecuted against the state whose judgment is so far re-examined. Nothing is demanded from the state. No claim against it of any description is asserted or prosecuted. The party is not to be restored to the possession of anything. . . . Whether it be by writ of error or appeal, no claim is asserted, no demand is made by the original defendant; he only asserts the constitutional right to have his defense examined by that tribunal whose province it is to construe the Constitution and laws of the Union.

It is, then, the opinion of the Court, that the defendant who removes a judgment rendered against him by a State court into this Court, for the purpose of re-examining the question, whether that judgment be in violation of the Constitution or laws of the United States, does not commence or prosecute a suit against the State, whatever may be its opinion where the effect of the writ may be to restore the party to the possession of a thing which he demands. . . .''

Corollary cases

Muskrat v. United States, 219 U.S. 346 (1911)
Marbury v. Madison, 1 Cranch 137 (1803)
Chisholm v. Georgia, 2 Dallas 431 (1793)
Monaco v. Mississippi, 292 U.S. 313 (1934)
Martin v. Hunter's Lessee, 1 Wheaton 304 (1816)

Note—Reasserted the Doctrine of *Marbury* v. *Madison*, 1 Cranch 137 (1802). In *Martin* v. *Hunter's Lessee*, 1 Wheaton 304 (1816) the Court held that the Constitution (in order to bring uniformity into our jurisprudence) extends the appellate jurisdiction of the Supreme Court to cases in state courts that involve the Constitution, laws, and treaties of the United States; and in *Cohens* when a state has obtained a judgment against an individual in a state court over a defense based on the Constitution or laws of the United States, the Supreme Court may review the decision.

Osborn v. Bank of the United States, 9 Wheaton 738; 6 L. Ed. 204 (1824)

The state of Ohio levied an annual tax on the Bank of the United States of $50,000. Officers of the bank refused to pay

the tax and the state officials collected by force. The Bank
of the United States was chartered by Congress, and brought
suit in the federal Circuit Court of Ohio, as authorized by its
charter, to recover the funds collected and restrain Osborn,
Auditor of Ohio, and other state officials from collecting the
tax.

OPINION BY MR. CHIEF JUSTICE MARSHALL
(Vote: 6-1)

Question—Could Congress give the bank authorization to sue
state officials in the Circuit Courts?

Decision—Yes.

Reason—In this case the Court reiterated the doctrine of
McCulloch v. *Maryland* that Congress can establish a bank
and that a state may not tax that bank. The Court then went
on to answer the question noted above. It was held that the
state was not a party on the record, so the case could not be
construed as a violation of the Eleventh Amendment. "If the
person who is the real principal, the person who is the true
source of the mischief, by whose power and for whose advantage it is done, be himself above the law, be exempt from all
judicial process, it would be subversive of the best established
principles, to say, that the law could not afford the same
remedies against the agent employed in doing the wrong,
which they would afford against him, could his principal be
joined in the suit."

A corporation chartered by Congress has the right to invoke
the protection of the federal courts in any matter properly
within the jurisdiction of the Court—a matter under Article
III, Section 2 of the Constitution. "The constitution establishes the supreme court, and defines its jurisdiction. It enu-
merates cases in which its jurisdiction is original and exclusive;
and then defines that which is appellate, but does not insinuate
that, in any such case, the power cannot be exercised in its
original form, by courts of original jurisdiction. It is not
insinuated, that the judicial power, in cases depending on the
character of the cause, cannot be exercised, in the first instance, in the courts of the union, but must first be exercised

in the tribunals of the state; tribunals over which the government of the union has no adequate control, and which may be closed to any claim asserted under a law of the United States. We perceive, then, no ground on which the proposition can be maintained, that congress is incapable of giving the circuit court original jurisdiction, in any case to which the appellate jurisdiction extends.''

Corollary cases

McCulloch v. Maryland, 4 Wheaton 316 (1819)
Ableman v. Booth, 21 Howard 506 (1859)
Ex parte McCardle, 7 Wallace 506 (1869)
Muskrat v. United States, 219 U.S. 346 (1911)
Ex parte Ayers, 123 U.S. 443 (1887)

Note—*Osborn* strongly reiterated *McCulloch* v. *Maryland*, 4 Wheaton 316 (1819). It not only sustained the doctrine of ''implied powers'' (Art. I, Section 8, Clause 18) but also recognized an implied limitation on the states. Subsequent decisions recognized the doctrine of ''resulting power,'' that is, power derived from a combination of two or more specific powers.

Ableman v. Booth, 21 Howard 506; 16 L. Ed. 169 (1859)

Booth was held in the custody of Ableman, a United States marshal, pending his trial in a district court of the United States on the charge of having aided the escape of a fugitive slave from the custody of a deputy marshal in Milwaukee. The Supreme Court of Wisconsin issued a writ of habeas corpus.

OPINION BY MR. CHIEF JUSTICE TANEY

(No evidence from the report that the decision was not unanimous.)

Question—Can a state court grant a writ of habeas corpus to a prisoner arrested under the authority of the United States and in federal custody?

Decision—No.

Reason—No state judge or court, after being judicially informed that the party is imprisoned under the authority of the

United States, has the right to interfere with him, or to require him to be brought before them. And if the authority of the state, in the form of judicial process or otherwise, should attempt to control the marshal or other authorized officer or agent of the United States in any respect, in the custody of his prisoner, it would be his duty to resist it, and to call to his aid any force that might be necessary to maintain the authority of federal law against illegal interference. No judicial process, whatever form it may assume, can have any lawful authority outside the limits of the jurisdiction of the court or judge by whom it is issued; and an attempt to enforce it beyond these boundaries is nothing less than lawless violence.

Corollary cases

Tennessee v. Davis, 100 U.S. 257 (1880)
Tarble's Case, 13 Wallace 397 (1872)
In re Neagle, 135 U.S. 1 (1890)

Note—Emphasized our dual form of government and the independence of state and federal courts from one another.

Ex parte McCardle, 7 Wallace 506; 19 L. Ed. 264 (1869)

The Constitution assigns appellate jurisdiction to the Supreme Court with "such exceptions and under such regulations, as the Congress shall make." In February 1867 Congress passed an act providing for the exercise by the Supreme Court of appellate jurisdiction in the matter of writs of habeas corpus in cases where persons were restrained in violation of the Constitution, or of any treaty or law of the United States. McCardle was held in custody by military authority for trial before a military commission for the publication of incendiary and libelous articles in a newspaper that he edited. Before the judges acted upon his appeal, the act providing for the appellate jurisdiction was repealed.

OPINION BY MR. CHIEF JUSTICE CHASE
(No evidence from the report that the decision was not unanimous.)

Question—Does the Court have appellate jurisdiction in a case after the act pertaining to such jurisdiction has been repealed?

Decision—No.

Reason—Appellate jurisdiction is granted the Court by the Constitution, but with exceptions and regulations by Congress. This does not imply that Congress grants appellate jurisdiction, but that it can make exceptions to that power. Therefore, the act of 1868 repealing the act of 1867 deprived the Court of jurisdiction in this case. The general rule followed was that when an act is repealed, it must be considered, except as to transactions past and closed, as if it never existed.

The Court then had no choice but to decline jurisdiction of this case. This does not imply that the entire appellate jurisdiction of this Court over cases of habeas corpus was denied, but only appeals from the Circuit Courts under the act of 1867

Corollary cases

Durousseau v. United States, 6 Cranch 312 (1810)
Ex parte Yerger, 8 Wallace 85 (1869)
Norris v. Crocker, 13 Howard 429 (1852)
Maryland v. Baltimore Radio Show, 338 U.S. 912 (1950)
Massachusetts v. Mellon, 262 U.S. 447 (1923)
Powell v. McCormack, 395 U.S. 486 (1969)
Zurcher v. United States, 436 U.S. 547 (1978)

Note—Article III, clause 2 of the Constitution is an accordion-like grant of appellate power to Congress, and the Court made the issue moot and saved the Reconstruction Acts. All groups controlling Congress at one time or another have attempted to expand or contract this jurisdiction. Congress thus reacted swiftly to *Zurcher* v. *California* (1978) and prohibited federal courts from issuing warrants to search newsrooms. After *Jencks* v. *United States,* 353 U.S. 657 (1957) Congress enacted the "Jencks Law" that regulated the procedure for securing information in government files. In the wake of *Mallory* v. *United States,* 354 U.S. 449 (1957) and *Miranda* v. *Arizona,* 384 U.S. 436 (1966) Congress in 1968, following the assassinations of Robert Kennedy and Martin L. King, passed the Omnibus Crime Control and Safe Streets Act.

Ex parte Albert Levitt, 302 U.S. 633, 58 S. Ct. 1, 82 L. Ed. 493 (1937)

Levitt, a lawyer, asked leave of the Supreme Court to file a petition for an order requiring Associate Justice Hugo

Black of the U.S. Supreme Court to show cause why he should be permitted to serve as an associate justice of the Court. Two grounds were stated. Levitt contended that under Article I, Section 6, no senator should be appointed to any civil office under the authority of the United States, the salary whereof had been increased during the time for which he was elected. While Black was a senator, Congress had enacted a measure whereby a justice could retire without discontinuance of the salary that he received as an active member of the Court. The second ground for the suit was that, since Justice Van Devanter had not resigned, but had merely retired, there was no vacancy on the Court to which Black might be appointed.

OPINION—PER CURIAM
(No evidence from the report that the decision was not unanimous.)

Question—Were there grounds sufficient for action by the Supreme Court?

Decision—No.

Reason—The Court stated that the petitioning lawyer had shown no interest in the matter other than that of a citizen and a member of the bar of the Court. Such an interest was insufficient to enable him to secure action from the Court. It was an established principle that, to entitle a private individual to invoke judicial power to determine the validity of executive or legislative action, he must show that he had sustained, or was in immediate danger of sustaining a direct injury as the result of that action. It was not sufficient that he had merely a general interest common to all members of the public.

Corollary cases

Tyler v. Judges of Ct. of Registration, 179 U.S. 405 (1900)
Southern R. R. Co. v. King, 217 U.S. 524 (1910)
Fairchild v. Hughes, 258 U.S. 126 (1922)
Massachusetts v. Mellon, 262 U.S. 447 (1923)

Note—There is nothing in the Constitution about disqualification of justices. It is a matter left entirely up to the responsibility of the justice; there is no statute on the subject and the Court, while internally it wrangled over specific cases, has never ruled on it. Justice Rehnquist, however, has left an important memorandum on the entire issue. *Laird* v. *Tatum*, 409 U.S. 824 (1972)

Erie Railroad Co. v. Tompkins, 304 U.S. 64; 58 S. Ct. 817; 82 L. Ed. 1188 (1938)

Tompkins, a citizen of Pennsylvania, was injured on a dark night by a passing freight train of the Erie Railroad Co. while walking along its right of way at Hughestown in the state. He claimed that the accident occurred through negligence in the operation or maintenance of the train; that he was rightfully on the premises as licensee because he was on a commonly used footpath that ran for a short distance along-side the tracks; and that he was struck by something which looked like a door projecting from one of the moving cars. To enforce that claim he brought an action in the federal court for southern New York, which had jurisdiction because the company is a corporation of that state. The Erie insisted that its duty to Tompkins was no greater than that owed to a trespasser. It contended among other things, that its duty to Tompkins and hence its liability, should be determined in accordance with the Pennsylvania law; that under the law of Pennsylvania, as declared by the highest court, persons who use pathways along the railroad right of way are to be deemed trespassers; and that the railroad is not liable. Tompkins denied that any such rule had been established, and contended that since there was no statute of the state on the subject, the railroad's duty and liability was to be determined in federal courts as a matter of general law.

OPINION BY MR. JUSTICE BRANDEIS
(Vote: 6-2)

Question—Is the federal court bound by the alleged rule of Pennsylvania's common law as declared by the highest court of that state or free to exercise an independent judgment as to what the common law of the state is or should be?

Decision—Federal court bound by declaration of highest state court on the state law.

Reason—Except in matters governed by the federal Constitution or by acts of Congress, the substantive law to be applied in any case is the law of the state. And whether the law of the state shall be declared by its legislature in a statute or by its highest court in a decision is not a matter of federal concern. There is no federal general common law. Congress has no power to declare substitute rules of common law applicable in a state whether they be local in their nature or "general," be they commercial law or part of the law of torts. And no clause of the Constitution purports to confer such a power upon the federal courts. The common law so far as it is enforced in the state is not common law generally but the law of that state existing by the authority of the state without regard to what it may have been in England or anywhere else. The authority and only authority is the state, and, if that be so, the voice adopted by the state as its own should utter the last word.

Corollary cases

Swift v. Tyson, 16 Peter 1 (1842)
Black and White Taxicab & Transfer Co. v. Brown and Yellow Taxicab & Transfer Co., 276 U.S. 518 (1928)
Baltimore and Ohio R. R. Co. v. Baugh, 149 U.S. 368 (1893)
Rubbin v. New York Life Insurance Co., 304 U.S. 202
Guaranty Trust Co. of New York v. York, 326 U.S. 99 (1945)
Meredith v. City of Winter Haven, 320 U.S. 228 (1943)

Note—*Erie Railroad* overruled *Swift* v. *Tyson,* which said there was a federal common law. This problem so plagued the federal courts for more than one hundred years that the Supreme Court grasped the *Erie* case to change the law. The Court held—apparently for the first time—that a prior court had acted in an unconstitutional manner in interpreting the Judiciary Act (1789) at the expense of the states.

Testa v. Katt, 330 U.S. 386; 67 S. Ct. 810; 91 L. Ed. 967 (1947)

The World War II Federal Emergency Price Control Act provided that persons charged over ceiling prices could sue for damages "in any court of competent jurisdiction." The defendant charged the plaintiff $210 in excess of the ceiling price on an automobile, and the plaintiff sued in a Rhode Island state court. Rhode Island held that its courts need not try the case, on the ground that the act was a "penal statute in the international sense."

OPINION BY MR. JUSTICE BLACK
(No evidence from the report that the decision was not unanimous.)

Question—Does a state court have the power and the jurisdiction to enforce federal laws

Decision—Yes.

Reason—The Court could not accept the mandate of the Rhode Island Supreme Court that it had no more obligation to enforce a valid penal law of the United States than it would have had to enforce a penal law of another state, or of a foreign country. Article VI of the Constitution provides that "this Constitution, and the laws of the United States which shall be made in pursuance thereof; and all treaties made, or which shall be made, under the authority of the United States, shall be the supreme law of the land; and the judges in every State shall be bound thereby, anything in the Constitution or laws of any State to the contrary notwithstanding."

Historically, there were no precedents for such an opinion as the state court handed down. The very first Congress conferred jurisdiction upon the state courts to enforce important federal laws. This was challenged, but in *Claflin* v. *Houseman* the Court reiterated, in a unanimous decision, that the Constitution and the laws pursuant are the supreme law of the land, binding alike upon states, courts, and people.

In the *Mondou* case, the Court held that Connecticut had no right to decline such action, since, when Congress speaks, it speaks and establishes a policy for all. Here Rhode Island likewise could hold no established policy by its courts against enforcing statutes of other states and of the United States. Her courts had adequate jurisdiction under established local law to judge this case.

Corollary cases

Claflin v. Houseman, 93 U.S. 130 (1876)
Mondou v. New York, N. H. & H. R.R. Co., 223 U.S. 1 (1912)
Minneapolis & St. Louis R.R. Co. v. Bombolis, 241 U.S. 211 (1916)
Prigg v. Pennsylvania, 16 Peters 539 (1842)
United States v. Jones, 109 U.S. 513 (1883)
Robertson v. Baldwin, 165 U.S. 275 (1897)

Holmgren v. United States, 217 U.S. 509 (1910)
McKnett v. St. Louis and S. F. Ry. Co., 292 U.S. 230 (1934)
Jennings v. Illinois, 343 U.S. 104 (1952)
Ware v. Aylton, 3 Dall 199 (1796)
Martin v. Hunter's Lessee, 1 Wheaton 304 (1816)
Cohens v. Virginia, 6 Wheaton 264 (1821)
McCarty v. McCarty, 69 L. Ed. 2d 589 (1981)

Note—This obligation forced on state courts to carry out federal law is of long standing—as in the Fugitive Slave Act of 1793, and the Alien Enemies Act of 1798. Reliance was placed on state courts to enforce Jefferson's Embargo Acts. The states, as can be expected, were hostile to this federal supremacy.

Illinois v. Allen, 397 U.S. 337; 90 S. Ct. 1057; 25 L. Ed. 2d 353 (1970)

Allen had been convicted of armed robbery. During the trial he had been removed from the courtroom because of his repeated interference with the procedure of the trial including the use of vile and abusive language, this in spite of repeated warnings by the judge. After conviction Allen filed a petition for a writ of habeas corpus in federal court alleging that he had been deprived of his right under the Sixth and Fourteenth Amendments to remain present throughout his trial and thus confront the witnesses against him.

OPINION BY MR. JUSTICE BLACK
(Vote: 8-0)

Question—Is a defendant's right to be present during his trial so absolute that regardless of his conduct he can never be held to have lost the right so long as he insists on it?

Decision—No.

Reason—Certainly the defendant can lose the right by conduct that is disruptive of trial procedure. It is essential to the proper administration of criminal justice that elementary standards of dignity, order, and decorum be maintained. Trial judges faced with disruptive conduct must be given sufficient discretion to meet the circumstances of each case. There are at least three constitutionally permissible ways for a trial judge to handle an obstreperous defendant: (1) bind and gag him, thereby keeping him present; (2) cite him for contempt; (3) take him out of the courtroom until he promises to conduct himself properly.

Corollary cases

Pointer v. Texas, 380 U.S. 400 (1965)
Diaz v. United States, 223 U.S. 442 (1912)
Mayberry v. Pennsylvania, 400 U.S. 455 (1971)
Dutton v. Evans, 400 U.S. 74 (1970)
Chandler v. Florida, 449 U.S. 560 (1981)
Ohio v. Roberts, 448 U.S. —; 65 L. Ed. 2d 597 (1980)
Davis v. Alaska, 415 U.S. 308 (1974)

Note—Does the Court's answer to a contumacious witness run the possibility of reversal, for example, denying a defendant under the Sixth Amendment the right to present his own defense witnesses? If the defendant's counsel were expelled, could the defendant claim that he lacked counsel?

Stump v. Sparkman, 435 U.S. 349; 55 L. Ed. 2d 331; 98 S. Ct. 1099 (1978)

A mother, under the cloak of an Indiana Circuit Court order, had her "somewhat retarded" daughter of 15 sterilized. When she was admitted to the hospital she was told it was to remove her appendix. A couple of years later she got married and her inability to conceive revealed the previous sterilization. She filed suit against those involved—her mother, her mother's attorney, the Circuit Court Judge Stump, who issued the order, the doctors who performed or assisted, and the hospital. Holding that the constitutional claims required "state action," the district court dismissed the suit against all the other defendants except the judge and held in his case that he was absolutely immune from suit under the doctrine of judicial immunity. The Court of Appeals reversed the decision.

OPINION BY MR. JUSTICE WHITE
(Vote: 5-3)

Question—Is the Indiana Circuit Court Judge who approved a mother's permission to have a minor daughter sterilized immune from a damage suit?

Decision—Yes.

Reason—It is an old and general principle of the highest importance for the proper administration of justice that a judge, in exercising the authority vested in him, "be free to act upon his own convictions, without apprehension of personal consequences to himself." A judge will not be deprived of immunity "because the action he took was in error, was done maliciously, or was in excess of his authority." The judge will be subject to liability "only when he has acted in the 'clear absence of all jurisdiction.' " Judge Stump did not act beyond his jurisdiction because in 1971 there was no Indiana statute and no case law prohibiting a Circuit Court, a court of general jurisdiction, from considering petitions of this sort. "A judge is absolutely immune from liability for his judicial acts even if his exercise of authority is flawed by the commission of grave procedural errors."

Corollary cases

Bradley v. Fisher, 13 Wall. 335 (1871)
Pierson v. Ray, 286 U.S. 547 (1967)
In re Summers, 325 U.S. 561 (1945)
Ferri v. Ackerman, 444 U.S. 193 (1979)
Polk County v. Dodson, —U.S.—; 70 L. Ed. 2d 509 (1981)
Martinez v. California, 444 U.S. 277 (1980)
United States v. Helstoski, —U.S.—; 61 L. Ed. 2d 12 (1979)
Hutchinson v. Proxmire, 443 U.S. 111 (1979)
Imbler v. Pachtman, 424 U.S. 609; 47 L. Ed. 2d 128 (1976)

Note—*Stump* is one of those cases in which the principle is right but the results are wrong. A suit can be maintained against a state official acting "under color of the law" as in *Screws* v. *United States,* 325 U.S. 91 (1945), but immunity covers judges for acts done beyond their jurisdiction or done maliciously or corruptly. Congressmen, of course, are protected by the "speech and debate clause;" they "shall not be questioned in any other place." Unlike appointed-for-life tenured judges, though, congressmen can (a) be censured or expelled by the chamber, and (b) retired in a subsequent election.

POLITICAL QUESTIONS

Luther v. Borden, 7 Howard 1; 12 L. Ed. 581 (1849)

In 1841 the people of the state of Rhode Island were still operating under the old colonial charter with a few minor revisions, using it as their state constitution. This constitution strictly limited the right to vote. Led by a man named Dorr, the people at various mass meetings throughout the state instituted a new constitution whereby suffrage was greatly increased. The state government claimed that this was an insurrection and appealed to the President to declare martial law. However, no federal forces were used. Members of the state militia led by Borden forced their way into the house of Luther, a Dorr adherent, who sued for trespass. Luther moved to Massachusetts in order to legalize a suit on the basis of diversity of citizenship.

OPINION BY MR. CHIEF JUSTICE TANEY
(Vote: 8-1)

Question—Can the Court decide as to the guaranty of a republican form of a state's government in accordance with Article IV, Section 4?

Decision—No.

Reason—This is a purely political question and must be left in the hands of the political branches of the government to decide. Their decision moreover may not be questioned in a judicial tribunal. It would constitute a usurpation of power for the Supreme Court to attempt to decide the question. The enforcement of the guarantee of a republican form of government rests with the president or Congress.

Corollary cases

Martin v. Mott, 12 Wheaton 19 (1827)
Ex parte Dorr, 3 Howard 103 (1847)
Coleman v. Miller, 307 U.S. 433 (1939)
Colegrove v. Green, 328 U.S. 549 (1946)
Pacific States Telephone and Telegraph Co. v. Oregon, 223 U.S. 118 (1912)

Note—The first and thus a leading case on the meaning of a political question; in *Powell* v. *McCormack,* 396 U.S. 486

(1969) there is an excellent statement on the yardstick the Court will use to determine the political question doctrine.

Muskrat v. United States, 219 U.S. 346; 31 S. Ct. 250; 55 L. Ed. 246 (1911)

An act of Congress authorized Muskrat and others to bring suit in the federal Court of Claims, with an appeal to the federal Supreme Court to determine the validity of certain acts of Congress that altered terms of certain prior allotments of Cherokee Indian lands.

OPINION BY MR. JUSTICE DAY

(No evidence from the report that the decision was not unanimous.)

Question—Is the Supreme Court able to judge the validity of an act of Congress as an abstract question rather than as an actual controversy or case?

Decision—No.

Reason—This is an attempt by Congress to have the Court pass upon the validity of laws before they are properly brought to the Court. Federal judicial power extends only to "cases" and "controversies," defined by Marshall as suits "instituted according to the regular course of judicial procedure." This matter is not presented in such a "case" or "controversy." "The whole purpose of the law is to determine the constitutional validity of this class of legislation, in a suit not arising between parties concerning a property right necessarily involved in the decision in question, but in a proceeding against the government in its sovereign capacity, and concerning which the only judgment required is to settle the doubtful character of the legislation in question. . . . If such actions as are here attempted, to determine the validity of legislation, are sustained, the result will be that this court, instead of keeping within limits of judicial power, and deciding cases or controversies arising between opposing parties, as the Constitution intended it should, will be required to give opinions in the nature of advice concerning legislative action,—a function never conferred upon it by the Constitution."

Corollary cases

Marbury v. Madison, 1 Cranch 137 (1803)
United States v. Ferreira, 13 Howard 40 (1852)
Altvater v. Freeman, 319 U.S. 359 (1943)
United States v. Evans, 213 U.S. 297 (1909)
Alabama State Federation of Labor v. McAdory, 325 U.S. 450 (1945)
Aetna Life Insurance Co. v. Haworth, 300 U.S. 227 (1937)
Nashville, C. and St. Louis R.R. Co. v. Wallace, 288 U.S. 249 (1933)
Orr v. Orr, 440 U.S. 268 (1979)

Note—Although still good law, *Muskrat,* however, is not to be confused with a declaratory judgment, an actual case between contesting parties. A declaratory judgment is binding on the parties to the suit, which distinguishes it from an advisory opinion. The line, however, between an actual case or controversy and an advisory opinion is a thin one. A justiciable controversy must be real, substantial, definite, concrete, touching legal relations of parties' legal interests.

Baker v. Carr, 369 U.S. 186; 82 S. Ct. 691; 7 L. Ed. 2d 663 (1962)

This was a civil action alleging that the apportionment of the Tennessee General Assembly by means of a 1901 statute debased the votes of the plaintiffs and denied them equal protection of the law under the Fourteenth Amendment. The Constitution of Tennessee mandates a decennial reapportionment but all proposals for such since 1901 have failed to pass the General Assembly. In this period the relative standings of Tennessee counties in terms of qualified voters have changed significantly. The appellants asserted that the voters in certain counties have been placed in a position of constitutionally unjustified inequality *vis-à-vis* voters in irrationally favored counties. The appellants claimed injunctive and declaratory judgment relief. The plaintiffs alleged that any change in the apportionment that would be brought about by legislative action would be difficult or impossible.

OPINION BY MR. JUSTICE BRENNAN
(Vote: 6-2)

Questions—1. Do federal courts have jurisdiction of cases involving state legislative reapportionment?

2. Does the case state a justiciable cause of action?

Decisions—1. Yes.

2. Yes.

Reason—This is a cause of action that arises under the Constitution according to Article III, Section 2 since the complaint alleges an apportionment that deprives the appellants of the equal protection of the laws in violation of the Fourteenth Amendment. Further, the claim is not "so attenuated and unsubstantial as to be absolutely devoid of merit." Moreover, "the appellants do have standing to maintain this suit. Our decisions plainly support this conclusion." Voters who allege facts showing disadvantage to themselves as individuals have standing to sue. Finally, the matter presented is justiciable. The mere fact that a suit seeks protection of a political right does not mean that it presents a nonjusticiable political question. The nonjusticiability of a political question is primarily a function of the separation of powers, the relationship between the judiciary and the coordinate branches of the federal government, and not the federal judiciary's relationship to the states.

The case was remanded to the district court for trial and further proceedings consistent with this opinion.

Corollary cases

Scholle v. Hare, 369 U.S. 429 (1962)
W.M.C.A., Inc. v. Simon, 370 U.S. 190 (1964)
Wesberry v. Sanders, 376 U.S. 1 (1964)
Reynolds v. Sims, 377 U.S. 533 (1964)
Avery v. Midland County, Texas, 390 U.S. 474 (1968)
United States v. Nixon, 418 U.S. 683 (1974)
Colegrove v. Green, 328 U.S. 549 (1946)
Luther v. Borden, 7 Howard 1 (1849)
Pacific States Telephone and Telegraph Co. v. Oregon, 223 U.S. 118 (1912)
Hadley v. Junior College District, 397 U.S. 50 (1970)
Whitcomb v. Chavis, 403 U.S. 124 (1971)
Sixty-Seventh Minnesota State Senate v. Beens, 406 U.S. 187 (1972)
Mahan v. Howell, 410 U.S. 315 (1973)

Note—*Baker* is a seminal case. In reversing *Colegrove* v. *Green,* 328 U.S. 549 (1946) the Supreme Court opened the federal courts to challenges of apportionment of legislative districts.

Powell v. McCormack, 395 U.S. 486; 89 S. Ct. 1944; 23 L. Ed. 2d 491 (1969)

Adam Clayton Powell, Jr. had been elected from the Eighteenth Congressional District of New York to serve in the United States House of Representatives of the Ninetieth Congress. When he was not permitted to take his seat, Powell brought suit in federal district court. He contended that the House could exclude him only if it found that he failed to meet the requirements of age, citizenship, and residence as stated in Article I, Section 2 of the Constitution.

OPINION BY MR. CHIEF JUSTICE WARREN
(Vote: 8-1)

Question—Can the House or Representatives exclude a duly elected member for reason other than failure to meet the qualifications set forth in the Constitution?

Decision—No.

Reason—Both the intentions of the framers of the Constitution and the basic principles of our democratic system "persuade us that the Constitution does not vest in the Congress a discretionary power to deny membership by a majority vote." The Court noted further that the provisions of Article I, Section 5 empowering each House to judge the qualifications of its own members is at most a "textually demonstrable commitment" to Congress to judge only the qualifications expressly set forth in the Constitution.

Corollary cases

Bond v. Floyd, 385 U.S. 116 (1966)
Alejandrino v. Quezon, 271 U.S. 528 (1926)
Barry v. United States, 279 U.S. 597 (1929)
Baker v. Carr, 369 U.S. 186 (1962)
Tenney v. Brandhove, 341 U.S. 367 (1951)
Barr v. Matteo, 360 U.S. 564 (1959)
United States v. Brewster, 408 U.S. 501 (1972)
Gravel v. United States, 408 U.S. 606 (1972)
Doe v. McMillan, 412 U.S. 306 (1973)

Note—Congress has a strong tradition of refusing to seat victors. In 1900 the House refused to seat Brigham H. Roberts of Utah as a polygamist, in 1919 Victor L. Berger of Milwaukee convicted of sedition, and in 1926 William S. Vare of Pennsylvania and Frank Smith of Illinois in the Senate because of campaign indiscretions. *Powell* has an excellent discussion of the elements constituting a "political question," especially as it concerns a coordinate branch.

FEDERALISM

**Equal Employment Opportunity Commission v. Wyoming, 460
U.S. 226; 75 L. Ed. 2d 18; 103 S. Ct. 1054 (1983)**

A supervisor for a state game and fish department was
dismissed on reaching the age of 55. With the approval of
his employer he could have been kept on. He claimed that
the dismissal violated the Age Discrimination in Employment Act (ADEA). As it applied to local and state government, the United States District Court dismissed the complaint partly on the basis that the Act violated the Tenth
Amendment doctrine of immunity. It was appealed to the
Supreme Court.

OPINION BY MR. JUSTICE BRENNAN
(Vote: 5-4)

Question—Whether Congress acted constitutionally when, in
1974, it extended the definition of "employer" under . . .
the Act to include state and local governments.

Decision—Yes.

Reason—Efforts in Congress to prohibit arbitrary age discrimination date back at least to the 1950s and surfaced in floor
debates in what became Title VII of the Civil Rights Act of
1964. Protection from age discrimination was subsequently
raised to age 70 in 1978. Originally the Age Discrimination in
Employment Act passed in 1967 did not apply to the federal
government, to the states, their political subdivisions, or to
employers with fewer than 25 employees. In 1974 the act was
amended to include federal, state, and local governments, and
employers with fewer than 20 employees. The appellees have
not claimed that Congress exceeded the reach of the commerce power in enacting the ADEA but as to the Wyoming
state game warden, the act "is precluded by virtue of external
constraints imposed by Congress's commerce powers by the
Tenth Amendment. The principle of state immunity articulated
in the *National League of Cities* v. *Usery* (1964) is not meant
to create a sacred province of state autonomy but to ensure
the unique benefits of a federal system in which the states

enjoy a "separate and independent existence." The state still assesses the fitness of a game warden and dismisses those wardens which appear unfit. "We conclude that the degree of federal intrusion in this case is sufficiently less serious than it was in *National League of Cities* so as to make it unnecessary for us to override Congress's express choice to extend its regulatory authority to the states."

Corollary cases

National League of Cities v. Usery, 426 U.S. 833, 49 L. Ed. 2d 245, 96 S. Ct. 2465 (1976)

Maryland v. Wirtz, 392 U.S. 183, 20 L. Ed. 2d 1020, 88 S. Ct. 2017 (1968)

Lane County v. Oregon, 74 U.S. 71, 19 L. Ed. 101 (1869)

FERC v. Mississippi, 456 U.S. 742, 72 L. Ed. 2d 532, 102 S. Ct. 2126 (1982)

United Transportation Union v. Long Island R. Co., 455 U.S. 678, 71 L. Ed. 2d 547, 102 S. Ct. 1349 (1982)

Hodel v. Virginia Surface Mining & Reclamation Association, 459 U.S. 264, 69 L. Ed. 2d 1, 101 S. Ct. 2352 (1981)

Note—Justice Stevens, in his concurring opinion, stressed that the commerce clause was the framers' response to the central problem under the Constitution, and that *National League of Cities* v. *Usery* (49 L. Ed. 2d 245, 1976) was wrongly decided in the spirit of the discredited Articles of Confederation and ought to be reversed. Two years later in *Garcia* v. *San Antonio* (83 L. Ed. 1016, 1985) the Court reversed *Usery*. In a strong dissent, the point was made that (1) the Constitution does not mandate how a state should select its employees, (2) Stevens's view set no limitation on the ability of Congress to override state sovereignty, and (3) Congress has not equally placed restrictions on itself in the exercise of its own sovereign powers.

Slaughterhouse Cases, 16 Wallace 36; 21 L. Ed. 394 (1873)

These cases arose under a measure enacted in 1869 by the legislature of Louisiana. The act regulated the business of slaughtering livestock in New Orleans. It required that such activities for the city and for a vast area surrounding it should be restricted to a small section below the city of New Orleans, and provided that the slaughtering should be done in the houses of one corporation. The effect was virtually a monopoly grant of the business, even though the corporation was required to permit other butchers to have access to their facilities on payment of a reasonable fee.

OPINION BY MR. JUSTICE MILLER
(Vote: 5-4)

Question—Were the butchers of New Orleans denied rights under the Fourteenth Amendment?

Decision—No.

Reason—The Court declared that a glance at the Thirteenth, Fourteenth, and Fifteenth Amendments disclosed a unity of purpose. That purpose was the achievement of the freedom of the slave race, the security and firm establishment of that freedom, and the protection of the new freemen and citizens from oppression by their former owners. The Court held that the rights of others were not impaired because these amendments did not speak of rights of citizens of the states. A sharp distinction was drawn between rights that were derived from state citizenship and those that were derived from citizenship of the United States. The Court held that the citizen derived his civil rights from state citizenship and therefore those rights were not protected by the Fourteenth Amendment against state action.

Corollary cases

Paul v. Virginia, 8 Wallace 180 (1869)
Crandall v. Nevada, 6 Wallace 36 (1868)
Colgate v. Harvey, 296 U.S. 404 (1935)
Austin v. New Hampshire, 420 U.S. 656 (1975)
Madden v. Commonwealth of Kentucky, 309 U.S. 83 (1940)
Edwards v. California, 314 U.S. 160 (1941)
Twining v. New Jersey, 211 U.S. 78 (1908)
Baldwin v. Montana Fish, Game Commissioner, 420 U.S. 656 (1978)
Minor v. Happersett, 21 Wallace 162 (1875)
Jones v. Helms, 69 L. Ed. 2d 118 (1981)
Hicklin v. Orbeck, 437 U.S. 518 (1978)

Note—The *Slaughterhouse Cases* were decided only five years after the adoption of the Fourteenth Amendment (1868) and were the first interpretation of the amendment. Privileges and immunities occur in Article IV, Section 2, and in the Four-teenth Amendment, Section 1. In the former the phrase seems restricted to the concept of federalism and the obligations of states to one another, and in the latter to political rights of national citizenship already possessed by citizens.

Beginning with the *Slaughterhouse Cases* (16 Wallace 36, 1873) the Court has been skittish in utilizing the privileges and immunities clause of the Fourteenth Amendment despite the plea of Justice R. Jackson in *Edwards* v. *California* (86 L. Ed. 119, 1941)—"This Court should . . . hold squarely that it is a privilege of citizenship . . . to enter any state of the union, either for temporary sojourn or for establishment of permanent residence." A change might be taking place, for in *Hicklin* v. *Orbeck* (57 L. Ed. 2d 397, 1978) the Court voided the "Alaska Hire" Act as a violation of the privileges and immunities clause; in *Supreme Court of New Hampshire* v. *Piper* (84 L. Ed. 2d 205, 1985) on similar grounds it held that New Hamp-shire's residency requirement for lawyers was void; and still more recently in *Supreme Court of Virginia* v. *Friedman* (101 L. Ed. 2d, 1988) the Court held that a residency requirement to practice law for an already practicing lawyer violates the privileges and immunities guarantees of the Fourteenth Amendment.

Puerto Rico v. Branstad, 483 U.S. _____; 97 L. Ed. 2d 187; 107 S. Ct. 2802 (1987)

Ronald Calder, a civilian air traffic controller, struck two persons with his automobile. Army Villalba was killed and her husband who had quarreled with respondent Calder earlier, was deliberately run over. On bail, Calder was charged for murder and attempted murder. He fled to Iowa. The governor of Puerto Rico requested Calder's extradition and was refused. Puerto Rico sought a mandamus in the district court holding that Iowa violated the extradition clause and the Federal Extradition Act. Resting on *Kentucky* v. *Dennison* (1861), the district court held that the federal courts had no power to order a governor to fulfill the state's obligation under the extradition clause (Art. 4, Sec. 2). The Court of Appeals affirmed. Supreme Court granted certio-rari.

<u>OPINION BY MR. JUSTICE MARSHALL</u>
(Vote: 8-0)

Question—Whether the propositions concerning the limitations of federal judicial power stated in *Kentucky* v. *Dennison* in 1861 retain their validity today.

Decision—No.

Reason—*Dennison*, like today's *Branstad* case, involves extradition. It was much related to recession, a threatening civil war, and free and slavery states. Representatives of the Deep South withdrew from Congress and Justice Campbell resigned from the Supreme Court. "The Court firmly rejected the position taken by *Dennison* and the governors of other free states that the extradition clause requires only the delivery of fugitives charged with acts which would be criminal by the law of the asylum state." Despite the Court's belief that the extradition clause was absolutist, the Court concluded that "the words 'it shall be the duty' were not used as mandatory and compulsory, but as declaratory of the moral duty" created by the Constitution. Thus for over 125 years *Kentucky* v. *Dennison* has stood for two propositions, first that the Extradition Clause creates a mandatory duty to deliver up fugitives "on demand" and, second, that the federal courts cannot compel performance of this ministerial duty. We hold that "the commands of the Extradition Clause are mandatory, and afford no discretion to the executive officers or courts of the asylum state." The fundamental premise of *Dennison* that in all circumstances the states and the federal government must be viewed as coequal sovereigns "is not representative of the law today." *Kentucky* v. *Dennison* is the product of another time and hence the Court of Appeals is reversed.

Corollary cases

Kentucky v. Dennison, 24 Howard 66, 16 L. Ed. 717 (1861)
Michigan v. Doran, 439 U.S. 282, 58 L. Ed. 2d 521, 99 S. Ct. 530 (1978)
Biddinger v. Commissioner of Police, 245 U.S. 1281, 62 L. Ed. 193, 38 S. Ct. 41 (1917)
Appleyard v. Massachusetts, 203 U.S. 222, 51 L. Ed. 161, 27 S. Ct. 122 (1906)

California v. Superior Court of California, 482 U.S. ——, 96 L. Ed. 2d 332,
    107 S. Ct. —— (1987)
Board of Liquidation v. McComb, 92 U.S. 531, 23 L. Ed. 623 (1876)
Ex parte Young, 209 U.S. 123, 52 L. Ed. 714, 28 S. Ct. 441 (1908)
Brown v. Board of Education, 349 U.S. 294, 99 L. Ed. 1083, 75 S. Ct. 753
    (1954)
Cooper v. Aaron, 358 U.S. 1, 3 L. Ed. 2d 5, 78 S. Ct. 1401 (1958)
FERC v. Mississippi, 456 U.S. 742, 72 L. Ed. 2d 532, 102 S. Ct. 2126 (1982)
Green v. County School Board, 391 U.S. 430, 20 L. Ed. 2d 716, 88 S. Ct.
    1689 (1968)
Examining Board of Engineers, Architects and Surveyors v. Flores de Otero,
    426 U.S. 572, 49 L. Ed. 2d 65, 96 S. Ct. 2264 (1976)
New York ex rel Kopel v. Bingham, 211 U.S. 468, 53 L. Ed. 286, 29 S. Ct.
    190 (1909)

Note—*Kentucky* v. *Dennison* (24 Howard 66, 1861) had lost
some of its bite since the Fugitive Felon and Witness Act of
1934. A point was made but easily rejected by the Court that
regardless of whether the extradition clause applied directly to
Puerto Rico as a "commonwealth" rather than as a "state,"
the Extradition Act applies to territories as well as to states.
Note that the Court—reminiscent of its view in *Garcia* v. *San
Antonio* (83 L. Ed. 2d 1016, 1985) disavows a static historical
view as immune from federal regulation—in reversing *Dennison* simply says the states are not co-equal with the national
government in this area and that *Dennison* "is the product of
another time."

Virginia v. Tennessee, 148 U.S. 503; 13 S. Ct. 728; 37 L. Ed. 537 (1893)

Virginia brought this suit to have the true boundary line
between herself and Tennessee established. In 1801, some
commissioners, appointed with the approval of both states,
established a boundary, and subsequently in 1803 both legislatures approved the boundary. Since that date, the boundary established had been adhered to by both states and was
recognized by Congress in districting for judicial, revenue,
and federal election purposes. In this case, Virginia sought
to have the agreement declared null and void as having been
entered into without the consent of Congress. The Constitution provides that "no state shall, without the consent of
Congress . . . enter into any agreement or compact with
another state, or with a foreign power. . . ."

Opinion by Mr. Justice Field
(No evidence from the report that the decision was not unanimous.)

Question—Is the agreement, made without the consent of Congress between Virginia and Tennessee, to appoint commissioners to run and mark the boundary line between them, within the prohibition of the clause stated in the Constitution.

Decision—No.

Reason—It was the opinion of the Court that what the Constitution implied by "agreement or compact" was any compact or agreement that endangered the power of the federal government, such as a war alliance or increasing the political power in the states. The Court further noted that the clause in the Constitution did not state when Congress should approve of a compact or agreement. The approval by Congress of the compact entered into between the states upon their ratification of the action of their commissioners is fairly implied from its subsequent legislation and proceedings. The exercise of jurisdiction by Congress over the country as a part of Tennessee on one side, and as a part of Virginia on the other, for a long succession of years, without question or dispute from any quarter, is as conclusive proof of assent to it by that body as can usually be obtained from its most formal proceedings.

"Looking at the clause in which the terms 'compact' or 'agreement' appear, it is evident that the prohibition is directed to the formation of any combination tending to the increase of political power in the states, which may encroach upon or interfere with the just supremacy of the United States."

Corollary cases

Rhode Island v. Massachusetts, 4 Howard 591 (1838)
Holmes V. Jennison, 14 Peters 540 (1840)
Green v. Biddle, 8 Wheaton 1 (1823)
Virginia v. West Virginia, 11 Wallace 39 (1871)
South Carolina v. Georgia, 93 U.S. 4 (1876)
West Virginia v. Sims, 341 U.S. 22 (1951)
New York v. New Jersey, 256 U.S. 296 (1921)
Hinderlider v. La Plata Co., 304 U.S. 92 (1938)

Kentucky v. Indiana, 281 U.S. 163 (1930)
Lake Country Estates Inc. v. Tahoe Regional Planning Agency, 59 L. Ed. 2d
  401 (1979)
New Hampshire v. Maine, 426 U.S. 363 (1976)
U.S. Steel Corp. v. Multistate Tax Commission, 434 U.S. 452 (1978)
Nebraska v. Iowa, 406 U.S. 117 (1972)
Cuyler v. Adams, 449 U.S. 433 (1981)

Note—Article I, Section 10, Clause 1 prohibits a state from
entering into treaties or to form an alliance or confederation.
This limitation is absolute and unconstitutional. In Clause 3,
however, the prohibition that a state cannot enter into an
agreement or compact without the permission of Congress is
less strict. As the Court says in *Virginia,* "the Constitution
does not state when the consent of Congress shall be given,
whether it shall precede or may follow the compact made, or
whether it shall be expressed or may be implied." Thus in
New Hampshire v. *Maine,* locating a boundary between them
did not require congressional consent nor was consent necessary when twenty-one states, *Multistate Tax Commission*
(1978) set up an administrative unit to collect taxes. Disputes
over compacts or agreements are subject to the Court's original jurisdiction.

United States v. Lanza, 260 U.S. 377; 43 S. Ct. 141; 67 L. Ed. 314 (1922)

> The state of Washington passed a prohibition law before
> the passage of the National Prohibition Act. Lanza was
> charged in the federal court of Washington and in the su-
> preme court of Whatcom County, Washington for the viola-
> tion of each of the respective acts. He was accused of
> making, selling, and transporting liquor and of having a still
> and material for the manufacture of liquor. He brought suit
> in the federal court to dismiss the suit of the United States
> on the grounds that he was placed in double jeopardy.

OPINION BY MR. CHIEF JUSTICE TAFT
(No evidence from the report that the decision was not unanimous.)

Question—Can the United States punish someone for an act
for which the state has already punished him?

Decision—Yes.

Reason—We have two sovereignties, deriving power from different sources, capable of dealing with the same subject matter within the same territory. Each may, without interference from the other, enact laws determining what shall be an offense against its peace and dignity. In doing this, each is exercising its own sovereignty, not that of the other.

It follows that an act denounced as a crime by both national and state sovereignties is an offense against the peace and dignity of both and may be punished by each. The Fifth Amendment applies only to proceedings of the federal government, and the double jeopardy covered therein forbids a second prosecution under the authority of the federal government after a first trial for the same offense under the same authority. Here the same act was an offense against the state of Washington because of a violation of its laws and also an offense against the United States under the National Prohibition Act. The defendants thus committed two different offenses by the same act and a conviction by a court of Washington together with conviction in the federal court was not double jeopardy.

Corollary cases

Barron v. Baltimore, 7 Peters 243 (1833)
National Prohibition Cases, 253 U.S. 350 (1920)
Wolf v. Colorado, 338 U.S. 25 (1949)
Palko v. Connecticut, 302 U.S. 319 (1937)
Screws v. United States, 325 U.S. 91 (1945)
Waller v. Florida, 397 U.S. 387 (1970)
United States v. Wilson, 420 U.S. 332 (1975)
Breed v. Jones, 421 U.S. 519 (1975)
Burks v. United States, 57 L. Ed. 2d 1 (1978)
Abbate v. United States, 359 U.S. 187 (1959)
Bartkus v. Illinois, 359 U.S. 121 (1959)
United States v. Jorn, 400 U.S. 479 (1971)
Robinson v. Neil, 409 U.S. 505 (1973)
Ludwig v. Massachusetts, 427 U.S. 618
United States v. Wheeler, 254 U.S. 281 (1920)
Benton v. Maryland, 395 U.S. 784 (1969)

Note—Although often criticized, *Lanza* is still good law and reaffirmed in *Abbate* v. *United States* (1959) and *Bartkus* v.

Illinois (1959), which maintains the "double-prosecution-is-not-double-jeopardy" rule. Again in 1985, the Court in *Heath* v. *Alabama* reinforced it.

Tigner v. State of Texas, 310 U.S. 141; 60 S. Ct. 879; 84 L. Ed. 1124 (1940)

> Tigner was charged with participation in a conspiracy to fix the retail price of beer. Such a conspiracy was made a criminal offense under the Texas penal code. Because the provisions of this law did not apply to agricultural products or livestock in the hands of the producer or raiser, Tigner challenged the validity of the entire statute and sought release in the local courts by habeas corpus. He contended that the law was offensive to the equal protection of the laws that the Fourteenth Amendment safeguards.

OPINION BY MR. JUSTICE FRANKFURTER
(Vote: 8-1)

Question—Could Texas promote its policy of freedom for economic enterprise by utilizing the criminal law against various forms of combination and monopoly, but exclude from criminal punishment corresponding activities of agriculture?

Decision—Yes.

Reason—The Constitution does not require things that are different in fact or opinion to be treated in law as though they were the same. So the Court concluded that to write into law the differences between agriculture and other economic pursuits was within the power of the Texas legislature. At the core of the law was a conception of price and production policy for agriculture very different from that which underlies the demands made upon industry and commerce by antitrust laws. Agriculture expresses functions and forces different from the other elements in the total economic process. Therefore, equal protection of the laws was not denied.

Corollary cases

Connolly v. Union Sewer Pipe Co., 184 U.S. 540 (1902)
Mulford v. Smith, 307 U.S. 38 (1939)

United States v. Rock Royal Co-op., 307 U.S. 533 (1939)
Nebbia v. New York, 291 U.S. 502 (1934)
Liberty Warehouse Co. v. Burley, 276 U.S. 71 (1928)
Frost v. Corporation Comm. of Oklahoma, 278 U.S. 515 (1929)
Rostker v. Goldberg, 453 U.S. —; 69 L. Ed. 2d (1981)
Vance v. Bradley, 440 U.S. 93 (1979)
Fullilove v. Klutznick, 448 U.S. 448 (1980)
Regents of the Univ. of California v. Bakke, 438 U.S. 265 (1978)
Reed v. Reed, 404 U.S. 71 (1971)
Craig v. Boren, 429 U.S. 190 (1977)

Note—The equal protection clause does not rule out classifications that are reasonable, rational, or rest on some compelling state interest. Thus, Congress can register men but not women as potential soldiers (*Rostker* v. *Goldberg,* 1981), set a different retirement age for foreign service personnel than used elsewhere in the federal civil service (*Vance* v. *Bradley,* 1979), and use racial quotas on certain public works projects (*Fullilove* v. *Klutznick,* 1980). Similarly a state can allow a medical school to take into account in applications race (*Bakke,* 1978) and treat men and women differently under a rape statute, (*Michael M.* v. *Superior Court of Sonoma County,* 1981). But classifications that cannot show compelling state need are void. Thus a separated mother and father of an interstate child cannot be treated unequally (*Reed* v. *Reed,* 1971) nor can a state have an alcoholic drinking law for men and another for women (*Craig* v. *Boren,* 1977).

Monaco v. Mississippi, 292 U.S. 313; 54 S. Ct. 745; 78 L. Ed. 1282 (1934)

The principality of Monaco asked leave to bring suit in the Supreme Court against the state of Mississippi over the nonpayment of bonds issued by the state, and alleged to be absolute property of the Principality. The bonds were issued in 1833, were due in 1861 and 1866, issued in 1838 and due in 1850, issued in 1838 and due in 1858. They were handed down in a family of the state, but since private citizens cannot sue a state they were given to Monaco to use for the betterment of their country, on the theory that, since Monaco was a foreign country, it would be able to sue the state.

Opinion by Mr. Justice Hughes
(No evidence from the report that the decision was not unanimous.)

Question—Can the state of Mississippi be sued by the principality of Monaco without that state's consent?

Decision—No.

Reason—The Court ruled that the states of the union retain the same immunity to suits by a foreign state that they enjoy with respect to suits by individuals whether citizens of the United States or subjects of a foreign power. The foreign state enjoys a similar immunity and without her consent cannot be sued by a state of the union. The principle of the Eleventh Amendment applies to suits against a state by a foreign state.

Corollary cases

Williams v. United States, 289 U.S. 553 (1951)
Hans v. Louisiana, 134 U.S. 1 (1890)
South Dakota v. North Carolina, 192 U.S. 286 (1904)
Cohens v. Virginia, 6 Wheaton 264 (1821)
New Hampshire v. Louisiana, 108 U.S. 76 (1883)
North Dakota v. Minnesota, 263 U.S. 365 (1923)
Chisholm v. Georgia, 2 Dallas 419 (1793)
Virginia v. West Virginia, 246 U.S. 565 (1871)
Wisconsin v. Illinois, 278 U.S. 367 (1929)
Maine v. Thiboutot, 448 U.S. 1 (1980)
Lake Country Estates v. Tahoe Regional Planning Agency, 440 U.S. 391 (1979)
Nevada v. Hall, 440 U.S. 410 (1979)

Note—If a suit by a state is an honest one in its behalf and not in behalf of some client, the Court will take jurisdiction declaring it is outside the prohibition of the Eleventh Amendment, as in *South Dakota* v. *North Carolina* (1904) and *Nevada* v. *Hall* (1979). Although the Eleventh Amendment retrieved *Chisholm* v. *Georgia* (1793) an individual can sue an officer of the state and also go into federal court on a Fourteenth Amendment claim or a violation of federal law, as in *Maine* v. *Thiboutot* (1980).

Sherrer v. Sherrer, 334 U.S. 343; 68 S. Ct. 1087; 92 L. Ed. 1429 (1948)

A wife went from her Massachusetts home to Florida and sued for a divorce in a court of that state after the expiration of the 90-day period of residence required by Florida law. Her husband appeared and denied all the allegations in the complaint, including that of the wife's Florida residence. The wife introduced evidence establishing her residence, and the husband did not cross-examine. The court found that the wife was a bona fide resident of Florida and granted the divorce. The husband did not appeal. The wife married again and subsequently returned to Massachusetts. Her former husband then introduced proceedings in a Massachusetts court attacking the Florida decree. The Massachusetts court found that the wife under Massachusetts law was never domiciled in Florida and held the divorce void.

OPINION BY MR. CHIEF JUSTICE VINSON
(Vote: 7-2)

Question—Did the Massachusetts judgment deny full faith and credit to the Florida judgment, contrary to Article IV, Section 1, of the Constitution?

Decision—Yes.

Reason—The Court reasoned that the husband had his day in court in Florida with respect to every issue involved in the litigation, and there is nothing in the concept of due process that demands that he be given a second opportunity to litigate the existence of the jurisdictional facts. The Court went on to say that if the application of the full faith and credit clause to cases of this nature requires that local policy be subordinated, that is a part of the price of our federal system. That vital interests are involved in divorce litigation makes it a matter of greater rather than lesser importance that, under the circumstances of this case, the litigation end in courts of the state in which the decree was rendered.

Corollary cases

Davis v. Davis, 305 U.S. 32 (1938)
Williams v. North Carolina, 325 U.S. 226 (1945)

Haddock v. Haddock, 201 U.S. 562 (1906)
Poppvici v. Agler, 280 U.S. 379 (1930)
Andrews v. Andrews, 188 U.S. 14 (1903)
Sosna v. Iowa, 419 U.S. 393 (1975)
Bell v. Bell, 181 U.S. 175 (1901)
Estin v. Estin, 334 U.S. 541 (1948)
May v. Anderson, 345 U.S. 528
Kulko v. California Superior Court, 436 U.S. —; 56 L. Ed. 2d 132 (1978)
Hisquierdo v. Hisquierdo, 439 U.S. 572 (1979)
McCarthy v. McCarthy, 453 U.S. —; 69 L. Ed. 2d 589 (1981)
Ridgway v. Ridgway, 454 U.S. —; 70 L. Ed. 2d 39 (1981)
Orr v. Orr, 440 U.S. 268 (1979)
Mathews v. Castro, 429 U.S. 181 (1976)
United Airlines v. Evans, 431 U.S. —; 52 L. Ed. 2d 617 (1977)

Note—As someone noted, divorce cases are a judicial titling field. The best view now is that an ex parte divorce will be honored in the domicilary state and in all likelihood all other states, but it does not alter the rights of property, alimony, or custody of a spouse not served personally and who did not appear in court.

Pennsylvania v. Nelson, 350 U.S. 497; 76 S. Ct. 477; 100 L. Ed. 640 (1956)

An acknowledged member of the Communist party, Steve Nelson was convicted in Allegheny County, Pennsylvania, of violation of the Pennsylvania Sedition Act. He was sentenced to imprisonment and fine. While the Pennsylvania statute proscribes sedition against either the government of the United States or the Commonwealth of Pennsylvania, this case was concerned only with alleged sedition against the United States.

Opinion by Mr. Chief Justice Warren
(Vote: 6-3)

Question—Does the Smith Act of 1940, which prohibits the knowing advocacy of the overthrow of the government of the United States by force and violence, supersede the enforceability of the Pennsylvania Sedition Act.

Decision—Yes.

Reason—The Court examined the various federal acts on the subject, including the Internal Security Act of 1950 and the Communist Control Act of 1954, as well as the Smith Act, and concluded that Congress had intended to occupy the entire field of sedition. These acts, taken as a whole, "evince a congressional plan which makes it reasonable to determine that no room has been left for the states to supplement it. . . . 'Sedition against the United States is not a *local* offense. It is a crime against the *Nation*'. . . . It is not only important but vital that such prosecutions should be exclusively within the control of the federal government." The Court went on to note that enforcement of state sedition statutes would present a serious danger of conflict with the administration of the federal program and would produce conflicting or incompatible court decisions.

"Since we find that Congress has occupied the field to the exclusion of parallel state legislation, that the dominant interest of the federal government precludes state intervention, and that administration of state acts would conflict with the operation of the federal plan, we are convinced that" the state statute cannot stand. "Without compelling indication to the contrary, we will not assume that Congress intended to permit the possibility of double punishment."

Corollary cases

United States v. Lanza, 260 U.S. 377 (1922)
Fox v. Ohio, 5 Howard 410 (1847)
Gilbert v. Minnesota, 254 U.S. 325 (1920)
Adler v. Board of Education of the City of New York, 342 U.S. 485 (1952)
Campbell v. Hussey, 368 U.S. 297 (1961)
American Communications Association v. Douds, 339 U.S. 382 (1950)
Dennis v. United States, 341 U.S. 494 (1951)
Hines v. Davidowitz, 312 U.S. 52 (1941)
Rice v. Santa Fe Elevator Corp., 331 U.S. 218 (1947)

Note—The political fallout on the Warren Court was heavy as regards *Nelson,* but all the opinion did was reaffirm the view of the Supreme Court of Pennsylvania. *Nelson* reaffirmed the doctrine of federal "supersession" and thus reversed *Gilbert v. Minnesota,* 254 U.S. 325 (1920). Sensitive to the issue of state sovereignty, the Court, in the *National League of Cities* v. *Usery*, 426 U.S. 833 (1976), held that federal minimum wage laws are not binding on state and local governments.

By 1985, the Court was less sensitive to precedent and federalism claims for in *Garcia* v. *San Antonio Metropolitan Transit Authority* (83 L. Ed. 2d 1016) it reversed *Usery*. The cases are only ten years apart. The Court went the other way and in *Puerto Rico* v. *Branstad* (97 L. Ed. 187, 1987), it reversed *Dennison* v. *Kentucky* (16 L. Ed. 717, 1861) after 126 years.

In an earlier case along the same reasoning, *Ashton* v. *Cameron County Water Improvement District One*, 298 U.S. 513 (1936), the Court said that in the exercise of its bankruptcy powers Congress must not transgress the Fifth and Tenth Amendments or subject the fiscal powers of a state to the control of a bankruptcy court.

Hicklin v. Orbeck, 437 U.S. 518; 57 L. Ed. 2d 397; 98 S. Ct. 2482 (1978)

> In 1972 Alaska attempted—in a popularly known "Alaska Hire" Act—to reduce employment within the state by requiring that all Alaskan oil and gas leases, easements, or right-of-way permits for oil and gas pipelines and unitization agreements contain a requirement that qualified Alaskan residents be hired in preference to nonresidents. The Supreme Court of Alaska upheld that part of the act that gave preference to Alaskan residents over nonresidents but ruled the one-year durational residency part void.

OPINION BY MR. JUSTICE BRENNAN
(Vote: 9-0)

Question—Is the "Alaska Hire" Act a violation of the privileges and immunities clause and the equal protection clause?

Decision—Yes.

Reason—The "Alaska Hire" Act discriminates against nonresidents and cannot stand constitutional scrutiny. ". . . the act is an attempt to force virtually all businesses that benefit in some way from the economic ripple effect of Alaska's decision to develop her oil and gas resources to bias their employment practices in favor of the state's residents. We believe that Alaska's ownership of the oil and gas that is the subject matter of Alaska Hire simply constitutes insufficient justification for the pervasive discrimination against nonresidents that the act mandates." No state can prefer its own economic well-being to that of the nation as a whole. Pennsylvania might keep its coal, the Northwest its timber, mining states their minerals so that "embargo may be retaliated with embargo" with the result that commerce would be halted at state lines." The commerce clause circumscribes a state's ability to prefer its own citizens in the utilization of natural resources found within its borders, but destined for interstate commerce. The Constitution was framed upon the theory "that the peoples of the several states must sink or swim together, and that in the long run prosperity and salvation are in union and not division."

Corollary cases

Baldwin v. Montana Fish and Game Commission, 420 U.S. 656 (1978)
Paul v. Virginia, 8 Wall 168 (1869)
Toomer v. Witsell, 334 U.S. 385 (1948)
Mullaney v. Anderson, 342 U.S. 415 (1952)
Edwards v. California, 314 U.S. 160 (1941)
Pennsylvania v. West Virginia, 262 U.S. 553 (1923)
Zobel v. Williams, 457 U.S. 672; 72 L. Ed. 2d 672 (1982)
United Bldg. & Construction Trades Council v. Camden, 79 L. Ed. 2d 249
    (1984)

Garcia v. San Antonio Metropolitan Transit Authority, 469 U.S. 528; 83 L. Ed. 2d 1016; 105 S. Ct. 1005 (1985)

The San Antonio Metropolitan Transit Authority (SAMTA) is a public mass transit authority. The Department of Labor held that SAMTA's operations are not immune from the minimum wage and overtime requirements of the Fair Labor Standards Act (FLSA) under the *National League of Cities* v. *Usery* (426 U.S. 833, 49 L. Ed. 2d 245, 96 S. Ct. 2465, 1976). It was held that the commerce clause does not empower Congress to enforce such requirements against the states in an area of "traditional governmental function." The district court held that a mass transit system is a traditional governmental function and under the *Usery* decision is exempt from the obligations imposed by the FLSA.

Opinion by Mr. Justice Blackmun
(Vote: 5-4)

Question—Whether or not the principles of the Tenth Amendment as set forth in *National League of Cities* v. *Usery* (1976) should be reconsidered.

Decision—Yes.

Reason—We feel that the attempt to draw "the boundaries of state regulatory immunity in terms of traditional governmental function" is not only unworkable but collide with the federalist principles. This being so, the case of *National League of Cities* (1976) accordingly is overruled. During the pendency of *Garcia* "the Court ruled that a community rail service provided by the state-owned Long Island Rail Road did not constitute a 'traditional governmental function' and hence did not enjoy constitutional immunity. . . ." It long has been settled that Congress's authority "under the Commerce Clause extends to intrastate economic activities that affect interstate Commerce." Although the Court has difficulty drawing the line on what is or is not a governmental function—the only case to address this problem is *Long Island*—still "we simultaneously disavow 'a static historical view of state functions generally immune from federal regulation.' " Any rule of state immunity that looks to the "traditional," "integral," or "necessary" nature of governmental functions inevitably invites an unelected federal judiciary to make decisions about which state policies it favors and which ones it dislikes." The judgment of the district court is reversed.

Corollary cases

National League of Cities v. Usery, 426 U.S. 833, 49 L. Ed. 2d 245, S. Ct. 2465 (1976)

Transportation Union v. Long Island R. Co., 455 U.S. 678, 71 L. Ed. 2d 547, 102 S. Ct. 1349 (1982)

Hodel v. Virginia Surface Mining & Recl. Assn., 452 U.S. 246, 69 L. Ed. 2d 1, 101 S. Ct. 2352 (1981)

Heart of Atlanta Motel v. United States, 379 U.S. 241, 13 L. Ed. 2d 258, 85 S. Ct. 348 (1964)

Wickard v. Filburn, 317 U.S. 111, 87 L. Ed. 122, 63 S. Ct. 82 (1942)

United States v. Darby, 312 U.S. 100, 85 L. Ed. 609, 61 S. Ct. 451 (1941)

Fry v. United States, 421 U.S. 542, 44 L. Ed. 2d 363, 95 S. Ct. 1792 (1975)

South Carolina v. United States, 199 U.S. 437, 50 L. Ed. 261, 26 S. Ct. 110 (1905)

Collector v. Day, 11 Wall 113, 20 L. Ed. 122 (1870)

New York v. United States, 326 U.S. 572, 90 L. Ed. 326, 66 S. Ct. 310 (1946)

Ohio v. Helvering, 292 U.S. 360, 78 L. Ed. 1307, 54 S. Ct. 725 (1934)

EEOC v. Wyoming, 460 U.S. 226, 75 L. Ed. 2d 18, 103 S. Ct. 1054 (1983)

Note—*Garcia* seems to settle the zig-zag course of the Court as regarding the sovereignty of the states in as much as Blackmun noted it would no longer accept a static historical view of state functions, generally immune from federal regulation. In 1968 in *Maryland* v. *Wirtz* (20 L. Ed. 2d 1020, 1968) the Court held the extension of minimum wage standards to employees of state schools and hospitals; but in 1976 the Court reversed its position in *National League of Cities* v. *Usery* and, in turn, reverses *Usery*. On a somber note, Justice Powell says that for all its genuflecting before the Tenth Amendment, that in this 5-4 ruling, the Court's words are "meaningless rhetoric." Continuing its course as though the Tenth Amendment did not exist, the Court in *South Carolina* v. *Baker,* (99 L. Ed. 2d 592, 1988) held that Congress can impose a federal tax on interest from state and municipal bonds and in doing so not violate the intergovernmental tax immunity doctrine.

CONSTITUTIONAL AMENDMENTS

Hollingsworth v. Virginia, 3 Dallas 378; 1 L. Ed. 644 (1798)

The decision of the Court in the case of *Chisholm* v. *Georgia* produced a proposition in Congress for amending the Constitution so that no state could be sued by citizens of another state, or by citizens or subjects of a foreign state. Upon its adoption this became the Eleventh Amendment.

OPINION BY MR. JUSTICE CHASE
(No evidence from the report that the decision was not unanimous.)

Question—Is the amendment valid since the original was never submitted to the president for his approbation?

Decision—Yes.

Reason—There is no necessity for an amendment to be shown to the president. The Constitutional requirement of presidential signature applies only to ordinary legislation. The action of Congress in proposing an amendment is a constituent rather than a legislative act.

Corollary cases

Chisholm v. Georgia, 2 Dallas 419 (1793)
National Prohibition Cases, 253 U.S. 350 (1920)
Dillon v. Gloss, 256 U.S. 368 (1921)
Hawke v. Smith, 253 U.S. 221 (1920)
United States v. Sprague, 282 U.S. 716 (1931)
Leser v. Garnett, 258 U.S. 130 (1922)
United States v. Chambers, 291 U.S. 217 (1934)
Coleman v. Miller, 307 U.S. 433 (1939)
Edwards v. United States, 286 U.S. 482 (1932)
The Pocket Veto Case, 279 U.S. 655 (1929)

Note—It is not settled whether or not a state governor has a veto over state ratifying resolutions. In a recent (1977) advisory opinion to the Massachusetts State Senate, the Supreme Judicial Court said the governor plays no role in the amending process.

Coyle v. Smith, 221 U.S. 559; 31 S. Ct. 688; 55 L. Ed. 853 (1911)

When Oklahoma was admitted as a state in 1906, Congress provided that the capital should be located at Guthrie until the year 1913. In 1910 the Oklahoma legislature passed an act providing for the removal of the capital to Oklahoma City. Suit was brought to stop the move.

OPINION BY MR. JUSTICE LURTON
(Vote: 7-2)

Questions—1. May Congress, under penalty of denying admission, impose limitations on a new state at the time of admission?

2. Will those limitations be binding after admission as a state?

Decisions—1. Yes.
2. No.

Reasons—1. "The constitutional provisions concerning the admission of new states is not a mandate, but a power to be exercised with discretion." Therefore, Congress, in the exercise of this discretion, may impose conditions that a state-to-be must meet before Congress grants approval to its admission.

2. Any restraints imposed by Congress on a new state before its admission can be ignored with impunity by that state after admission except such as have some bases in the Constitution. Congress has no power to limit the rights of a state. The constitutional duty of guaranteeing to each state a republican form of government does not allow Congress to place limits on them that would deprive them of equality with other states. The constitutional power of admission of states is based on the assumption that the new states will be on a par with other states. This is a union of equal states. If Congress could lay down binding conditions, as the one involved in this case on an incoming state, then the United States would include states unequal in power. When a state enters the Union, she at once becomes "entitled to and possessed of all the rights of dominion and sovereignty which belonged to the original states. She was admitted, and could be admitted, only on the same footing with them."

A clear distinction should be drawn between a matter involving political inequality of a new state (as here, and which is not binding after admission) and a matter involving a quid pro quo contractual relation (which is binding after admission).

Corollary cases

Stearns v. Minnesota, 179 U.S. 223 (1900)
Van Brocklin v. Tennessee, 117 U.S. 151 (1886)
Willmette Iron Bridge Co. v. Hatch, 125 U.S. 1 (1888)
Pollard v. Hagan, 3 Howard 212 (1885)
Escanaba and L. M. Transportation Co. v. Chicago, 107 U.S. 678 (1883)
Permiol v. New Orleans, 3 Howard 589 (1845)
Texas v. White, 7 Wallace 700 (1869)
Ervien v. United States, 251 U.S. 41 (1919)

Note—The admission standards for states after the original thirteen and the longevity of such "standards" had not been tested until *Coyle*.

Pacific States Telephone and Telegraph Co. v. State of Oregon, 223 U.S. 118; 32 S. Ct. 224; 56 L. Ed. 377 (1912)

In 1902 Oregon amended its constitution to give the people of the state the right of direct legislation through the initiative and the referendum. A tax law in 1906 was passed by the initiative under which corporations of certain types were assessed 2 percent of their gross receipts, and the Pacific States Telephone and Telegraph Co. refused to pay it.

OPINION BY MR. CHIEF JUSTICE WHITE
(No evidence from the report that the decision was not unanimous.)

Question—Does this use of the initiative and referendum destroy the republican form of government in Oregon?

Decision—It is a political question and the Court has no jurisdiction in this case.

Reason—The case in question was not against the legality of the tax as such but was concerned with the framework and political character of the government by which the statute levying the tax was passed. It was the government, the political entity, that was called to the bar of the Court, not for the purpose of testing judicially some exercise of power assailed on the ground that its exertion has injuriously affected the rights of an individual because of some repugnancy to some constitutional limitation, but to demand of the state that it establish its right to exist as a state, republican in form.

These issues were political and governmental and out of the jurisdiction of this Court.

Corollary cases

Luther v. Borden, 7 Howard 1 (1849)
Colegrove v. Green, 328 U.S. 549 (1946)
Georgia v. Stantor, 6 Wallace 50 (1868)
South v. Peters, 339 U.S. 276 (1950)
McDougall v. Green, 335 U.S. 281 (1948)
Coleman v. Miller, 307 U.S. 433 (1939)

Note—Article IV, Section 4 says the United States will guarantee to every state a republican form of government. What is a republican form of government has never been defined and is unlikely to be so. It is a "political question." It is hard to imagine what would not be since, presumably, the United States was a republican form of government during the time of slavery and before the Nineteenth Amendment. The argument that ours is a "republican" but not a "democratic" government, is a sterile one based more on words than on fact.

National Prohibition Cases (Rhode Island v. Palmer), 253 U.S. 350; 40 S. Ct. 486; 64 L. Ed. 946 (1920)

The National Prohibition Cases consisted of seven cases of the same nature, and therefore were subject to the same interpretation. These cases questioned the constitutionality and legality of the Eighteenth Amendment and of the Volstead Act to enforce that amendment, and had asked the lower courts for a restraining order against the Volstead Act.

OPINION BY MR. JUSTICE VAN DEVANTER
(Vote: 7-2)

Question—Is the Eighteenth Amendment within the power to amend reserved by Article Five?

Decision—Yes.

Reason—The power to amend the Constitution was reserved by Article Five. The Court noted the following points:

"1. The adoption by both Houses of Congress, each by a two-thirds vote, of a joint resolution proposing an amendment to the Constitution, sufficiently shows that the proposal was deemed necessary by all who voted for it. An express declaration that they regarded it as necessary is not essential. None of the resolutions whereby prior amendments were proposed contained such a declaration.

2. The two-thirds vote in each House, which is required in proposing an amendment is a vote of two-thirds of the members present—assuming the presence of a quorum—and not a vote of two-thirds of the entire membership, present and absent. . . .

3. The referendum provisions of state constitutions and statutes cannot be applied, consistently with the Constitution of the United States, in the ratification or rejection of amendments to it. . . .

4. The prohibition of manufacture, sale, transportation, importation, and exportation of intoxicating liquors for beverage purposes, as embodied in the Eighteenth Amendment, is within the power to amend reserved by Article Five of the Constitution.

5. That amendment, by lawful proposal and ratification, has become a part of the Constitution, and must be respected and given effect the same as other provisions of that instrument."

According to the Constitution, this amendment had been legally proposed by a two-thirds vote of the members present in each house, assuming the presence of a quorum, and ratified by a majority of the legislatures in three-fourths of the states. Incorporated into that amendment was the provision "that Congress and the several states shall have concurrent power to enforce this article by appropriate legislation." This Section Two of the amendment therefore authorized the Volstead Act. The words "concurrent power," giving concurrent power to Congress and the states to enforce that amendment, do not mean a joint power or require that legislation thereunder by

Congress, to be effective, shall be approved or sanctioned by the several states or any of them, and is in no wise dependent on or affected by action, or inaction, on the part of the states or any of them.

Corollary cases

Hawke v. Smith, 253 U.S. 221 (1920)
Missouri Pacific R.R. Co. v. Kansas, 248 U.S. 276 (1919)
United States v. Sprague, 282 U.S. 716 (1931)
Leser v. Garnett, 258 U.S. 130 (1922)
Coleman v. Miller, 307 U.S. 433 (1939)
Hollingsworth v. Virginia, 3 Dallas 378 (1798)

Hawke v. Smith, 253 U.S. 221; 40 S. Ct. 495; 64 L. Ed. 871 (1920)

Hawke, a citizen of Ohio, filed a petition for an injunction, seeking to enjoin the secretary of state of Ohio from spending public money in preparing and printing forms of ballots for submission of a referendum to the electors of the state on the question of the ratification that the General Assembly had made of the proposed Eighteenth Amendment to the federal Constitution. The petition was sustained, this judgment was affirmed by the court of appeals and supreme court of Ohio, and then the Supreme Court of the United States was asked to decide the correctness of the judgment.

OPINION BY MR. JUSTICE DAY

(No evidence from the report that the decision was not unanimous.)

Question—Is the provision of the Ohio Constitution, extending the referendum to the ratification by the General Assembly of proposed amendments to the federal Constitution, in conflict with Article V of the Constitution of the United States?

Decision—Yes.

Reason—Article V of the federal Constitution says that, "The Congress, whenever two-thirds of both Houses shall deem it necessary, shall propose Amendments to this Constitution, or, on the application of the legislatures of two-thirds of the several states, shall call a convention for proposing amend-

ments, which, in either case, shall be valid . . . when ratified
by the legislatures of three-fourths of the several states, or by
conventions in three-fourths thereof. . . .'' Article V is for the
purpose of establishing an orderly manner in which changes in
the Constitution can be accomplished. Ratification by a state
of a constitutional amendment is not an act of legislation in the
proper sense of the word. It is but an expression of the assent
of the state to a proposed amendment. The power to legislate
in the enactment of the laws of a state is derived from the
people of the state, but the power to ratify a proposed amendment to the Constitution has its source in the federal Constitution. The act of ratification by the state derives its authority
from the federal Constitution, to which the states and its
people alike assent. The method of ratification is left to the
choice of Congress. The determination of ratification is the
exercise of a national power specifically granted by the Constitution. The language of Article V is plain. It is not the function
of courts or legislative bodies, national or state, to alter
methods that the Constitution has fixed.

Corollary cases

Coleman v. Miller, 307 U.S. 433 (1939)
Chandler v. Wise, 307 U.S. 474 (1939)
United States v. Sprague, 282 U.S. 716 (1931)
Leser v. Garnett, 258 U.S. 130 (1922)
National Prohibition Cases, 253 U.S. 350 (1920)

Dillon v. Gloss, 256 U.S. 368; 41 S. Ct. 513; 65 L. Ed. 994 (1921)

Dillon was taken into custody under Section 26 of Title 2
of the National Prohibition Act of October 28, 1919 on the
charge of transporting intoxicating liquor in violation of
Section 3 of Title 2. He petitioned the court and sought to
be discharged on a writ of habeas corpus from the court on
grounds: (1) that the Eighteenth Amendment was invalid
because the Congressional resolution proposing the amendment declared that it should be inoperative unless ratified
within seven years, and (2) that the act which he was charged
with violating, and under which he was arrested, had not
gone into effect at the time of the asserted violation nor at

the time of the arrest. The Eighteenth Amendment was ratified January 16, 1919 but it was not proclaimed by the secretary of state until January 29, 1919. Dillon committed the violation on January 17, 1920. By the terms of the act it was to have gone into effect one year after being ratified. Dillon asserted it should have gone into effect one year after being proclaimed by the secretary of state which would have been January 29, 1920.

OPINION BY MR. JUSTICE VAN DEVANTER
(No evidence from the report that the decision was not unanimous.)

Questions—1. Can Congress set a reasonable time limit on the ratification of an amendment?

2. On what date does the ratification take effect?

Decisions—1. Yes.
2. The day the last required state ratifies the amendment is the date the amendment becomes part of the Constitution.

Reasons—1. Article Five discloses that it is intended to invest Congress with a wide range of power in proposing amendments. That the Constitution contains no express provision on the time limit for ratification is not in itself controlling, for with the Constitution, as with a statute or other written instruments, what is reasonably implied is as much a part of it as what is expressed. Proposal and ratification are but necessary steps in a single endeavor. There is a fair implication that ratification must be sufficiently contemporaneous in the required number of states to reflect the will of the people in all sections at relatively the same period, and hence that ratification must be within some reasonable time after the proposal.

The court held that Article Five impliedly gives Congress a wide range of power in proposing amendments, and therefore a time limit of seven years for ratification is a reasonable use of this power.

2. The Court held that the amendment takes effect the day the last state ratifies it, that is, the state that gives the amendment the required majority. It is not necessarily the date when the secretary of state proclaims the amendment.

Corollary cases

Ex parte Yarbrough, 110 U.S. 651 (1884)
South Carolina v. United States, 199 U.S. 437 (1905)
Luria v. United States, 231 U.S. 9 (1913)
National Prohibition Cases, 253 U.S. 350 (1920)
United States v. Sprague, 282 U.S. 716 (1931)
Hawke v. Smith, 253 U.S. 221 (1920)
Coleman v. Miller, 307 U.S. 433 (1939)
Hollingsworth v. Virginia, 3 Dallas 378 (1798)
Leser v. Garnett, 258 U.S. 130 (1922)

Coleman v. Miller, 307 U.S. 433; 59 S. Ct. 972; 83 L. Ed. 1385 (1939)

In June 1924 Congress proposed an amendment to the Constitution known as the Child Labor Amendment. In January 1925 the legislature of Kansas adopted a resolution rejecting the proposed amendment, and a certified copy was sent to the secretary of state of the United States. In January 1937 a resolution was introduced in the Senate of Kansas ratifying the proposed amendment. There were forty Senators, twenty in favor, and twenty rejecting it. The lieutenant governor, presiding officer of the Senate, cast his vote in favor of the resolution, which was later adopted by a majority of the members of the House of Representatives.

Petition was then brought challenging the right of the lieutenant governor to cast the deciding vote. The petition also challenged the vitality of the amendment, stating that a reasonable amount of time for ratification had elapsed.

OPINION BY MR. CHIEF JUSTICE HUGHES
(Vote: 7-2)

Questions—Two major issues were involved: (1) Can a state whose legislature has formally rejected a federal amendment later ratify it? (2) Do proposed amendments die of old age, if they remain before the states for too long a time?

Decisions—The Court decided that the case held enough interest for consideration. It upheld, without considering the merits, the decision of the state supreme court that the lieutenant governor had the authority to break the tie.

(1) The question of ratification in the light of previous rejec-

tion, or attempted withdrawal should be regarded as a political question, with ultimate authority for its decision residing in Congress.

(2) Congress, likewise, has the final say in the determination of whether or not an amendment has lost its vitality before the required ratifications.

Reasons—Article V of the Constitution says nothing of rejection, but only of ratification. The power to ratify is conferred upon a state by the Constitution and persists even if previously rejected.

The political departments of the government dealt with previous rejection and attempted withdrawal in the adoption of the Fourteenth Amendment. Both were considered ineffectual in the presence of an actual ratification. This is a political question pertaining to the political departments, with final authority for the matter in the hands of Congress.

Regarding the vitality of the amendment, an amendment is not open for ratification for all time, since amendments are prompted by necessity. However, if Congress does not set a limit, as it did in the Eighteenth Amendment (7 years), the Court may not take upon itself the responsibility of deciding what constitutes a reasonable time. No criteria for a judicial determination of any kind of time limit exist in the Constitution.

Congress has the power under Article V to fix a reasonable time limit. If the time is not fixed in advance, it is open for determination at the time of promulgating the adoption of the amendment. This decision of Congress would not be subject to review by the Court. These questions are essentially political and are not justiciable.

Corollary cases

Dillon v. Gloss, 256 U.S. 368 (1921)
United States v. Sprague, 282 U.S. 716 (1931)
Hawke v. Smith, 253 U.S. 221 (1920)
Luther v. Borden, 7 Howard 1 (1849)
Pacific States Telegraph and Telephone Co. v. State of Oregon, 223 U.S. 118 (1912)
Leser v. Garnett, 258 U.S. 130 (1922)

Note—The doctrine of "political questions" is thrown into considerable doubt by the Court's recent forays in *Baker* v. *Carr,* 369 U.S. 186 (1962) and *Powell* v. *McCormack,* 393 U.S. 486 (1969). Moreover, the defeated Equal Rights Amendment generated new questions involving constitutional amendments: thus, how can the President's role in the amending process be erased even though Article I, Section 7 requires—contrary to the view in *Hollingsworth*—that bills passed by Congress must be presented to the President? *Hollingsworth* itself is considered an aberration inasmuch as there never was a reason for its holding. The Court, in *Dillon,* furthermore, said that "a time limit of seven years for ratification is a reasonable use of this power"—a view from which the Court retreated in *Coleman* as bordering on an advisory opinion. The Equal Rights Amendment was extended from 7 years to 10½ years before its time ran out. Discussion still rages over its constitutionality.

INTERSTATE COMMERCE

Gibbons v. Ogden, 9 Wheaton 1; 6 L. Ed. 23 (1824)

The state of New York gave exclusive navigation rights to all water within the jurisdiction of the state of New York to R. R. Livingston and R. Fulton, who assigned Ogden the right to operate between New York City and New Jersey ports. Gibbons owned two steamships running between New York and Elizabethtown, which were licensed under act of Congress. Ogden gained an injunction against Gibbons, who appealed.

OPINION BY MR. CHIEF JUSTICE MARSHALL
(No evidence from the report that the decision was not unanimous.)

Question—Can a state grant exclusive rights to navigate its waters?

Decision—No.

Reason—Congressional power to regulate commerce is unlimited except as prescribed by the Constitution. Commerce is more than traffic; it is intercourse and it is regulated by prescribing rules for carrying on that intercourse. Regulating power over commerce between states does not stop at jurisdictional lines of states, and may be exercised within a state, but it does not extend to commerce wholly within a state. When the state law and federal law conflict on this subject, federal law must be supreme. Thus the act of the state of New York was unconstitutional. Any matter that affects interstate commerce is within the power of Congress.

This case is noteworthy because it was the first one ever to go to the Court under the commerce clause.

Corollary cases

Wilson v. Blackbird Creek Marsh Co., 2 Peters 245 (1829)
Cooley v. Board of Wardens of the Port of Philadelphia, 12 Howard 299 (1851)
Baldwin v. Seelig, 294 U.S. 511 (1935)
H. P. Hood and Sons v. Du Mond, 336 U.S. 525 (1949)
United States v. South-Eastern Underwriters Association, 322 U.S. 533 (1944)

Note—The principles of *Gibbons* (1824) and *Cooley* (1851) are seminal and are the beginning of any discussion of national and local commerce. *Gibbons*, argued for by Daniel Webster, was the first even to go to the Court under the commerce clause and was Chief Justice Marshall's most popular opinion.

Brown v. Maryland, 12 Wheaton 419; 6 L. Ed. 678 (1827)

There was a law in Maryland requiring all importers of foreign goods to have a license issued by the state. The indictment in this case charged Brown with having imported and sold some foreign goods without having a license to do so.

OPINION BY MR. CHIEF JUSTICE MARSHALL
(Vote: 6-1)

Question—Can the legislature of a state constitutionally require the importer of foreign goods to take out a license from the state before he shall be permitted to sell the goods imported?

Decision—No.

Reason—The powers remaining with the states as a result of the Constitution may be so exercised as to come in conflict with those vested in Congress. When this happens, that which is not supreme must yield to that which is supreme. It results necessarily from this principle that the taxing power of the states must have some limits. Here the Court held that the Maryland statute authorizing a tax on imports interfered with the federal government's control of commerce with foreign countries. Although not denying the right of a state to tax property within the state, the Court felt in this case the taxing of imports would obviously derange the measures of Congress to regulate commerce, and affect materially the purpose for which that power was given. "It is sufficient for the present to say, generally, that when the importer has so acted upon the thing imported, that it has become incorporated and mixed up with the mass of property in the country, it has, perhaps, lost its distinctive character as an import, and has become subject to the taxing power of the state; but while remaining the property of the importer, in his warehouse, in the original form or package in which it was imported, a tax upon it is too plainly a duty on imports to escape the prohibition in the Constitution.'' The Court held the action of Maryland also to be contrary to the provision in the Constitution expressly forbidding states to tax imports.

Corollary cases

McCulloch v. Maryland, 4 Wheaton 316 (1819)
Anglo-Chilean Nitrate Sales Corp. v. Alabama, 288 U.S. 218 (1933)
Hooven and Allison Co. v. Evatt, 324 U.S. 652 (1945)
Baldwin v. Seelig, 294 U.S. 511 (1935)
Leisy v. Hardin, 135 U.S. 100 (1890)
Woodruff v. Parham, 8 Wallace 123 (1869)
Youngstown Sheet and Tube Co. v. Bowers, 358 U.S. 534 (1959)
Michelin Tire Corp. v. Wages, 423 U.S. 276 (1976)

Note—The "original package" case, *Brown* covers commerce from *abroad* to the states, as *Leisy* v. *Hardin,* 135 U.S. 100 (1890) covers commerce *among* the American states.

Cooley v. The Board of Wardens of the Port of Philadelphia, 12 Howard 299; 13 L. Ed. 996 (1851)

The Board of Wardens of the port of Philadelphia, acting under a statute of the state of Pennsylvania that established an elaborate system of regulations regarding pilots in the port including monetary penalties for failure to comply with the regulations, attempted to enforce the regulations. Cooley violated the regulations and when tried alleged that they were unconstitutional.

OPINION BY MR. JUSTICE CURTIS
(Vote: 7-2)

Question—Is the power of Congress entirely exclusive in the regulation of commerce?

Decision—No.

Reason—The grant of this power to Congress does not contain any terms that expressly exclude the states from exercising any authority over this subject matter. Although Congress has the power to regulate pilots, its legislation manifests an intention not to regulate this subject but to let the states do it.

"Whatever subjects of this power are in their nature national, or admit only the one uniform system, or plan of regulation, may justly be said to be of such a nature as to require exclusive legislation by Congress. That this cannot be affirmed of laws for the regulation of pilots and pilotage, is plain."

Corollary cases

License Tax Cases, 5 Wallace 462 (1867)
Louisiana Public Service Comm. v. Texas and N.O.R. Co., 284 U.S. 125 (1931)
Gilman v. Philadelphia, 3 Wallace 713 (1866)
City of Burbank v. Lockheed Air Terminal, Inc., 411 U.S. 624 (1973)
Escanaba and L. M. Transportation Co. v. Chicago, 107 U.S. 678 (1883)
Port Richmond and Bergen Point Ferry Co. v. Board of Chosen Freeholders of Hudson County, 234 U.S. 317 (1914)
Hall v. De Cuir, 95 U.S. 785 (1878)

Note—The Court adopted a "selective exclusiveness doctrine" in which Congress would regulate commerce that was national and uniform and the states local. *Gibbons* deals with the positive power of Congress and *Cooley* with the negative phase.

Munn v. Illinois, 94 U.S. 113; 24 L. Ed. 77 (1877)

Ira Y. Munn, *et al.*, were grain warehousemen in Chicago, Illinois, and were sued by Illinois for transacting business without a state license in violation of a state statute that provided a maximum of charges for the storage of grain in a warehouse. The defendants admitted the facts charged, but alleged that the statute requiring said license was unconstitutional for attempting to fix that maximum rate of storage, on the ground that it was repugnant to the Constitution, which confers upon Congress the power to regulate commerce with foreign states and among the several states.

OPINION BY MR. CHIEF JUSTICE WAITE
(Vote: 7-2)

Question—Can the General Assembly of Illinois, under the limitations upon the legislative powers of the states imposed by the Constitution, fix by law regulations for the storage of grain in warehouses at Chicago and other places in the state?

Decision—Yes.

Reason—The Court reasoned that it has always been an established principle that where the public has a definite and positive interest in a business, they have a right to regulate the operations of that business. The Court held that such was the case here, and it did not matter that these plaintiffs had built their warehouses and established their business before the regulations complained of were adopted. What they did was from the beginning always subject to possible regulations promoting the common good. They entered upon their business and provided themselves with the means to carry it on, subject to this condition. If they did not wish to submit themselves to such interference, they should not have clothed the public with an interest in their concerns. "Property does become clothed with a public interest when used in a manner to make it of public consequence, and affect the community at large. When, therefore, one devotes his property to a use in which the public has an interest, he, in effect, grants to the public an interest in the use, and must submit to be controlled by the public for the common good, to the extent of the interest he has thus created. He may withdraw his grant by discontinuing the use; but so long as he maintains the use, he must submit to the control. We know that this is a power which may be abused; but that is no argument against its existence. For protection against abuses by legislatures the people must resort to the polls, not to the courts."

Corollary cases

Brown v. Maryland, 12 Wheaton 448 (1827)
Gibbons v. Ogden, 9 Wheaton 232 (1824)
Osborne v. Mobile, 16 Wallace 481 (1873)
Nebbia v. New York, 291 U.S. 502 (1934)
Peik v. Chicago & N.W.R. Co., 94 U.S. 164 (1877)
Olsen v. Nebraska, 313 U.S. 236 (1941)
Cooley v. Wardens of the Port of Philadelphia, 12 Howard 299 (1851)
Brass v. North Dakota, 153 U.S. 391 (1894)

Note—The principle in *Munn* that the state could regulate only businesses "affected with the public interest" was finally discarded in *Nebbia* v. *New York,* (1934) upholding a New York law setting milk prices.

Leisy v. Hardin, 135 U.S. 100; 10 S. Ct. 681; 34 L. Ed. 128 (1890)

> Leisy, a brewer of Peoria, Illinois, brought an action to recover a quantity of barrels and cases of beer that had been seized in a proceeding on behalf of the state, for violating the Iowa statute prohibiting the sale of intoxicating liquors in the state. The beer in question was shipped from Illinois and sold in the original packages.

OPINION BY MR. CHIEF JUSTICE FULLER
(Vote: 6-3)

Question—Can a state prohibit articles of commerce from being imported into the state, in the absence of legislation on the part of Congress?

Decision—No.

Reason—The power of Congress to regulate commerce is unlimited, except for those restrictions specified in the Constitution. If Congress does not regulate concerning certain phases of interstate commerce, that commerce shall be free and unhampered. Beer, therefore, may be brought into the state and sold, after which time it becomes mingled in the common mass of property of the state, and subject to its control. The right to sell any article brought into a state is an inseparable incident to the right to import the article.

Corollary cases

Brown v. Maryland, 12 Wheaton 419 (1827)
License Cases, 5 Howard 504 (1847)
Bowman v. Chicago & N. Ry. Co., 125 U.S. 465 (1888)
South Carolina State Highway Department v. Barnwell Bros., 303 U.S. 177 (1938)
In re Rahrer, 140 U.S. 545 (1891)
Clark Distilling Co. v. Western Maryland Ry. Co., 242 U.S. 311 (1917)
United States v. Hill, 248 U.S. 420 (1919)

Rhodes v. Iowa, 170 U.S. 412 (1898)
Whitfield v. Ohio, 297 U.S. 431 (1956)
Kentucky Whip and Collar Co. v. Illinois Central R.R. Co., 299 U.S. 334
  (1937)

Note—The original package doctrine as regards foreign imports, *Brown* v. *Maryland*, 12 Wheaton 419 (1827) was carried over and covered interstate commerce in *Leisy*. In *Leisy*, though, the Court invited Congress to enact legislation giving the states some power to regulate articles involved in interstate commerce, which it did in 1890 in the Wilson Act, subsequently validated in *In re Rahrer*, 140 U.S. 545 (1891).

In re Debs, 158 U.S. 564; 15 S. Ct. 900; 39 L. Ed. 1092 (1895)

Eugene V. Debs and associates, officers of the American Railway Union, had instituted a strike against the Pullman Co. of Chicago. To enforce their demands they picketed the railway cars of that company and would not allow them either to enter or leave Chicago. In doing this they stopped interstate commerce and also the cars carrying United States mail. The company was granted an injunction by the federal court against the union picketing and when the order was not carried out Debs and the other officers of the union were convicted in contempt of it.

OPINION BY MR. JUSTICE BREWER
(No evidence from the report that the decision was not unanimous.)

Question—Is the federal government able to prevent a forcible obstruction of interstate commerce and of the mails?

Decision—Yes.

Reason—"The entire strength of the nation may be used to enforce in any part of the land the full and free exercise of all national powers and the security of all rights entrusted by the Constitution to its care. The strong arm of the national government may be put forth to brush away all obstructions to the freedom of interstate commerce or the transportation of the mails. If the emergency arises, the army of the nation, and all its militia, are at the service of the nation to compel obedience to its laws."

"It is obvious from these decisions that while it is not the province of the government to interfere in any mere matter of private controversy between individuals, or to use its great powers to enforce the rights of one against another, yet, whenever the wrongs complained of are such as affect the public at large, and are in respect of matters which by the Constitution are entrusted to the care of the nation, and concerning which the nation owes the duty to all the citizens of securing to them their common rights, then the mere fact that the government has no pecuniary interest in the controversy is not sufficient to exclude it from the courts, or prevent it from taking measures therein to fully discharge those constitutional duties.''

Corollary cases

United States v. San Jacinto Tin Co., 125 U.S. 273 (1888)
Coppage v. Kansas, 236 U.S. 1 (1915)
Duplex Printing Press Co. v. Deering, 254 U.S. 443 (1921)
Loewe v. Lawlor, (Danbury Hatter's Case), 208 U.S. 274 (1908)
Bedford Cut Stone Co. v. Journeymen Stone Cutter's Association, 274 U.S. 37 (1927)

Note—Governor Altgeld of Illinois strongly protested the introduction of troops to break up the strike, as did, years later, Governor O. Faubus of Arkansas when President Eisenhower sent troops to Little Rock to control violence and assist in school integration. When President John Kennedy dispatched federal troops to Mississippi to force the state university to admit James Meredith, a black student, Governor Ross Barnett protested vehemently. The president, of course, is responsible for faithfully executing the law.

United States v. E. C. Knight Co., 156 U.S. 1; 15 S. Ct. 249; 39 L. Ed. 325 (1895)

The government charged that the E. C. Knight Company, with four others, had contracted with the American Sugar Refining Company for the purchase by the latter of the stocks and properties of these corporations, and for the issuance of stock in the American Sugar Refining Co. It charged that this transaction was intended to bring about control of the price of sugar in the United States, together with a monopoly of the manufacture and sale of refined sugar in this country, in violation of the Sherman Anti-Trust Act.

OPINION BY MR. CHIEF JUSTICE FULLER
(Vote: 8-1)

Question—Assuming the existence of a monopoly in manufacture, can the monopoly be directly suppressed under the act of Congress in the manner attempted by this action?

Decision—No.

Reason—The power to control manufacturing involves in a certain sense the control of its disposition, but only in a secondary sense. The exercise of that power brings the operation of commerce into play, but only indirectly. The regulation of commerce applies to subjects of commerce, not to those of internal police. The fact that an article is manufactured with an intent of export to another state does not of itself make such an article an item of interstate commerce. It becomes so when it begins its journey in interstate commerce.

The act of 1890 did not attempt to deal with monopolies as such, but with conspiracies to monopolize trade among the several states. In the case at hand, the object was private gain from manufacture of the commodity, not control of interstate or foreign commerce. There was nothing in the proofs to indicate any intention to put a restraint upon trade or commerce.

Corollary cases

Coe v. Errol, 116 U.S. 517 (1886)
Kidd v. Pearson, 128 U.S. 1 (1888)
Standard Oil Co. v. United States, 221 U.S. 1 (1911)
United States v. American Tobacco Co., 221 U.S. 106 (1911)
Swift and Co. v. United States, 196 U.S. 375 (1905)
United States v. Northern Securities Co., 193 U.S. 197 (1904)
Loewe v. Lawlor (Danbury Hatters' Case), 208 U.S. 274 (1908)
N.L.R.B. v. Jones and Laughlin Steel Corp., 301 U.S. 1 (1937)

Note—*E. C. Knight* was reversed in *N.L.R.B.* v. *Jones and Laughlin Steel Corp.* (1937). *Knight* was the first big interpretation of the Sherman Antitrust Act (1890). The practical effect of *Knight* was a legal "no man's land"—the doctrine of "dual federalism" that was ultimately erased in *United States* v. *Darby Lumber Co.,* 312 U.S. 100 (1941).

Champion v. Ames (The Lottery Case), 188 U.S. 321; 23 S. Ct. 321; 47 L. Ed. 492 (1903)

> Congress passed legislation in 1895 for the suppression of lottery traffic through national and interstate commerce and the postal service. The regulation was, in effect, a prohibition, since the law provided a prison term for each violation. Charles Champion was arrested for violating the act and he appealed that the act was unconstitutional since the commerce clause granted Congress only the power to regulate not to prohibit.

OPINION BY MR. JUSTICE HARLAN
(Vote: 5-4)

Question—Did Congress exceed its power in passing the legislation in question?

Decision—No.

Reason—Congress by the act did not assume to interfere with traffic or commerce in lottery tickets carried on exclusively within the limits of any state, but had in view only commerce of that kind among the several states. As a state may, for the purpose of guarding the morals of its own people, forbid all sales of lottery tickets within its limits, so Congress, for the purpose of guarding the people of the United States against the "widespread pestilence of lotteries" and to protect the commerce that concerns all the states, may prohibit the carrying of lottery tickets from one state to another. Congress alone has the power to occupy by legislation the whole field of interstate commerce. If the carrying of lottery tickets from one state to another be interstate commerce, and if Congress is of the opinion that an effective regulation for the suppression of lotteries, carried on through such commerce, is to make it a criminal offense to cause lottery tickets to be carried from one state to another, the Court knew of no authority to hold that the means was not appropriate. The Court held "that lottery tickets are subject to traffic among those who choose to sell or buy them; that the carriage of such tickets by independent carriers from one state to another is therefore interstate commerce; that under its power to regulate commerce among the several states Congress—subject to the limitations imposed by the Constitution upon the exercise of the powers granted—has plenary authority over such commerce, and may prohibit the carriage of such tickets from state to state; and that legislation to that end, and of that character, is not inconsistent with any limitation or restriction imposed upon the exercise of the powers granted to Congress."

Corollary cases

Phalen v. Virginia, 8 Howard 163 (1850)
Stone v. Mississippi, 101 U.S. 814 (1880)
Douglas v. Kentucky, 168 U.S. 488 (1897)
Allgeyer v. Louisiana, 165 U.S. 578 (1897)
Hoke v. United States, 227 U.S. 308 (1913)
Brooks v. United States, 267 U.S. 432 (1925)
Gooch v. United States, 297 U.S. 124 (1936)
United States v. Darby, 312 U.S. 100 (1941)

Note—The first recognition of federal "police powers." Together with the commerce power Congress has virtual control over the economic life of the nation.

Houston, E. & W. Texas Ry. Co. v. United States (The Shreveport Case), 234 U.S. 342; 34 S. Ct. 833; 58 L. Ed. 1341 (1914)

This case involved the power of Congress and its agent, the Interstate Commerce Commission, to control railroad rates between points within the same state. The commission had fixed rates between the city of Shreveport, Louisiana, and certain points in eastern Texas for which Shreveport is the natural trade center. Motivated by a natural desire to keep Texas trade safe for the Texans, the government of that state had endeavored to fix the rates between the eastern Texas points and such cities as Dallas and Houston so low that these eastern points would trade with the Texas cities even though they were farther away than was Shreveport. At this point the ICC ordered the intra-Texas rates raised to the same level as the interstate Texas-Louisiana rates.

OPINION BY MR. JUSTICE HUGHES
(Vote: 7-2)

Question—Under any conditions can Congress regulate local and intrastate commerce?

Decision—Yes.

Reason—The Supreme Court upheld the right of the federal government to regulate the local or intrastate commerce in this case on the theory that it had such a close and substantial relation to interstate commerce that the satisfactory control of one required the simultaneous and identical control of the other. "Congress, in the exercise of its paramount power, may prevent the common instrumentalities of interstate and intrastate commercial intercourse from being used in their intrastate operations to the injury of interstate commerce. This is not to say that Congress possesses the authority to regulate the internal commerce of a state, as such, but that it does possess the power to foster and protect interstate commerce, and to take all measures necessary or appropriate to that end, although intrastate transactions or interstate carriers may thereby by controlled."

Corollary cases

The Daniel Ball, 10 Wallace 557 (1871)
Mobile County v. Kimball, 102 U.S. 691 (1881)
Second Employers' Liability Cases, 223 U.S. 1 (1912)
Complete Auto Transit, Inc. v. Brady, 97 S. Ct. 1076 (1977)
Minnesota Rate Cases, 230 U.S. 352 (1913)
Wisconsin R.R. Commission v. C. B. & Q. R.R. Co., 257 U.S. 563 (1922)
New York v. United States, 257 U.S. 591 (1922)

Note—The Court adopts the "Shreveport Rule" and abandons the concept of two mutually exclusive areas of intrastate and interstate commerce. For all practical purposes the clause is unlimited.

Stafford v. Wallace, 258 U.S. 495; 42 S. Ct. 397; 66 L. Ed. 735 (1922)

Stafford and Company, engaged in the buying and selling of livestock, brought suit against Secretary of Agriculture H. C. Wallace in order to prohibit him from enforcing the Packers and Stockyards Act of 1921, which they contended was unconstitutional. The act provided for the supervision by federal authority of the business of the commission men and of the livestock dealers in the great stockyards of the country. Congress passed the act because, after extensive investigation, it found that the "Big Five" meat packers of the nation were engaged in a conspiracy in violation of the Anti-Trust Law, to control the business of the purchase of livestock, their preparation for use in meat products, and the distribution and sale thereof in this country and abroad.

OPINION BY MR. CHIEF JUSTICE TAFT
(Vote: 7-1)

Question—Did Congress have the authority under the commerce clause to supervise the activities of the meat packers?

Decision—Yes.

Reason—The Court reasoned that Congress was exercising its established authority over interstate commerce. The stockyards are not a place of rest or final destination. Thousands of head of livestock arrive daily by carload and must be promptly sold and disposed of and moved out to give place to the constantly flowing traffic that presses behind. The stockyards are but a throat through which the current flows, and the transactions that occur therein are only incident to this current from the west to the east, and from one state to another. Such transactions cannot be separated from the movement to which they contribute, and necessarily take on its character. The commission men are essential in making the sales without which the flow of the current would be obstructed, and this, whether they are made to packers or dealers. The dealers are essential to the sales to the stock farmers and feeders. The sales are not in this aspect merely local transactions. They create a local change of title, but they do not stop the flow; they merely change the private interests in the subject of the current, not interfering with, but on the contrary, being indispensable to its continuity. The origin of the livestock is in the west, its ultimate destination known to, and intended by all engaged in the business is in the middle west and east, either as meat products or stock for feeding and fattening. The stockyards and the sales are necessary factors in the middle of this current of commerce.

Corollary cases

Munn v. Illinois, 94 U.S. 113 (1877)
Swift & Co. v. United States, 196 U.S. 375 (1905)

Note—The "stream of commerce" concept was developed by Justice Oliver Wendell Holmes when he wrote in *Swift and Co. v. United States:* "Commerce among the states is not a technical legal conception, but a practical one, drawn from the course of business." Activities that closely affect the "stream of commerce" may be made subject to federal regulation even though the activities take place wholly within a state. *Stafford* follows logically from *Shreveport,* which allowed Congress power to regulate intrastate railroad rates when necessary for effective regulation of interstate rates.

Baldwin v. G.A.F. Seelig, Inc., 294 U.S. 511; 55 S. Ct. 497; 79 L. Ed. 1032 (1935)

G.A.F. Seelig, Inc. was engaged as a milk dealer in the city of New York. It bought its milk, including cream, in Fair Haven, Vt. from the Seelig Creamery Corporation, which in turn bought from the producers on the neighboring farms. Upon arrival in New York, about 90 percent was sold to customers in the original cans. About 10 percent was bottled in New York and sold to customers in bottles.

The New York Milk Control Act set up a system of minimum prices to be paid by dealers to producers. A protective provision prohibited the sale of milk brought in from outside the state unless the price paid to the producers was one that would be lawful within the state.

Seelig bought its milk from the creamery in Vermont at prices lower than the minimum in New York. The commissioner of farms and markets refused to license the transaction unless Seelig conformed to the New York regulations.

OPINION BY MR. JUSTICE CARDOZO
(No evidence from the report that the decision was not unanimous.)

Question—Is the New York law an unreasonable interference with interstate commerce?

Decision—Yes.

Reason—(1) New York has no power to project its legislation into Vermont. Such a power sets up a barrier in trade as effective as a customs duty. The imposition of imposts or duties upon commerce is placed without exception by the Constitution beyond the power of the states. The case in question is not one in which the state may regulate for the prevention of disease or to protect its inhabitants against fraudulent deception.

(2) The "original package" is not inflexible and final as regards interstate commerce. It is a convenient concept, and sufficient, except in exceptional cases. However, neither the police power nor the power to tax may be used with the aim or effect of setting up economic barriers against competition with the products of another state.

Corollary cases

International Textbook Co. v. Pigg, 217 U.S. 91 (1910)
Asbell v. Kansas, 209 U.S. 251 (1908)
Plumley v. Massachusetts, 155 U.S. 461 (1894)
Brown v. Maryland, 12 Wheaton 419 (1827)
Hood and Sons v. Du Mond, 336 U.S. 525 (1949)
Gibbons v. Ogden, 9 Wheaton 1 (1824)
Minnesota v. Clover Leaf Creamery Co., 449 U.S. 456 (1981)
Reeves v. Stake, 65 L. Ed. 2d 244 (1980)

Note—The people of the several states must "sink or swim" together and "that in the long run prosperity and salvation are in union and not in division." This also was the message recently in *Hicklin* v. *Orbeck,* 437 U.S. 518 (1978) in voiding Alaska's attempt in its 1972 "Alaska Hire" act to corner employment for Alaskans. The Supreme Court held in *Friedman (Supreme Court of Virginia* v. *Friedman,* 101 L. Ed. 2d 56, 1988) that Virginia's residency requirement for admission to the bar without examination of a lawyer practicing in another state violated the privileges and immunities clause.

Ashwander v. Tennessee Valley Authority, 297 U.S. 288; 56 S. Ct. 466; 80 L. Ed. 688 (1936)

The TVA, an agency of the federal government, entered into a contract with the Alabama Power Company, providing for the purchase by the TVA, among other items, of certain transmission lines and real property. Also included in the contract were the interchange of hydroelectric energy and the sale by the TVA to the power company of the surplus power from the Wilson Dam. The plaintiffs, who held preferred stock in the power company, were unable to get results in protesting the contract to the power company. Therefore, they sought a decree restraining these activities as repugnant to the Constitution. The district court issued a decree annulling the contract and the circuit court of appeals reversed.

OPINION BY MR. CHIEF JUSTICE HUGHES
(Vote: 8-1)

Question—Is the contract of the TVA with the Alabama Power Co. beyond the constitutional power of the federal government?

Decision—No.

Reason—The Court first considered the constitutional authority for the construction of the Wilson Dam, which was supported on the grounds that it was constructed under the exercise of war and commerce powers, that is, for the purpose of national defense and the improvement of navigation.

Secondly, the Court considered the constitutional authority to dispose of electric energy generated at the Wilson Dam. Here it was held that the authority to dispose of property constitutionally acquired by the United States is expressly granted to Congress by Section 3 of Article 4 of the Constitution. This section provides: "The Congress shall have power to dispose of and make all needful rules and regulations respecting the territory or other property belonging to the United States; and nothing in this Constitution shall be so construed as to prejudice any claims of the United States, or of any particular state.''

Corollary cases

Dodge v. Woolsey, 18 Howard 331 (1856)
Pollock v. Farmers' Loan & Trust Co., 157 U.S. 429 (1895)
McCulloch v. Maryland, 4 Wheaton 316 (1819)
Green Bay & M. Canal Co. v. Patten Paper Co., 172 U.S. 58 (1898)
United States v. Chandler-Dunbar Water Power Co., 229 U.S. 53 (1913)
Kaukauna Water-Power Co. v. Green Bay & M. Canal Co., 142 U.S. 254 (1819)
Tennessee Electric Power Co. v. TVA, 306 U.S. 118 (1939)

Note—Brandeis's concurrence set out the ''Ashwander Rules,'' since augmented, in which the Court defines its jurisdiction.

Kentucky Whip and Collar Co. v. Illinois Central R.R. Co., 299 U.S. 334; 57 S. Ct. 277; 81 L. Ed. 270 (1937)

The Ashurst-Sumners Act of 1935 makes it unlawful to ship in interstate commerce goods made by convict labor into any state where the goods are intended to be received, possessed, sold, or used in violation of its laws. Packages containing convict-made goods must be plainly labeled so as to show the names and addresses of shipper and consignee, the nature of the contents, and the name and location of the penal or reformatory institution where the article was produced. The petitioner manufactures in Kentucky, with convict labor, horse collars, harness, and strap goods that are marketed in various states. The Illinois Central received twenty-five separate shipments, for transportation in interstate commerce, none of which was labeled as required. The respondent refused to accept the shipments, and the petitioner brought suit for a mandatory injunction to compel shipment.

OPINION BY MR. CHIEF JUSTICE HUGHES
(Vote: 8-0)

Question—Does Congress have the power to prohibit in interstate commerce useful and harmless articles made by convict labor?

Decision—Yes.

Reason—The congressional power to regulate commerce is complete in itself, acknowledging no other limitations than those prescribed by the Constitution. The question here is whether this statute goes beyond the authority to "regulate."

The power to prohibit interstate transportation has been upheld in many cases. In fact, in the exercise of its control over interstate commerce, Congress may have the quality of police regulations. In so regulating, Congress may shape its policy to aid valid state laws in the protection of persons and property. Therefore, Congress may prevent transportation in interstate commerce of articles in which the state has the constitutional authority to forbid traffic in its internal commerce.

The Ashurst-Sumners Act has substantially the same provisions as the Webb-Kenyon Act. The subject matter is different, the effects are different, but the principle is the same. Where the subject of commerce is one on which the power of a state may be constitutionally exerted, Congress may, if it so chooses, put forth its power to prevent interstate commerce from being used to frustrate the state policy.

As far as the labels are concerned, they are but a reasonable provision for carrying out the purposes of the act.

Corollary cases

Gibbons v. Ogden, 9 Wheaton 1 (1824)
In re Rahrer, 140 U.S. 545 (1891)
United States v. Hill, 248 U.S. 420 (1919)
Whitfield v. Ohio, 297 U.S. 431 (1936)
Rhodes v. Iowa, 170 U.S. 412 (1898)
Clark Distilling Co. v. Western Maryland Railway Co., 242 U.S. 311 (1917)

United States v. Carolene Products Co., 304 U.S. 144; 58 S. Ct. 778; 82 L. Ed. 123 (1938)

In March 1923 Congress passed the "Filled Milk Act," that prohibited the shipment in interstate commerce of skimmed milk compounded with any fat or oil other than milk fat, so as to resemble milk or cream. The appellee was indicted in southern Illinois for shipping in interstate commerce certain packages of a filled milk compound.

OPINION BY MR. JUSTICE STONE
(Vote: 6-1)

Question—Is this regulation beyond the power of Congress over interstate commerce, and is this a deprivation of property without due process of law?

Decision—No.

Reason—Filled milk is described by the statute as an adulterated article of food, injurious to health, and a fraud upon the public. "Even in the absence of such aids the existence of facts supporting the legislative judgment is to be presumed, for regulatory legislation affecting ordinary commercial transactions is not to be pronounced unconstitutional unless in the light of the facts made known or generally assumed it is of such a character as to preclude the assumption that it rests upon some rational basis within the knowledge and experience of the legislators."

In this case, it is at least debatable whether commerce in filled milk should be left unregulated, partially restricted, or entirely prohibited. That was a decision for Congress, and as such, the prohibition of shipment in interstate commerce of this product was a constitutional exercise of the power to regulate interstate commerce. Congressional power to regulate commerce is the power to prescribe the rules by which commerce is to be governed. This extends to the prohibition of shipments in such commerce. This power is complete and unlimited, except as limited by the Constitution. Congress is free to exclude from interstate commerce articles whose use in states may be injurious to public health, morals, or welfare, or that contravene the policy of the state of their destination.

Corollary cases

O'Gorman and Young v. Hartford Fire Insurance Co., 282 U.S. 251 (1931)
Daniel v. Family Security Life Insurance Co., 336 U.S. 220 (1949)
United States v. Bass, 404 U.S. 336 (1972)
Champion v. Ames, 188 U.S. 321 (1903)
Brooks v. United States, 227 U.S. 308 (1925)

Note—*Carolene* contains the now-famous footnote four of Chief Justice Stone that set forth for perhaps the first time the "preferred freedoms" of the First Amendment. Justice Roberts had hinted at it in *Herndon* v. *Lowry,* 301 U.S. 242 (1927), and more explicitly by Justice Cardozo in *Palko* v. *Connecticut,* 302 U.S. 319 (1937) to his honor roll of superior rights. What footnote four in effect did was to set up a double standard of adjudication in which (a) economic legislation would be presumed constitutional unless on its face it obviously was not, and (b) legislation touching the Bill of Rights would not be so generously presumed as valid. The reason for the difference is that where rights involve the political process itself they should be more protected than economic rights.

Ziffrin v. Reeves, 308 U.S. 132; 60 S. Ct. 103; 84 L. Ed. 128 (1939)

Appellant, an Indiana corporation, had, since 1933, been receiving whisky from distillers in Kentucky for direct carriage to consigness in Chicago. It had permission under the Federal Motor Carriers Act of 1935 to operate as a contract carrier, and claimed the right to transport whisky in spite of the prohibitions of the Kentucky Alcoholic Beverages Control Law of 1938. It now sought to restrain the state from enforcing the contraband and penal provisions of the law. The Kentucky law forbade the carriage of intoxicating liquors by carriers other than licensed common carriers, and forbade distillers to deliver to an unauthorized carrier. Constant state control was exercised over the manufacture, sale, transportation, and possession of whisky. The corporation was denied a common carrier's certificate and transportation license by Kentucky. The corporation claimed that the law was unconstitutional because it was repugnant to the commerce, due process, and equal protection clauses.

OPINION BY MR. JUSTICE MCREYNOLDS
(Vote: 8-0)

Question—Is the Kentucky law unconstitutional?

Decision—No.

Reason—The Twenty-First Amendment sanctions the right of the state to legislate concerning intoxicating liquor brought from without, unfettered by the commerce clause. Without doubt a state may absolutely prohibit the manufacture of intoxicants, their transportation, sale, or possession, irrespective of when or where produced or obtained or the use to which they are put. Further, she may adopt measures reasonably appropriate to effectuate these inhibitions and exercise full police authority in respect of them. Under its police power, the state of Kentucky can permit the manufacture and sale of liquors only under certain conditions and regulate the way in which they are sold. In this way they cannot properly be regarded as an article of commerce.

The record shows no violation of the equal protection clause. A licensed common carrier is under stricter control than an ordinary contract carrier and may be entrusted with privileges forbidden to the latter.

The Motor Carrier Act of 1935 is said to secure the appellant the right claimed, but the Court could find nothing there that undertakes to destroy state power to protect her people against the evils of intoxicants or to sanction the receipt of articles declared contraband. The act has no such purpose or effect.

Corollary cases

South Carolina Highway Dept. v. Barnwell Bros., 303 U.S. 177 (1938)
Kidd v. Pearson, 128 U.S. 1 (1880)
Finch Co. v. McKittrick, 305 U.S. 395 (1939)
Duckworth v. Arkansas, 314 U.S. 390 (1941)
Carter v. Virginia, 321 U.S. 131 (1941)
United States v. Frankfort Distilleries, 324 U.S. 293 (1945)

Note—"Because of the sweep of the Twenty-first Amendment, the state is unfettered by traditional commerce clause limitations. Thus, while some activity might survive as First Amendment rights when it is related to the Twenty-first Amendment, however, it is controllable . . . forbidding liquor where food is not sold, where dancing is permitted or near a church, school, or bar with nude live entertainment." *New York State Liquor Authority* v. *Bellanca,* 69 L. Ed. 2d 357 (1981)

United States v. Appalachian Electric Power Co., 311 U.S. 377; 61 S. Ct. 291; 85 L. Ed. 243 (1940)

On June 25, 1925 the predecessor of the respondent Appalachian Electric Power Co. initiated the Radford Dam

Project. There was some difficulty in determining whether the New River was navigable or not, so, in order to expedite matters, the respondent applied for a license that could be withdrawn if it was found that no federal license was required. This application was later withdrawn. On October 12, 1932, without notice, the Federal Power Commission pronounced the river navigable. The respondent began construction about June 1, 1934. On May 6, 1935 the United States filed this bill for an injunction against the construction or maintenance of the proposed dam otherwise than under a license from the Federal Power Commission and for a mandatory order of removal.

OPINION BY MR. JUSTICE REED
(Vote: 6-2)

Question—Was the New River navigable, and, if so, is the licensing power of the Federal Power Commission valid?

Decision—Yes.

Reason—"The plenary federal power over commerce must be able to develop with the needs of that commerce which is the reason for its existence. It cannot properly be said that the federal power over navigation is enlarged by the improvements to the waterways. It is merely that improvements make applicable to certain waterways the existing power over commerce. In determining the navigable character of the New River it is proper to consider the feasibility of interstate use after reasonable improvement which might be made.

"The state and respondent alike, however, hold the waters and the land under them subject to the power of Congress to control the waters, for the purpose of commerce. The power flows from the grant to regulate, i.e., to 'prescribe the rule by which commerce is to be governed'. This includes the protection of navigable waters in capacity as well as use. This power of Congress to regulate commerce is so unfettered that its judgment as to whether a structure is or is not a hindrance is conclusive. Its determination is legislative in character. The federal government has domination over the water power inherent in the flowing stream. It is liable to no one for its use or non-use. The flow of navigable stream is in no sense private property. . . . Exclusion of riparian owners from its benefits without compensation is entirely within the government's discretion. . . .

"The point is that navigable waters are subject to national planning and control in the broad regulation of commerce granted the federal government. The license conditions to which objection is made have an obvious relationship to the exercise of the commerce power. Even if there were no such relationship the plenary power of Congress over navigable waters would empower it to deny the privilege of constructing an obstruction in those waters. It may likewise grant the privilege on terms. . . ."

Corollary cases

Gibbons v. Ogden, 9 Wheaton 1 (1824)
Oklahoma v. Guy F. Atkinson Co., 313 U.S. 508 (1941)
The Thomas Jeffferson, 10 Wheaton 428 (1825)
The Genesee Chief v. Fitzhugh, 12 Howard 443 (1852)
Arizona v. California, 283 U.S. 423 (1941)
Montana v. United States, 450 U.S. —; 61 L. Ed. 2d 493 (1981)
Vaughn v. Vermilion Corp., 444 U.S. 206 (1979)
United States v. New Mexico, 438 U.S. —; 57 L. Ed. 2d 1052 (1978)
Oregon v. Corvallis Sand and Gravel Co., 429 U.S. 363 (1977)
Douglas v. Seacoast Products, 431 U.S. 265 (1977)

Note—The term "navigable" has lost all meaning in the sense of limiting federal control. It is enough for a waterway to be *potentially* navigable for it to be federally controlled.

Despite the sweep of the above, the Court in *South Dakota v. Dole* (97 L. Ed. 171, 1987) held that the federal government directing the reduction of highway funds to states having the minimum drinking age set below the age of 21 was a valid exercise of Congress's spending powers.

Edwards v. California, 314 U.S. 160; 62 S. Ct. 164; 86 L. Ed. 119 (1941)

Edwards was a citizen of the United States and a resident of California. He left Marysville, Calif., for Spur, Texas with the intention of bringing his wife's brother, Frank Duncan, to Marysville. Duncan was a resident of Texas. Edwards knew that Duncan was employed by the WPA and was aware that he was an indigent person throughout the case. They went to California in Edwards's car. Duncan had about $20 when he left Texas and nothing when he arrived in California. He lived unemployed with Edwards ten days, then received assistance from the Farm Security Administration. The district court decided that Edwards violated the Welfare and Institutions Code of California by knowingly bringing into the state a nonresident indigent person.

OPINION BY MR. JUSTICE BYRNES
(No evidence from the report that the decision was not unanimous.)

Question—Is this law a valid exercise of the police power of the state of California?

Decision—No.

Reason—The California statute concerning the entry of indigent persons was a violation of the commerce clause of the federal Constitution. The passage of persons from state to state constitutes interstate commerce within the provisions of Article I, Section 8 of the Constitution delegating to Congress the authority to regulate interstate commerce, and the California law imposed an unconstitutional burden on such commerce. The concurring opinion noted that the right to move freely from state to state is an incident of national citizenship protected by the privileges and immunities clause of the Fourteenth Amendment against state interference.

Corollary cases

Hague v. C.I.O., 307 U.S. 496 (1939)
Baldwin v. Seelig, 294 U.S. 511 (1935)
City of New York v. Miln, 11 Peters 102 (1837)
Milk Control Board of Eisenberg Farm Products, 306 U.S. 346 (1939)
Crandall v. Nevada, 6 Wallace 35 (1868)
Zemel v. Rusk, 381 U.S. 1 (1965)
Kent v. Dulles, 357 U.S. 116 (1958)
Southern Railway Co. v. King, 217 U.S. 524 (1910)
South Carolina State Highway Dept. v. Barnwell Bros., 303 U.S. 177 (1938)
Southern Pacific Co. v. Arizona, 325 U.S. 761 (1945)

Note—The Court struck down California's "anti-Okie" law as an impermissible obstruction of interstate commerce and, despite four concurring opinions, refused to apply the privileges and immunities of the national citizenship provision of the Fourteenth Amendment.

United States v. F. W. Darby Lumber Co., 312 U.S. 100; 61 S. Ct. 451; 85 L. Ed. 609 (1941)

The appellee was engaged, in the state of Georgia, in the business of acquiring raw materials, which he manufactured into finished lumber with the intention of shipping it in interstate commerce to customers outside the state. Numerous counts charged the appellee with the shipment of lumber in interstate commerce from Georgia to points outside the state and that he employed workmen at less than the prescribed minimum wage or more than the prescribed maximum hours without payment of any wage for overtime. Another count charged the appellee with failure to keep records showing the hours worked each day a week by his employees, as required by the regulation of the administrator. The appellee sought to sustain the decision on the grounds that the prohibition of Congress was unauthorized by the commerce clause, and was prohibited by the Fifth Amendment.

OPINION BY MR. JUSTICE STONE
(No evidence from the report that the decision was not unanimous.)

Question—Has Congress the constitutional power to prohibit the shipment in interstate commerce of lumber manufactured by employees whose wages are less than a prescribed minimum or whose weekly hours are greater than a prescribed maximum and to prohibit the employment of workmen in the production of goods for "interstate commerce" at other than prescribed wages and hours?

Decision—Yes.

Reason—The manufacture of goods in itself is not a matter of interstate commerce, but the shipment of such articles is. It was contended that the regulations of Congress in the matter of wages and hours belong properly to the states. However, the power of Congress to regulate interstate commerce is complete in itself, with no other limitations except those prescribed in the Constitution.

The motive and purpose of the act in question was to keep interstate commerce from being an instrument in the distribution of goods produced under substandard conditions, as such competition would be injurious to interstate commerce. This was a matter of legislative judgment perfectly within the bounds of congressional power, and over which the courts are given no control.

Congress has the power to regulate not only commerce between the states, but such intrastate activities that so affect interstate commerce as to make their regulation means to a legitimate end. As regards the congressional policy of excluding from interstate commerce all goods manufactured under substandards, the enforcement of wages and hours, even though intrastate, are a valid means of protection, and therefore, within the reach of the commerce power.

Corollary cases

Gibbons v. Ogden, 9 Wheaton 1 (1824)
Kentucky Whip & Collar Co. v. Illinois Central R.R. Co., 229 U.S. 334 (1937)
McGray v. United States, 195 U.S. 27 (1904)
Sonzinsky v. United States, 300 U.S. 506 (1937)
Veazie Bank of Fenno, 8 Wallace 533 (1869)
National League of Cities v. Usery, 426 U.S. 833 (1976)
United States v. Carolene Products Co., 304 U.S. 144 (1938)
Kidd v. Pearson, 128 U.S. 1 (1888)
United States v. Rock Royal Co-op., 307 U.S. 533 (1939)
Sunshine Anthracite Coal Co. v. Adkins, 310 U.S. 381 (1940)
Warren-Bradshaw Co. v. Hall, 317 U.S. 88 (1942)

Note—*Darby* reversed *Hammer* v. *Dagenhart,* 247 U.S. 251 (1918). In upholding the Fair Labor Standards Act of 1938, *Darby,* in effect, ruled that the proposed Child Labor Amendment of 1924 was still unratified as well as unneeded. *Darby* closed the era of laissez faire in which the Court restricted the economic powers of Congress. It now returned to Marshall's view of a broad, almost unlimited, commerce power.

Wickard v. Filburn, 317 U.S. 111; 63 S. Ct. 82; 87 L. Ed. 122 (1942)

The appellee for many years owned and operated a small farm in Montgomery County, Ohio, maintaining a herd of dairy cattle, selling milk, raising poultry, and selling poultry and eggs. He was accustomed to raising a small acreage of winter wheat, of which a portion was sold, part fed to poultry and livestock, part used for making flour for home consumption, and the rest kept for seeding the following year.

In 1940, according to the Agricultural Adjustment Act, he was given a wheat acreage of 11.1 acres and a normal yield of 20.1 bushels of wheat an acre. He sowed, however, 23 acres, and harvested from his excess acreage 239 bushels, which was subject to a penalty of 49 cents a bushel, or $117.11 in all. Filburn claimed that the excess wheat was not produced for the purpose of marketing but for his own consumption on his farm. He refused to pay the penalty, or to store the excess according to regulations.

OPINION BY MR. JUSTICE JACKSON
(No evidence from the report that the decision was not unanimous.)

Question—Does Congress possess the power under the commerce clause of the Constitution to regulate the production and consumption of wheat destined for personal use on the farm when the effect upon interstate commerce is at most indirect?

Decision—Yes.

Reason—Marketing, according to the act, included, in addition to the conventional meaning, whatever might be consumed on the premises. Questions of federal power cannot be side-stepped by calling such activities indirect.

Whether the appellant's activity was local, or whether it was regarded as commerce or not, if it exerted a substantial economic effect on interstate commerce, such activity could be regulated by Congress. The consumption of homegrown wheat is the most variable factor in the disappearance of the wheat crop. Even though the appellant's contribution to the demand for wheat may have been trivial, it did not remove him from the field of federal regulation. His contribution, together with others in similar circumstances, had a substantial influence on price and market conditions. Therefore, homegrown wheat competes with commercially grown wheat in commerce. The stimulation of commerce is a regulatory function clearly within the power of Congress.

Corollary cases

Mulford v. Smith, 307 U.S. 38 (1939)
United States v. Butler, 297 U.S. 1 (1936)
United States v. Darby, 312 U.S. 100 (1941)
Gibbons v. Ogden, 9 Wheaton 1 (1824)
United States v. E. C. Knight Co., 156 U.S. 1 (1895)
Swift and Co. v. United States, 196 U.S. 375 (1905)
Shreveport Rate Cases, 234 U.S. 342 (1914)
N.L.R.B. v. Fainblatt, 306 U.S. 601 (1939)

Note—*Filburn* represents a high watermark of commerce clause expansionism with the distinction between "commerce" and "production." Today, few areas involving the commerce clause are beyond congressional reach.

United States v. Southeastern Underwriters Ass'n., 322 U.S. 533; 64 S. Ct. 1162; 88 L. Ed. 1440 (1944)

The Southeastern Underwriters Association represented private stock companies in the business of selling fire insurance in six southeastern states. They were indicted in a federal district court for violations of the Sherman Antitrust Act by fixing and maintaining arbitrary and noncompetitive premium rates on fire insurance, and by monopolizing the trade and commerce in that line of insurance in and among the same states. They contended that selling insurance was not commerce and, therefore, did not come under the interstate commerce regulations.

OPINION BY MR. JUSTICE BLACK
(Vote: 4-3)

Question—Do fire insurance transactions that stretch across state lines constitute "commerce among the several states" so as to make them subject to regulation by Congress under the commerce clause?

Decision—Yes.

Reason—The Court reasoned that the basic responsibility in interpreting the commerce clause is to make certain that the power to govern intercourse among the states remains where the Constitution placed it. That power, as held by the Supreme Court from the beginning, is vested in Congress, available to be exercised for the national welfare as Congress shall deem necessary. No commercial enterprise of any kind that conducts its activities across state lines has been held to be wholly beyond the regulatory power of Congress under the commerce clause. The Court concluded that they could not make an exception of the insurance business.

Corollary cases

Paul v. Virginia, 8 Wallace 168 (1869)
Hooper v. California, 155 U.S. 648 (1895)
New York Life Insurance Co. v. Deer Lodge Company, 231 U.S. 495 (1913)
Lottery Case, 188 U.S. 321 (1903)
Hoke v. United States, 227 U.S. 308 (1913)
United States v. Simpson, 252 U.S. 465 (1920)
Toolson v. New York Yankees, 346 U.S. 356 (1953)
Flood v. Kuhn, 407 U.S. 258 (1972)
Allstate Insurance Co. v. Hague, 449 U.S. 302 (1981)
Western & Southern Life Insurance Co. v. State Board of Equalization, 68 L. Ed. 2d 514 (1981)

Note—*Southeastern* reversed the long-standing precedent, *Paul* v. *Virginia,* 8 Wallace 168 (1869). Congress reacted by passing the McCarran Act permitting the states to continue to regulate insurance and it was upheld in *Prudential Insurance Co.* v. *Benjamin,* 328 U.S. 408 (1946). The results of the McCarran Act make it appear that the issue in *Southeastern* had never been decided.

Southern Pacific Co. v. Arizona, 325 U.S. 761; 65 S. Ct. 1515; 89 L. Ed. 1915 (1945)

The Arizona Train Limit Law required that any person or corporation operating within the state a railroad train with more than fourteen passenger cars or more than seventy freight cars would pay a penalty for each violation of the act.

OPINION BY MR. CHIEF JUSTICE STONE
(Vote: 7-2)

Question—Does the statute contravene the commerce clause of the federal Constitution?

Decision—Yes.

Reason—The Court reasoned that the Arizona law, viewed as a safety measure, afforded at most slight and dubious advantage, if any, over unregulated train lengths, because it resulted in an increase in expense and in the number of trains and train operations and a consequent increase in train accidents of a character generally more severe than those due to slack action. Its effect on commerce was regulation without securing uniformity of the length of trains operated in interstate commerce. Thus it prevented the free flow of commerce by delaying it and by substantially increasing its cost and impairing its efficiency.

Corollary cases

Kelly v. Washington, 302 U.S. 1 (1937)
Cooley v. Board of Wardens, 12 Howard 299 (1851)
South Carolina Highway Dept. v. Barnwell Bros., 303 U.S. 177 (1938)
Gibbons v. Ogden, 9 Wheaton 1 (1824)
New York, N.H. H. R.R. Co. v. New York, 165 U.S. 628 (1897)

Note—Contrast train regulation—here denied—and automobile regulation in *South Carolina State Highway Department* v. *Barnwell Bros., 303 U.S. 177 (1938).*

Heart of Atlanta Motel, Inc. v. United States, 379 U.S. 241; 85 S. Ct. 348; 13 L. Ed. 2d 258 (1964)

The owner of a large motel in Atlanta, Georgia, which restricted its clientele to white persons, brought suit for a declaratory judgment and for an injunction to restrain enforcement of Title II of the Civil Rights Act of 1964, which outlawed distinguishing on the basis of race, color, religion, or national origin in making available public accommodations.

OPINION BY MR. JUSTICE CLARK
(Vote: 9-0)

Question—Does Congress have the power to enact this type of legislation under the power to regulate interstate commerce?

Decision—Yes.

Reason—The power of Congress over interstate commerce includes the power to regulate local incidents and activities in both the states of origin and destination of the commerce that might have a substantial and harmful effect on that commerce. The Court concluded that "the action of the Congress in the adoption of the act as applied here to a motel which concededly serves interstate travelers is within the power granted it by the Commerce Clause of the Constitution as interpreted by this Court for 140 years." The Court made brief mention of the power to enforce the Fourteenth Amendment, but its decision was basically that the commerce power was here being exercised.

Corollary cases

The Civil Rights Cases, 109 U.S. 3 (1883)
Hall v. De Cuir, 95 U.S. 485 (1878)
Boynton v. Virginia, 364 U.S. 454 (1960)
Bob-Lo Excursion Co. v. Michigan, 333 U.S. 28 (1948)
Wickard v. Filburn, 317 U.S. 11 (1942)
Moose Lodge No. 107 v. Irvis, 407 U.S. 163 (1972)
N.L.R.B. v. Jones and Laughlin Steel Corp., 301 U.S. 1 (1937)
Burton v. Wilmington Parking Authority, 365 U.S. 715 (1961)
Schechter v. United States, 295 U.S. 495 (1935)
Daniel v. Paul, 395 U.S. 298 (1969)
Jones v. Alfred H. Mayer, 392 U.S. 409 (1968)
Tillman v. Wheaton-Haven Recreational Association, Inc., 410 U.S. 431 (1973)

Note—This decision reversed the *Civil Rights Cases,* 109 U.S. 3 (1883). This same doctrine was applied in *Katzenbach* v. *McClung,* 379 U.S. 294 (1964), involving a restaurant that purchased much of its food through interstate commerce.

CONTRACTS

Fletcher v. Peck, 6 Cranch 87; 3 L. Ed. 162 (1810)

John Peck deeded to Robert Fletcher lands in the state of Georgia, which had been bought from the state of Georgia. The contract was executed in the form of a bill passed through the Georgia legislature in 1795. The next legislature rescinded the act and took possession of the land. Fletcher sued Peck to regain the purchase price.

OPINION BY MR. CHIEF JUSTICE MARSHALL
(No evidence from the report that the decision was not unanimous.)

Question—Can an executed contract in the form of a legislative grant of land by the state itself through its legislature be rescinded later by the state?

Decision—No.

Reason—A valid contract was executed. The state of Georgia was restrained either by general principles that are common to our free institutions or by particular provisions of the Constitution of the United States, from passing a law whereby the estate of the plaintiff in the premises so purchased could be constitutionally and legally impaired and rendered null and void. "One legislature is competent to repeal any act which a former legislature was competent to pass; and that one legislature cannot abridge the powers of a succeeding legislature." However, ". . . if an act be done under a law, a succeeding legislature cannot undo it. . . . When, then, a law is in its nature a contract, when absolute rights have vested under that contract, a repeal of the law cannot divest those rights; and the act of annulling them, if legitimate, is rendered so by a power applicable to the case of every individual in the community."

Corollary cases

Green v. Biddle, 8 Wheaton 1 (1823)
Trustees of Dartmouth College v. Woodward, 4 Wheaton 518 (1819)
Charles River Bridge v. Warren Bridge, 11 Peters 420 (1837)
Ogden v. Saunders, 12 Wheaton 213 (1827)

Note—*Peck,* an unpopular decision, was the first case in which the Court held a state law contrary to the Constitution. As the country developed economically so the Court maintained an unswaying view of the contract clause in Article I, Section 10. But in *Charles River* (1837) it adopted the view that contracts must be viewed narrowly and nothing is given by implication. In *Blaisdell* (1934) the contract must bend under the onslaught of an economic upheaval. Chief Justice Hughes found it untenable that the clause prevented dealing with a great public calamity such as a fire, flood, or an earthquake.

Trustees of Dartmouth College v. Woodward, 4 Wheaton 518; 4 L. Ed. 629 (1819)

In 1769 Dartmouth College was chartered by the English Crown. Later, in 1816, the state legislature of New Hampshire passed a law completely reorganizing the government of the college and changing the name to Dartmouth University. The old trustees of the college brought an action of trover against Woodward, who was secretary and treasurer of the college and had joined in the new university movement. He held the seal, records, and account books. The state decided against the old college trustees.

OPINION BY MR. CHIEF JUSTICE MARSHALL
(Vote: 5-1)

Questions—1. Is this contract protected by the Constitution of the United States?

2. Does the act of 1816 impair the original charter, as contended by the old college trustees?

Decisions—1. Yes.
2. Yes.

Reason—"This is plainly a contract to which the donors, the trustees, and the crown (to whose rights and obligations New Hampshire succeeds) were the original parties. It is a contract made on a valuable consideration. It is a contract for the security and disposition of property. . . . It is then a contract within the letter of the Constitution, and within its spirit also.''

The act of 1816 by the New Hampshire legislature gave the college a public and civil status, increased the number of trustees, and, therefore, in essence impaired the operations of the college as originally intended by the founders. The founders sought the charter in good faith, thus making a legally binding contract. Under the act of 1816, the charter as originally intended no longer existed. Thus the New Hampshire legislature violated the Constitution of the United States, and the act of 1816 was unconstitutional and void.

Corollary cases

Providence Ban v. Billings, 4 Peters 514 (1830)
Stone v. Mississippi, 101 U.S. 814 (1880)
Charles River Bridge v. Warren Bridge, 11 Peters 420 (1837)
Ogden v. Saunders, 12 Wheaton 213 (1827)
Home Building and Loan Ass'n v. Blaisdell, 290 U.S. 398 (1934)
Fletcher v. Peck, 6 Cranch 87 (1810)
New Jersey v. Wilson, 7 Cranch 164 (1812)
Pennsylvania Hospital v. Philadelphia, 245 U.S. 20 (1917)
Long Island Water Supply Co. v. Brooklyn, 166 U.S. 685 (1897)
United States Trust Co. v. New Jersey, 431 U.S. 1 (1979)
Allied Structural Steel Co. v. Spannaus, 437 U.S. —; 57 L. Ed. 2d 727 (1978)

Note—*Dartmouth* not only came down on the sanctity of contracts—in this case for the college—but for business and corporate interests. Daniel Webster argued for the college, and his final words have echoed through the ages: "It is, sir, . . . a small college, and yet there are those that love it."

Charles River Bridge v. Warren Bridge, 11 Peters 420; 9 L. Ed. 773 (1837)

This was an action by the Charles River Bridge Company to stop the construction of the Warren Bridge on the ground that the act authorizing its erection impaired the obligation of the contract between the Charles River Bridge Company and Massachusetts. The defendant received permission to erect another bridge of similar span within a few rods of the original bridge and was to give it to the state when paid for. The contention was that an original grant of ferry privileges to Harvard College in 1650 and a charter of 1785 incorporating the Proprietors of the Charles River Bridge (to which were transferred the rights of the College under the grant of

1650) constituted a contract whereby the plaintiffs were vested with an exclusive right to maintain a bridge "in that line of travel." Thus the Charles River Bridge Company implied that the privileges originally granted to Harvard College were transferred to them by means of the charter of 1785.

OPINION BY MR. CHIEF JUSTICE TANEY
(Vote: 5-2)

Question—Does the charter contain such a contract on the part of the state?

Decision—No.

Reason—"If a contract on that subject can be gathered from the charter, it must be by implication, and cannot be found in the words used. . . . In charters of this description, no rights are taken from the public, or given to the corporation, beyond those which the words of the charter, by their natural and proper construction, purport to convey." Implied privileges could prove to be unfavorable to the public and to the rights of the community; therefore it has always been the general operation of the Court to rule in favor of the public where an ambiguity exists in a contract between private enterprises and the public.

Corollary cases

The Binghamton Bridge, 3 Wallace 51 (1865)
Bridge Proprietors v. Hoboken Co., 1 Wallace 116 (1863)
Larson v. South Dakota, 278 U.S. 429 (1929)
Ogden v. Saunders, 12 Wheaton 213 (1827)
West River Bridge v. Dix, 6 Howard 507 (1848)
Long Island Water Supply Co. v. Brooklyn, 166 U.S. 685 (1897)

Note—This rule of the strict construction of public contracts or grants was reaffirmed in a strikingly similar case in *Larson* v. *South Dakota*, 278 U.S. 429 (1929).

Stone v. Mississippi, 101 U.S. 814; 25 L. Ed. 1079 (1880)

The legislature of Mississippi passed an act, approved Feb. 16, 1867, entitled "An act incorporating the Mississippi

Agricultural and Manufacturing Aid Society." Actually it
was nothing but a lottery enterprise. The Constitution of the
state, adopted in convention May 15, 1868, and ratified by
the people Dec. 1, 1869, forbade the legislature to authorize
any lottery. Criminal suit was brought against the lottery
"society," which argued that it was operating under its
charter.

OPINION BY MR. CHIEF JUSTICE WAITE

(No evidence from the report that the decision was not unanimous.)

Question—Was this impairment of the obligation of contract?

Decision—No.

Reason—Whether the contract existed depended on the authority of the legislature to bind the state and people of the
state in this way in this case. A legislature cannot bargain away
the police power of a state, which pertains to all matters
affecting public health or morals. In their Constitution the
people have expressed their wishes in this matter, so that no
legislature can, by chartering a lottery company, defeat their
wishes.

The contracts protected by the Constitution are property
rights, not governmental rights. Lotteries are a species of
gambling, which would disturb a well-ordered community. The
right to suppress them is governmental, and may be invoked
at will. Such an arrangement as this "is a permit, good as
against existing laws, but subject to future legislative and
constitutional control or withdrawal."

Corollary cases

Boston Beer Co. v. Massachusetts, 97 U.S. 25 (1878)
United States Trust Co. v. New Jersey, 431 U.S. 1 (1977)
Pennsylvania Hospital v. Philadelphia, 245 U.S. 20 (1917)
Long Island Water Supply Co. v. Brooklyn, 166 U.S. 685 (1897)
Texas and N. O. R.R. Co. v. Miller, 221 U.S. 408 (1911)
Allied Structural Steel Co. v. Spannaus, 437 U.S. —; 57 L. Ed. 2d 727 (1978)

Note—In general the police power of the state cannot be
circumscribed by the contract clause. The general welfare
takes precedence over the rights of individuals. Therefore,
proper state legislation affecting contracts between individuals
is valid. The contract clause has lost some of its force today in

as much as what formerly was covered by it is now covered by the due process clause. In *Spannaus* (1978) and *U.S. Trust Co.* (1977) the Court said the contract clause was "not a dead letter" but neither is it in fighting shape.

Home Building and Loan Association v. Blaisdell, 290 U.S. 398; 54 S. Ct. 231; 78 L. Ed. 413 (1934)

The Home Building and Loan Association held a mortgage on the land of Blaisdell, the said mortgage containing a valid power of sale by advertisement, and, by reason of default, the mortage was foreclosed. Blaisdell appealed to the Supreme Court of Minnesota, which affirmed his claim on the grounds that an act passed by the state legislature entitled "The Minnesota Mortgage Moratorium Law" provided that one who is unable to pay or retire a mortgage at the date of redemption can, by petitioning the court, be granted a moratorium from foreclosure sales. The Home Building and Loan Association appealed to the Supreme Court of the United States.

OPINION BY MR. CHIEF JUSTICE HUGHES
(Vote: 5-4)

Questions—1. Is the act contrary to the due process and equal protection clauses of the Fourteenth Amendment?

2. Does it violate the contract clause of the Constitution?

Decisions—1. No.
2. No.

Reasons—The obligations of a contract are impaired by a law that renders them invalid or releases or extinguishes them. Here the integrity of the mortgage indebtedness was not impaired; interest continued to run, the mortgagor was to pay the rental value of the premises as ascertained in judicial proceedings. The obligation remained.

Also, not only are existing laws read into contracts in order to fix obligations as between the parties, but the reservation of essential attributes of sovereign power is also read into contracts as a postulate of the legal order. This power—called the police power—is paramount to any right under contracts between individuals. "An emergency existed in Minnesota which furnished a proper occasion for the exercise of the reserved power of the state to protect the vital interests of the commu- nity."

Corollary cases

Wilson v. New, 243 U.S. 332 (1917)
East New York Savings Bank v. Hahn, 326 U.S. 230 (1945)
Sturges v. Crowninshield, 4 Wheaton 122 (1819)
Von Hoffman v. City of Quincy, 4 Wallace 535 (1867)
Bronson v. Kinzie, 1 Howard 311 (1843)
Boston Beer Co. v. Massachusetts, 97 U.S. 25 (1878)
Manigault v. Springs, 199 U.S. 473 (1905)
Honeyman v. Jacobs, 306 U.S. 539 (1939)
Gelfert v. National City Bank, 313 U.S. 221 (1941)
Providence Bank v. Billings, 4 Peters 514 (1830)
Stone v. Mississippi, 101 U.S. 814 (1880)
Charles River Bridge v. Warren Bridge, 11 Peters 420 (1837)
Ogden v. Saunders, 12 Wheaton 213 (1827)
Fletcher v. Peck, 6 Cranch 87 (1810)
New Jersey v. Wilson, 7 Cranch 164 (1812)
Pennsylvania Hospital v. Philadelphia, 245 U.S. 20 (1917)
Long Island Water Supply Co. v. Brooklyn, 155 U.S. 685 (1897)
Trustees of Dartmouth College v. Woodward, 4 Wheaton 518 (1819)
El Paso v. Simmons, 379 U.S. 497 (1965)
United States Trust Co. v. New Jersey, 431 U.S. 1 (1977)

Note—While an emergency does not create power, it does furnish the occasion for its exercises. Congress has done this by resuscitating dormant powers and the novel application of ordinary powers during wars, depressions, and crises. The contract clause that prohibits the states from enacting any law that will impair the obligation of contracts does not, however, apply to the federal government.

Norman v. Baltimore & Ohio Railroad Co., 294 U.S. 240; 55 S. Ct. 407; 79 L. Ed. 885 (1935)

> The Baltimore and Ohio Railroad issued bonds that were to be paid in gold coin of the United States of or equal to the standard of weight and fineness existing on Feb. 1, 1930. In 1933, by a joint resolution, Congress nullified the gold clause in existing contractual obligations. The resolution provided

that payment in gold was against public policy and that from then on all debts should be paid in the legal tender then in use in the United States.

OPINION BY MR. CHIEF JUSTICE HUGHES
(Vote: 5-4)

Question—Can Congress deny effect to "gold clauses" in existing contracts?

Decision—Yes.

Reason—The obligation is for payment of money and not for a specific number of grains of gold. Nor did the conditions specify gold value as claimed. Congress is empowered to coin money and to control its value. Even though the gold clauses in the bonds were a measure to avoid the payment of devalued money and were constitutional at the time they were made, the Congress has the power to devalue the dollar at its pleasure. Congress possesses this power as a delegated power, and even though it may invalidate certain contracts, it may exercise this power. The existence of such contracts cannot act as a bar to Congress in the exercise of its powers. Admission of the gold clauses in spite of the law would only tend to produce the opposite effect from that intended by Congress. Further it would place an unjust obligation on corporations, municipalities, and others whose sources of revenue, while being based on one standard, would have too many interests and debts on another standard.

Corollary cases

Perry v. United States, 294 U.S. 330 (1935)
Nortz v. United States, 294 U.S. 317 (1935)
Smyth v. United States, 302 U.S. 329
Guaranty Trust Co. v. Henwood, 307 U.S. 247
Craig v. Missouri, 4 Peters 410 (1830)
Poindexter v. Greenhow, 114 U.S. 270 (1885)

Note—Dissenting in *Norman,* Justice Reynolds said from the bench: "As for the Constitution, it does not seem too much to say that it is gone." But the federal government's power to borrow money prohibits it from abrogating such clauses in government bonds and contracts.

Snepp v. U.S., 444 U.S. 507; 62 L. Ed. 2d 704; 100 S. Ct. 763 (1980)

As a condition of his employment with the CIA in 1968, Frank Snepp executed an agreement promising that he would "not . . . publish . . . any information relating to the agency, its activities or intelligence activities either during or after the term of (his) employment . . . without specific prior approval of the agency." Though Snepp had pledged not to divulge classified information and not to publish any information without prepublication review, he published a book concerning certain CIA activities in South Vietnam without submitting it to the agency for approval.

OPINION: PER CURIAM
(Vote: 6-3)

Questions—1. Did Snepp breach his fiduciary obligation owed to the CIA by publishing the book without obtaining prepublication review?

2. Could a constructive trust be created allowing the U.S. government to benefit on all profits that Snepp might earn from publishing the book?

Decisions—1. Yes.
        2. Yes.

Reasons—"Snepp's employment with the CIA involved an extremely high degree of trust. He deliberately and surreptitiously violated his obligation to submit all material for prepublication review. Thus, he exposed the classified information with which he had been entrusted to the risk of disclosure. Whether Snepp violated his trust does not depend upon whether his book actually contained classified information. . . . The government simply claims that, in light of the special trust reposed in him and the agreement that he signed, Snepp should have given the CIA an opportunity to determine whether the material he proposed to publish would compromise classified information or sources. . . . [A] CIA agent's violation of his obligation to submit writings about the agency for prepublication review impairs the CIA's ability to perform its statutory duties. . . .

"A constructive trust . . . protects both the Government and the former agent from unwarranted risks. . . . It deals fairly with both parties by conforming relief to the dimensions of the wrong. If the agent secures prepublication clearance, he can publish with no fear of liability. If the agent publishes unreviewed material in violation of his fiduciary and contractual obligation, and the trust remedy simply requires him to disgorge the benefits of his faithlessness."

Corollary cases

United States Civil Service Commission v. National Association of Letter
  Carriers, 413 U.S. 548 (1973)
Buckley v. Valco, 424 U.S. 1 (1976)
Greer v. Spock, 424 U.S. 828 (1976)
New York Times Co. v. United States, 403 U.S. 713 (1971)
Nebraska Press Association v. Stuart, 427 U.S. 539 (1976)

THE PRESIDENCY

Martin v. Mott, 12 Wheaton 19; 6 L. Ed. 537 (1827)

In August 1814, the governor of the state of New York, in compliance with a request from the president of the United States, ordered certain companies of militia to assemble in the city of New York for the purpose of entering the service of the United States. The president acted in accordance with a federal statute empowering him to call the militia wherever there shall be danger of invasion. Mott, a private in one of the companies called, refused to comply with the order of the governor. In 1818 a court martial imposed on him a fine of $96, and when he refused to pay he was sentenced to twelve months imprisonment. Martin, deputy United States marshal, seized certain goods of Mott, which Mott sought to recover by action of replevin.

OPINION BY MR. JUSTICE STORY
(No evidence from the report that the decision was not unanimous.)

Question—Can the president, under the law, call forth the militia of the states when no invasion has taken place?

Decision—Yes.

Reason—One of the best means to repel invasion is to provide the necessary forces before the enemy has reached the soil. Who shall judge whether a state of emergency has arisen, if not the president? If any officer or inferior soldier were permitted to decide for himself, where would the case end? The power invested in the president for the faithful execution of his responsibility constitutes him the best judge of the facts. "Whenever a statute gives a discretionary power to any person, to be exercised by him, upon his own opinion of certain facts, it is a sound rule of construction, that the statute constitutes him the sole and exclusive judge of the existence of those facts. . . . It is no answer, that such a power may be abused, for there is no power which is not susceptible of abuse."

Corollary cases

Houston v. Moore, 5 Wheaton 1 (1820)
Luther v. Borden, 7 Howard 1 (1849)

Sterling v. Constantin, 287 U.S. 378 (1932)
Laird v. Tatum, 408 U.S. 1 (1972)

Note—This is a good case to contrast the discretion vested in the president in an emergency to call out the troops and the War Powers Act of 1973, born out of the Vietnam War, to restrict the power of the president. Although untested, some scholars believe the act might be unconstitutional. In the light of *INS v. Chadha* (72 L Ed 2d 317, 1983) in which the legislative veto was unconstitutional on the grounds of violating the doctrine of separation of powers—some 200 acts, among them the War Powers Act of 1973—are likely invalid. In *Chadha* the Court said Congress can reverse a presidential veto by a ⅔ vote but it cannot—one house action as regard treaties—deprive the president of his veto prerogative.

Ex parte Merryman, 17 Fed. Cas. No. 9487 (1861)

> The petitioner, a citizen of Baltimore, was arrested by a military officer acting on the authority of his commanding officer. The petitioner was accused of treason against the United States. The chief justice of the United States, while on circuit court duty, issued a writ of habeas corpus directing the commanding officer to deliver the prisoner, and this was refused on the grounds that the officer was authorized by the president to suspend the writ.

OPINION BY MR. CHIEF JUSTICE TANEY WHILE ON CIRCUIT COURT DUTY

Question—Can the president suspend the writ of habeas corpus?

Decision—No.

Reason—The Court held that the petitioner was entitled to be set free on the grounds that (1) the president, under the Constitution cannot suspend the privilege of the writ of habeas corpus. This can be done under the Constitution only by Congress, since the provision appears in the article of the Constitution dealing with Congress, and in a list of limitations on Congress. (2) A military officer cannot arrest a person not subject to the rules and articles of war, except in the aid of civil authority when the individual has committed an offense against the United States. In such a case the military officer must deliver the prisoner immediately to civil authority to be dealt with according to law.

Corollary cases

Ex parte Bollman and Swartwout, 4 Cranch 75 (1807)
Ex parte Milligan, 4 Wallace 2 (1866)
Mississippi v. Johnson, 4 Wallace 475 (1867)
Ex parte McCardle, 7 Wallace 506 (1869)
Ex parte Vallandigham, 1 Wallace 243 (1864)
Duncan v. Kahanamokv, 327 U.S. 304 (1946)

Note—Chief Justice Taney's opinion did not explicitly settle the question. Congress subsequently passed an act allowing the president to lift the writ whenever, in his judgment, the public safety may require it, although it is unclear that he was "authorized" by the act or by the Constitution itself. In three instances Congress did suspend the writ: in 1871 in South Carolina involving the Ku Klux Klan; in 1905 in an injunction in the Philippines; and in World War II in Hawaii.

Mississippi v. Johnson, 4 Wallace 475; 18 L. Ed. 437 (1867)

This case involved a bill in equity by which the state of Mississippi sought to enjoin President Andrew Johnson and the general in command of the military district of Mississippi and Arkansas from enforcing the Reconstruction Acts of 1867.

OPINION BY MR. CHIEF JUSTICE CHASE
(No evidence from the report that the decision was not unanimous.)

Question—Can the president be restrained by injunction from carrying into effect an act of Congress?

Decision—No.

Reason—The Congress is the legislative department of the government. The president is the executive department. Neither can be restrained in its action by the judicial department, though the acts of both, when performed are, in proper cases, subject to its cognizance. The impropriety of such interference, the Court held, could be clearly seen upon consideration of its possible consequences. If the injunction were granted, the Court would have no power to enforce it. If the president did not enforce the bill according to the wishes of this Court, he would be subject to impeachment by the Congress and the Court could not stop the proceedings. "It is true that a state may file an original bill in this Court. And it may be true, in some cases, that such a bill may be filed against the United States. But we are fully satisfied that this Court has no jurisdiction of a bill to enjoin the president in the performance of his official duties, and that no such bill ought to be received by us."

Corollary cases

Georgia v. Stanton, 6 Wallace 50 (1868)
Marbury v. Madison, 1 Cranch 137 (1803)
Kendall v. United States, 12 Peters 524 (1838)

Note—*Mississippi* was highly charged politically since Congress believed the defeated rebels would recover in court what they lost on the battlefield. The Court might have reached its decision to stay out of it by recalling Chief Justice Marshall's difficulties with Thomas Jefferson during the Aaron Burr treason trial.

In re Neagle (Cunningham v. Neagle), 135 U.S. 1; 10 S. Ct. 658; 34 L. Ed. 55 (1890)

David Neagle was a deputy United States marshal traveling with Mr. Justice Field, who was holding Circuit Court, and whose life had been threatened by one Terry, who had been imprisoned on sentence imposed by Justice Field. Neagle was assigned by the attorney general to accompany and protect Field. Mr. Justice Field was attacked by this man, whereupon Neagle shot and killed him. Neagle was arrested by local authorities for murder but was released on a writ of habeas corpus by the federal Circuit Court on the grounds that he was held for "an act done or omitted in pursuance of a law of the United States," within the meaning of the federal statute providing for the issuance of the writ in such cases. However, the law under which Neagle acted was an executive order of the president.

OPINION BY MR. JUSTICE MILLER
(Vote: 6-2)

Question—Was the federal Circuit Court interfering with the state in too great a degree?

Decision—No.

Reason—"It would be a great reproach to the system of government of the United States, declared to be within its sphere sovereign and supreme, if there is to be found within the domain of its powers no means of protecting the judges, in the conscientious and faithful discharge of their duties, from the malice and hatred of those upon whom their judgments may operate unfavorably. . . ."

Just as a sheriff must keep the peace of the state and local laws of California, thus Neagle, a United States deputy marshal was bound to keep the peace in regard to the federal laws. The attack on Mr. Justice Field was the breaking of the peace of the United States and it was a duty of Neagle to keep that peace.

"We cannot doubt the power of the president to take measures for the protection of a judge of one of the courts of the United States, who, while in the discharge of the duties of his office, is threatened with a personal attack which may probably result in his death. . . ."

Corollary cases

Tennessee v. Davis, 100 U.S. 257 (1880)
Johnson v. Maryland, 254 U.S. 51 (1920)
Tarble's Case, 13 Wallace 397 (1872)
Martin v. Hunter, 1 Wheaton 304 (1816)
In re Debs, 158 U.S. 564 (1895)
United States v. United Mine Workers, 330 U.S. 258 (1947)

Note—President Truman in *Youngstown Sheet & Tube Co.* v. *Sawyer,* 343 U.S. 579 (1952) cited the "inherent power" doctrine in *Neagle* but lost on narrower grounds of statutory interpretation over the provisions of the Taft-Hartley Act (1947). It was under statutes passed by Congress to counter combinations too powerful for the ordinary course of law that

President Eisenhower ordered troops to Little Rock, Arkansas in 1957, and President John Kennedy to do likewise in Mississippi and Alabama in 1962 and 1963 respectively.

Ex parte Grossman, 267 U.S. 87; 45 S. Ct. 332; 69 L. Ed. 527 (1925)

> Philip Grossman was sued for violation of the National Prohibition Act. An injunction against him had been granted by the District Court of Chicago. Two days later an information was filed against him that he had violated the temporary order, and he was arrested, tried, found guilty of contempt, and sentenced to one year and $1,000 fine. The president granted a pardon, on the condition that the fine be paid. After he was released, he was sent by the court to the House of Correction to serve the sentence, in spite of the pardon.

OPINION BY MR. CHIEF JUSTICE TAFT
(No evidence from the report that the decision was not unanimous.)

Question—Does the president have power to pardon this type of offense?

Decision—Yes.

Reason—Contempts are crimes even though no trial by jury is allowed, as they are infractions of the laws and are intended as efforts to defeat the operation of a court order. That which violates the dignity and authority of federal courts, such as an intentional effort to defeat their decrees, violates a law of the United States and so is an offense against the United States. "For civil contempts, the punishment is remedial and for the benefit of the complainant, and a pardon cannot stop it. For criminal contempts, the sentence is punitive in the public interest to vindicate the authority of the court and to deter other like derelictions. . . . The executive can reprieve or pardon all offenses after their commission, either before trial, during trial or after trial, by individuals, or by classes, conditionally or absolutely, and this without modification or regulation by Congress."

Corollary cases

United States v. Wilson, 7 Peters 150 (1833)
Gompers v. Buck's Stove and Range Co., 221 U.S. 418 (1911)
Ex parte Garland, 4 Wallace 333 (1867)
Schick v. Reed, 419 U.S. 256 (1974)
United States v. Klein, 13 Wallace 128 (1872)
Biddle v. Perovich, 274 U.S. 480 (1927)
Brown v. Walker, 161 U.S. 591 (1896)
Burdick v. United States, 236 U.S. 79 (1915)
Carlesi v. New York, 233 U.S. 51 (1914)

Note—The president's pardoning power is found in the Constitution (Article 2, Section 2, clause 1): "The power flows from the Constitution alone . . . and . . . it cannot be modified, abridged, or diminished by the Congress," *Schick* v. *Reed*, 419 U.S. 256 (1974). In 1977 President Carter issued a blanket pardon to Vietnam draft dodgers but not to servicemen who deserted. The United States District Court for the Western District of Michigan rejected a challenge of President Ford's pardon of Richard Nixon in *Murphy* v. *Ford*, 390 F. Supp. 1372 (1975).

Myers v. United States, 272 U.S. 52; 47 S. Ct. 21; 71 L. Ed. 160 (1926)

As a result of the president having exercised complete power of removal of officials from appointed offices, Congress passed the Tenure of Office Act, which sought to prevent the removal of any official for whose appointment the concurrence of the Senate was required, without in turn obtaining Senatorial approval for his dismissal. This formula was subsequently re-enacted in a statute of 1876 pertaining to postmasters of the first three classes, concurrence of the Senate being stipulated as necessary for removal as well as appointment. In 1920, Myers, the postmaster of Portland, Oregon, was removed by President Wilson without the consent of the Senate being obtained or even requested. Myers claimed that, under the terms of the 1876 statute, his removal was unlawful and sued for salary due him.

OPINION BY MR. CHIEF JUSTICE TAFT
(Vote: 6-3)

Question—May Congress limit the president's removal power?

Decision—No.

Reason—Section 6 of the act of July 12, 1876, under which Myers was appointed provided that: "Postmasters of the first, second and third classes shall be appointed and may be removed by the president by and with the consent of the Senate, and shall hold their offices for four years unless sooner removed or suspended according to law." The Court referred to Madison's opinion given in the House of Representatives during the First Congress on Tuesday, May 18, 1789. The vesting of the executive power in the president was essentially a grant of the power to execute the laws. But the president alone and unaided cannot execute the laws. He must execute them by the assistance of subordinates. This view has since been repeatedly affirmed by the Court. The further implication must be, in the absence of any express limitation respecting removals, that as the president's selection of administrative officers is essential to the execution of the laws by him, so in his power of removing those for whom he cannot continue to be responsible.

The power to prevent the removal of an officer who has served under the president is different from the authority to consent to or reject his appointment. When a nomination is made, it may be presumed that the Senate is, or may become, as well advised as to the fitness of the nominee as the president, but in the nature of things defects in ability or intelligence or loyalty in the administration of the laws of one who has served under the president are facts as to which the president or his trusted subordinates must be better informed than the Senate, and the power to remove him may therefore be regarded as confined, for very sound practical reasons, to the governmental authority that has administrative control. The power of removal is incident to the power of appointment, not to the power of advising and consenting to appointment, and when the grant of the executive power is enforced, by the express mandate to take care that the laws be faithfully executed, it emphasizes the necessity for including within the executive power as conferred the exclusive power of removal. Such an opinion was held by all branches of the government for more than seventy-four years (1789–1863). The Court concluded that, for the reasons given, it must therefore hold that the provision of the law of 1876 by which the unrestricted power of removal of first-class postmasters was denied to the president was in violation of the Constitution and invalid.

Corollary cases

Kendall v. United States, 12 Peters 624 (1838)
Kilbourn v. Thompson, 103 U.S. 168 (1881)
Wilcox v. Jackson, 13 Peters 498 (1839)
Rathbun, Humphrey's Executor v. United States, 295 U.S. 602 (1935)
Morgan v. United States, 312 U.S. 701 (1941)
Shurtleff v. United States, 189 U.S. 311 (1903)
In re Neagle, 135 U.S. 1 (1890)

Note—*Humphrey's Executor* v. *United States,* 295 U.S. 602 (1935) sharply reduced the extent of *Myers.* Together both cases comprehensively cover the president's removal power. What about agencies that exercise quasi-judicial or administrative power? Even though the statute was silent, as in the case of the war claims commission, the Court limited Eisenhower's removal power in *Wiener* v. *United States,* 357 U.S. 349 (1958).

Rathbun, Humphrey's Executor v. United States, 295 U.S. 602; 55 S. Ct. 869; 79 L. Ed. 1611 (1935)

> William E. Humphrey on December 10, 1931 was nominated by President Hoover to succeed himself as a member of the Federal Trade Commission, and was confirmed by the Senate. He was duly commissioned for a term of seven years, ending on September 25, 1938. On July 25, 1933 President Roosevelt asked the commissioner for his resignation, on the grounds that the aims of the administration would be carried out more effectively by his own personnel. Humphrey refused and was removed by the president on October 7, 1933. Suit was brought by Samuel F. Rathbun, executor of the deceased Humphrey's estate.

OPINION BY MR. JUSTICE SUTHERLAND
(No evidence from the report that the decision was not unanimous.)

Question—Do the provisions of the Federal Trade Commission Act stating that "any commissioner may be removed by the president for inefficiency, neglect of duty, or malfeasance in office'' restrict the power of the president to remove a commissioner except for one or more of the causes named, and, if so, is such a restriction valid under the Constitution?

Decision—Yes.

Reason—In the act setting up the Federal Trade Commission the term of office was set at seven years because the exacting and difficult character of the work made it desirable that the commissioners have an opportunity to acquire the expertness that comes from experience.

It was also the intention of Congress to create a commission not subject to the government, nor under any political domination or control, but separate from any existing department. It is clear that the length and certainty of tenure was considered a vital factor in setting up the commission, and that therefore executive removal power is limited to the causes mentioned.

As to the contention that the restriction is an unconstitutional interference with the executive power of the president, the government pointed to the *Myers* v. *United States* case. However, Myers was a postmaster, which is an executive function, subject to the control of the chief executive, which differs greatly from a commissioner having legislative and judicial power.

The power of Congress to create such quasi-legislative or quasi-judicial agencies cannot be doubted, nor the authority to fix the period of office and to forbid their removal, except for specified causes. The *Myers* decision affirms the power of the president to remove purely executive officers, but for officers under consideration in this case, no removal may be made except for the causes mentioned. ''We think it plain under the Constitution that illimitable power of removal is not possessed by the president in respect of officers of the character of those just named. The authority of Congress, in creating quasi-legislative or quasi-judicial agencies, to require them to act in discharge of their duties independently of executive control cannot well be doubted, and that authority includes, as an appropriate incident, power to fix the period during which they shall continue, and to forbid their removal except for cause in the meantime.''

Corollary cases

Shurtleff v. United States, 189 U.S. 311 (1903)
Federal Trade Commission v. Raladam Co., 283 U.S. 643
Train v. City of New York, 420 U.S. 35 (1975)
Myers v. United States, 272 U.S. 52 (1926)
Wiener v. United States, 357 U.S. 349 (1958)
United States v. Nixon, 418 U.S. 683 (1974)

United States v. Curtiss-Wright Export Corp., 299 U.S. 304; 57 S. Ct. 216; 81 L. Ed. 255 (1936)

Curtiss-Wright Export Corp. sold to Bolivia, a country then engaged in armed conflict in the Chaco, certain arms of war. The sale was completed in the United States. The company was charged with violating the joint resolution of Congress empowering the president to forbid the sale of any articles of war to countries engaged in armed conflict if this prohibition of sale would act in the intent of peace between the combatants. This applied to sales within the United States. The president issued such a proclamation and made violation of it punishable as a crime.

Opinion by Mr. Justice Sutherland
(Vote: 7-1)

Question—Is this joint resolution of Congress an illegal delegation of legislative power to the president?

Decision—No.

Reason—"It is important to bear in mind that we are here dealing not alone with an authority vested in the president by an exertion of legislative power; but with such an authority plus the very delicate, plenary and exclusive power of the president as the sole organ of the federal government in the field of international relations—a power which does not require as a basis for its exercise an act of Congress, but which, of course, like every other governmental power, must be exercised in subordination to the applicable provisions of the

Constitution. It is quite apparent that if, in the maintenance of our international relations, embarrassment—perhaps serious embarrassment—is to be avoided and success for our aims achieved, congressional legislation which is to be made effective through negotiation and inquiry within the international field must often accord to the president a degree of discretion and freedom from statutory restriction which would not be admissible were domestic affairs alone involved. . . .

"Practically every volume of the United States Statutes contains one or more acts or joint resolutions of Congress authorizing action by the President in respect of subjects affecting foreign relations which either leave the exercise of the power to his unrestricted judgment, or provide a standard far more general than that which has always been considered requisite with regard to domestic affairs. . . . A legislative practice such as we have here, evidenced not by only occasional instances, but marked by the movement of a steady stream for a century and a half of time, goes a long way in the direction of proving the presence of unassailable ground for the constitutionality of the practice, to be found in the origin and history of the power involved, or in its nature, or in both combined. . . ."

Corollary cases

Field v. Clark, 143 U.S. 649 (1892)
Jones v. United States, 137 U.S. 202 (1890)
Panama Refining Co. v. Ryan, 293 U.S. 388 (1935)
Schechter Poultry Corp. v. United States, 295 U.S. 495 (1935)
Industrial Union Dept. v. American Petroleum, 65 L. Ed. 2d 1010 (1979)

Note—*Curtiss-Wright* is often linked to *Missouri* v. *Holland,* 252 U.S. 416 (1920) in terms of foreign policy and treaty powers. A good deal of *Curtiss-Wright* is expansive and *dicta,* but, except for the inherent power doctrine, more clearly noted in *In re Neagle,* 135 U.S. 1 (1890) and rejected in *Youngstown Sheet and Tube* v. *Sawyer,* 343 U.S. 579 (1952), not repudiated. The War Powers Act of 1973 is still another attempt to contain *Curtiss-Wright.* Article I, Section 8 clearly sets out Congress's delegated powers. Congress can use or not use its powers but cannot violate the axiom "delegata potestas non potest delegari"—delegated power cannot be redelegated. But a delegated power is possible in which Congress sets up the objective and then authorizes an administration or commission to carry it out and allows an administrator to determine and act when certain conditions exist.

Youngstown Sheet & Tube Co. v. Sawyer, 343 U.S. 579; 72 S. Ct. 863; 96 L. Ed. 817 (1952)

In the latter part of 1951 a dispute arose between the steel companies and their employees over terms and conditions that should be included in new collective bargaining agreements. Long-continued conferences failed to settle the dispute. On Dec. 18, 1951, the employees' representative, United Steel Workers of America, CIO gave notice of an intention to strike when the agreements expired on Dec. 31. The Federal Mediation and Conciliation Service intervened, but unsuccessfully, and the president then referred the dispute to the Federal Wage Stabilization Board to investigate and make recommendations for fair and equitable terms of settlement. This failing, the union gave notice of a nationwide strike called to begin at 12:01 A.M., April 9. The indispensability of steel led President Truman to believe that the proposed strike would immediately jeopardize our national defense, and he issued an executive order directing Secretary of Commerce Sawyer to take possession of the steel mills and keep them running.

OPINION BY MR. JUSTICE BLACK
(Vote: 6-3)

Question—Is the seizure order within the constitutional power of the president?

Decision—No.

Reason—The power of the president to issue such an order must stem from an act of Congress or from the Constitution itself. Only two statutes authorize seizure under certain conditions, but the government admitted these conditions were not met, since the procedure involved was too cumbersome and time-consuming. Moreover, in the consideration of the

Taft-Hartley Act, the Congress rejected an amendment authorizing governmental seizures in an emergency.

Nor is there any provision in the Constitution that would warrant this seizure. As commander-in-chief of the Armed Forces the president still has no right to seize private property to keep labor disputes from stopping production. This was a matter of Congress only, not for military authorities. Neither does the Constitution permit the president to legislate—a function that belongs only to Congress, in good times or in bad times. "This seizure order cannot stand."

Corollary cases

Hooe v. United States, 218 U.S. 322 (1910)
United States v. North American Co., 253 U.S. 330 (1920)
Larson v. Domestic & Foreign Corp., 337 U.S. 682 (1949)
United States v. Curtiss-Wright Export Corp., 299 U.S. 304 (1936)
United States v. Russell, 13 Wallace 623 (1871)
United States v. Causby, 328 U.S. 256 (1946)
United States v. Caltex, 344 U.S. 149 (1952)
Haig v. Agee, 69 L. Ed. 2d 640 (1981)
Rostker v. Goldberg, 453 U.S. 57 (1981)
Dames & Moore v. Regan, 453 U.S. 654 (1981)

Note—*Youngstown* continues to generate controversy and already there is a body of literature; for example, Grant McConnell, *Steel and the Presidency* (1963). Does the president have inherent power, as in *In re Neagle,* 135 U.S. 1 (1890)? While conceding he does, *Youngstown* nevertheless said no in this case since Congress had foreclosed seizure authority in the Taft-Hartley Act (1947).

United States v. Richard M. Nixon, 418 U.S. 683; 94 S. Ct. 3090; 41 L. Ed. 2d 1039 (1974)

As a result of the break-in of the Democratic National Committee headquarters at the Watergate complex in Washington, D.C., the investigations and subsequent trial of a number of persons brought out the fact that President Nixon had taped an indefinite number of conversations in the Oval Office of the White House. Realizing the potential in an examination of the tapes, Special Prosecutor Leon Jaworski had a subpoena *duces tecum* issued to President Nixon. This ordered the surrender of certain of the tapes and papers to federal District Judge John J. Sirica for his judgment as to what portions of the tapes were irrelevant and inadmissible. The President's claim was that these materials were immune from subpoena under the theory of executive privilege.

OPINION BY MR. CHIEF JUSTICE BURGER
(No evidence from the report that the decision was not unanimous.)

Question—Can a federal court order the chief executive of the United States to surrender to that court materials that the president wishes to withhold as a matter of executive privilege?

Decision—Yes.

Reason—The Constitution does not contain any explicit reference to an executive privilege of confidentiality yet there is constitutional basis for this if it involves the effective discharge of the president's powers. Here there was involved a criminal trial, and the needs of fair administration of justice had to be balanced against the importance of the president's general privilege of confidentiality. While taking note of the doctrine of separation of powers, the Court observed that there is no unqualified presidential privilege of immunity from judicial process under all circumstances. "To read the Art. II powers of the president as providing an absolute privilege as against a subpoena essential to enforcement of criminal statutes on no more than a generalized claim of the public interest in confidentiality of nonmilitary and nondiplomatic discussions would upset the constitutional balance of 'a workable government' and gravely impair the role of the courts under Art. III."

Corollary cases

Ex parte Merryman, 17 Fed. Cas. No. 9487 (1861)
Mississippi v. Johnson, 4 Wallace 475 (1867)
In re Neagle, 135 U.S. 1 (1890)
Myers v. United States, 272 U.S. 52 (1926)
Nixon v. Warner Communications Incorporated, 435 U.S. 589 (1978)
Rathbun, Humphrey's Executor v. United States, 295 U.S. 602 (1935)
Youngstown Sheet & Tube Co. v. Sawyer, 343 U.S. 579 (1952)
Train v. City of New York, 420 U.S. 35 (1975)

Note—The political overtones loomed large and obviously it is a landmark case. But it is narrow in its application, limited to a situation involving criminal prosecution, nonmilitary, and nondiplomatic matters.

Dames & Moore v. Regan, 453 U.S. 654; 69 L. Ed. 2d 918; 101 S. Ct. 2972 (1981)

Pursuant to the International Economic Powers Act, President Carter declared a national emergency on November 14, 1979, and blocked the removal or transfer of all property and interests in property of the government of Iran that were subject to the jurisdiction of the United States. This was in retaliation—the Court calls it a "bargaining chip"—of the Iranian seizure of the American Embassy and the capture of our diplomatic personnel as hostages. On January 19, 1981, the American hostages were released following an executive agreement—authorized by Congress—by President Carter and "ratified" by President Reagan, that obligated the United States to terminate all legal proceedings in United States courts involving Iran and to bring about the termination of such claims through arbitration in an Iran-United States Claims Tribunal. Dames & Moore, who had a nearly $1,000,000 claim against Iran, contested the constitutionality of the agreement.

OPINION BY MR. JUSTICE REHNQUIST
(Vote: 9–0)

Question—Is the agreement concluded with Iran to terminate the hostage crisis in which claims between the two countries will be transferred from American courts to an Iran-United States Claims Tribunal constitutionally infirm?

Decision—No.

Reason—Our decision rests "on the narrowest possible ground capable of deciding the case . . . we attempt to lay down no general 'guidelines' covering other situations not involved here, and attempt to confine the opinion only to the very questions necessary to decision of the case." Moreover, ". . . decisions of the Court in this area have been rare, episodic, and affords little precedential value for subsequent cases." The president acted with the expressed authorization of Congress and thus his actions merit the strongest presumption and the widest latitude of judicial interpretation. "We think both the legislative history and cases interpreting the TWEA (Trading with the Enemy Act) fully sustain the broad authority of the executive when acting under this congressional grant of power. The statutes support a broad scope for executive action in circumstances under review. Though settlements have been made by treaty "there is also a long standing practice of settling such claims by executive agreement without the advice and consent of the Senate." Since 1952 the president has entered into at least ten binding settlements with foreign nations, including an $80 million settlement with the People's Republic of China. Nor has the president divested the federal courts of jurisdiction inasmuch as "those claims not within the jurisdiction of the claims tribunal will 'revive' and become judicially enforceable in United States Courts."

Corollary cases

United States v. Pink, 315 U.S. 203 (1942)
Youngstown Street & Tube Co. v. Sawyer, 343 U.S. 579 (1952)
Ashwanda v. TVA, 297 U.S. (1936)
United States v. Curtiss-Wright Export Corp., 299 U.S. 304 (1936)
Springer v. Philippine Islands, 277 U.S. 189 (1928)
Proper v. Clark, 337 U.S. 472 (1949)
Orvis v. Brownell, 345 U.S. 183 (1953)
Zittman v. McGrath, 341 U.S. 446 (1951)

Haig v. Agee, 453 U.S.—; 69 L. Ed. 2d 640; 101 S. Ct. 2766 (1981)

Agee, an American citizen and a former employee of the CIA, announced a campaign "to expose CIA officers and agents and to take measures necessary to drive them out of the countries where they are operating." Because Agee's activities abroad resulted in the identification of alleged undercover CIA agents and intelligence sources in foreign countries, Secretary of State Haig revoked Agee's passport, explaining that a regulation authorized the secretary of state to revoke a passport where the secretary determines that an American citizen's activities abroad causes or is likely to cause serious damage to the national security or the foreign policy of the United States. Agee brought suit contending that the revocation would violate a Fifth Amendment interest in a right to travel and a First Amendment right to criticize government policies.

OPINION BY MR. CHIEF JUSTICE BURGER
(Vote: 7–2)

Question—Does the president, acting through the secretary of state, have authority to revoke a passport on the ground that the citizen's activities abroad are causing or are likely to cause serious damage to the national security or foreign policy of the United States?

Decision—Yes.

Reason—"The Passport Act does not in so many words confer upon the secretary a power to revoke a passport, nor, . . . does it expressly authorize denials of passport applications. Neither, however, does any statute expressly limit those powers. It is beyond dispute that the secretary has the power to deny a passport for reasons not specified in the statutes. The history of passport controls since the earliest days of the Republic shows congressional recognition of executive authority to withhold passports on the basis of substantial reasons of national security and foreign policy. It is 'obvious and unarguable' that no governmental interest is more compelling than the security of the nation. Protection of the foreign policy of the United States is a governmental interest of great importance, since foreign policy and national security considerations cannot neatly be compartmentalized. Agee . . . endangered the interests of countries other than the United States, thereby creating serious problems for American foreign relations and foreign policy. Restricting Agee's foreign travel, although perhaps not certain to prevent all of Agee's harmful activities, is the only avenue open to the government to limit these activities."

Corollary cases

Zemel v. Rusk, 381 U.S. 1 (1965)
Kent v. Dulles, 357 U.S. 116 (1958)
U.S. v. Curtiss-Wright Export Corp., 299 U.S. 304 (1936)
Lorillard v. Pons, 434 U.S. 575 (1978)
Aptheker v. Secretary of State, 378 U.S. 500 (1964)
Califano v. Aznavorian, 439 U.S. 170 (1978)

WAR AND THE MILITARY

The Prize Cases, 2 Black 635; 17 L. Ed. 459 (1863)

> By proclamations of April 15, April 19, and April 27, 1861, President Lincoln established a blockade of southern ports. These cases were brought to recover damages suffered by ships carrying cargoes to the Confederate states during the blockade. The blockade was declared before Congress had a chance to assemble and take action on the matter. These ships had been raided by public ships of the United States.

OPINION BY MR. JUSTICE GRIER
(Vote: 5–4)

Question—Did a state of war exist at the time this blockade was instituted that would justify a resort to these means of subduing the hostile force?

Decision—Yes.

Reason—Although a civil war is never publicly proclaimed, *eo nomine,* against insurgents, its actual existence is a fact in our domestic history that the Court is bound to notice and to know. By the Constitution, Congress alone has the power to declare a national or foreign war. It cannot declare war against a state or any number of states, by virtue of any clause in the Constitution. The Constitution confers on the president the whole executive power. He is bound to take care that the laws be faithfully executed. He is commander-in-chief of the army and navy of the United States, and of the militia of the several states when called into the service of the United States. He has no power to initiate or declare war, either against a foreign nation or a domestic state. But he is authorized to call out the militia and use the military and naval forces of the United States in case of invasion by foreign nations, and to suppress insurrection against the government of a state or of the United States.

If a war be made by invasion by a foreign nation, the president is not only authorized but bound to resist force by force. He does not initiate the war, but is bound to accept the challenge without waiting for any special legislative authority.

And whether the hostile party be a foreign invader or domestic states organized in rebellion, it is none the less a war, although the declaration of it be unilateral.

"The greatest of civil wars was not gradually developed by popular commotion, tumultuous assemblies, or local unorganized insurrections. However long may have been its previous conception, it nevertheless sprung forth suddenly from the parent brain, a Minerva in the full panoply of *war*. The president was bound to meet it in the shape it presented itself, without waiting for Congress to baptize it with a name; and no name given to it by him or them could change the fact. . . . Whether the president in fulfilling his duties, as commander-in-chief, in suppressing an insurrection, has met with such armed hostile resistance, and a civil war of such alarming proportions as will compel him to accord to them the character of belligerents, is a question to be decided by him, and this court must be governed by the decision and acts of the political department of the government to which this power was entrusted. 'He must determine what degree of force the crisis demands.' The proclamation of blockade is, itself, official and conclusive evidence to the court that a state of war existed which demanded and authorized a recourse to such a measure, under the circumstances peculiar to the case."

Corollary cases

Ex parte Milligan, 4 Wallace 2 (1866)
Ex parte Quirin, 317 U.S. 1 (1942)
Duncan v. Kahanamoku, 327 U.S. (1945)

Note—The Korean and Vietnam wars involved the nation as though they had been congressionally "declared," but when attempts were made to get the Court to come out clearly on the issue, it refused to do so, as in *Massachusetts* v. *Laird*, 400 U.S. 886 (1970). In 1973 Congress passed the War Powers Act, a constitutionally questionable attempt to deprive the president of his full powers in foreign affairs. As already noted, this attempt on the part of Congress to affect the president's ability to make foreign affairs decisions was rejected in *INS* v. *Chadha* (77 L. Ed. 2d 317, 1983). Along similar lines, moreover, several governors went to the Court to prevent the National Guard from being called to duty beyond state boundaries, specifically, to Central America, but the Court rejected this challenge as well.

Ex parte Milligan, 4 Wallace 2, 18 L. Ed. 281 (1866)

> Milligan, who was not and never had been in the military service of the United States, was tried, convicted, and sentenced to be hanged by a military commission established under presidential authority. The sentence was approved by the president. In a proceeding for a writ of habeas corpus, Milligan contended the commission had no jurisdiction over him and that he was not accorded a jury trial. The Circuit Court asked the Supreme Court for an opinion.

OPINION BY MR. JUSTICE DAVIS
(No evidence from the report that the decision was not unanimous.)

Question—Did the military tribunal have any legal power and authority to try and to punish this man?

Decision—No.

Reason—The Court stated that every trial involves the exercise of judicial power. No part of the judicial power of the country was conferred on the military commission because the Constitution expressly vests it "in one supreme court and in such inferior courts as the Congress may from time to time ordain and establish." The military cannot justify action on the mandate of the president because he is controlled by law, and has his appropriate sphere of duty, which is to execute, not make, the laws. The Court stated that in times of grave emergencies the Constitution allows the government to make arrests without a writ of habeas corpus but it goes no further; that is, that the citizen might be tried otherwise than by the course of the common law.

The Court further stated that martial law can be applied only when there is real necessity, such as during an invasion that would effectually close the courts and civil administration. However, as long as the civil courts are operating, as they were in this case, then the accused is entitled to a civil trial by jury.

"The Constitution of the United States is a law for rulers and people, equally in war and in peace, and covers with the shield of its protection all classes of men, at all times, and under all circumstances. No doctrine involving more pernicious consequences, was ever invented by the wit of men than that any of its provisions can be suspended during any of the great exigencies of government."

Corollary cases

Ex parte Quirin, 317 U.S. 1 (1942)
In re Yamashita, 327 U.S. 1 (1946)
Duncan v. Kahanamoku, 327 U.S. 304 (1945)
Korematsu v. United States, 323 U.S. 214 (1944)
Hirabayashi v. United States, 320 U.S. 81 (1940)
Ex parte Endo, 323 U.S. 283 (1944)
Ex parte Merryman, 17 Fed. Cas. No. 9487 (1861)
United States ex rel. Toth v. Quarles, 350 U.S. 11 (1955)
Wilson v. Girard, 354 U.S. 524 (1957)
Kinsella v. United States ex rel. Singleton, 361 U.S. 234 (1960)
Reid v. Covert, 354 U.S. 1 (1957)
O'Callahan v. Parker, 395 U.S. 258 (1969)

Note—Not only was *Milligan* decided 9 to 0, but five justices, a majority, believed even the president and Congress together could not authorize military commissions to try civilians that were not in the war zone. In a special session of the Supreme Court, *Ex parte Quirin,* 317 U.S. 1 (1942), a military commission named by the president to try German saboteurs was permitted.

Selective Draft Law Cases (Arver v. United States) 245 U.S. 366; 38 S. Ct. 159; 62 L. Ed. 349 (1918)

By the act of May 18, 1917, Congress provided that all male citizens between the ages of 21 and 30, with certain exceptions, should be subject to military service, and authorized the president to select from them a body of one million men. All persons made liable to service by the act were required to present themselves at a time appointed by the president for registration. The plaintiffs in error failed to present themselves as required and were prosecuted and convicted. They contended that Congress had no power to compel military service by selective draft.

OPINION BY MR. CHIEF JUSTICE WHITE
(No evidence from the report that the decision was not unanimous.)

Question—Does Congress have constitutional authority to draft men to raise military forces?

Decision—Yes.

Reason—The Court unanimously held that the power of conscription is included in the constitutional power to raise armies. The power is not limited by the fact that other powers of Congress over state militia are narrower in scope than powers over the regular army. The Court stated that when the Constitution came to be formed, one of the recognized necessities for its adoption was the want of power in Congress to raise an army and the dependence upon the states for their quotas. In supplying the power it was manifestly intended to give Congress all and leave none to the states, since, besides the delegation to Congress of authority to raise armies, the Constitution prohibited the states, without the consent of Congress, from keeping troops in time of peace or engaging in war.

"Finally, as we are unable to conceive upon what theory the exaction by government from the citizen of the performance of his supreme and noble duty of contributing to the defense of the rights and honor of the nation, as the result of a war declared by the great representative body of the people, can be said to be the imposition of involuntary servitude in violation of the prohibition of the Thirteenth Amendment, we are constrained to the conclusion that the contention to that effect is refuted by its mere statement."

Corollary cases

Cox v. Wood, 247 U.S. 3 (1918)
United States v. Williams, 302 U.S. 46 (1937)
Northern Pacific Ry. v. North Dakota, 250 U.S. 135 (1919)
Reitman v. Mulkey, 387 U.S. 369 (1967)
Estep v. United States, 327 U.S. 114 (1946)
Falbo v. United States, 320 U.S. 549 (1944)

United States v. Seeger, 380 U.S. 163 (1965)
Rostker v. Goldberg, 453 U.S.—; 69 L. Ed. 2d 478 (1981)

Note—Despite the numerous wars in which the United States was involved throughout its history, the Court only recently decided on the issue of conscription war power. The Court no doubt assumed that Congress had the power to do what was necessary for victory. Of the eighteen powers granted Congress, no fewer than six deal with military matters. Tested often, the Court has held that the war power does not encroach upon the state militia, does not violate "establishment clause" by exceptions to the clergy and to conscientious objectors, and does not establish peonage in violation of the Thirteenth Amendment. In *Rostker,* the Court held that Congress can require males but not females to register for potential conscription.

Hamilton v. Kentucky Distilleries & Warehouse Co., 251 U.S. 146; 40 S. Ct. 106; 64 L. Ed. 194 (1919)

On November 11, 1918, the armistice with Germany was signed. On November 21, 1918, Congress passed and the president approved the War-Time Prohibition Act, which provided that alcoholic beverages held in bond should not be moved therefrom except for export. The purpose was to conserve the manpower of the nation and to increase the efficiency of war production. The Kentucky Distilleries contended that the act was invalid since hostilities had ceased, thus bringing an end to the wartime powers. Furthermore, they held that the government could not enforce such an act since the police power was reserved to the states.

OPINION BY MR. JUSTICE BRANDEIS
(No evidence from the report that the decision was not unanimous.)

Question—Was the War-Time Prohibition Act valid?

Decision—Yes.

Reason—The Court reasoned that the United States lacks general police power, and that this was reserved to the states by the Tenth Amendment. However, it is nonetheless true that when the United States exerts any of the powers conferred upon it by the Constitution, no valid objection can be based upon the fact that such exercise may be attended by the same incidents that attend the exercise by a state of its police power, or that it may tend to accomplish a similar purpose. As to the validity of the act after cessation of hostilities, the Court held that the power of wartime emergencies is not limited to victories in the field and the dispersion of the insurgent forces. It inherently carries with it the power to guard against the immediate renewal of the conflict and to remedy the evils that have arisen from its rise and progress. The Court was of the opinion that since the security of the nation was involved, the government had to be given a wide latitude of discretion as to the limitations of war powers.

Corollary cases

Woods v. Miller, 333 U.S. 138 (1948)
Fleming v. Mohawk Wrecking and Lumber Co., 331 U.S. 111 (1947)
Stewart v. Kahn, 11 Wallace 493 (1871)
United States v. Central Eureka Mining Co., 357 U.S. 155 (1958)
Jacob Ruppert, Inc. v. Caffery, 251 U.S. 264 (1920)
Yakus v. United States, 321 U.S. 414 (1944)
Parker v. Levy, 417 U.S. 733 (1974)
Lichter v. United States, 334 U.S. 742 (1948)
Rostker v. Goldberg, 453 U.S. 57 (1981)
Dames & Moore v. Regan, 453 U.S. 654 (1981)

Note—Cicero's phrase *inter arma silent leges* (the laws are silent in times of war) has some validity here. The Court assumes that Congress has the power to do what is necessary to achieve victory.

Ex Parte Quirin, 317 U.S. 1; 63 S. Ct. 1; 87 L. Ed. 3 (1942)

The petitioners were all born in Germany. All lived in the United States and returned to Germany between 1933 and 1941, where they attended sabotage school. After completing this training, Quirin and two others boarded a submarine and proceeded to Amagansett Beach, N.Y. They landed on or about June 13, 1942, carrying a supply of explosives and wearing German infantry uniforms. They buried their uniforms and proceeded to New York City. The four remaining petitioners proceeded by submarine to Ponte Vedra Beach,

Florida. These men were wearing caps of German marine infantry and carrying explosives. They buried uniform parts and proceeded to Jacksonville, Florida, and thence to various points in the United States. All were taken in custody by agents of the FBI. All had received instructions to destroy war industries and war facilities in the United States. The president of the United States by order of July 2, 1942 appointed a military commission and directed it to try the petitioners for offenses against the law of war and Articles of War, and prescribed regulations on trial and review of record of the trial and any decision handed down by the commission.

OPINION BY MR. CHIEF JUSTICE STONE
(Vote: 8–0)

Question—Was trial by a military commission without jury legal?

Decision—Yes.

Reason—It is necessary for the federal government to provide for the common defense. The president has the power to carry into effect all laws that Congress passes regarding the conduct of the war and all laws defining and punishing offenses against the law of nations, including those that pertain to the conduct of the war. These men were nothing more than spies. They fall under this category by their actions. "It has not hitherto been challenged, and, so far as we are advised, it has never been suggested in the very extensive literature of the subject that an alien spy, in time of war, could not be tried by military tribunal without a jury.

"We conclude that the Fifth and Sixth Amendments did not restrict whatever authority was conferred by the Constitution to try offenses against the law of war by military commission, and that petitioners, charged with such an offense not required to be tried by jury at common law, were lawfully placed on trial by the Commission without a jury."

Corollary cases

Ex parte Milligan, 4 Wallace 2 (1866)
Ludecke v. Watkins, 335 U.S. 160 (1948)
In re Yamashita, 327 U.S. 1 (1946)

Hirabayashi v. United States, 320 U.S. 81 (1943)
Korematsu v. United States, 323 U.S. 214 (1944)
Ex parte Endo, 323 U.S. 283 (1944)
Duncan v. Kahanamoku, 327 U.S. 304 (1946)
United States ex rel. Toth v. Quarles, 350 U.S. 11 (1955)
Reid v. Covert, 354 U.S. 1 (1957)
McElroy v. United States ex rel. Guagliardo, 361 U.S. 281 (1960)
Grisham v. Hogan, 361 U.S. 278 (1960)
O'Callahan v. Parker, 395 U.S. 258 (1969)
Middendorf v. Henry, 425 U.S. 25 (1976)

Note—This case was decided during a special session of the Court that looked into and upheld the right of a military commission to try the seven Nazi saboteurs. The Court distinguished this case from *Ex parte Milligan,* 4 Wallace 2 (1866).

Goldman v. Weinberger, 475 U.S. 475 U.S. 3, 89 L. Ed. 2d. 478; 106 S. Ct. 1310 (1986)

The petitioner is an ordained Orthodox Jew and a commissioned officer in the U.S. Air Force. In uniform and on duty but in violation of Air Force dress regulations, Goldman claimed that Air Force regulations prevented him from wearing his yarmulke (skullcap) in violation of his First Amendment right to freedom of religion. Continued violation of the Air Force dress regulations, he was warned, would lead to a courtmartial. Goldman brought suit against the secretary of defense and others. The United States District Court granted Goldman injunctive relief against the application of dress regulations but the United States Court of Appeals reversed it. The Supreme Court granted certiorari.

OPINION BY CHIEF JUSTICE REHNQUIST
(Vote: 5–4)

Question—Is it a First Amendment right for a Jewish officer who is also a rabbi to wear a yarmulke or skullcap in violation of an Air Force dress regulation?

Decision—No.

Reason—The Court has repeatedly held that "the military is, by necessity, a specialized society separate from civilian society" and "the military must insist upon a respect for duty and discipline without counterpart in civilian life." The military need not encourage debate or tolerate protest to the extent "that such tolerance is required of the civilian state by the First Amendment." To accomplish its mission "the military must foster instinctive obedience, unity, commitment, and an esprit de corps." Courts must give great deference concerning the relative importance of a particular military interest." Uniforms encourage a sense "of hierarchical unity by tending to eliminate outward individual distinctions except for those of rank. The Air Force considers them as vital during peace time as during war . . . habits of discipline and unity must be developed in advance of trouble." But whether or not expert witnesses "may feel that religious exceptions . . . are desirable is quite besides the point. The desirability of dress regulations in the military is decided by the appropriate military officials, and they are under no constitutional mandate to abandon their considered professional judgment."

Corollary cases

Sherbert v. Verne, 374 U.S. 398, 10 L. Ed. 2d 965, 83 S. Ct. 1790 (1963)
Thomas v. Review Board, 450 U.S. 707, 67 L. Ed. 2d 624, 101 S. Ct. 1425 (1981)
Wisconsin v. Yoder, 406 U.S. 205, 32 L. Ed. 2d 15, 92 S. Ct. 1526 (1972)
Parker v. Levy, 412 U.S. 733, 41 L. Ed. 2d 439, 94 S. Ct. 2547 (1974)
Chappell v. Wallace, 462 U.S. 296, 76 L. Ed. 2d 586, 103 S. Ct. 2362 (1983)
Schlesinger v. Councilman, 420 U.S. 738, 43 L. Ed. 2d 591, 95 S. Ct. 1300 (1975)
Orloff v. Willoughby, 345 U.S. 83, 97 L. Ed. 842, 73 S. Ct. 534 (1953)
Greer v. Spock, 424 U.S. 828, 47 L. Ed. 2d 505, 96 St. Ct. 1211 (1976)
Rostker v. Goldberg, 453 U.S. 57, 69 L. Ed. 2d 478, 101 S. Ct. 2646 (1981)

Korematsu v. United States, 323 U.S. 214; 65 S. Ct. 193; 89 L. Ed. 194 (1944)

> Korematsu, an American citizen of Japanese ancestry, remained in California after it had been ordered cleared of all persons of Japanese descent under Executive Order 34, itself based on an act of Congress. He refused to leave and was convicted under the law.

OPINION BY MR. JUSTICE BLACK
(Vote: 6–3)

Question—Was this a proper exercise of the war power?

Decision—Yes.

Reason—"Korematsu was not excluded from the Military Area because of hostility to him or his race. He was excluded because we are at war with the Japanese Empire, because the properly constituted military authorities feared an invasion of our West Coast and felt constrained to take proper security measures, because they decided that the military urgency of the situation demanded that all citizens of Japanese ancestry be segregated from the West Coast temporarily, and finally, because Congress, reposing its confidence in this time of war in our military leaders—as inevitably it must—determined that they should have the power to do just this. There was evidence of disloyalty on the part of some, the military authorities considered that the need for action was great, and time was short. We cannot—by availing ourselves of the calm perspective of hindsight—now say that at that time these actions were unjustified."

Corollary cases

Hirabayashi v. United States, 320 U.S. 81 (1940)
Chastleton Corporation v. Sinclair, 264 U.S. 543 (1924)
Block v. Hirsh, 256 U.S. (1921)
Ex parte Endo, 323 U.S. 283 (1944)
Duncan v. Kahanamoku, 327 U.S. 304 (1945)

Note—The only question presented here was the right of the military to evacuate persons. Rather than martial law, the war power was used. Had it been the former, it would have applied to all citizens and possibly in conflict with *Ex parte Milligan,* 4 Wallace 2 (1866). The Court refused to rule on the basic constitutional issues of the relocation, confinement, and segregation of Japanese Americans. The order was lifted by President Truman on December 31, 1946. In April 1976, President Ford more formally lifted the relocation order.

Korematsu has been a controversial opinion from its inception. By the middle of the 1980s criticism of the law portion escalated to include alleged racialism. At this writing the story is not finished but by 1989 Congress was convinced to pay damages for formerly interned American Japanese but it balked in extending an official apology.

Duncan v. Kahanamoku, 327 U.S. 304; 66 S. Ct. 606; 90 L. Ed. 688 (1946)

Immediately following the Pearl Harbor attack, Governor Poindexter of the Territory of Hawaii proclaimed martial law, suspended the writ of habeas corpus, closed the local courts, and turned over the powers of government to the commanding general of the United States Army in Hawaii. The president approved the measure, and the military ruled Hawaii until October 24, 1944, with minor relaxations.

The procedure aroused much opposition, and suits were brought to test the validity of the convictions of civilians by the military courts. In February 1944, Duncan, a civilian shipfitter employed by the Navy, was convicted of assault for engaging in a brawl with two Marine sentries. He was tried by a military tribunal rather than by a civil court.

OPINION BY MR. JUSTICE BLACK
(Vote: 6–2)

Question—Is the military government of Hawaii valid under the Hawaiian Organic Act?

Decision—No.

Reason—Civilians in Hawaii are entitled to their constitutional privilege of a fair trial. In 1900, when Congress passed the Hawaiian Organic Act, it never intended to overstep the boundaries of military and civilian power. Martial law was never intended, in the meaning of the act, to supersede the civilian courts, but only to come to the assistance of the government, and maintain the defense of the island.

Corollary cases

Ex parte Milligan, 4 Wallace 2 (1866)
Ex parte Quirin, 317 U.S. 1 (1942)
Korematsu v. United States, 323 U.S. 214 (1944)

Note—The Court very deliberately skirted the constitutional issue. As in the case of *Ex parte Milligan* (1866), *Duncan* reached the Court after hostilities ceased.

Woods v. Cloyd W. Miller Co., 333 U.S. 138; 68 S. Ct. 421; 92 L. Ed. 596 (1948)

The District Court for the Northern District of Ohio declared unconstitutional Title II of the Housing and Rent

Act of 1947, which continued in force rent control provisions of previous legislation. The act became effective on July 1, 1947, and the following day the appellee demanded of its tenants 40 percent and 60 percent increases for rental accommodations in the Cleveland Defense-Rental Area. This was an admitted violation of the act. The district court declared the act an unconstitutional violation of congressional war power.

OPINION BY MR. JUSTICE DOUGLAS
(No evidence from the report that the decision was not unanimous.)

Question—Does the right of Congress to establish rent controls by virtue of its war powers carry beyond the cessation of hostilities?

Decision—Yes.

Reason—The war power of Congress includes the power "to remedy the evils which have arisen from its rise and progress." This power continues for the duration of the emergency and does not necessarily end with the cessation of hostilities. The deficit in housing caused by the heavy demobilization of veterans and the reduction of residential construction due to lack of materials during the period of hostilities still continued. Since the war effort contributed heavily to that deficit, Congress might retain controls, even after the cessation of hostilities.

War powers, used indiscriminately, may swallow up all the powers of Congress, as well as the Ninth and Tenth Amendments. Any power can be abused. Such was not, however, the case in this situation. Also, questions as to whether or not Congress has overstepped its war powers are open to judicial inquiry.

Corollary cases

Hamilton v. Kentucky Distilleries Co., 251 U.S. 146 (1919)
Block v. Hirsh, 256 U.S. 135 (1921)
Yakus v. United States, 321 U.S. 414 (1944)
Bowles v. Willingham, 321 U.S. 503 (1944)
Fleming v. Mohawk Wrecking and Lumber Co., 331 U.S. 111 (1947)
Ruppert v. Caffey, 251 U.S. 264 (1920)
Arver v. United States, 245 U.S. 366 (1918)

Note—Since it can be said that we are either preparing for a possible war, engaged in war, or recovering from the ravages of a past war, the longevity of federal war powers is strong and its effect pervasive. Federal war power, as decided in *Woods* v. *Miller,* 333 U.S. 138 (1948), extends to whatever is necessary to bring hostilities to a close and to treat the consequences of war.

Welsh v. United States, 398 U.S. 333; 90 S. Ct. 1792; 26 L. Ed. 2d 308 (1970)

Welsh was convicted in federal court for refusing to submit to induction into the armed forces. His application for conscientious objector classification had been denied. Under the statute this status is accorded to those persons who by reason of "religious training and belief" are conscientiously opposed to participation in war in any form. Specifically excluded by the statute from such training and belief are "essentially political, sociological, or philosophical views or a merely personal code." Welsh based his claim on his belief that it is wrong to participate in any war but he stated that his views were not religious. He was not a member of any organized religion at that time.

OPINION BY MR. JUSTICE BLACK
(Vote: 5–3)

Question—Does the statutory exclusion include such situations as this?

Decision—No.

Reason—Even though Welsh's conscientious objection to war was undeniably based in part on his perception of world politics, the statute should not be read to exclude from classification as conscientious objectors those who hold strong beliefs about our domestic and foreign affairs or even those whose conscientious objection to participation in all wars is founded to a substantial extent upon considerations of public policy. The beliefs involved must be held with the strength of more traditional religious convictions.

Corollary cases

United States v. Seeger, 380 U.S. 163 (1965)
United States v. Macintosh, 283 U.S. 605 (1931)

Sherbert v. Verner, 374 U.S. 398 (1963)
Parisi v. Davidson, 405 U.S. 34 (1972)
Selective Draft Law Cases, 245 U.S. 366 (1918)
Braunfield v. Brown, 366 U.S. 599 (1961)
Clay v. United States, 403 U.S. 698 (1971)
Rostker v. Goldberg, 453 U.S. 57 (1981)

Note—Originally used only by those claiming a conscientious objector status on religious grounds, in *United States* v. *Seeger,* 380 U.S. 128 (1965), the exception grounds were expanded to include deeply held moral and philosophical views. When, however, in reaction to the unpopularity of the Vietnam War, a claim was made only for a specific war, the Court refused. In *Gillette* v. *United States,* 401 U.S. 437 (1971), in dealing with issues growing out of the Vietnam conflict, the Court handed down some important decisions. Thus, in *Oestereich* v. *Selective Service Board,* 393 U.S. 233 (1962), the Court held a draft board could not withdraw a divinity student's classification because he participated in an antiwar rally, or accelerate an inductee call because he turned in his draft card, as in *Gunecht* v. *United States,* 396 U.S. 295 (1970), and that a draft board must honor a nonfrivolous request to re-examine a classification, as in *Mulloy* v. *United States,* 398 U.S. 410 (1970).

Rostker v. Goldberg, 453 U.S. 57; 69 L. Ed. 2d 478; 101 S. Ct. 1 (1981)

The Military Selective Service Act authorizes the president to require the registration for possible military service of males but not females. In 1980, President Jimmy Carter reactivated the registration process for both male and females. Congress allocated only those funds necessary for the men, despite Carter's requested funding for both sexes. Suit was brought by three men, claiming the act's gender based discrimination violated the due process clause of the Fifth Amendment to the Constitution.

OPINION BY MR. JUSTICE REHNQUIST
(Vote: 6–3)

Question—Is the Military Selective Service Act in violation of the Fifth Amendment?

Decision—No.

Reason—"Congress is a co-equal branch of government whose members take the same oath we do to uphold the Constitution. . . . This Court has consistently recognized Congress's 'broad constitutional power' to raise and regulate armies and navies." Moreover, just as Congress's scope of power in this area is broad, "the lack of competence on the part of the courts is marked." While the Court does not abdicate its responsibility to decide constitutional questions, "the Constitution itself requires such deference to congressional choice." This case "is quite different from several of the gender-based discrimination cases . . . and the decision to exempt women from registration was not the 'accidental by-product of a traditional way of thinking about women.' The purpose of the registration, therefore, was to prepare for a draft of *combat troops*. Women as a group . . . unlike men as a group, are not eligible for combat. . . . Congress's decision to authorize the registration of only men, therefore, does not violate the due process clause."

Corollary cases

Schlesinger v. Ballard, 95 S. Ct. 572 (1976)
Craig v. Boren, 97 S. Ct. 451 (1976)

Note—Despite a number of decisions favorable to women on equal protection grounds, just to cite a few, *Craig v. Boren* (429 U.S. 190, 1977), *Stanton v. Stanton* (421 U.S. 7, 1975), *Dothard v. Rawlingson* (473 U.S. 321, 1977) and *Califano v. Goldfarb* (430 U.S. 199, 1977) the Court has never said that sex is a "suspect" classification. Cohen and Kaplan, *Constitutional Law* (1982 2d edition), correctly wrote: None of the Justices writing in *Rostker* . . . "questioned the constitutional validity of a practice of reserving combat military roles to men." The dissenters argued that "it was unconstitutional to limit selective service registration to men even if combat was limited to men."

TREATIES AND EXECUTIVE AGREEMENTS

Head Money Cases (Edye v. Robertson) 112 U.S. 580; 5 S. Ct. 247; 28 L. Ed. 798 (1884)

In 1882 Congress passed an act providing that a duty of fifty cents should be collected for each and every passenger who was not a citizen of the United States, coming from a foreign port to any port within the United States. Individuals and steamship companies brought suit against the collector of customs at New York, Mr. W. H. Robertson, for the recovery of the sums of money collected. The act was challenged on the grounds that it violated numerous treaties of our government with friendly nations.

OPINION BY MR. JUSTICE MILLER
(No evidence from the report that the decision was not unanimous.)

Question—Is this act void because of conflict with a treaty?

Decision—No.

Reason—A treaty is a compact between independent nations, which depends for its enforcement upon the interest and honor of the governments that are parties to the treaty. Treaties that regulate the mutual rights of citizens and subjects of the contracting nations are in the same category as acts of Congress. When these rights are of such a nature as to be enforced by a court of justice, the court resorts to the treaty as it would to a statute. However, the Constitution gives a treaty no superiority over an act of Congress. "In short, we are of the opinion, that, so far as a treaty made by the United States with a foreign nation can become the subject of judicial cognizance in the courts of this country, it is subject to such acts as Congress may pass for its enforcement, modification or repeal."

Corollary cases

The Cherokee Tobacco Case, 11 Wallace 616 (1870)
United States v. McBratney, 104 U.S. 621 (1882)
State Railroad Tax Cases, 92 U.S. 612 (1876)
Chae Chan Ping v. United States, 130 U.S. 581 (1889)
Whitney v. Robertson, 124 U.S. 190 (1888)

Asakura v. Seattle, 265 U.S. 332 (1924)
Tucker v. Alexandroff, 183 U.S. 424 (1902)
Nielsen v. Johnson, 279 U.S. 47 (1929)
United States v. Belmont, 301 U.S. 324 (1937)
Missouri v. Holland, 252 U.S. 416 (1920)
Dames and Moore v. Regan, 453 U.S.—; 69 L. Ed. 2d 918 (1981)

Note—Although treaties and statutes are equal in case of conflict, the one most recently passed is binding, as decided in *Whitney v. Robertson,* 124 U.S. 190 (1888). In *United States v. Pink,* 315 U.S. 203 (1942), the Court virtually placed executive agreements on the same level with treaties.

Missouri v. Holland, 252 U.S. 416; 40 S. Ct. 382; 64 L. Ed. 641 (1920)

The United States entered into a treaty with Great Britain for the protection of migratory birds. In the treaty was a provision that each of the contracting powers undertake to pass laws that would forbid the killing, capturing, or selling of the birds except in accordance with certain regulations. Congress enacted legislation and Missouri brought suit, saying its reserved powers under the Tenth Amendment were violated by the act and treaty.

OPINION BY MR. JUSTICE HOLMES
(Vote: 7–2)

Question—Do the treaty and statute interfere invalidly with the rights reserved to the states by the Tenth Amendment?

Decision—No.

Reason—Acts of Congress must be made in pursuance of the Constitution, but treaties are valid when made under the authority of the United States. "We do not mean to imply that there are no qualifications to the treaty-making power; but they must be ascertained in a different way. It is obvious that there may be matters of the sharpest exigency for the national well-being that an act of Congress could not deal with but that a treaty followed by such an act could, and it is not lightly to be assumed that, in matters requiring national action, 'a power which must belong to and somewhere reside in every civilized government' is not to be found. . . . Here a national interest of very nearly the first magnitude is involved. It can be protected only by national action in concert with that of another power. The subject matter is only transitorily within the state and has no permanent habitat therein.

"If the treaty is valid there can be no dispute about the validity of the statute under Article I, Section 8, as a necessary and proper means to execute the powers of the government."

Corollary cases

Nielson v. Johnson, 279 U.S. 47 (1929)
Hauenstein v. Lynham, 100 U.S. 483 (1880)
Massachusetts v. Laird, 400 U.S. 886 (1970)
Orlando v. Laird, 404 U.S. 869 (1971)
Attlee v. Richardson, 411 U.S. 94 (1973)
Geofrey v. Riggs, 133 U.S. 258 (1890)
United States v. Belmont, 301 U.S. 324 (1937)
United States v. Pink, 315 U.S. 203 (1942)
Dames & Moore v. Regan, 453 U.S. 654 (1981)

Note—*Missouri* seems to hold that Congress might do by treaty what is inadmissible by law. This view was attacked in 1954 by the proposed Bricker Amendment, which was defeated after a close vote. Had it been adopted it would: (a) have reduced a treaty to the status of a law, (b) brought the House into the treaty process, and (c) reversed *Missouri* v. *Holland*.

CONGRESSIONAL POWERS

McCulloch v. Maryland, 4 Wheaton 316; 4 L. Ed. 579 (1819)

Congress incorporated the Bank of the United States, a branch of which was established in Baltimore. The state of Maryland required all banks not chartered by the state to pay a tax on each issuance of bank notes. McCulloch, the cashier of the Baltimore branch of the Bank of the United States, issued notes without complying with the state law. Action was brought on the part of Maryland to recover the penalties.

OPINION BY MR. CHIEF JUSTICE MARSHALL

(No evidence from the report that the decision was not unanimous.)

Question—1. Has Congress power to incorporate a bank?

2. May the state of Maryland tax a branch of the United States Bank located in Maryland?

Decisions—1. Yes.
2. No.

Reason—1. The Constitution empowers the government with the right to lay and collect taxes; to borrow money; to regulate commerce; to declare and conduct war; and to raise the support armies and navies. Congress has also been granted the power "to make all laws which shall be necessary and proper for carrying into execution" the expressed powers in the Constitution. Therefore, by incorporating a bank, Congress is creating the means to attain the goals of the powers entrusted to them.

2. The Court contended that the Constitution and the laws made in pursuance thereof are supreme and cannot be controlled by the various states. If the state of Maryland could regulate the laws of the federal government to its own convenience, then the Constitution and federal laws would soon lose their significance. "Let the end be legitimate, let it be within the scope of the Constitution, and all means which are appropriate, which are plainly adapted to that end, which are not prohibited, but consist with the letter and spirit of the Consti-

tution, are constitutional.'' The Court stated that when Maryland taxed the operations of the federal government, it acted upon institutions created not by their own constituents, but by people over whom they claimed no control. The power to tax involves the power to destroy. Such a tax could be used to destroy an institution vitally necessary to carry out the operations of the federal government, and therefore is unconstitutional and void.

Corollary cases

United States v. Fisher, 2 Cranch 358 (1805)
Osborn v. The Bank of the United States, 9 Wheaton 738 (1824)
Dobbins v. Commissioners of Erie County, 16 Peters 435 (1842)
Collector v. Day, 11 Wallace 113 (1871)
Graves v. New York ex rel. O'Keefe, 306 U.S. 466 (1939)

Note—*McCulloch* will be found in any list of the "great cases." A good deal of Hamiltonian theory became law. It proclaimed the doctrine of federal supremacy. In the *Legal Tender Cases,* 12 Wallace 457 (1871), and in *Juilliard* v. *Greenman,* 110 U.S. 421 (1884), *McCulloch* was supplemented by the development of the doctrine of "resulting" (or resultant) powers.

Baldrige v. Shapiro, 455 U.S.—; 71 L. Ed. 2d 199, 102 S. Ct. 1103 (1982)

> After concluding the 1980 census, the Bureau of Census related to officials in Denver and Essex County, New Jersey, that their areas, along with some fifty others, had lost population. Under bureau procedures, these areas challenged the census figures as erroneous classifications and sought to compel disclosure of a portion of the address lists used by the government. The bureau resisted claiming that the law prohibited disclosure of raw census data and under exemptions of the Freedom of Information Act. The district court agreed with Denver and Essex County. The United States Court of Appeals affirmed the Supreme Court on certiorari reversed.

OPINION BY MR. CHIEF JUSTICE BURGER
(No evidence from the report that the decision was not unanimous.)

Question—Are lists of addresses collected and utilized by the Bureau of Census exempt from disclosure, by way of civil discovery under the Freedom of Information Act or under the confidentiality provisions of the Census Act.

Decision—Yes.

Reason—Under the Constitution, said the Court, responsibility for conducting the decennial census rests with Congress. "The broad mandate of the Freedom of Information Act (FOIA) is to provide open disclosure of public information. The act expressly recognizes, however, that public disclosure is not always in the public interest and consequently provides that agency records may be withheld from disclosure under any one of the nine exemptions. . . . Under Exemption 3 disclosure need not be made as to information 'specifically exempted from disclosure by statute'. . . . [T]he national census . . . fulfills many important and valuable functions for the benefit of the Country as a whole. . . . Although Congress has broad power to require individuals to submit responses, an accurate census depends in large part on public cooperation. To stimulate that cooperation Congress had provided assurances that information furnished to the secretary by individuals is to be treated as confidential. . . . We hold that whether sought by way of requests under the FOIA or by way of discovery rules, raw data reported by or on behalf of individuals need not be disclosed."

Corollary cases

St. Regis Paper Co. v. United States, 368 U.S. 208 (1961)
NLRB v. Sears, Roebuck & Co., 421 U.S. 132 (1975)
Renegotiation Board v. Bannercroft Clothing Co., 415 U.S. 1 (1974)

Note—If this case had been decided differently, it is not hard to imagine the political hazards a future census would encounter. Has the government, as some have claimed, lost control of our borders? If so, it is difficult to conceive resident undocumented aliens participating in the census. Anything less than the strict confidentiality of *Baldrige* would have subjected them to possible deportation.

CONGRESSIONAL INVESTIGATIONS

McGrain v. Daugherty, 273 U.S. 135; 47 S. Ct. 319; 71 L. Ed. 580 (1927)

The Senate decided to investigate the activities and inactivities of Harry M. Daugherty, former attorney general of the United States. In the investigations they subpoenaed Mally S. Daugherty, a brother of the former attorney general, to appear before the committee that was conducting the hearings. He refused, and the Senate issued a warrant to compel him to appear and testify. The Senate sent McGrain, its deputy sergeant-at-arms, to arrest him. Daugherty applied for and received a writ of habeas corpus to discharge him from custody on the ground that the Senate exceeded its powers under the Constitution.

OPINION BY MR. JUSTICE VAN DEVANTER
(Vote: 8–0)

Question—May either the Senate or House of Representatives compel a private individual to appear before it or one of its committees and give testimony?

Decision—Yes.

Reason—The power to legislate carries with it by necessary implication information needed in the rightful exercise of that power and to employ compulsory process for that purpose. Although it was investigating the former attorney general, and the resolution that brought the committee into existence had not in turn avowed that it was intended to be in aid of legislation, plainly the subject was such that the information received could be of valuable help in enacting further laws.

Corollary cases

Anderson v. Dunn, 6 Wheaton 204 (1821)
In re Chapman, 266 U.S. 661 (1897)
Marshall v. Gordon, 243 U.S. 521 (1917)
Barry v. United States ex rel. Cunningham, 279 U.S. 597 (1929)
Jurney v. MacCracken, 294 U.S. 125 (1935)
Sinclair v. United States, 279 U.S. 263 (1929)
Kilbourn v. Thompson, 103 U.S. 168 (1881)
United States v. Rumely, 345 U.S. 41 (1953)

Watkins v. United States, 354 U.S. 178 (1957)
Ullman v. United States, 350 U.S. 422 (1956)
Barenblatt v. United States, 360 U.S. 109 (1959)
Eastland v. United States Serviceman's Fund, 421 U.S. 491 (1975)

Note—In a very early case involving the power of Congress to punish, *Anderson* v. *Dunn,* 6 Wheaton 204 (1821), the Court noted that: (1) only obstructions to the legislative power come within the investigative power, and (2) imprisonment for contempt could not exceed the life of the session.

United States v. Lovett, 328 U.S. 303; 66 S. Ct. 1073; 90 L. Ed. 1252 (1946)

> Lovett, Watson, and Dodd had been working for the government for several years, and the government agencies that had lawfully employed them were fully satisfied with their work and wished to keep them employed. In 1943 Congress passed the Urgent Deficiency Appropriation Act, which provided that no salary should be paid respondents unless they were reappointed to their jobs by the president with the advice and consent of the Senate. Notwithstanding the failure of the president to reappoint them, they continued at their jobs and sued for their salaries.

OPINION BY MR. JUSTICE BLACK
(Vote: 8–0)

Question—Is this a bill of attainder, which is forbidden by the Constitution?

Decision—Yes.

Reason—In *Cummings* v. *Missouri* the Court said, "A bill of attainder is a legislative act which inflicts punishment without a judicial trial." If the punishment be less than death, the act is termed a bill of pains and penalties, but both are included in the meaning of the Constitution.

Lovett, Watson, and Dodd were mentioned by Congressman Dies with thirty-six other named government employees as "irresponsible, unrepresentative, crackpot, radical bureaucrats" and affiliates of "communist front organizations." He urged that Congress refuse to appropriate money for their salaries. This in effect would force the governmental agencies to discharge them and stigmatize their reputations, which would seriously impair their chances to earn a living. This clearly punished the individuals without a judicial trial, which is forbidden by the Constitution.

Corollary cases

Cummings v. Missouri, 4 Wallace 277 (1867)
Ex parte Garland, 4 Wallace 333 (1867)
Duncan v. Kahanamoku, 327 U.S. 304 (1946)
United States v. Brown, 381 U.S. 437 (1965)

Note—Relatively few bill of attainder cases have come before the Supreme Court. In the Test Oath Cases—*Cummings* v. *Missouri,* 4 Wallace 277 (1867) and *Ex parte Garland,* 4 Wallace 333 (1867)—the Court struck down bills of attainder, and more recently it declared a section of the Landrum-Griffin Labor Act (1959) void, in *United States* v. *Brown,* 381 U.S. 437 (1965). Instead of deciding *Lovett* as a bill of attainder case (the practical effect of which was to guarantee a job at public expense), it might have decided it on grounds that it violated the president's power of removal as set out in *Humphrey. Lovett* also represents the principle of partial invalidity.

The Department of Defense Authorization Act denied federal financial assistance (under the Higher Education Act of 1965) to male students who failed to register for the draft. The Court held that the act (1) was not a bill of attainder since it did not single out any identifiable group, (2) did not violate the self-incrimination clause, (3) did not violate the self-protection clause, and (4) that the Act carried out a legitimate government objective. *Selective Service System* v. *Minnesota Public Interest Research Group,* 82 L. Ed. 2d 632 (1984).

Watkins v. United States, 354 U.S. 178; 77 S. Ct. 1173; 1 L. Ed. 2d 1273 (1957)

John T. Watkins, a labor union organizer, appeared as a witness in compliance with a subpoena issued by a Sub-Committee of the Committee on Un-American Activities of the House of Representatives. Although Watkins indicated he would answer questions about his relations with the Communist party as well as questions concerning acquaintances currently members, he refused to answer those questions involving persons whom he believed had separated from the party on the ground that these were not relevant to the work of this committee and beyond the authority of the committee to demand. He was indicted and convicted for contempt of Congress under a statute making criminal refusal to answer "any questions pertinent to the question under inquiry."

OPINION BY MR. CHIEF JUSTICE WARREN
(Vote: 6–1)

Question—May a witness at a congressional committee hearing properly refuse to answer questions on the basis of their lack of pertinency?

Decision—Yes.

Reason—While the power of Congress to conduct investigations is inherent in the legislative process and is a broad power, the inquiry "must be related to and in furtherance of a legitimate task of the Congress." The Bill of Rights is applicable to investigations as to all forms of governmental actions, so the First Amendment freedoms of speech, press, religion, and political belief and association must not be abridged. Further, the First Amendment may be invoked against infringement of the protected freedoms by law or by lawmaking.

There is a freedom *not* to speak. "Protected freedoms should not be placed in danger in the absence of a clear determination by the House or the Senate that a particular inquiry is justified by a specific legislative need." This requires that the instructions to an investigating committee spell out that group's jurisdiction and purpose with sufficient particularity. "There is no congressional power to expose for the sake of exposure."

In this instance, none of the several sources—the authorizing resolution, the remarks of the chairman, or the remarks of members of the committee—was adequate to convey sufficient information as to the pertinency of the questions. Watkins was thus "not accorded a fair opportunity to determine whether he was within his rights in refusing to answer, and his conviction is necessarily invalid under the Due Process Clause of the Fifth Amendment."

Jencks v. United States, 353 U.S. 657; 77 S. Ct. 1007; 1 L. Ed. 2d 1103 (1957)

> The president of a labor union, Clinton E. Jencks, had been convicted of falsely swearing that he was not a member of the Communist party. The government's principal witnesses, Harvey F. Matusow and John W. Ford, were Communist party members paid by the Federal Bureau of Investigation. These men had made regular oral and written reports to the FBI on the matters about which they had testified. The accused had demanded that these reports be produced in court for inspection with a view to their possible use by the defense in impeaching the testimony. This motion was denied.

OPINION BY MR. JUSTICE BRENNAN
(Vote: 7–1)

Question—Is an accused person entitled to inspect relevant statements and reports of government witnesses in the possession of the government?

Decision—Yes.

Reason—Only the defense is adequately equipped to determine the effective use of such statements and reports for the purpose of discrediting the government's witnesses. "Justice requires no less. . . . The burden is the government's, not to be shifted to the trial judge, to decide whether the public prejudice of allowing the crime to go unpunished is greater than that attendant upon the possible disclosure of state secrets and other confidential information in the government's possession." The Court noted also that a trial judge can determine the admissibility of government documents and reports as evidence only after inspection by the accused.

Corollary cases

Goldman v. United States, 316 U.S. 129 (1942)
Berger v. United States, 295 U.S. 78 (1935)

Goldberg v. United States, 425 U.S. 94 (1976)
United States v. Reynolds, 345 U.S. 1 (1953)
Roviaro v. United States, 353 U.S. 53 (1957)
Hannah v. Larche, 363 U.S. 420 (1960)

Note—As a consequence of the political fallout of *Jencks,* Congress enacted the "Jencks law," which regulated the procedure for securing information in government files. It was now to be accomplished by a judge rather than solely by request of the defendant. This restored the previous practice of the lower courts.

Branzburg v. Hayes, 408 U.S. 205; 92 S. Ct. 2646; 33 L. Ed. 2d 626 (1972)

> On November 15, 1969, the *Louisville Courier-Journal* carried a story under Paul Branzburg's byline describing in detail the drug activities of two persons. He was subpoenaed by the Jefferson County grand jury, but he refused to identify the two hashish makers since he had promised them not to reveal their identity. Branzburg maintained that if forced to reveal confidential sources, reporters would be measurably deterred from furnishing publishable information, and that this would work to the detriment of a free press.

OPINION BY MR. JUSTICE WHITE
(Vote: 5–4)

Question—Do reporters have an obligation to respond to grand jury subpoenas and to answer questions relevant to an investigation into the commission of a crime?

Decision—Yes.

Reason—The great weight of authority is that newsmen are not exempt from the normal duty of appearing before a grand jury and answering such questions. The First Amendment interest asserted by newsmen is outweighed by the general obligation of citizens to appear before a grand jury or at trial, pursuant to a subpoena, and to give what information they possess. Public interest in law enforcement and in ensuring effective grand jury proceedings outweighs the consequential but uncertain burden on news gathering.

Corollary cases

New York Times Co. v. United States, 403 U.S. 713 (1971)
Toledo Newspaper Co. v. United States, 247 U.S. 402 (1918)
United States v. Bryan, 339 U.S. 323 (1950)
Near v. Minnesota, 283 U.S. 697 (1931)
Herbert v. Lando, 441 U.S. 153 (1979)
Houchins v. KQED, 438 U.S. 1 (1978)
Whalen v. Roe, 429 U.S. 589 (1977)
United States v. Caldwell, 408 U.S. 665 (1972)

Note—As one consequence of *Branzburg,* some states have passed "shield laws" that extend privileged communication to journalists as it has been open to spouses, doctors, lawyers, and clergymen. Reporters are on the losing side of case law when they argue that they can make an ex parte agreement to keep their news sources "confidential" or else these sources will "dry up". The prevailing view is that the First Amendment "does not guarantee the press a constitutional right of special access to information not available to the public generally . . ." *Branzburg v. Hayes* (1972).

IMPROPER DELEGATION OF POWER

J. W. Hampton, Jr., & Co. v. United States, 276 U.S. 394; 48 S. Ct. 348; 72 L. Ed. 624 (1928)

> The J. W. Hampton, Jr., and Co. imported some goods at a New York port and was assessed a rate higher than fixed by statute. The collector of the port assessed the increase under authority of a proclamation by the president. The basis of the tariff was an act of Congress setting up a Tariff Commission under the executive branch of the government. The act gave the president the power to fix and change duties on imports after investigation by the commission and notice given to all parties interested to produce evidence. This was the so-called flexible tariff provision. The law provided that the increase or decrease of the tariff duties should not exceed 50 percent of the rate set by Congress. The Hampton Co. contended that the act gave the president the power to legislate and therefore was unconstitutional.

OPINION BY MR. CHIEF JUSTICE TAFT
(No evidence from the report that the decision was not unanimous.)

Question—Does the act invoke improper delegation of legislative power?

Decision—No.

Reason—The Court held that the true distinction is between the delegation of power to make the law, which necessarily involves a discretion as to what it shall be, and conferring an authority or discretion as to its execution, to be exercised under and in pursuance of the law. The first cannot be done; the second, as was the case here, is valid.

The Court referred to the reasoning in *Field* v. *Clark,* 143 U.S. 649, to substantiate the point that Congress did not delegate legislative powers to the president, because nothing involving the contents of the law was left to the determination of the president. The legislative power was performed when Congress passed an act setting up the Tariff Commission as a part of the executive branch, placing the power to execute the law in the hands of the president, and setting down the general rules of action under which both the commission and the president should proceed.

"What the president was required to do was merely in execution of the act of Congress. It was not the making of law. He was the mere agent of the lawmaking department to ascertain and declare the event upon which its expressed will was to take effect."

The Court also upheld the protection features of the tariff act as a proper exercise of its power over foreign commerce, as well as on the basis of action by the First Congress, which was composed, in part, of framers of the Constitution.

Corollary cases

Buttfield v. Stranahan, 192 U.S. 649 (1904)
Interstate Commerce Commission v. Goodrich Transit Co., 224 U.S. 194 (1912)
Field v. Clark, 143 U.S. 649 (1892)
Panama Refining Co. v. Ryan, 293 U.S. 388 (1935)
Ambach v. Norwich, 60 L. Ed. 2d 49 (1979)
Schechter Poultry Corp. v. United States, 295 U.S. 495 (1936)
Yakus v. United States, 321 U.S. 414 (1944)
Opp Cotton Mills v. Administrator, 312 U.S. 126 (1941)
United States v. Curtiss-Wright Export Corp., 299 U.S. 304 (1936)
California Bankers Ass'n. v. Schultz, 416 U.S. 21 (1974)

A.L.A. Schechter Poultry Corp. v. United States, 295 U.S. 495; 55 S. Ct. 837; 79 L. Ed. 1570 (1935)

The A.L.A. Schechter Poultry Corp. was convicted in the United States District Court for the Eastern District of New York on an indictment charging violations of what was known as the "Live Poultry Code," established by executive order under the National Industrial Recovery Act (NRA). The circuit court of appeals sustained the conviction in the district court on sixteen counts for violation of the code, but reversed the conviction on two counts that charged violation of requirements as to minimum wages and maximum hours of labor, as these were not deemed to be within the congressional power of regulation.

The NRA provided for the setting up of codes that would establish certain standards that were to be upheld under force of civil and criminal action. If an industry did not set up its own code, it would be up to the president to impose a code upon it. Schechter was a poultry dealer in New York City and disregarded the code. When tried, he was found guilty on eighteen counts. He then took the case to the Supreme Court.

OPINION BY MR. CHIEF JUSTICE HUGHES
(No evidence from the report that the decision was not unanimous.)

Questions—1. Was the act an illegal delegation of legislative powers?

2. Was the poultry in this case considered within the domain of the interstate commerce power of Congress?

Decisions—1. Yes.
            2. No.

Reason—1. The act set no standard nor rules of conduct to be followed. It was too broad a declaration, leaving the president too much room for discretion. The act left virtually untouched the field of policy. The president in approving a code could impose his own conditions. It was an unconstitutional delegation of legislative power.

The Constitution provides that "all legislative powers herein granted shall be vested in a Congress of the United States, which shall consist of a Senate and House of Representatives," and the Congress is authorized "to make all laws which shall be necessary and proper for carrying into execution" its general powers. The Congress is not permitted to abdicate or to transfer to others the essential legislative functions with which it is thus vested.

2. Although the poultry came from various states, when it arrived in New York it remained there and was processed. Congress could regulate it until it reached New York, after that it was intrastate commerce and as such it could not be controlled by Congress.

Corollary cases

See Panama Refining Co. v. Ryan and cases there cited.
Hampton, Jr., and Co. v. United States, 276 U.S. 394 (1928)
McKinley v. United States, 249 U.S. 397 (1919)
United States v. Grimaud, 220 U.S. 506 (1911)

Hood and Sons v. United States, 307 U.S. 588 (1939)
Sunshine Anthracite Coal Co. v. Adkins, 310 U.S. 381 (1940)
New York Central Securities Corp. v. United States, 287 U.S. 12 (1932)
United States v. Rock Royal Cooperative, 307 U.S. 533 (1939)

Note—Sometimes called the "sick chicken case." Two other notables in which the New Deal era Supreme Court voided on improper delegation of power were *United States* v. *Butler,* 297 U.S. 1 (1936) and *Panama Refining Co.* v. *Ryan,* 293 U.S. 388 (1935). In the field of foreign relations, the Court has sanctioned a large dose of delegated power to the president, as it did in *United States* v. *Curtiss-Wright Export Corp.,* 299 U.S. 304 (1936).

Panama Refining Co. v. Ryan, 293 U.S. 388; 55 S. Ct. 241; 79 L. Ed. 446 (1935)

Section 9 (c) of the National Industrial Recovery Act (NIRA) had given the President the power to forbid the transportation in interstate commerce of oil produced or withdrawn from storage in violation of state law. The Panama Refining Company, as owner of an oil refining plant in Texas, sued to restrain the defendants, who were federal officials, from enforcing regulations from the Department of Interior based on the National Industrial Recovery Act, on the grounds that Section 9 (c) of the act was unconstitutional.

OPINION BY MR. CHIEF JUSTICE HUGHES
(Vote: 8–1)

Question—Does Section 9 (c) of the National Industrial Recovery Act delegate legislative power to the president?

Decision—Yes.

Reason—The statute did not contain any definition of the circumstances or conditions in which the transportation was to be permitted or prohibited. In other words, the power of the president was purely discretionary. He was not merely filling in the details of a legislative policy, since no legislative policy was outlined to guide or control him. Therefore, the Court noted that, while very broad powers of administrative regulation may be delegated to the president, there must still be a legislative statement of policy sufficiently definite to prevent the exercise upon his part of pure discretion. Section 9 (c) of the NIRA in essence delegates the power to legislate to the President and is therefore unconstitutional and void.

Corollary cases

Wichita Railroad & Light Co. v. Public Utilities Commission, 260 U.S. 48 (1922)

Mahler v. Eby, 264 U.S. 32 (1924)

Opp Cotton Mills v. Administrator of Wage and Hour Division, 312 U.S. 126 (1941)

United States v. Curtiss-Wright Export Corp., 299 U.S. 302 (1934)

Yakus v. United States, 321 U.S. 414 (1944)

Bowles v. Willingham, 321 U.S. 503 (1944)

Norwegian Nitrogen Products Co. v. United States, 288 U.S. 294 (1933)

Carter v. Carter Coal Co., 298 U.S. 238 (1936)

Eubank v. Richmond, 226 U.S. 137 (1912)

Washington ex rel. Seattle Trust Co. v. Roberge, 278 U.S. 116 (1928)

A.L.A. Schechter Poultry Corp. v. United States, 295 U.S. 495 (1935)

Note—Known as the "Hot Oil Case" in reference to oil produced or withdrawn from storage in violation of state law. This was the first New Deal statute declared void as an unconstitutional delegation of power. The well-known maxim *delegata potestas non potest delegari* (delegated power cannot be redelegated) is the basis of the decision. Delegated power to the president in foreign affairs has escaped Court censure, as in *United States* v. *Curtiss-Wright Export Corp.,* 299 U.S. 304 (1936), but is still denied to the states, as decided in *Knickerbocker Ice Co.* v. *Stewart,* 253 U.S. 149 (1920).

Yakus v. United States, 321 U.S. 414; 64 S. Ct. 660; 88 L. Ed. 834 (1944)

The petitioner was tried and convicted for the willful sale of wholesale cuts of beef prices above the maximum prices prescribed by the price regulations set down by the federal Price Administrator under the authority of the Emergency Price Control Act of January 30, 1942, and as amended by the Inflation Control Act of October 2, 1942.

OPINION BY MR. CHIEF JUSTICE STONE
(Vote: 6–3)

Question—Do the acts in question involve an unconstitutional delegation to the Price Administrator of the legislative power of Congress to control prices?

Decision—No.

Reason—"The essentials of the legislative function are the determination of the legislative policy and its formulation and promulgation as a defined and binding rule of conduct—here the rule, with penal sanctions, that prices shall not be greater than those fixed by maximum price regulations which conform to standards and will tend to further the policy which Congress has established. These essentials are preserved when Congress has specified the basic conditions of fact upon whose existence or occurrence, ascertained from relevant data by a designated administrative agency, it directs that its statutory command shall be effective. It is no objection that the determination of facts and the inferences to be drawn from them in the light of the statutory standards and declaration of policy call for the exercise of judgment, and for the formulation of subsidiary administrative policy within the prescribed statutory framework. . . . The standards prescribed by the present Act, with the aid of the 'statement of the considerations' required to be made by the administrator, are sufficiently definite and precise to enable Congress, the courts, and the public to ascertain whether the administrator, in fixing the designated prices, has conformed to those standards. Hence we are unable to find in them an unauthorized delegation of legislative power."

Corollary cases

Field v. Clark, 143 U.S. 649 (1892)
Hampton, Jr., & Co. v. United States, 276 U.S. 394 (1928)
Mulford v. Smith, 307 U.S. 38 (1939)
United States v. Rock Royal Co-op., 307 U.S. 533 (1939)
Sunshine Anthracite Coal Co. v. Adkins, 310 U.S. 381 (1940)
Opp Cotton Mills v. Administrator, 312 U.S. 190 (1941)
Kiyoshi Hirabayashi v. United States, 320 U.S. 81 (1943)

Union Bridge Co. v. United States, 204 U.S. 364 (1907)
Bowles v. Willingham, 321 U.S. 503 (1944)
Currin v. Wallace, 306 U.S. 15 (1959)
Panama Refining Co. v. Ryan, 293 U.S. 388 (1935)
Schechter Poultry Corp. v. United States, 295 U.S. 495 (1935)
Woods v. Miller, 333 U.S. 138 (1948)
National Broadcasting Co. v. United States, 319 U.S. 190 (1943)

FREEDOM OF SPEECH

Schenck v. United States, 249 U.S. 47; 39 S. Ct. 247; 63 L. Ed. 470 (1919)

Schenck was the general secretary of the Socialist party. He sent out about 15,000 leaflets to men who had been called to military service, urging them to assert their opposition to the Conscription Act. He was indicted on three counts under the Espionage Act of 1917: (1) conspiracy to cause insubordination in the military service of the United States, (2) using the mails for the transmission of matter declared to be nonmailable by the Espionage Act, and (3) the unlawful use of the mails for the transmission of the same matter as mentioned above.

OPINION BY MR. JUSTICE HOLMES
(No evidence from the report that the decision was not unanimous.)

Question—Does the statute in question violate the freedom of speech and the press guaranteed by the First Amendment?

Decision—No.

Reason—The defendants claimed that the tendency of the circular to obstruct the draft was protected by the First Amendment. That would be true in normal circumstances, but the character of every act must be judged according to the circumstances in which it was done. What must be ascertained is whether the words are used in such circumstances as "to create a clear and present danger" that would have brought about substantive evils that Congress had a right to prevent. It is a question of proximity and degree. Many things that may be of no consequence in time of peace may not be said when a nation is at war. "The most stringent protection of free speech would not protect a man in falsely shouting fire in a theatre and causing a panic." The statute punishes conspiracies to obstruct as well as actual obstruction. There are no grounds for saying that success alone makes the action a crime.

Corollary cases

Gitlow v. New York, 268 U.S. 652 (1925)
Bridges v. California, 314 U.S. 252 (1941)

Gompers v. Bucks Stove and Range Co., 221 U.S. 418 (1911)
Terminiello v. City of Chicago, 337 U.S. 1 (1940)
Abrams v. United States, 250 U.S. 616 (1919)
Herndon v. Lowry, 301 U.S. 242 (1937)
Pennekamp v. Florida, 328 U.S. 331 (1946)
Near v. Minnesota, 283 U.S. 697 (1931)
Grosjean v. American Press Co., 297 U.S. 233 (1936)

Note—This is the famous "clear and present danger" doc-trine—the rule of proximate causation. In *Schaefer* v. *United States,* 251 U.S. 466 (1920), the Court resorted to the "bad tendency" test, and in *Dennis* v. *United States,* 341 U.S. 494 (1951), it adopted a "clear and probable danger" test.

Cantwell v. Connecticut, 310 U.S. 296; 60 S. Ct. 900; 84 L. Ed. 1213 (1940)

Newton Cantwell and others, members of the Jehovah's Witnesses, went from house to house in New Haven, Conn., selling books. They were equipped with a record player that described the books. They asked each householder for per-mission to play the record before doing so. They were convicted under a statute that said that no person could solicit money for alleged religious purposes from someone not of their sect unless they have first secured a permit from the secretary of the Public Welfare Council. The secretary passed on all permits that were given.

Opinion by Mr. Justice Roberts
(No evidence from the report that the decision was not unanimous.)

Question—Does this statute deprive the appellants of their liberty and freedom of religion in violation of the First Amendment as guaranteed by the Fourteenth Amendment?

Decision—Yes.

Reason—The act required an application to the secretary of the Public Welfare Council of the state. He was empowered to determine whether the cause was a religious one, and the issuance of a certificate depended upon his affirmative action. If he found that the cause was not one of religion, it then became a crime to solicit for the cause. He did not issue the certificate as a matter of course. He must first appraise the facts, exercise judgment, and formulate an opinion. He was authorized to withhold certification if he believed the cause not to be religious. Such a censorship of religion as the means of determining its right to survive is a denial of liberty protected by the First Amendment as applied to the states by the Fourteenth Amendment.

Corollary cases

Cox v. New Hampshire, 312 U.S. 569 (1941)
Chaplinsky v. New Hampshire, 315 U.S. 568 (1942)
Murdock v. Pennsylvania, 319 U.S. 105 (1943)
Martin v. Struthers, 319 U.S. 141 (1943)
Follett v. Town of McCormick, 321 U.S. 573 (1943)
Marsh v. Alabama, 326 U.S. 501 (1946)
Tucker v. Texas, 326 U.S. 517 (1946)
Prince v. Massachusetts, 321 U.S. 158 (1944)
Kedroff v. St. Nicholas Cathedral of Russian Orthodox Church in North
    America, 344 U.S. 94 (1960)
Fowler v. State of Rhode Island, 345 U.S. 67 (1953)
Poulos v. State of New Hampshire, 345 U.S. 395 (1953)
Kunz v. New York, 340 U.S. 290 (1951)
Epperson v. Arkansas, 393 U.S. 97 (1968)
Widmar v. Vincent, 70 L. Ed. 2d 440 (1981)
Heffron v. International Society for Krishna Consciousness, 69 L. Ed. 2d 298
    (1981)

Note—*Cantwell* was the first case to apply the "Gitlow doctrine" to religious guarantees of the First Amendment.

Cox v. New Hampshire, 312 U.S. 569; 61 S. Ct. 762; 85 L. Ed. 1049 (1941)

Cox, a member of the "Jehovah's Witnesses," was convicted of violating a city ordinance of the city of Manchester, New Hampshire, that forbade any parade or procession upon a public street unless a license had been obtained from the selectmen of the town. Cox said that he and the defendants did not have a parade, but they also claimed that this ordinance was invalid under the Fourteenth Amendment of the Federal Constitution in that it deprived the appellants of their right of freedom of worship, freedom of speech and press, and freedom of assembly, vested unreasonable and unlimited arbitrary and discriminatory powers in the licensing authority, and was vague and indefinite. Each of the defendants claimed to be a minister ordained to preach the gospel in accordance with his belief.

OPINION BY MR. CHIEF JUSTICE HUGHES

(No evidence from the report that the decision was not unanimous.)

Question—Is this ordinance a valid exercise of the police power of the state and not in conflict with the Constitution?

Decision—Yes.

Reason—The facts concerned here are not with the depriving of Cox of freedom of worship but of the ordinance governing the use of public streets. They were not prosecuted for anything other than that. Civil liberties, as guaranteed by the Constitution, imply the existence of an organized society maintaining public order, without which liberty itself would be lost in the excess of unrestrained abuses. The use of the power of the local authorities is not inconsistent with civil liberties but a means of safeguarding them. The Court felt that the licensing was necessary to afford opportunity for proper policing.

"One would not be justified in ignoring the familiar red traffic light because he thought it his religious duty to disobey the municipal command or sought by that means to direct public attention to an announcement of his opinion. . . . We find it impossible to say that the limited authority conferred by the licensing provisions of the statute in question as thus construed by the state court contravened any constitutional right."

Corollary cases

Thornhill v. Alabama, 310 U.S. 88 (1940)
Hague v. C.I.O., 307 U.S. 496 (1939)
Cantwell v. Connecticut, 310 U.S. 296 (1940)
Chaplinsky v. New Hampshire, 315 U.S. 568 (1942)
Saia v. People of State of New York, 334 U.S. 558 (1948)
Kovacs v. Cooper, 336 U.S. 77 (1949)
Schaumburg v. Citizens for a Better Environment, 440 U.S. 620 (1980)
Federal Communications Commission v. Pacifica Foundation, 438 U.S. 726;
    57 L. Ed. 2d 1073 (1978)

Richmond Newspapers, Inc. v. Virginia, 448 U.S. 555; 65 L. Ed. 2d 973
(1980)
Metromedia, Inc. v. San Diego, 69 L. Ed. 2d 800 (1981)
Heffron v. International Soc. for Krishna Consciousness, Inc., 452 U.S.—;
69 L. Ed. 2d 298 (1981)

Note—This is a case of "speech plus," in which the Court makes a distinction between *speech*, which is protected by the First Amendment, and *conduct*, which is subject to state police power.

Bridges v. California (Times-Mirror Co. v. Superior Court of California) 314 U.S. 252; 62 S. Ct. 190; 86 L. Ed. 892 (1941)

While a motion for a new trial was pending in a case involving a dispute between an AFL and a CIO union of which Bridges was an officer, he either caused to be published or acquiesced in the publication of a telegram which he had sent to the secretary of labor. The telegram referred to the judge's decision as "outrageous," said that attempted enforcement of it would tie up the port of Los Angeles and involve the entire Pacific Coast, and concluded with the announcement that the CIO union did "not intend to allow state courts to override the majority vote of members in choosing its officers and representatives and to override the National Labor Relations Board."

Involved also were newspaper editorials that commented on pending action before the same court. "The editorial thus distinguished was entitled 'Probation for Gorillas?' After vigorously denouncing two members of a labor union who had previously been found guilty of assaulting nonunion truck drivers, it closed with the observation: "Judge A. A. Scott will make a serious mistake if he grants probation to Matthew Shannon and Kennan Holmes. This community needs the example of their assignment to the jute mill."

Both Bridges and the newspaper were cited for contempt and convicted.

OPINION BY MR. JUSTICE BLACK
(Vote: 5–4)

Question—Do the convictions violate rights of free speech and due process as guaranteed by the First Amendment made applicable to the States by the Fourteenth Amendment?

Decision—Yes.

Reason—The telegram that Bridges sent to the secretary of labor criticizing the decision of the court was merely a statement of the facts that the secretary of labor was entitled to receive regarding an action that might result in a strike. "Again, we find exaggeration in the conclusion that the utterance even 'tended' to interfere with justice. If there was electricity in the atmosphere, it was generated by the facts; the charge added by the Bridges telegram can be dismissed as negligible."

The influence of the editorials was likewise minimized by the Court: "This editorial, given the most intimidating construction it will bear, did no more than threaten future adverse criticism which was reasonably to be expected anyway in the event of a lenient disposition of the pending case. To regard it, therefore, as in itself of substantial influence upon the course of justice would be to impute to judges a lack of firmness, wisdom, or honor, which we cannot accept as a major premise."

Corollary cases

Cantwell v. Connecticut, 310 U.S. 296 (1940)
Gitlow v. New York, 268 U.S. 652 (1925)
Toledo Newspaper Co. v. United States, 247 U.S. 402 (1918)
Pennekamp v. Florida, 328 U.S. 331 (1946)
Schenck v. United States, 249 U.S. 47 (1919)
Abrahams v. United States, 250 U.S. 616 (1919)
Garrison v. Louisiana, 379 U.S. 64 (1964)
Craig v. Harney, 331 U.S. 367 (1947)
Wood v. Georgia, 370 U.S. 375 (1962)
Stroble v. California, 343 U.S. 181 (1951)
Irvin v. Dowd, 366 U.S. 717 (1961)
Beck v. Washington, 369 U.S. 541 (1962)
Rideau v. Louisiana, 373 U.S. 723 (1963)

Murdock v. Commonwealth of Pennsylvania, 319 U.S. 105; 63 S. Ct. 870; 87 L. Ed. 1292 (1943)

The city of Jeannette, Pennsylvania, had an ordinance for forty years requiring that all persons soliciting get a license from the treasurer of the borough before doing so. The petitioners were Jehovah's Witnesses, who were arrested for asking people to purchase certain religious books, as they distributed literature.

OPINION BY MR. JUSTICE DOUGLAS
(Vote: 5–4)

Question—Is this an abridgement of the freedom of religion?

Decision—Yes.

Reason—It would hardly be denied that a tax laid specifically on the freedom of the First Amendment would be unconstitutional. Yet the license tax in this case was just that in substance. The custom of hand-distribution of religious literature is an old one and has the same claim to protection as other conventional exercises of religion. In this case payment of the license tax is a condition for pursuing their religious activities.

"The fact that the ordinance is 'nondiscriminatory' is immaterial. The protection afforded by the First Amendment is not so restricted. A license tax certainly does not acquire constitutional validity because it classifies the privileges protected by the First Amendment along with the wares and merchandise of hucksters and peddlers and treats them all alike. Such equality in treatment does not save the ordinance. Freedom of press; freedom of speech, freedom of religion are in a preferred position. . . .

"Jehovah's Witnesses are not 'above the law.' But the present ordinance is not directed to the problems with which the police power of the state is free to deal. It does not cover, and petitioners are not charged with, breaches of the peace. They are pursuing their solicitations peacefully and quietly. . . ."

Corollary cases

Jones v. Opelika, 316 U.S. 584 (1943)
Jamison v. Texas, 318 U.S. 413 (1943)
Douglas v. City of Jeannette, 319 U.S. 157 (1942)
Tucker v. Texas, 326 U.S. 517 (1946)
Cox v. New Hampshire, 312 U.S. 564 (1941)
Chaplinsky v. New Hampshire, 315 U.S. 568 (1942)
Martin v. Struthers, 319 U.S. 141 (1943)

Follett v. Town of McCormick, 321 U.S. 573 (1943)
Marsh v. Alabama, 326 U.S. 501 (1946)
Prince v. Massachusetts, 321 U.S. 158 (1944)
Cantwell v. Connecticut, 310 U.S. 296 (1940)
Lovell v. Griffin, 303 U.S. 444 (1938)
Minersville School District v. Gobitis, 310 U.S. 586 (1940)
West Virginia State Board of Education v. Barnette, 319 U.S. 624 (1943)
Largent v. Texas, 318 U.S. 418 (1943)
Niemotko v. Maryland, 340 U.S. 268 (1951)
Breard v. Alexandria, 341 U.S. 622 (1951)
Heffron v. International Society for Krishna Consciousness, Inc., 69 L. Ed.
  2d 298 (1981)

Note—*Murdock* specifically reversed *Jones* v. *Opelika*, (1942). We find for the first time the concept that the guarantees of religion, speech, and press are in a "preferred position." Statutes that restrict civil rights are not to be accorded even a presumption of constitutionality.

Thomas v. Collins, 323 U.S. 516; 65 S. Ct. 315; 89 L. Ed. 430 (1945)

A Texas statute required that all persons soliciting members for a labor organization obtain an organizer's card from the secretary of state. Thomas, president of the International Union UAW (United Automobile, Aircraft, and Agricultural Implements Workers) and a vice-president of the CIO, was asked to address a mass meeting where the Oil Workers Industrial Union (OWIU) was campaigning to organize Local No. 1002. Thomas arrived in Houston on the evening of September 21 for the meeting, which was to be held on September 23. His address had been announced in advance and wide publicity was given to the meeting. On the afternoon of September 23 at about 2:30 he was served with a restraining order.

Thomas consulted his attorneys and went ahead with the meeting as planned, regarding the law and the citation as a restraint upon free speech and free assembly. The meeting was orderly and peaceful. Thomas closed his address with a general invitation to all who were not members of a union to join Local No. 1002, and solicited orally one Pat O'Sullivan. After the address, Thomas was arrested, and contempt proceedings filed for violation of the temporary restraining order.

Opinion by Mr. Justice Rutledge
(Vote: 5–4)

Question—Does the statute in question violate the First and Fourteenth Amendments by imposing a previous restraint upon freedom of speech and free assembly?

Decision—Yes.

Reason—Thomas based his case on the rule that requires that a clear and present danger must be evident to sustain a restriction upon freedom of speech or assembly. Texas contended that the statute was similar to statutes directed at business practices like selling insurance, dealing in securities, acting as a commission merchant, or pawnbroking, and that the appropriate standard was the commerce clause, which sustains state statutes regulating transportation. The Court was confronted with the delicate question of where the individual's freedom ends and the state's power begins, and, as in such cases, it is the character of the right, not of the limitation, that determines which standard to apply.

Restrictions upon these liberties must be justified by clear public interest; not by doubtful or remote threats, but by clear and present danger. Only the gravest abuses can give grounds for permissible limitations, especially when the right is exercised within a peaceable assembly. "If one who solicits support for the cause of labor may be required to register as a condition to the exercise of the rights to make a public speech, so may he who seeks to rally support for any social, business, religious or political cause. We think a requirement that one must register before he undertakes to make a public speech to enlist support for a lawful movement is quite incompatible with the requirements of the First Amendment.

"Once the speaker goes further, however, and engages in conduct which amounts to more than the right of free discussion comprehends, as when he undertakes the collection of funds or securing subscriptions, he enters a realm where a reasonable registration or identification requirement may be imposed. In that context such solicitation would be quite different from the solicitation involved here. . . ."

Corollary cases

Cantwell v. Connecticut, 310 U.S. 296 (1940)
United States v. Carolene Products Co., 304 U.S. 144 (1938)
De Jonge v. Oregon, 299 U.S. 353 (1937)
Schneider v. State, 308 U.S. 147 (1939)
Lovell v. Griffin, 303 U.S. 444 (1938)
Hague v. C.I.O., 307 U.S. 496 (1939)
Schenck v. United States, 249 U.S. 296 (1940)
Gitlow v. New York, 268 U.S. 652 (1925)
Herndon v. Lowry, 301 U.S. 242 (1937)
Terminiello v. City of Chicago, 337 U.S. 1 (1940)
Thornill v. Alabama, 310 U.S. 88 (1940)
Carlson v. California, 310 U.S. 106 (1940)
United States Postal Service v. Council of Greenburgh Civil Association,
    69 L. Ed. 2d 517 (1981)
Heffron v. International Society for Krishna Consciousnes, 69 L. Ed. 2d 298
    (1981)
Carey v. Brown, 65 L. Ed. 2d 263 (1980)
Detroit Edison Co. v. NLRB, 440 U.S. 301 (1979)
Pruneyard Shopping Center v. Robbins, 447 U.S. 74 (1980)

Note—Justice Rutledge said: "We think the controlling principle is stated in *De Jonge* v. *Oregon.* . . ." *De Jonge,* a seminal
case, applied the "Gitlow doctrine" to freedom of assembly.

Marsh v. State of Alabama, 326 U.S. 501; 66 S. Ct. 276; 90 L. Ed. 265 (1946)

> Grace Marsh, a member of Jehovah's Witnesses, was
> distributing religious literature on the street of a privately
> owned town that adjoined the municipality of Mobile, Ala-
> bama, known as Chickasaw, and owned by the Gulf Ship-
> building Corporation. She was warned that she could not
> distribute literature without a permit and she would not be
> issued a permit. She refused to obey and was arrested for
> violation of the Alabama Code, which makes it a crime to
> enter upon or remain on the premises of another after being
> warned not to do so.

OPINION BY MR. JUSTICE BLACK
(Vote: 5–3)

Question—Is the Alabama statute constitutional?

Decision—No.

Reason—The Court took the view that a state statute seeking to punish the distribution of religious literature clearly violates the First and Fourteenth Amendments to the Constitution. The Court reasoned that one may remain on private property against the will of the owner and contrary to the law of the state so long as the only objection to his presence is that he is exercising an asserted right to spread his religious views.

"When we balance the Constitutional rights of owners of property against those of the people to enjoy freedom of press and religion, as we must here, we remain mindful of the fact that the latter occupy a preferred position. As we have stated before, the right to exercise the liberties safeguarded by the First Amendment 'lies at the foundation of free government by free men' and we must in all cases 'weigh the circumstances and . . . appraise . . . reasons in support of the regulation . . . of the rights,' *Schneider* v. *State,* 308 U.S. 147. In our view the circumstances that the property rights to the premises where the deprivation of liberty, here involved, took place, were held by others than the public, is not sufficient to justify the state's permitting a corporation to govern a community of citizens so as to restrict their fundamental liberties and the enforcement of such restraint by the application of a state statute. In so far as the state has attempted to impose criminal punishment on appellant for undertaking to distribute religious literature in a company town, its action cannot stand."

Corollary cases

Martin v. Struthers, 319 U.S. 141 (1943)
Tucker v. Texas, 326 U.S. 517 (1946)
Prince v. Massachusetts, 321 U.S. 158 (1944)
Lloyd Corporation, Ltd. v. Tanner, 407 U.S. 551 (1972)
McDaniel v. Patty, 55 L. Ed. 2d 593 (1978)
Cantwell v. Connecticut, 310 U.S. 296 (1940)
Amalgamated Food Employees Union Local 59 v. Logan Valley Plaza, Inc., 391 U.S. 308 (1968)
Heffron v. International Society for Krishna Consciousness, 69 L. Ed. 2d 298 (1981)
Beth Israel Hospital v. N.L.R.B., 437 U.S. 483 (1978)

Note—In *Marsh* a company town was performing a public function that was governmental. Free speech, thus, was protected by the First Amendment. In *Amalgamated Food Employees Union* v. *Logan Valley Plaza*, (1968), the Court held that picketing of a private shopping center was like picketing at a downtown "business block." Four years later in *Lloyd Corporation* v. *Tanner*, (1972), the Court retreated, holding that a private mall may prohibit handbill distribution when they are unrelated to the shopping center. Four years later again in *Hudgens* v. *N.L.R.B.*, 424 U.S. 507 (1976), the Court overruled *Logan Valley*. Finally, in *Pruneyard Shopping Center* v. *Robins*, 447 U.S. 74 (1980), the Court returned to the *Marsh* principle by upholding a California Supreme Court decision on expansive state free speech grounds. Contrast *Board of Airport Commissioners* v. *Jews For Jesus*, 96 L. Ed. 2d 500 (1987).

Kovacs v. Cooper, 336 U.S. 77; 69 S. Ct. 448; 93 L. Ed. 513 (1949)

> An ordinance of Trenton, New Jersey makes it unlawful to play, use, or operate for advertising or any other purpose on public streets, alleys, or thoroughfares, sound trucks, loud speakers, sound amplifiers, calliopes, or any instrument that emits "loud and raucous noises."

OPINION BY MR. JUSTICE REED
(Vote: 5–4)

Question—Does this ordinance violate the right of freedom of speech and assembly, and the freedom to communicate information and opinions to others?

Decision—No.

Reason—Freedom of speech is not beyond control. The Court held that the legislation against "loud and raucous noises" is a permissible exercise of municipal authority. The citizen in his home or on the street is not in the position of the passerby who can refuse a pamphlet. He is helpless to escape this interference with his privacy except through the protection of the municipality.

"The preferred position of freedom of speech in a society

that cherishes liberty for all does not require legislators to be insensible to claims by citizens to comfort and convenience. To enforce freedom of speech in disregard of the rights of others would be harsh and arbitrary in itself." This is not a restriction upon communication of ideas, but a reasonable protection from distraction.

Corollary cases

Winters v. New York, 333 U.S. 507 (1948)
Saia v. New York, 334 U.S. 558 (1948)
Martin v. Struthers, 319 U.S. 141 (1943)
Grayned v. City of Rockford, 408 U.S. 104 (1972)
Palko v. Connecticut, 302 U.S. 319 (1937)
Public Utilities Commission of the District of Columbia v. Pollak, 343 U.S. 451 (1952)
Greer v. Spock, 424 U.S. 828 (1976)
Kunz. v. New York, 340 U.S. 290 (1951)
Brandenburg v. Ohio, 395 U.S. 444 (1969)
Coates v. Cincinnati, 402 U.S. 611 (1971)
Carey v. Brown, 65 L. Ed. 2d 263 (1980)

Note—Although concurring in *Kovacs,* Justice Frankfurter included a catalog of *instances* where the Court used the "preferred freedoms" approach prior to 1945. Apparently a city may regulate the place, time, and volume of sound trucks but may not ban them. The Court has a sharp eye for distinguishing laws that suffer from the "voice of vagueness," as in *Kunz* v. *New York,* 340 U.S. 290 (1951), and those that are more narrowly drawn, as in *Kovacs.* For a comment on relevant authorities on the vice of vagueness, see Note #12, *City of Mesquite* v. *Aladdin's Castle,* 71 L. Ed. 2d 152 (1982).

American Communications Association v. Douds, 339 U.S. 382; 70 S. Ct. 674; 94 L. Ed. 925 (1950)

Section 9 (h) of the Taft-Hartley Act, the Labor-Management Relations Act of 1947, provides that no investigation shall be made by the National Labor Relations Board of any question unless all officers of a labor organization concerned in the dispute sign an affidavit that they are not Communists and that they are not advocates of overthrowing the United States government by force or by illegal means.

Opinion by Mr. Chief Justice Vinson
(Vote: 5–1)

Question—Is Section 9 (h) of the Taft-Hartley Act contrary to the First Amendment of the Constitution?

Decision—No.

Reason—The freedoms of speech, press, or assembly, established in the First Amendment, are dependent on the power of constitutional government to survive. If it is to survive it must have power to protect itself against unlawful conduct. Thus freedom of speech does not comprehend the right to speak on any subject at any time. Also, this is not merely a matter of speech. The government's interest "is in protecting the free flow of commerce from what Congress considers to be substantial evils of conduct that are not the products of speech at all. Section 9 (h) . . . regulates harmful conduct which Congress has determined is carried on by persons who may be identified by their political affiliations and beliefs. . . . Section 9 (h) is designed to protect the public not against what Communists and others identified therein advocate or believe but against what Congress has concluded they have done and are likely to do again." There was no violation of the ex post facto prohibition because here the law was intended to prevent future action rather than to punish past action.

Corollary cases

Dennis v. United States, 339 U.S. 162 (1950)
Whitney v. California, 274 U.S. 357 (1927)
Hague v. CIO, 307 U.S. 496 (1939)
Bridges v. California, 314 U.S. 252 (1941)
Thomas v. Collins, 323 U.S. 516 (1945)
Terminiello v. Chicago, 337 U.S. 1 (1949)
United States v. Brown, 381 U.S. 427 (1965)
Killian v. United States, 368 U.S. 231 (1961)

Note—The "balancing test" of *Barenblatt* v. *United,* 360 U.S. 109 (1959), is that when the interests and rights of both individuals and the government are at stake, the more necessary gets the weight.

Dennis v. United States, 341 U.S. 494; 71 S. Ct. 857; 95 L. Ed. 1137 (1951)

Eleven leaders of the Communist party were convicted of violating the 1940 Smith Act. The defendants were convicted of conspiring to organize the Communist party for the purpose of having it teach and advocate the overthrow and destruction of the United States government by force and violence. They claimed Articles Two and Three of the act to be unconstitutional as violating the First Amendment and other provisions of the Bill of Rights and also as violative of the First and Fifth Amendments because of indefiniteness.

OPINION BY MR. CHIEF JUSTICE VINSON
(Vote: 6–2)

Questions—1. Did the act violate the right of free speech?

2. Did it, because of indefiniteness, also violate the First and Fifth Amendments?

Decisions—1. No.
2. No.

Reasons—The Congress has the power to protect the United States government from armed rebellion, and the defendants were advocating the violent overthrow of the government. This law was not directed at discussion but against the advocacy of violence. These persons intended to overthrow the United States government as soon as conditions would permit. This represented a clear and present danger to the government. It was the existence of the highly organized conspiracy that created the danger. "Whatever theoretical merit there may be to the argument that there is a 'right' to rebellion against dictatorial government is without force where the existing structure of the government provides for peaceful and orderly change. We reject any principle of governmental helplessness in the face of preparation for revolution, which principle, carried to its logical conclusion, must lead to anarchy."

Corollary cases

Frohwerk v. United States, 249 U.S. 204 (1919)
Debs v. United States, 249 U.S. 211 (1919)

Gitlow v. New York, 268 U.S. 652 (1925)
Schaefer v. United States, 251 U.S. 466 (1920)
American Communications Association v. Douds, 339 U.S. 382 (1950)
Whitney v. California, 274 U.S. 357 (1927)
Wieman v. Updegraff, 344 U.S. 183 (1952)
Brandenburg v. Ohio, 395 U.S. 444 (1969)
Yates v. United States, 354 U.S. 298 (1957)
Communist Party of the United States v. Subversive Activities Control
    Board, 367 U.S. 1 (1961)
Scales v. United States, 367 U.S. 203 (1961)
Aptheker v. Secretary of State, 378 U.S. 500 (1964)
Zemel v. Rusk, 381 U.S. 1 (1965)
United States v. Robel, 389 U.S. 258 (1967)
Schneider v. Smith, 390 U.S. 17 (1968)
Herbert v. Lando, 441 U.S. 153; 60 L. Ed. 2d 115 (1979)
Haig v. Agee, 69 L. Ed. 2d 640 (1981)
Snepp v. United States, 444 U.S. 507 (1980)

Note—The time element of the *Holmes-Brandeis* "clear and present danger" rule was omitted and a "clear and probable danger" rule substituted. The teeth was taken out of *Dennis* in *Yates* v. *U.S.,* 354 U.S. 298 (1957), the decision turning not on "conduct" but on "advocacy."

Feiner v. New York, 340 U.S. 315; 71 S. Ct. 303; 95 L. Ed. 295 (1951)

Irving Feiner, a student at Syracuse University, addressed a street meeting of about seventy-five people, urging them to attend a meeting that night on the subject of civil rights. He made derogatory remarks about President Truman, the American Legion, the mayor of Syracuse, and other local political officials. The police arrived and noted the restlessness of the crowd. Feiner was asked several times to stop talking and was then arrested. He was convicted of creating a breach of the peace. Three lower courts in New York upheld his conviction.

OPINION BY MR. CHIEF JUSTICE VINSON
(Vote: 6–3)

Question—If the police stop a lawful assembly when it passes the limits of persuasion and undertakes incitement to riot, is this contrary to the right of free speech as guaranteed by the First and Fourteenth Amendments?

Decision—No.

Reason—The officers making the arrest were concerned only with the preservation of law and order and not with the suppression of Feiner's views and opinions. The deliberate defiance of Feiner and the imminent danger of reaction in the crowd constituted sufficient reason for state police action. The guarantee of free speech does not include the license of incitement to riot. Moreover, the state courts' approval of the action of the local police was entitled to the utmost consideration.

Corollary cases

Sellers v. Johnson, 322 U.S. 851 (1948)
Terminiello v. Chicago, 337 U.S. 1 (1940)
Cantwell v. Connecticut, 310 U.S. 296 (1940)
Chaplinski v. New Hampshire, 315 U.S. 568 (1942)
United States v. O'Brien, 391 U.S. 367 (1968)
Street v. New York, 394 U.S. 576 (1969)

Note—*Feiner* represents a departure from the previous views of the Court that free speech was almost an absolute right.

Keyishian v. Board of Regents, 385 U.S. 589; 87 S. Ct. 675; 17 L. Ed. 2d 629 (1967)

> Faculty members of the State University of New York at Buffalo refused to sign, as regulations then in effect required, a certificate that they were not, and had never been, Communists. Each was notified that his failure to sign the certificate would require his dismissal. Action was brought by the faculty members for declaratory and injunctive relief. Those bringing the suits were in the English and philosophy departments of the state university.

(OPINION BY MR. JUSTICE BRENNAN
(Vote: 5–4)

Question—Does this state program violate the First Amendment made applicable to the states by the due process provision of the Fourteenth Amendment?

Decision—Yes.

Reason—There can be no doubt of the legitimacy of New York's interest in protecting its education system from subversion. Nevertheless, First Amendment freedoms need breathing space to survive, and therefore government may regulate in the area only with narrow specificity. New York's complicated and intricate scheme plainly violates that standard. Vagueness of wording is aggravated by prolixity; by a profusion of statutes, regulations, and administrative machinery; and by manifold cross-references to interrelated enactments and rules. The Court noted that there was "extraordinary ambiguity" in terms used in the regulations and that the whole was unconstitutionally vague. Such regulations have a chilling effect on the exercise of First Amendment rights.

The Court overruled its holding in *Adler* v. *Board of Education,* 342 U.S. 485 (1952), noting that "constitutional doctrine which has emerged since that decision has rejected its major premise. That premise was that public employment, including academic employment, may be conditioned upon the surrender of constitutional rights which could not be abridged by direct government action."

The Court concluded that mere membership without a specific intent to further the unlawful aims of an organization is not a constitutionally adequate basis for exclusion from such positions as were here involved. Thus, these regulations infringed on the freedom of association.

Corollary cases

Elfbrandt v. Russell, 384 U.S. 11 (1966)
Cramp v. Board of Public Instruction, 368 U.S. 278 (1961)
Baggett v. Bullitt, 377 U.S. 360 (1964)
Aptheker v. Secretary of State, 378 U.S. 500 (1964)
United States v. Robel, 389 U.S. 258 (1967)
Wieman v. Updegraff, 344 U.S. 183 (1952)
Gerende v. Board of Supervisors, 341 U.S. 56 (1951)
Garner v. Board of Public Works, 341 U.S. 716 (1951)
Lerner v. Casey, 357 U.S. 468 (1958)
Beilan v. Board of Education, 357 U.S. 399 (1958)
De Jonge v. Oregon, 299 U.S. 353 (1937)
Dennis v. United States, 341 U.S. 494 (1951)
Bond v. Floyd, 385 U.S. 116 (1966)
Elrod v. Burns, 427 U.S. 347 (1975)

Federal Communications Commission v. Pacifica Foundation, 438 U.S. 726; 57 L. Ed. 2d 1073; 98 S. Ct. 3026 (1978)

A satiric humorist, George Carlin, recorded a twelve-minute monologue entitled "Filthy words" before a live audience in a California theatre. He noted that these were the sort of words one could not repeat on the airwaves. He repeated these words in a variety of colloquialisms. In October 1973, a New York radio station broadcast the monologue at 2 p.m., which was heard by a father and son while in a car. The father complained to the FCC and following some correspondence between the FCC and the Pacifica Foundation, the monologue was judged "patently offensive" though not necessarily "obscene," and because the broadcast was a time when children are an audience, banned the monologue. A three-judge panel of the court of appeals reversed.

OPINION BY MR. JUSTICE STEVENS
(Vote: 5–4)

Question—Has the Federal Communications Commission any power to regulate a radio broadcast that is indecent but not obscene?

Decision—Yes.

Reason—Although the commission held the monologue "patently offensive" and not "obscene," it was not its intention to "censor" material but to "channel" it beyond the exposure of children who constitute a daytime audience. Broadcasting requires special treatment because: children have access to radios and are often unsupervised by parents, radios are in homes and people's privacy is "entitled to extra deference," unconsenting adults can tune in without any warning that offensive language is being broadcast, and because there is a scarcity of spectrum space the government can license in the public interest. Although the FCC cannot edit broadcasts, it cannot be denied its statutory power "to review the content of completed broadcasts in the performance of its regulatory duties." The commission's ruling covers "patently offensive references to excretory and sexual organs and activities" and will not restrict serious communication by the use of less offensive language. "We simply hold that when the commission finds that a pig has entered the parlor, the exercise of its regulatory power does not depend on the proof that the pig is obscene."

Corollary cases

Columbia Broadcasting System, Inc. v. Democratic National Committee, 412 U.S. 94 (1973)

Red Lion Broadcasting Co., Inc. v. FCC, 395 U.S. 367 (1969)

Young v. American Mini Theatres, 427 U.S. 50 (1976)

Bates v. State Bar, 43 U.S. 350 (1977)

Chaplinsky v. New Hampshire, 315 U.S. 568 (1942)

Miller v. California, 413 U.S. 15 (1973)

Roth v. United States, 354 U.S. 476 (1957)

Cohen v. California, 403 U.S. 15 (1971)

Joseph Burstyn, Inc. v. Wilson, 343 U.S. 495 (1952)

Ginzburg v. New York, 390 U.S. 629 (1966)

Nixon v. Warner Communications, Inc., 435 U.S. 589 (1978)

Bethel Sch. Dist. v. Fraser, 92 L Ed 2d 549 (1986)

Chandler v. Florida, 449 U.S. 560 (1981)

CBS v. Federal Communications Commission, 69 L. Ed. 2d 706 (1981)

Herbert v. Lando, 441 U.S. 153; 60 L. Ed. 2d 115 (1979)

Post Co. v. National Citizens Committee for Broadcasting, 56 L. Ed. 2d 697 (1978)

Note—In an earlier case involving zoning, *Village of Euclid, Ohio* v. *Ambler Reality Co.,* 272 U.S. 365 (1926), the Court said, "a nuisance may merely be a right thing in the wrong place, like a pig in the parlor instead of the barnyard." It was daytime scheduling that the Court found offensive.

Herbert v. Lando, 441 U.S. 153; 60 L. Ed. 2d 115; 99 S. Ct. 1635 (1979)

Anthony Herbert, a retired army officer, received substantial publicity when in 1969–1970 he accused his superiors of covering up war atrocities. Three years later, a producer of a CBS program, Barry Lando, broadcasted a report on Herbert and his accusations and also published a related article in *Atlantic Monthly*. Herbert sued for defamation in a federal district court, claiming the television program and the magazine article falsely and maliciously portrayed him as a liar. He conceded he was a "public figure" and the First and Fourteenth Amendments preclude recovery absent proof that Lando had published damaging falsehoods with "actual malice," that is, with knowledge that the statements were false or with reckless disregard of whether they were false or not. Lando refused to answer questions on First Amendment grounds involving the editorial process and the state of mind of those who edit, produce, or publish. The district court upheld Herbert, but it was reversed in the court of appeals.

OPINION BY MR. JUSTICE WHITE
(Vote: 6–3)

Question—Claiming First Amendment protection, can a reporter, accused of damaging falsehoods and injury to someone's reputation, be required to reveal his "state of mind" when preparing his material?

Decision—Yes.

Reason—The Court is "being asked to modify firmly established constitutional doctrine by placing beyond reach a range of direct evidence relevant to proving knowing or reckless falsehood by the publisher of the alleged libel. . . ." The Court rejects this view and ". . . according an absolute privilege to the editorial process of a media defendant on a libel case is not required, authorized or presaged by our prior cases, and would substantially enhance the burden of proving actual malice. . . . Courts have traditionally admitted any direct or indirect evidence relevant to the state of mind . . . without encountering constitutional objections. . . . Spreading false information in and of itself carries no First Amendment credentials."

Corollary cases

New York Times v. Sullivan, 376 U.S. 254 (1964)
Curtis Publishing Co. v. Butts, 388 U.S. 130 (1967)
Gertz v. Robert Welch, Inc., 418 U.S. 323 (1974)
Beauharnais v. Illinois, 343 U.S. 250 (1952)
Roth v. United States, 354 U.S. 476 (1957)
Chaplinsky v. New Hampshire, 315 U.S. 568 (1942)
Near v. Minnesota, 283 U.S. 697 (1931)
Time v. Hill, 385 U.S. 374 (1967)
Miami Herald Publishing Co. v. Tornillo, 418 U.S. 241 (1974)
CBS v. Democratic National Committee, 412 U.S. 94 (1973)

Time, Inc. v. Firestone, 424 U.S. 448 (1976)
United States v. Nixon, 418 U.S. 683 (1974)
Herbert v. Lando, 441 U.S. 153 (1979)
Houchins v. KQED, 438 U.S. 1 (1978)
Whalen v. Roe, 429 U.S. 589 (1977)
United States v. Caldwell, 408 U.S. 665 (1972)

Branti v. Finkel, 445 U.S. 507; 63 L. Ed. 2d 574; 100 S. Ct. 1287 (1980)

Finkel and Tabakman, two Republican assistant public defenders, were about to be discharged by Branti, the newly appointed county public defender, who was a Democrat. Upon his formal appointment, Branti began issuing termination notices for six of the nine assistants then in office. With one possible exception, the nine who were to be appointed or retained were all Democrats and were selected by Democratic legislators and town chairmen. Finkel and Tabakman brought suit to enjoin Branti, contending they had been selected for discharge solely because of their Republican party status.

OPINION BY MR. JUSTICE STEVENS
(Vote: 6–3)

Question—Do the First and Fourteenth Amendments to the Constitution protect an assistant public defender who is satisfactorily performing his job from discharge solely because of his political beliefs?

Decision—Yes.

Reason—"If the First Amendment protects a public employee from discharge based on what he has said, it must also protect him from discharge on what he believes." Unless the government can demonstrate an overriding interest of vital importance, "requiring that a person's private beliefs conform to those of the hiring authority, his beliefs cannot be the sole basis depriving him of continued public employment." Party affiliation may be an acceptable requirement for some types of government employment. "[I]f an employee's private political beliefs would interfere with the discharge of his public duties, his First Amendment Rights may be required to yield to the

State's vital interest in maintaining governmental effectiveness and efficiency. . . . [T]he ultimate inquiry is not whether the label 'policymaker' or 'confidential' fits a particular position; rather, the question is whether the hiring authority can demonstrate that party affiliation is an appropriate requirement for the effective performance of the public office involved. . . . The primary . . . responsibility of an assistant public defender is to represent individual citizens in the controversy with the state. . . . [W]hatever policymaking occurs in the public defender's office must relate to the needs of individual clients and not to any partisan political interests. It would undermine, rather than promote, the effective performance of an assistant public defender's office to make his tenure dependent on his allegiance to the dominant political party."

Corollary cases

Elrod v. Burns, 427 U.S. 347 (1976)
Perry v. Sindermann, 408 U.S. 593 (1972)

Village of Schaumburg v. Citizens for a Better Environment, 444 U.S. 620; 63 L. Ed. 2d 73; 100 S. Ct. 826 (1980)

A Schaumburg, Illinois, ordinance provided that every charitable organization that desired to solicit contributions by utilizing public streets and public ways or by door-to-door solicitations had to apply for a permit. The permit application had to contain satisfactory proof that at least 75 percent of the proceeds of such solicitations would be used directly for the charitable purpose of the organization, excluding salaries and administrative expenses. Citizens For A Better Environment (CBE) is a nonprofit corporation organized for the purpose of promoting environmental protection. CBE requested permission to solicit contributions in Schaumburg but was denied a permit as the organization could not prove that 75 percent of its receipts would be used for "charitable purposes" as required of Schaumburg's code.

OPINION BY MR. JUSTICE WHITE
(Vote: 8–1)

Question—Is the 75 percent requirement of Schaumburg's code a violation of Freedom of Expression as guaranteed by the First and Fourteenth Amendments?

Decision—Yes.

Reason—"The 75 percent limitation is a direct and substantial limitation on protected activity that cannot be sustained unless it serves a sufficiently strong, subordinating interest that the village is entitled to protect. . . . The village may serve its legitimate interests but it must do so by narrowly drawn regulations designed to serve those interests without unnecessarily interfering with First Amendment freedoms. . . . We also fail to perceive any substantial relationship between the 75 percent requirement and the protection of public safety or of residential privacy. The 75 percent requirement is related to the protection of privacy only in the most indirect of ways. . . . The ordinance is not directed to the unique privacy interests of persons residing in their homes because it applies not only to door-to-door solicitation, but also to solicitation on 'public streets and public ways.'. . . The 75 percent requirement in the village ordinance plainly is insufficiently related to the governmental interest in its support to justify its interference with protected speech.''

Corollary cases

Schneider v. States, 308 U.S. 147 (1939)
Lovell v. Griffin, 303 U.S. 444 (1938)
Cantwell v. Connecticut, 310 U.S. 296 (1940)
Virginia Pharmacy Board v. Virginia Consumer Council, 425 U.S. 748 (1976)
Valentine v. Chrestensen, 316 U.S. 52 (1942)
Jamison v. Texas, 318 U.S. 413 (1943)
Murdock v. Pennsylvania, 319 U.S. 105 (1943)
Thomas v. Collins, 323 U.S. 516 (1945)
Breard v. Alexandria, 341 U.S. 622 (1951)
Hynes v. Mayor of Oradell, 425 U.S. 610 (1976)
Bates v. State Bar of Arizona, 433 U.S. 350 (1977)

Note—In *Secretary of Maryland* v. *Joseph H. Munson* (81 L. Ed. 2d 786, 1984) the Court invalidated as unconstitutionally overbroad a statute that prohibited a fund raising charitable organization from paying or agreeing to pay more than 25% of the amount raised. The Court struck down a North Carolina law that set a limit on solicitations of charitable contributions by professional fund raisers (*Riley* v. *National Association of*

Blind, 101 L. Ed. 2d 699, 1988). The Court held that the acts' provisions violated First Amendment free speech by regulating content, and the state's interest was marginal. In a far-reaching decision that involved an attempt by Lakewood, Ohio to give the mayor unfettered discretion to deny or permit placing newspapers in dispensing devices on public property, the Court strongly vetoed the ordinance in *Lakewood* v. *Plain Dealer* (100 L. Ed. 2d 771, 1988). This decision is especially important, for it reaffirms the right to challenge some laws that facially limit free speech rather than having to wait until the law is enforced.

FREEDOM OF PRESS

Abrams v. United States, 250 U.S. 616; 40 S. Ct. 17; 63 L. Ed. 1173 (1919)

In this case, Abrams and four other Russians were indicted for conspiring to violate the Espionage Act. They published two leaflets that denounced the efforts of capitalist nations to interfere with the Russian Revolution, criticized the president and the "plutocratic gang in Washington" for sending American troops to Russia, and urged workers producing munitions in the United States not to betray their Russian comrades.

OPINION BY MR. JUSTICE CLARKE
(Vote: 7–2)

Question—Does the Espionage Act violate the First Amendment?

Decision—No.

Reason—The Court reasoned that the plain purpose of their propaganda was to excite, at the supreme crisis of the war, disaffection, sedition, riots, and, as they hoped, revolution, in this country, for the purpose of embarrassing, and if possible defeating, the military plans of the government in Europe.

Corollary cases

Schenck v. United States, 249 U.S. 47 (1919)
Frohwerk v. United States, 249 U.S. 204 (1919)
Debs v. United States, 249 U.S. 211 (1919)
Stromberg v. California, 283 U.S. 359 (1931)
Herndon v. Lowry, 301 U.S. 242 (1937)
Schaefer v. United States, 251 U.S. 466 (1920)
Gorin v. United States, 312 U.S. 19 (1941)
Rosenberg v. United States, 346 U.S. 273 (1953)

Note—The majority opinion gave rise to a stinging dissent by Justice O. W. Holmes in behalf of the First Amendment. The "modern" espionage case involved the conviction and capital punishment of Julius and Ethel Rosenberg, *Rosenberg* v. *United States*, (1953).

**City of Lakewood v. Plain Dealer Pub. Co., 486 U.S. ____;
100 L. Ed. 2d 771; 108 S. Ct. 2138 (1988)**

OPINION BY JUSTICE BRENNAN
(Vote: 4–3)

Lakewood, Ohio, passed an ordinance giving the mayor unfettered discretion to control by licensing the placing of newspaper dispensing devices on public property. The mayor was empowered (1) to grant or deny applications for newspaper installation; (2) to state his reasons if he denied a license; (3) to permit him to enlarge the terms he thought "necessary and reasonable." The city's architectural board would police the design of the vendors and indemnify the city from any liability stemming from the vending bins. The district court upheld the ordinance but the United States Court of Appeals reversed the decision.

Question—Does Lakewood's ordinance over the placing (under a license) issued by sole authority of the mayor of newspaper vending machines on public property violate on its face the First Amendment?

Decision—Yes.

Reason—"Our cases have long held that when a licensing statute allegedly vests unbridled discretion in a government official over whether to permit or deny expressive activity, one who is subject to the law may challenge it facially without the necessity of first applying for, and being denied, a license." In the area of free expression "a licensing statute placing unbridled discretion in the hands of a government official or agency constitutes a prior restraint and may result in censorship. This condition "intimidates parties into censoring their own speech, even if the discretion and power are never actually abused." The absence of standards makes it difficult to distinguish between legitimate and illegitimate abuse of censorial power. A newspaper operating on a shoe-string budget and espousing an unpopular view might find it easy to capitulate. The entire regulatory scheme permits a facial challenge. Without standards "a government official may decide who may speak and who may not based upon the content of the speech or viewpoint of the speaker. It is not sufficient that the city claims are implicit in its law; they must be made explicit by textual incorporation, bending judicial or administrative construction, or well-established practices. The Lakewood ordinance is unconstitutional. Moreover, "we need not resolve the remaining questions presented for review as our conclusion regarding mayoral discretion will alone sustain the Court of appeals."

Corollary cases

Freedom v. Maryland, 380 U.S. 51, 56 L. Ed. 2d 649, 85 S. Ct. 734 (1965)
Thornhill v. Alabama, 310 U.S. 88, 84 L. Ed. 1093, 60 S. Ct. 736 (1940)
Shuttlesworth v. Birmingham, 394 U.S. 147, 22 L. Ed. 2d 162, 89 S. Ct. 935 (1969)
Jones v. Opelika, 316 U.S. 584, 86 L. Ed. 1691, 62 S. Ct. 1231 (1942)
Lovell v. Griffin, 303 U.S. 444, 82 L. Ed. 949, 58 S. Ct. 666 (1938)
Cox v. Louisiana, 379 U.S. 536, 13 L. Ed. 2d 471, 85 S. Ct. 453 (1965)
Staub v. City of Baxley, 355 U.S. 313, 2 L. Ed. 2d 302, 78 S. Ct. 277 (1958)
Kunz v. New York, 340 U.S. 290, 95 L. Ed. 280, 71 S. Ct. 312 (1951)
Niemotko v. Maryland, 340 U.S. 268, 95 L. Ed. 267, 71 S. Ct. 325 (1951)
Sala v. New York, 334 U.S. 558, 92 L. Ed. 1574, 68 S. Ct. 1148 (1948)
Cantwell v. Connecticut, 310 U.S. 296, 84 L. Ed. 1213, 60 S. Ct. 900 (1940)
Talley v. California, 362 U.S. 60, 4 L. Ed. 2d 559, 80 S. Ct. 536 (1960)
Martin v. Struthers, 319 U.S. 141, 87 L. Ed. 1313, S. Ct. 862 (1943)

Note—As in *Wallace v. Jaffree* (1985), the Court refuses to discuss an issue now moot. The Court will not decide a constitutional case unless absolutely required to do so, nor anticipate a question not directly before the Court. Thus in *Edwards v. Aguillard* (96 L. Ed. 2d 510, 1987) the Court said that if the first test of *Lemon v. Kurtzman,* (403 U.S. 602, 1971) involving the First Amendment were breached no consideration of the second or third *Lemon* criteria is necessary.

Near v. State of Minnesota ex rel. Olson, 283 U.S. 697; 51 S. Ct. 625; 75 L. Ed. 1357 (1931)

A Minnesota statute provided for the abatement, as a public nuisance, of a "malicious, scandalous and defamatory newspaper, magazine, or other periodical." The county attorney of Hennepin County brought action against a publication known as *The Saturday Press* published by the defendants in the city of Minneapolis. The periodical in various issues charged certain public officers with gross neglect of duty or grave misconduct in office.

OPINION BY MR. CHIEF JUSTICE HUGHES
(Vote: 5–4)

Question—Is this an infringement of the liberty of the press as guaranteed by the Fourteenth Amendment?

Decision—Yes.

Reason—It is no longer questioned that liberty of the press is one of the personal freedoms protected by the Fourteenth Amendment. However, the police powers of the state must be admitted and the limits determined.

The liberty of the press in the meaning of the Constitution is principally immunity from previous restraint. The statute cannot be justified by giving a publisher an opportunity to present his evidence. It would be only a step to a complete system of censorship. "The fact that the liberty of the press may be abused by miscreant purveyors of scandal does not make any the less necessary the immunity of the press from previous restraint in dealing with official misconduct. Subsequent punishment for such abuses as may exist is the appropriate remedy, consistent with constitutional privilege."

Scandal that tends to disturb the peace is a serious public evil, but the threat to liberty is an even more serious public evil. The Court held that the statute, by its operation and effect was unconstitutional, without any questioning of the truth of the charges contained in the particular periodical.

Corollary cases

Gompers v. Buck Stove & Range Co., 221 U.S. 418 (1911)
Schenck v. United States, 249 U.S. 47 (1919)
Patterson v. Colorado, 205 U.S. 454 (1907)
Grosjean v. American Press Co., 297 U.S. 233 (1936)
Craig v. Harney, 331 U.S. 367 (1947)
Associated Press v. United States, 326 U.S. 1 (1947)
Branzburg v. Hayes, 408 U.S. 665 (1972)
Roth v. United States, 354 U.S. 476 (1957)
Ginzburg v. United States, 383 U.S. 463 (1966)

New York Times Co. v. Sullivan, 376 U.S. 254 (1964)
Curtis Publishing Co. v. Butts, 388 U.S. 130 (1967)
Herbert v. Lando, 441 U.S. 153 (1979)
First Nation Band of Boston v. Bellott, 435 U.S. 765 (1978)
Landmark Communications, Inc. v. Virginia, 435 U.S. 829 (1978)
Miami Herald Publishing Co. v. Tornillo, 418 U.S. 241 (1974)
Nebraska Press Association v. Stuart, 427 U.S. 539 (1976)

Note—In *Near,* the Court applied the "Gitlow doctrine" to freedom of the press and held a statute void on that basis for the first time. Although prior censorship of the press is condemned, the chief justice does indicate when it would be admissible.

Grosjean v. American Press Co., 297 U.S. 233; 56 S. Ct. 444; 80 L. Ed. 660 (1936)

This suit was brought by a group of newspapers in the state of Louisiana to prevent enforcement of a statute levying a 2 percent gross receipts tax on them. The statute levied a tax only on newspapers having a circulation of 20,000 copies per week, making it applicable to only thirteen newspapers. Only one of these was not openly opposed to Senator Huey P. Long, under whose influence the law had been passed.

OPINION BY MR. JUSTICE SUTHERLAND
(No evidence from the report that the decision was not unanimous.)

Question—Does the Louisiana statute abridge the freedom of the press, being contrary to the due process clause of the Fourteenth Amendment?

Decision—Yes.

Reason—Justice Sutherland dealt at length with the various attempts in the history of the British government to tax newspapers. Inevitably such a tax produced two results, a hampering of the circulation, and more or less resistance on the part of citizens. The tax imposed by this statute was not one for the purpose of supporting the government, but a tax to limit the circulation of information to the public, which circulation is necessary for a free people and a free government. Even the form of this tax was suspicious, being based solely upon the amount of circulation.

Corollary cases

Twining v. New Jersey, 211 U.S. 78 (1908)
Near v. Minnesota, 283 U.S. 697 (1931)
Pennekamp v. Florida, 328 U.S. 331 (1946)
FCC v. National Citizens Committee for Broadcasting, 436 U.S. 775 (1978)
Winters v. New York, 333 U.S. 507 (1948)
Bridges v. California, 314 U.S. 252 (1941)
Associated Press v. NLRB, 301 U.S. 103 (1937)
Associated Press v. United States, 326 U.S. 1 (1945)
Metromedia, Inc. v. San Diego, 69 L. Ed. 2d 800 (1981)
Haig v. Agee, 69 L. Ed. 2d 640 (1981)
Snepp v. United States, 444 U.S. 507 (1980)
Smith v. Daily Mail Publishing Co., 443 U.S. 97 (1979)
Post Co. v. National Citizens Committee for Broadcasting, 56 L. Ed. 2d 697 (1978)

Note—The state of Louisiana used the tax power rather than police power and the Court went beyond the face of the statute to its true purpose. In *Arkansas Writer's Project v. Ragland* (95 L Ed 2d 209, 1987) the Court held void a tax which exempted some but not all classes of magazines. Although exempting newspapers, trade, professional and sports journals the Court still held the act violated the First Amendment and Arkansas had now shown a compelling state reason for this selective content-based tax.

Martin v. City of Struthers, Ohio, 319 U.S. 141; 63 S. Ct. 862; 87 L. Ed. 1313 (1943)

An ordinance of the city of Struthers made it unlawful for any person distributing circulars or handbills from door to door to ring the doorbell, sound the knocker, or in any way to summon the inmate of the residence to the door. The appellant, Thelma Martin, challenged this ordinance as violating the right of freedom of the press, and religion as guaranteed by the First and Fourteenth Amendments.

Opinion by Mr. Justice Black
(Vote: 6–3)

Question—Does the city possess the power so to legislate in the light of the constitutional guarantee of freedom of speech and press?

Decision—No.

Reason—The freedom of the First Amendment embraces the right to distribute literature, and protects the right to receive it. Here is a case in which the civil rights of an individual and the rights of the individual householder to determine his willingness to accept a message conflict with the ordinance of this city protecting the interests of all its citizens, whether they want that protection or not.

Freedom to distribute literature is clearly vital to the preservation of a free society. The city may set reasonable police and health regulations, but must leave the individual householder free to decide for himself whether he will receive or reject the stranger at his door. Stringent prohibition can serve no purpose but that forbidden by the Constitution, the naked restriction of the dissemination of ideas. "We conclude that the ordinance is invalid because in conflict with the freedom of speech and press."

Corollary cases

Lovell v. Griffin, 303 U.S. 444 (1938)
Schneider v. State, 308 U.S. 147 (1939)
Cantwell v. Connecticut, 310 U.S. 296 (1940)
Marsh v. Arizona, 326 U.S. 501 (1946)
Tucker v. Texas, 326 U.S. 517 (1946)
Prince v. Massachusetts, 321 U.S. 158 (1944)
Heffron v. International Society for Krishna Consciousness, 69 L. Ed. 2d 298 (1981)
Beth Israel Hospital v. NLRB, 437 U.S. 483 (1978)

Pennekamp v. Florida, 328 U.S. 331; 66 S. Ct. 1029; 90 L. Ed. 1295 (1946)

The petitioners, the publisher and associate editor of a newspaper, were responsible for the publication of two editorials and a cartoon criticizing certain action previously taken by a Florida trial court of general jurisdiction in certain nonjury proceedings as being too favorable to criminals and gambling establishments. Two of the cases involved were dismissed. The third, a rape case, was at first dismissed and then a new indictment was granted and a trial was pending. The petitioners were convicted of contempt of court in that the publication reflected upon and impugned the integrity of the court, tended to create a distrust for the court, and also tended to obstruct the fair and impartial justice of pending cases.

OPINION BY MR. JUSTICE REED
(Vote: 8–0)

Question—Was the petitioners' right of free speech and freedom of the press violated by this conviction?

Decision—Yes.

Reason—On the record, the danger to fair judicial administration in this case had not the necessary clearness and immediacy to close the door of permissible public comment. Since the publication was concerned with the attitude of the judge toward those charged with crime, not comments on rulings during a jury trial or on evidence, their effect on the juries that might try the case was too remote to be a clear and present danger to justice.

This criticism of the judge's inclination or action in pending nonjury proceedings could not directly affect the administration of justice, although the cases were still pending on other points or might be revived by rehearings.

"It may influence some judges more than others. Some are of a more sensitive fiber than their colleagues. The law deals in generalities and external standards and cannot depend on the varying degrees of moral courage or stability in the face of criticism which individual judges may possess any more than it generally can depend on the personal equations or individual idiosyncrasies of the tort-feasor. We are not willing to say under the circumstances of this case that these editorials are a clear and present danger to the fair administration of justice in Florida."

Corollary cases

Bridges v. California, 314 U.S. 252 (1941)
Near v. Minnesota, 293 U.S. 697 (1931)
Abrams v. United States, 250 U.S. 616 (1919)
Schenck v. United States, 249 U.S. 47 (1919)
Toledo Newspaper Co. v. United States, 247 U.S. 402 (1918)

New York Times Company v. United States, 403 U.S. 713; 91 St. Ct. 2140; 29 L. Ed. 2d 820 (1971)

The *New York Times* was enjoined by a federal district court injunction from publication of the "Pentagon Papers." Later this was abolished. These papers had been turned over to the *Times* and the *Washington Post* by Daniel Ellsberg, a Pentagon employee. The study was entitled, "History of the U.S. Decision-Making Process on Viet Nam Policy."

OPINION: PER CURIAM
(Vote: 6–3)

Question—Can the judiciary prevent the publication of material which the government deems harmful to the national interest in the absence of a statute on the matter?

Decision—No.

Reason—"The Bill of Rights changed the original Constitution into a new charter under which no branch of government could abridge the freedom of press, speech, religion, and assembly. . . . Both the history and language of the First Amendment support the view that the press must be left free to publish news, whatever the source, without censorship, injunction, or prior restraint. . . . To find that the president has the 'inherent power' to halt the publication of news by resort to the courts would wipe out the First Amendment and destroy the fundamental liberty and security of the very people the government hopes to make 'secure' . . . the word 'security' is a broad, vague generality whose contours should not be invoked to abrogate the fundamental law embodied in the First Amendment."

Corollary cases

Chaplinsky v. New Hampshire, 315 U.S. 568 (1942)
Cohen v. California, 403 U.S. 15 (1971)
Schacht v. United States, 398 U.S. 58 (1970)
Branzburg v. Hayes, 408 U.S. 205 (1972)
Bantam Books, Inc. v. Sullivan, 372 U.S. 58 (1963)
Near v. Minnesota, 283 U.S. 697 (1931)
Red Lion Broadcasting Co. v. FCC, 395 U.S. 367 (1969)
CBS v. Democratic National Committee, 412 U.S. 94 (1973)

Organization for a Better Austin v. Keefe, 402 U.S. 415 (1971)
New York Times v. Sullivan, 376 U.S. 254 (1964)
Gertz v. Robert Welch, Inc., 418 U.S. 323 (1974)
Miami Herald Publishing Co. v. Tornillo, 418 U.S. 241 (1974)
Cantrell v. Forest City Publishing Co., 419 U.S. 245 (1974)
Spence v. Washington, 418 U.S. 405 (1974)
Landmark Communications, Inc. v. Virginia, 435 U.S. 829 (1978)

Nebraska Press Association v. Stuart, 427 U.S. 539; 49 L. Ed. 2d 683; S. Ct. 2791 (1976)

On October 18, 1975, the police found six members of the Henry Kellie family murdered in their home in Sutherland, Nebraska, a town of about 800 persons. A suspect, Edwin Charles Simants, was made known to the press. Simants was arrested. The crime attracted very wide coverage. The county attorney and Simants jointly asked the judge for an order restricting the flow of news so as to guarantee the defendant a fair trial. The judge agreed. His order prohibited everyone in attendance from releasing or authorizing for public dissemination in any form or manner whatsoever any testimony given or evidence deduced. The judge's order prohibited the press from reporting in five areas. The Nebraska Supreme Court affirmed. The United States Supreme Court granted certiorari.

OPINION BY MR. CHIEF JUSTICE BURGER

(No evidence from the report that the decision was not unanimous.)

Question—Can a judge, in order to insure a defendant a fair trial under the guarantees of the Sixth Amendment, restrain the news media from reporting information as to pretrial events relating to a murder and in doing so not violate the First Amendment?

Decision—No.

Reason—The problems presented by this case, said the Court, are as old as the republic itself. From the very first days of the Constitution there was a potential conflict between the First and the Sixth Amendments. These problems have an impact and history outside the Court. "We cannot," said the Court, "resolve all of them, for it is not the function of this Court to write a code. We look instead to this particular case and the legal context in which it arise." Pretrial publicity, however, "does not inevitably lead to an unfair trial." What the judge says and how he acts also sets the tone of the trial and whether or not the defendant received a fair trial. "A prior restraint, by contrast and by definition, has an immediate and irreversible sanction. If it can be said that a threat of criminal or civil sanctions after publications 'chills' speech, prior restraint 'freezes' it at least for a time." The Court will not assign priorities between the First and Sixth Amendments. "There is no finding that alternative measures," said the Court, "would not have protected the defendant's rights."

Corollary cases

Irving v. Dowd, 366 U.S. 717 (1961)
Rideau v. Louisiana, 373 U.S. 723 (1963)
Estes v. Texas, 381 U.S. 532 (1965)
Marshall v. United States, 360 U.S. 310 (1959)
Sheppard v. Maxwell, 384 U.S. 333 (1966)
Stroble v. California, 343 U.S. 181 (1951)
Houchins v. KQED, Inc., 438 U.S. 1 (1978)
Murphy v. Florida, 421 U.S. 794 (1975)
Near v. Minnesota, 283 U.S. 697 (1931)
New York Times v. United States, 403 U.S. 713 (1971)
Cox Broadcasting v. Cohn, 420 U.S. 469 (1975)
Craig v. Harney, 331 U.S. 367 (1947)
Herbert v. Lando, 441 U.S. 153 (1979)
FCC v. National Citizens Committee for Broadcasting, 436 U.S. 775 (1978)

Gannett Co. v. DePasquale, 443 U.S. 368; 61 L. Ed. 2d 608; 99 S. Ct. 2898 (1979)

Two men committed murder. At their pretrial hearing their attorneys requested that the public and the press be excluded because of an alleged buildup of adverse publicity that had jeopardized the defendants' ability to receive a fair trial. The district attorney did not oppose the motion. A reporter who was employed by Gannett Co., the petitioner, was present in the courtroom but made no objection. Judge DePasquale granted the motion. The reporter wrote a letter to the judge the next day and requested access to the transcript, which was denied. DePasquale allowed another hearing, but refused to vacate the order or grant Gannett immediate access to the transcript, ruling that the interest of the press and the public was outweighed by the defendants' right to a fair trial. The Supreme Court of New York reversed the trial judge's order. Before the case was heard at the Appellate Division, the defendants pleaded guilty to lesser included offenses and a transcript of the suppression hearing was made available to Gannett. The New York Court of Appeals reversed the lower court and upheld the exclusion of the press and the public from the pretrial proceeding.

OPINION BY MR. JUSTICE STEWART
(Vote: 5–4)

Question—Does the state court order for protection of defendants' fair-trial rights in a murder case, agreed to by prosecution and defense, violate the Constitution in barring members of press and public from the pretrial suppression hearing?

Decision—No.

Reason—"To safeguard the due process rights of the accused, a trial judge has an affirmative constitutional duty to minimize the effects of prejudicial pretrial publicity. . . . And because of the Constitution's pervasive concern for these due process rights, a trial judge may surely take protective measures even when they are not strictly and inescapably necessary. . . . Among the guarantees that the amendment provides to a person charged with the commission of a criminal offense, and to him alone, is the 'right to a speedy and public trial, by an impartial jury.' The Constitution nowhere mentions any right of access to a criminal trial on the part of the public; its guarantee, like the others enumerated, is personal to the accused. . . . Several factors lead to the conclusion that the actions of the trial judge here were consistent with any right of access the petitioner may have had under the First and Fourteenth Amendments. First, none of the spectators present in the courtroom, including the reporter employed by the petitioner, objected when the defendants made the closure notice. . . . Furthermore, any denial of access in this case was not absolute but only temporary. Once the danger of prejudice had dissipated, a transcript of the suppression hearing was made available."

Richmond Newspapers, Inc. v. Commonwealth of Virginia, 448 U.S. 555; 65 L. Ed. 2d 973; 100 S. Ct. 2814 (1980)

Before the trial of a suspected murderer began, counsel for the defendant moved that the surroundings be closed to the public, thus excluding two Richmond newspaper reporters from the courtroom. There was no objection by the prosecution and the decision to clear the courtroom was left entirely to the discretion of the presiding judge. After the judge ordered that the courtroom be kept clear of all parties except the witnesses when they testified, Richmond Newspapers sought a hearing on a motion to vacate the order. The court denied the motion and ordered the trial to continue with the press and public excluded. The judge then granted a defense motion to strike the prosecution's evidence and found the defendant not guilty of murder, and the court granted the newspaper's motion to intervene in the case. The newspaper petitioned the Virginia Supreme Court for writs of mandamus and prohibition and filed an appeal from the trial court's closure order, but the Virginia Supreme Court dismissed the petitions and denied the appeal.

OPINION BY MR. CHIEF JUSTICE BURGER
(Vote: 7–1)

Question—Is the right of the public and press to attend criminal trials guaranteed under the United States Constitution?

Decision—Yes.

Reason—"The origins of the proceeding, which has become the modern criminal trial in Anglo-American justice can be traced back beyond reliable historical records. . . . [T]hroughout its evolution, the trial has been open to all who cared to observe . . . we are bound to conclude that a presumption of openness inheres in the very nature of a criminal trial under our system of justice. The Bill of Rights was enacted against the backdrop of the long history of trials being presumptively open. Public access to trials was then regarded as an important aspect of the process itself. . . . In guaranteeing freedoms such as those of speech and press, the First Amendment can be read as protecting the right of everyone to attend trials so as to give meaning to those explicit guarantees. . . . [T]he First Amendment guarantees of speech and press, standing alone, prohibit government from summarily closing courtroom doors which had long been open to the public at the time that amendment was adopted. . . . [A] trial courtroom . . . is a public place where the people generally—and representatives of the media—have a right to be present, and where their presence historically has been thought to enhance the integrity and quality of what takes place. We hold that the right to attend criminal trials is implicit in the guarantees of the First Amendment; without the freedom to attend such trials, . . . important aspects of freedom of speech and 'of the press could be eviscerated.' "

Corollary cases

In re Oliver, 333 U.S. 257 (1948)
Estes v. Texas, 381 U.S. 532 (1965)
Nebraska Press Association v. Stuart, 427 U.S. 539 (1976)
Sheppard v. Maxwell, 384 U.S. 333 (1966)
Faretta v. California, 422 U.S. 806 (1975)
Pell v. Procunier, 417 U.S. 817 (1974)
Houchins v. KQED, Inc., 438 U.S. 1 (1978)
Chandler v. Granger, 449 U.S. 560 (1981)
Richmond Newspapers v. Virginia, 448 U.S. 555 (1980)

Note—The Court reaffirmed its view of press exclusion legislation in *Globe Newspaper Co.* v. *Supreme Court,* 73 L. Ed. 2d 248 (1982). *Globe* involved a rape trial in which the public was barred and, although the exclusion order had expired, the Supreme Court noted that the matter was not moot because it was capable of repetition. The Sixth Amendment, which benefits the defendant, seems to conflict with the First Amendment guarantee of a free press. The Court opts for the defendant's rights. The right of a public trial belongs to the defendant and not to television crews nor does the press have rights to information superior to the public—as for example, the right, under the First Amendment—to interview prisoners. *Saxbe* v. *Washington Post,* 41 L. Ed. 2d 514, 1974). *Gannett* held that the judge could close a preliminary hearing a point underscored in *Richmond* v. *Virginia* (1980).

Chandler and Granger v. Florida, 449 U.S. 560; 66 L. Ed. 2d 740; 101 S. Ct. 802 (1981)

A canon of the Florida Code of Judicial Conduct permitted still photography and electronic media coverage of judicial proceedings subject to the control of the presiding judge. The trial judges were obliged to protect the fundamental right of the accused in a criminal case to a fair trial. Appellants Chandler and Granger, former Miami Beach policemen, who were charged with a crime that attracted media attention, were convicted by a jury in a Florida trial court over objections that the television coverage of parts of their trials denied them a fair and impartial trial.

Opinion by Mr. Chief Justice Burger
(Vote: 8–0)

Question—Does the televising of a criminal trial deny the accused of his fundamental right to a fair trial as is guaranteed by the due process clause of the Fourteenth Amendment?

Decision—No.

Reason—"An absolute constitutional ban on broadcast coverage of trials cannot be justified simply because there is a danger that, in some cases, prejudicial broadcast accounts of pretrial and trial events may impair the ability of jurors to decide the issue of guilt or innocence uninfluenced by extraneous matter. The risk of juror prejudice is present in any publication of a trial, but the appropriate safeguard against such prejudice is the defendant's right to demonstrate that the media's coverage of his case—be it printed or broadcast—compromised the ability of the particular jury that heard the case to adjudicate fairly. . . . The Florida guidelines place on trial judges positive obligations to be on guard to protect the fundamental right of the accused to a fair trial. . . . To demonstrate prejudice in a specific case a defendant must show something more than juror awareness that the trial is such as to attract the attention of broadcasters . . . unless we were to conclude that television coverage under all conditions is prohibited by the Constitution, the states must be free to experiment . . . because this court has no supervisory authority over state courts, our review is confined to whether there is a constitutional violation. We hold that the Constitution does not prohibit a state from experimenting with [its] program."

Corollary cases

Estes v. Texas, 381 U.S. 532 (1965)
Nebraska Free Press Association v. Stuart, 427 U.S. 539 (1975)
Murphy v. Florida, 421 U.S. 794 (1975)
Sheppard v. Maxwell, 384 U.S. 333 (1966)

Note—The Court noted that states must be free to experiment. Florida, a pioneer in judicial experiment, is currently using trials by television, that is, where defendants appear in court only on a large television screen. Can a defense attorney be in two places simultaneously, that is, next to his client and next to the jurors?

Hustler Magazine v. Falwell, 485 U.S. _____; 99 L. Ed. 2d 41; 108 S. Ct. 876, (1988)

In a district court a nationally known minister sought to recover damages for libel and intentional infliction of emotional distress arising from an advertisement "parody" that portrayed him in a drunken incestuous tryst with his mother in an outhouse. This "parody" featured in Hustler magazine was modeled on an advertisement for Compari Liqueur that played on the double entendre of "first times." Falwell, claiming an invasion of privacy and the intentional infliction of emotional distress, asked for libel damages. The district court discounted the libel and privacy claims but found with emotional distress. The United States Court of Appeals upheld with only the emotional distress. Supreme Court granted certiorari.

OPINION BY CHIEF JUSTICE REHNQUIST

Question—Does the First Amendment prohibit a public figure from recovering damages for the intentional infliction of emotional distress as a result of a parody?

Decision—Yes.

Reason—"Respondent would have us find that a state's interest in protecting public figures from emotional distress is sufficient to deny First Amendment protection . . . this we decline to do . . . the First Amendment recognizes no such thing as a 'false' idea." Criticism of public figures will not always be reasoned or moderate. They likely are subject to vehement and caustic, attacks. This does not mean all speech is immune. Under the Sullivan doctrine we have held that a speaker is liable for reputational damage caused by a defamatory falsehood but only if the statement was made "with knowledge that it was false or with reckless disregard of whether it was false or not." Although falsehoods have little value, they are nevertheless inevitable in free debate even "when a speaker or writer is motivated by hatred or ill-will." To hold otherwise cartoonists would continually be subject to suits—because "the art of the cartoonist is often not reasoned or even handed, but slashing and one sided." Outrageous speech in political and social discourse has an inherent subjectiveness about it which would allow a jury to impose liability on the basis of the jurors tastes or views or their dislike of a particular expression. The United States Supreme Court reversed.

Corollary cases

New York Times v. Sullivan, 376 U.S. 254, 11 L. Ed. 2d 686, 84 S. Ct. 710 (1964)

Bose Corp. v. Consumer's Union of United States, 466 U.S. 485, 80 L. Ed. 2d 502, 104 S. Ct. 1949 (1984)

Gertz v. Welch, 418 U.S. 323, 41 L. Ed. 2d 789, 94 S. Ct. 2997 (1974)

Abrams v. United States, 250 U.S. 616, 63 L. Ed. 1173, 40 S. Ct. 17 (1919)

Curtis Publishing Co., v. Butts, 388 U.S. 130, 18 L. Ed. 2d 1094, 87 S. Ct. 1975 (1967)

Baumgartner v. United States, 322 U.S. 665, 88 L. Ed. 1525, 64 S. Ct. 1240 (1944)

Monitor Patriot Co., v. Roy, 401 U.S. 265, 28 L. Ed. 2d 35, 91 S. Ct. 621 (1971)

Philadelphia Newspapers Incorporated v. Hepps, 475 U.S. 767, 89 L. Ed. 2d 783, 106 S. Ct. 1558 (1986)

Zacchini v. Scripps-Howard Broadcasting Co., 433 U.S. 562, 53 L. Ed. 2d 965, 97 S. Ct. 2849 (1977)

Garrison v. Louisiana, 379 U.S. 64, 13 L. Ed. 2d 125, 85 S. Ct. 209 (1964)

NAACP v. Claiborne Hardware Co., 458 U.S. 886, 73 L. Ed. 2d 1215, 102 S. Ct. 3409 (1982)

FCC v. Pacifica Foundation, 438 U.S. 726, 57 L. Ed. 2d 1073, 98 S. Ct. 3026 (1978)

Street v. New York, 394 U.S. 576, 22 L. Ed. 2d 572, 89 S. Ct. 1354 (1969)

Chaplinski v. New Hampshire, 315 U.S. 568, 86 L. Ed. 1031, 62 S. Ct. 766 (1942)

Dun & Bradstreet, Inc., v. Greenmoss Builders, 472 U.S. 749, 86 L. Ed. 593, 105 S. Ct. 2939 (1985)

COMMERCIAL SPEECH

**Virginia State Board of Pharmacy v. Virginia Citizens
Consumer Council, Inc., 425 U.S. 748; 48 L. Ed. 2d 346;
96 S. Ct. 1817 (1976)**

> The appellees, a consumer group, challenged a Virginia
> law that states that a pharmacist is guilty of unprofessional
> conduct if he "publishes, advertises or promotes, directly
> or indirectly, in any manner whatsoever, any amount, price,
> fee, premium, discount, rebate or credit terms . . . for any
> drugs which may be dispensed by prescription." The
> Virginia State Board of Pharmacy is the licensing authority,
> and a pharmacist is subject to a civil monetary penalty, or
> to revocation or suspension of his license.

OPINION BY MR. JUSTICE BLACKMUN
(Vote: 7–1)

Question—Is the Virginia statute making it unprofessional
conduct for a pharmacist to advertise prescription drug
prices a violation of the First Amendment rights of drug
consumers?

Decision—Yes.

Reason—Freedom of speech, noted the Court, "presupposes
a willing speaker. But where a speaker exists, as in the case
here, the protection afforded is to the communication, to its
source and to the recipients both." If there is a right to
advertise there is a reciprocal right to receive the advertising.
The contention that the advertisement of the prescription drug
prices is outside the First Amendment because it is "commercial speech" is rejected. The Court said it was not unmindful
of the fact that some commercial speech can be regulated by
the state, for example, untruthful speech or wholly false,
deceptive, or misleading advertising; and some other speech,
for example in the electronic broadcast media is outside the
confines of its decision. But society has a strong interest in the
free flow of commercial information. Virginia argues that it
would protect its citizens from fraud and maintain professional
standards but, in truth, its protectiveness, as to competing

drug prices, rests in large measure "on the advantages of their being kept in ignorance."

Corollary cases

Valentine v. Christensen, 316 U.S. 52 (1942)
Head v. New Mexico Board, 374 U.S. 424 (1963)
Willeamson v. Lee Optical Co., 348 U.S. 483 (1955)
Semler v. Dental Examiners, 294 U.S. 608 (1935)
Lamont v. Postmaster General, 381 U.S. 301 (1975)
Kleindienst v. Mandel, 408 U.S. 753 (1972)
Procunier v. Martinez, 416 U.S. 396 (1974)
Breard v. Alexandria, 341 U.S. 622 (1951)
Bigelow v. Virginia, 421 U.S. 809 (1975)
Pittsburgh Press Co. v. Pittsburgh Commission on Human Relations, 413 U.S. 376 (1973)
First National Bank of Boston v. Bellotti, 435 U.S. 765 (1978)
Metromedia v. San Diego, 69 L. Ed. 2d 800 (1981)
Schaumberg v. Citizens for Better Environment, 444 U.S. 620 (1980)
Central Hudson Gas & Electric Corp. v. Public Service Commission, 447 U.S. 557 (1980)
In re R.M.J., 71 L. Ed. 2d 64 (1982)

Note—*Virginia State Board* logically followed from *Bigelow* v. *Virginia* (1975), involving a newspaper advertisement. It, in turn, led to other commercial speech cases, such as contraception advertising in *Carey* v. *Population Services,* 431 U.S. 678; legal advertising, in *Bates* v. *State Bar,* 433 U.S. 350 (1977); and real estate "for sale" and "sold" signs in *Linmark Associates, Inc.* v. *Willingboro,* 431 U.S. 85 (1977). A novel case involving free speech and advertising occurred in *Posadas de Puerto Rico Associates* v. *Tourism Company of Puerto Rico* (92 L. Ed. 2d 266, 1986) in which the Court upheld a law restricting advertising by a legal gambling casino against the charge of free speech, due process, and equal protection. It was Puerto Rico's intention to appeal to tourists who want to gamble but not to citizens of Puerto Rico.

First National Bank of Boston v. Bellotti, 435 U.S. 765; 55 L. Ed. 2d 707; 98 S. Ct. 1407 (1978)

Appellants are national banking associations and business corporations that wanted to publicize their views. They opposed a referendum proposal to amend the Massachusetts Constitution that would allow the legislature to enact a graduated personal income tax. The attorney general of Massachusetts advised the corporation from making contributions or expenditures "for the purpose of influencing . . . or affecting the vote on any question submitted to the voters, other than the one materially affecting any of the property, business or assets of the corporation." The Supreme Judicial Court of Massachusetts held that the corporation could not claim First or Fourteenth Amendment protections for its speech or other activities entitling it to communicate its position on that issue to the general public. Although the 1976 referendum had passed the Court did not believe the question "moot" inasmuch as another referendum proposal is likely to arise.

OPINION BY MR. JUSTICE POWELL
(Vote: 5–4)

Question—Is the Massachusetts law that prohibits corporations from spending money to influence a referendum vote a violation of the First and Fourteenth Amendment?

Decision—Yes.

Reason—Freedom of speech and press embrace the liberty to discuss publicly and truthfully all matters of public concern without previous restraint or fear of subsequent punishment. If the speakers were not corporations no one would suggest that the state could silence their proposed speech. Speech is indispensable to decisionmaking in a democracy "and this is no less true because the speech comes from a corporation rather than an individual." Although the press is a recognized institution in informing and educating the public and in offering criticism and providing a forum for discussion and debate it "does not have a monopoly on either the First Amendment or the ability to enlighten." If a legislature may direct business corporations to "stick to business" it may also limit other corporations—religious, charitable, or civil—to their respective "business" when addressing the public. "Such power in government to channel the expression of views is unacceptable under the First Amendment."

Corollary cases

Thornhill v. Alabama, 310 U.S. 88 (1940)
Mills v. Alabama, 284 U.S. 214 (1966)
Burnstyn v. Wilson, 343 U.S. 495 (1952)
De Jonge v. Oregon, 299 U.S. 353 (1937)
Buckley v. Valeo, 424 U.S. 1 (1976)
Red Lion Broadcasting Co. v. FCC, 395 U.S. 367 (1969)
New York Times v. Sullivan, 376 U.S. 254 (1964)
Virginia State Board of Pharmacy v. Virginia Citizens Consumer Council,
   Inc., 425 U.S. 748 (1976)
Metromedia, Inc. v. San Diego, 69 L. Ed. 2d 800 (1981)
Central Hudson Gas & Electric Corp. v. Public Service Commission of New
   York, 447 U.S. 557 (1980)
Friedman v. Rogers, 440 U.S. 1 (1979)
Citizens Against Rent Control v. Berkeley, 70 L. Ed. 2d 492 (1981)

Note—The Court's view in *Bellotti* is not likely to change. In *Central Hudson Gas and Electric Corporation* v. *Public Service Commission* (65 L. Ed. 2d 341, 1980) the Court held in violation of the First Amendment an attempt by the state public service commission banning promotional advertising. In *Pacific Gas & Electric Co.* v. *Public Utilities* (89 L. Ed. 2d 1, 1986) the Court voided an attempt by a Public Utilities Commission to require the gas and electric company to allow a consumer group to "piggy-back" by utilizing "extra space" in its billing statement.

Sony Corporation v. Universal City Studios 464 U.S. _____; 78 L. Ed. 2d 574; 104 S. Ct. 774 (1984)

   Owners of copyrights on television programs sued the manufacturers of video cassette recorders alleging that individuals used the recorders to pirate copyright material on television and that the manufacturers were liable for such an infringement. They sought money damages, an equitable distribution of profits, and an injunction against the manufacture. The United States District Court denied all relief, the court of appeals reversed and for a second time the Supreme Court ordered a reargument.

OPINION BY JUSTICE STEVENS
(Vote: 5–4)

Questions—1. Is the taping of copyright material on television an infringement?

2. Is time shifting not fair use?
3. Were the manufacturers of recorders guilty of materially contributing to the infringement?

Decision—1. No.
   2. No.
   3. No.

Reason—There is no basis in "the Copyright Act upon which the respondents can hold petitioners liable for distributing VTR's (Video Tape Recorders) to the general public." Art. I, Sec. 8 of the Constitution provides that "the Congress shall have power . . . to promote the progress of science and useful Arts . . ." the monopoly privileges that Congress "may authorize are neither unlimited nor primarily designed to provide a special private benefit." The limited grant is a means by which an important public purpose may be achieved. "The copyright law, like the patent statute, makes reward to the owner a secondary consideration . . . it is Congress that has been assigned the task of defining the scope of the limited monopoly that should be granted to authors or inventors." Copyright work is to be encouraged and rewarded "but private motivation must ultimately serve the cause of promoting broad public availability of literature, music, and other arts . . . this protection has never accorded the copyright owner complete control over all possible uses of his work." Even if home recording of copyright material constitutes an infringement, there are many owners who do consent to copying copyright work and, furthermore, an "injunction would deprive the public of the ability" to use a recorder "for the noninfringing off-the-air recording." One may search the Copyright Act and not find that Congress outlawed time-shifting or would penalize the sale of machines that make copying possible.

Corollary cases

Fox Film Corp. v. Doyal, 286 U.S. 123, 76 L. Ed. 1010, 52 S. Ct. 546 (1932)
Thompson v. Hubbard, 131 U.S. 123, 33 L. Ed. 79, 9 S. Ct. 710 (1889)
Teleprompter Corp. v. CBS, 415 U.S. 394, 39 L. Ed. 2d 415, 94 S. Ct. 1129 (1974)
Fortnightly Corp. v. United Artists, 392 U.S. 390, 20 L. Ed. 2d 1176, 88 S. Ct. 2084 (1968)

White-Smith Music Publishing Co. v. Apollo Co., 209 U.S. 1, 52 L. Ed. 655, 285 S. Ct. 319 (1908)
Kalem Co. v. Harper Brothers, 222 U.S. 55, 56 L. Ed. 92, 32 S. Ct. 20 (1911)
Community Television of Southern California v. Gottfried, 464 U.S. _____ Note 12, 74 L. Ed. 2d 705, 103 S. Ct. 885 (1983)

FREEDOM OF ASSEMBLY

Frisby v. Schultz, 487 U.S. _____; 101 L. Ed. 2d 420; 108 S. Ct. 2495 (1988)

Brookfield, Wisconsin, is a residential suburb of Milwaukee. It has a population of about 5,000. Antiabortionists Sandra Schultz and Robert Braun, along with others, targeted the home of a doctor who allegedly performed abortions. The picketing was orderly and peaceful but generated substantial controversy and numerous complaints. The town board passed an ordinance that held: "It is unlawful for any person to engage in picketing before or about the residence or dwelling of any individual in the town of Brookfield," the federal district court granted appellees' motion for a preliminary injunction, concluding that the ordinance was not narrowly tailored enough to restrict protected speech in a public forum. The court of appeals ultimately affirmed.

OPINION BY JUSTICE O'CONNOR
(Vote: 6–3)

Question—Is the Brookfield ordinance that permits picketing "before or about" in violation of the First Amendment?

Decision—No.

Reason—The ordinance itself recites the primary purpose of the picket ban, namely, "the protection and preservation of the home." The practice of picketing before or about residences and dwellings causes emotional disturbance and distress to the occupants. The ordinance also evinces a concern for public safety. It is important that speech in public fora be uninhibited, and restrictions should be carefully scrutinized. A public street does not lose its status as a traditional public forum simply because it runs through a residential neighborhood. The ordinance is readily subject to a narrow construction for the words "residence" and "dwelling" are singular and suggest "that the ordinance is intended to prohibit only picketing focused on, and taking place in front of, a particular residence." We construe the ban to be a limited one—"only focused picketing taking place solely in front of a particular

216

residence." It does not cover marching through the area or walking in front of an entire block. There are other alternatives. Protesters can visit a neighborhood, singly or in groups, may go from door to door or distribute mail by hand or by delivery. "A statute is narrowly tailored if it targets and eliminates no more than exact source of the "evil" it seeks to remedy. Largely because of its narrow scope, the facial challenge to the ordinance must fail."

Corollary cases

Carey v. Brown, 447 U.S. 455, 65 L. Ed. 2d 263, 100 S. Ct. 2286 (1980)

Boos v. Barry, 485 U.S. _____, 99 L. Ed. 2d 333, 108 S. Ct. 1157 (1988)

Cornelius v. NAACP Legal Defense and Educational Fund, 473 U.S. 788, 87 L. Ed. 2d 567, 105 S. Ct. 3439 (1985)

Perry Education Association v. Perry Local Educators' Assn., 460 U.S. 37, 74 L. Ed. 2d 794, 103 S. Ct. 948 (1983)

Hague v. C10, 307 U.S. 496, 83 L. Ed. 1423, 59 S. Ct. 954 (1939)

Brockett v. Spokane Arcades, 472 U.S. 491, 86 L. Ed. 2d 394, 105 S. Ct. 2794 (1985)

Virginia v. American Booksellers Association, 484 U.S. _____, 98 L. Ed. 2d 782, 108 S. Ct. 636 (1988)

Erzoznik v. City of Jacksonville, 422 U.S. 205, 45 L. Ed. 2d 125, 95 S. Ct. 2268 (1975)

Cohen v. California, 403 U.S. 15, 29 L. Ed. 2d 284, 91 S. Ct. 1780 (1971)

Gregory v. Chicago, 394 U.S. 111, 22 L. Ed. 2d 134, 89 S. Ct. 946 (1969)

Rowan v. Post Office Dept., 397 U.S. 728, 25 L. Ed. 2d 736, 90 S. Ct. 1484 (1970)

Schneider v. State, 308 U.S. 147, 84 L. Ed. 155, 60 S. Ct. 146 (1939)

Martin v. Struthers, 319 U.S. 141, 87 L. Ed. 1313, 63 S. Ct. 862 (1943)

City Council of Los Angeles v. Taxpayers for Vincent, 466 U.S. 789, 80 L. Ed. 2d 772, 104 S. Ct. 2118 (1984)

Organization for a Better Austin v. Keefe, 402 U.S. 415, 29 L. Ed. 2d 1, 91 S. Ct. 1575 (1971)

Bolger v. Youngs Drug Products Corp., 463 U.S. 60, 77 L. Ed. 2d 469, 103 S. Ct. 2875 (1983)

Consolidated Edison Co. v. Public Service Comm'n of New York, 447 U.S. 530, 65 L. Ed. 2d 319, 100 S. Ct. 2326 (1980)

Note—Even the Supreme Court itself is not immune to litigation. A federal law prohibits the "display of any flag, banner, or device designed or adapted to bring into public notice any party, organization, or movement" in the Supreme Court building or on its grounds, which include the public sidewalks constituting the outer boundaries of the grounds. The Court held that the sidewalks are public areas under the free speech provision of the First Amendment. *United States* v. *Grace (75 L. Ed. 2d 736, 1983)*

De Jonge v. Oregon, 299 U.S. 353; 57 S. Ct. 255; 81 L. Ed. 278 (1937)

De Jonge was indicted in Multnomah County, Oregon, for the violation of the Criminal Syndicalism Law of the state. This law made the doctrine that advocates crime, physical violence, sabotage, or any unlawful acts as methods of accomplishing industrial change or political revolution a crime. De Jonge was a member of the Communist party and spoke at an advertised meeting sponsored by the Communist party.

OPINION BY MR. CHIEF JUSTICE HUGHES
(Vote: 8–0)

Question—Was this law a denial of due process?

Decision—Yes.

Reason—Apparently the only offense for which the accused was charged, convicted, and sentenced to imprisonment for seven years was taking part in a meeting held under the auspices of the Communist party. While the states are entitled to protect themselves and the privileges of our institutions from abuse, none of the court decisions go to the length of such a curtailment of the right of free speech as the Oregon statute demanded.

Freedom of speech, press, and peaceful assembly are fundamental rights safeguarded by the due process clause of the Fourteenth Amendment. Holding a peaceful public meeting for lawful discussion cannot be made a crime. The Court was not here upholding the objectives of the Communist party. The defendant was still entitled to his personal right of free speech, although he was a member of the Communist party, if the activity was carried on in a lawful manner, without incitement to violence or crime.

The Court held that the Oregon statute, as applied to the

particular charge here, was repugnant to the due process clause of the Fourteenth Amendment.

Corollary cases

Gitlow v. New York, 268 U.S. 652 (1925)
Whitney v. California, 274 U.S. 357 (1927)
Near v. Minnesota, 283 U.S. 697 (1931)
Grosjean v. American Press Co., 297 U.S. 233 (1936)
Healy v. James, 408 U.S. 169 (1972)
Hague v. CIO, 307 U.S. 496 (1939)
Herndon v. Lowry, 301 U.S. 242 (1937)
Fiske v. Kansas, 274 U.S. 380 (1927)
Stromberg v. California, 283 U.S. 359 (1931)
Bates v. Little Rock, 361 U.S. 516 (1960)
Terminiello v. Chicago, 337 U.S. 1 (1940)
Coates v. Cincinnati, 402 U.S. 611 (1971)
Democratic Party of the United States v. La Follette, 67 L. Ed. 2d 82 (1981)
Heffron v. International Society for Krishna Consciousness, Inc., 69 L. Ed. 2d 298 (1981)
Madison Joint School District v. Wisconsin Employment Relations Commission, 429 U.S. 167 (1976)

Note—In *De Jonge,* the "Gitlow doctrine" was applied to the First Amendment's freedom of assembly.

Hague v. Committee for Industrial Organization, 307 U.S. 496; 59 S. Ct. 954; 83 L. Ed. 1423 (1939)

This case involved the validity of an ordinance of Jersey City that prohibited assemblies "in or upon public streets, highways, public works, or public buildings" without a permit from the director of public safety. In reliance on this ordinance, the officers of the city had enforced a policy against the distribution of circulars, leaflets, and handbills of the CIO, which was then organizing in the city.

OPINION BY MR. JUSTICE ROBERTS
(Vote: 5–2)

Question—Does this ordinance violate the due process clause of the Fourteenth Amendment?

Decision—Yes.

Reason—Although it has been held that the Fourteenth Amendment created no rights in the citizen of the United

States but merely secured existing rights against state abridgment, it is clear that the right peaceably to assemble and discuss topics and to communicate respecting them, whether orally or in writing, is a privilege inherent in the citizenship of the United States that the amendment protects.

Citizenship of the United States would be little better than a name if it did not carry with it the right to discuss national legislation and the benefits, advantages, and opportunities that inure to citizens. However, the privileges and immunities section of the Fourteenth Amendment is applicable only to natural persons and not to artificial or legal persons.

Corollary cases

Slaughter House Cases, 16 Wallace 36 (1873)
United States v. Cruikshank, 92 U.S. 542 (1876)
Colgate v. Harvey, 296 U.S. 404 (1935)
Whitney v. California, 274 U.S. 357 (1927)
Madden v. Kentucky, 309 U.S. 83 (1940)
Crandall v. Nevada, 6 Wallace 35 (1868)
Edwards v. South Carolina, 372 U.S. 229 (1963)
De Jonge v. Oregon, 299 U.S. 353 (1937)
Terminiello v. Chicago, 337 U.S. 1 (1949)
Adderley v. Florida, 385 U.S. 39 (1966)
Gregory v. Chicago, 394 U.S. 111 (1969)
Cohen v. California, 403 U.S. 15 (1971)
Coates v. Cincinnati, 402 U.S. 611 (1971)

Note—As it was to do in numerous other cases—notably in *Edwards* v. *California,* 314 U.S. 160 (1941)—the Court refused, despite the views of three justices, to decide this case under the privileges and immunities doctrine.

Bowers v. Hardwick, 478 U.S. _____; 92 L. Ed. 2d 140; 106 S. Ct. 2841 (1986)

In August 1982 respondent was charged with violating a Georgia statute that had criminalized sodomy. He had committed this act with another male in the bedroom of his home. Respondent Hardwick brought suit in the district court challenging the constitutionality of the statute in so far as it criminalized consensual sodomy. The district court affirmed, the court of appeals reversed. On certiorari it went to the Supreme Court.

OPINION BY JUSTICE WHITE
(Vote: 5–4)

Question—Does the Fourteenth Amendment confer a fundamental right to engage in sodomy and hence invalidate state laws that criminalize such conduct and have done so for a long time?

Decision—No.

Reason—"We . . . register our disagreement with the Court of Appeals and with respondent that the Court's prior cases have construed the constitution to confer a right of privacy that extends to homosexual sodomy." The cases enumerated by the court of appeals bears no resemblance "to the claimed constitutional right of homosexuals to engage in acts of sodomy." Moreover, the claim made by this listing of cases "insulated from state proscription is unsupportable." The Court is "quite unwilling" to announce that homosexuals have a fundamental right of sodomy. Neither in the doctrines implicit in the concept of ordered liberty." nor "deeply rooted in this nation's history and tradition" is sodomy protected. Sodomy was a criminal offense at common law, forbidden by the original thirteen colonies, and with the adoption of the Fourteenth Amendment in 1868, all but 5 of the 37 states in the union had criminal sodomy laws. Today, 24 states plus the District of Columbia have criminalized sodomy. Such claims of freedom to engage in sodomy are "facetious." Finally, the

221

Court is not inclined to take a more "expansive view" of its "authority to discover new fundamental rights embedded in the due process clause."

Corollary cases

Griswold v. Connecticut, 381 U.S. 479, 14 L. Ed. 2d 510, 85 S. Ct. 1678 (1965)

Eisenstadt v. Baird, 405 U.S. 438, 31 L. Ed. 2d 349, 92 S. Ct. 1029 (1972)

Stanley v. Georgia, 394 U.S. 557, 22 L. Ed. 2d 542, 89 S. Ct. 1243 (1969)

Roe v. Wade, 410 U.S. 113, 35 L. Ed. 2d 147, 93 S. Ct. 705 (1973)

Carey v. Population Services International, 431 U.S. 678, 52 L. Ed. 2d 675, 97 S. Ct. 2010 (1977)

Pierce v. Society of Sisters, 268 U.S. 510, 69 L. Ed. 1070, 45 S. Ct. 571 (1925)

Mistretta v. United States, 488 U.S. 102 L. Ed. 2d 714, 109 S. Ct. (1989)

Meyer v. Nebraska, 262 U.S. 390, 67 L. Ed. 1042, 43 S. Ct. 625 (1923)

Prince v. Massachusetts, 321 U.S. 158, 88 L. Ed. 645, 64 S. Ct. 438 (1944)

Skinner v. Oklahoma ex rel. Williamson, 316 U.S. 535, 86 L. Ed. 1655, 62 S. Ct. 1110 (1942)

Loving v. Virginia, 388 U.S. 1, 18 L. Ed. 2d 1010, 87 S. Ct. 1817 (1967)

Palco v. Connecticut, 302 U.S. 319, 82 L. Ed. 288, 58 S. Ct. 149 (1937)

Moore v. East Cleveland, 431 U.S. 494, 52 L. Ed. 2d 531, 97 S. Ct. 1932 (1977)

Note—This decision was a surprise considering that "privacy" seemed already "anchored" in *Griswold* v. *Connecticut* (381 US 479, 1965) and *Roe* v. *Wade* (410 US 113, 1973). Here Justice White follows the law, upholds the state, and frankly rejects not only an "expansive" view but instead opts for "judicial restraint."

Village of Euclid, Ohio, v. Ambler Realty Co., 272 U.S. 365; 47 S. Ct. 114; 71 L. Ed. 303 (1926)

Appellee owned land within Euclid, Ohio. The village of Euclid passed a zoning law restricting the use of land to residential purposes. The Ambler Realty Company was holding it for industrial use because of its location and the resultant much higher value of the land than if used for residential lots.

OPINION BY MR. JUSTICE SUTHERLAND
(Vote: 6–3)

Question—Does the zoning ordinance take the company's property without due process of law contrary to the Fourteenth Amendment?

Decision—No.

Reason—The zoning ordinance is a valid exercise of the state's police power under which the state has the authority to abate a nuisance. Actually a nuisance may be merely a right thing in a wrong place. Noise, traffic, fire hazards, and the general desirability of an area for "residential" purposes, including the rearing of children, certainly come under the power of the state and its agencies to care for the public safety, health, morals, and general welfare. Concern for the common good may properly override an individual's property rights.

Corollary cases

Terrace v. Thompson, 263 U.S. 197 (1923)
Welch v. Swasey, 214 U.S. 91 (1909)
Hebe Co. v. Shaw, 248 U.S. 29 (1909)
Cusack Co. v. City of Chicago, 242 U.S. 526 (1917)
Village of Belle Terre v. Boraas, 416 U.S. 1 (1974)
Gorieb v. Fox, 274 U.S. 603 (1927)
Nectow v. City of Cambridge, 277 U.S. 183 (1928)
Queenside Hills Realty Co. v. Saxl, 328 U.S. 80 (1946)
Berman v. Parker, 348 U.S. 26 (1954)
Warth v. Selding, 422 U.S. 490 (1975)
Young v. American Mini Theatres, Inc., 427 U.S. 50 (1976)

Note—*Ambler* is often remembered for Justice Sutherland's sassy remark: "A nuisance may merely be a right thing in the wrong place, like a pig in the parlor instead of the barnyard." In *City of Renton* v. *Playtime Theatres* (89 L. Ed. 2d 29, 1986) the Court upheld a zoning law prohibiting an adult movie house from locating within 1,000 feet of a park, school, or residential home.

Tumey v. Ohio, 273 U.S. 510; 47 S. Ct. 437; 71 L. Ed. 749 (1927)

Tumey was arrested and brought before Mayor Pugh of the village of North College Hill in the state of Ohio on the charge of unlawfully possessing intoxicating liquor contrary to the prohibition act of that state. The mayor, under statutes of Ohio, had the authority to hear a case of one charged with violating this prohibition act. Tumey moved for a dismissal of the case because of the disqualification of the mayor to try him under the Fourteenth Amendment. The mayor denied the motion, proceeded to the trial, convicted Tumey of unlawfully possessing intoxicating liquor within Hamilton County, Ohio, fined him $100, and ordered that he be imprisoned until the fine and costs were paid. As a result of the conviction the mayor received a $12 fee from Tumey for his acting as judge in addition to his being mayor. The mayor would not have received this fee if the accused had not been convicted.

OPINION BY MR. CHIEF JUSTICE TAFT
(No evidence from the report that the decision was not unanimous.)

Question—Do certain statutes in Ohio, in providing for a trial by the mayor of a village of one accused of violating the prohibition act of the state deprive the accused of due process of law and violate the Fourteenth Amendment to the federal Constitution, because of the pecuniary and other interests that those statutes give the mayor in the result of the trial?

Decision—Yes.

Reason—"All questions of judicial qualification may not involve constitutional validity. Thus matters of kinship, personal bias, state policy, remoteness of interest would seem generally to be matters of legislative discretion. . . . But it certainly violates the Fourteenth Amendment and deprives a defendant in a criminal case of due process of law to subject his liberty or property to the judgment of a court, the judge of which has a direct, personal, substantial pecuniary interest in reaching a conclusion against him in his case."

No matter what the evidence against him, the defendant has the right to have an impartial judge.

Corollary cases

Powell v. Alabama, 287 U.S. 45 (1932)
Haley v. Ohio, 332 U.S. 596 (1948)
Ward v. Village of Monroeville, 409 U.S. 57 (1972)
Bute v. Illinois, 333 U.S. 640 (1948)
Dugan v. Ohio, 277 U.S. 61 (1928)
Hudson v. Louisiana, 450 U.S.—(1981); 67 L. Ed. 2d 30 (1981)

Carter v. Kentucky, 450 U.S.—(1981); 67 L. Ed. 2d 241 (1981)
Bordenkircher v. Hayes, 434 U.S. 357 (1978)
Little v. Streator, 452 U.S. 1; 68 L. Ed. 2d 627 (1981)
Memphis Light, Gas & Water Division v. Graff, 436 U.S. 1; 56 L. Ed. 2d 30
  (1978)

Note—The *Tumey* doctrine was reiterated in *Ward* v. *Monroe-ville* (1972), in which the mayor of an Ohio village convicted Ward of a traffic violation. The mayor was also responsible for the village finances and in that role held a mayor's court that collected fines and fees. In *Memphis Light* (1978), the Court held that due process requires a public utility to apprise its customers of the administrative procedure to consider complaints of erroneous billings.

O'Connor v. Donaldson, 422 U.S. 563; 95 S. Ct. 2486; 45 L. Ed. 2d 396 (1975)

> Kenneth Donaldson was confined as a mental patient in the Florida State Hospital at Chattahoochee "for care, maintenance and treatment" for almost fifteen years. He had made frequent requests for release; responsible persons had agreed to care for him if necessary; he was dangerous to no one, either himself or others; and he had not received treatment for any mental illness at the hospital. The alleged justification by Dr. O'Connor, the hospital superintendent during most of the period of confinement, for keeping Donaldson in the hospital was a state law that authorized indefinite custodial confinement of the "sick." Dr. O'Connor further maintained that the action was taken in good faith.

OPINION BY MR. JUSTICE STEWART
(No evidence from the report that the decision was not unanimous.)

Question—Was the state law valid under the Fourteenth Amendment?

Decision—No.

Reason—A state cannot constitutionally confine without consent a nondangerous individual who is capable of surviving safely in freedom by himself or with the help of willing and responsible family members or friends. This violates a person's right to liberty. "A finding of 'mental illness' alone cannot justify a state's locking a person up against his will and keeping him indefinitely in simple custodial confinement. Assuming that term can be given a reasonably precise content and that the 'mentally ill' can be identified with reasonable accuracy, there is still no constitutional basis for confining such persons involuntarily if they are dangerous to no one and can live safely in freedom.''

Corollary cases

Woods v. Strickland, 420 U.S. 308 (1975)
Scheuer v. Rhodes, 416 U.S. 232 (1974)
Jackson v. Indiana, 406 U.S. 715 (1972)
Humphrey v. Cady, 405 U.S. 504 (1972)
McNeil v. Director, Patuxent Institution, 407 U.S. 245 (1972)
Cohen v. California, 403 U.S. 15 (1971)
Coates v. City of Cincinnati, 402 U.S. 611 (1971)
Greenwood v. United States, 350 U.S. 366 (1957)
Drope v. Missouri, 420 U.S. 162 (1975)
Stump v. Sparkman, 435 U.S. 349 (1978)
Vitek v. Jones, 445 U.S. 480 (1980)
Parham v. J. R., 442 U.S. 584; 61 L. Ed. 2d 101 (1979)
Penhurst State School and Hospital v. Halderman, 451 U.S. 1 (1981)
Polk County v. Dodson, 70 L. Ed. 2d 509 (1981)

Note—Since commitment for mental illness significantly deprives a person of his liberty, the Court, in *Addington* v. *Texas,* 439 U.S. 908 (1979), held it must be done by clear and convincing evidence of that person's being a danger to society and not by evidence that was merely beyond a reasonable doubt.

Zablocki v. Redhail, 434 U.S. 374; 54 L. Ed. 2d 618; 98 S. Ct. 673 (1978)

Redhail, the appellee, was a Wisconsin resident who, under a paternity statute, was unable to marry in Wisconsin or elsewhere as long as he maintained a Wisconsin residence. In January 1972, when Redhail was a minor and a high school student, he was subject to a paternity suit and a court order, in May 1972, that ordered him to pay $109.00 monthly as support for the child until she reached 18 years of age. In September 1974, Redhail applied for a marriage license and Zablocki, the county clerk of Milwaukee

County, refused on the sole ground that Redhail had not obtained a court order granting him permission. Redhail had not satisfied his support obligations of his illegitimate child—in excess of $3,700—and the child had been a public charge since birth.

OPINION BY MR. JUSTICE MARSHALL
(Vote: 8–1)

Question—Can Wisconsin determine that members of a certain class of residents cannot marry in the state or elsewhere without first obtaining a court order?

Decision—No.

Reason—The Court has continuously confirmed the right to marry. The right to marry is of "fundamental importance for all individuals." The freedom of personal choice in matters of marriage and family life is one of the liberties protected by the due process clause of the Fourteenth Amendment. It is not suggested that every statute that relates to marriage must be subject to rigorous scrutiny. On the contrary, reasonable regulations that do not significantly interfere with the decision to marry may legitimately be imposed. But the statutory classification here clearly does interfere directly and substantially with the right to marry. "When a statutory classification significantly interferes with the exercise of a fundamental right, it cannot be upheld unless it is supported by sufficiently important state interests and is closely tailored to effect only those interests." The Wisconsin statute is both "grossly underinclusive" and "substantially overinclusive."

Corollary cases

Loving v. Virginia, 388 U.S. 1 (1967)
Meyer v. Nebraska, 262 U.S. 390 (1923)
Skinner v. Oklahoma, 316 U.S. 535 (1942)
Griswold v. Connecticut, 381 U.S. 479 (1965)
Carey v. Population Services International, 431 U.S. 678 (1977)
Eisenstadt v. Baird, 405 U.S. 438 (1972)
Prince v. Massachusetts, 321 U.S. 158 (1944)
Pierce v. Society of Sisters, 268 U.S. 510 (1925)
Roe v. Wade, 410 U.S. 113 (1973)

Note—While the older cases spoke of the family (*Meyer* v. *Nebraska*, *Pierce* v. *Society of Sisters*), under the liberty provision of the Fourteenth Amendment, the more recent cases in human sexuality and marriage issues speak of the individual under the equal protection clause (*Eisenstadt* v. *Baird*, 1972, and *Roe* v. *Wade*, 1973).

EQUAL PROTECTION

Board of Directors of Rotary International v. Rotary Club of Duarte, 481 U.S. _____; 95 L. Ed. 2d 474; 107 S. Ct. 1940 (1987)

Each local Rotary Club is a member of Rotary International in which (as of 1982) there were 19,788 clubs world wide in 157 countries with a total membership of a little more than 900,000 members. Individuals are admitted to membership according to a "classification system" that includes representatives of every worthy and recognized business, professional, or institutional activity in the community. The classification system permits additional members as associate, senior active, or past service, but is unlimited as to the number of clergymen, journalists, or diplomats. Each Rotary adopts its own rules. Rotary, however, is open only to men and although women are invited to attend various activities and can even form auxiliary units, they cannot be members. When the Duarte Rotary admitted women, the directors revoked their charter. Meanwhile the local Rotary went to the Court. After a bench trial in favor of Rotary, the California Court of Appeals reversed the decision. The Supreme Court assumed appellate jurisdiction.

OPINION BY JUSTICE POWELL
(Vote: 7–0)

Question—Whether the California statute (Unruh Act) that requires California Rotary Clubs to admit women members violates the First Amendment.

Decision—No.

Reason—The California Court of Appeals found that Rotary Clubs—although committed to humanitarian service, high ethical standards in all vocations, and a concern for good will and world peace—are business establishments and therefore subject to the Unruh Act. The trial court erred in holding that Rotary was only incidentally involved in business. The appeals court rejected the view that Rotary does not provide services or facilities to its members. Rotary is not a small intimate club

229

that gives rise to "continuous, personal, and social" relation-ships of a kind of which the Court is solicitous in protecting. Rotary does not fall in this category. In determining this protection "we consider factors such as size, purpose, selec-tivity and whether others are excluded. "Many of the Rotary Clubs central activities are carried on in the presence of visitors and strangers. Rather than keep an atmosphere of privacy they "seek to keep their windows and doors open to the whole world." The evidence fails "to demonstrate that admitting women to Rotary Clubs will affect in any significant way the existing members' ability to carry out their various purposes." The Unruh Act does not violate the right of expres-sive association afforded by the First Amendment."

Corollary cases

Roberts v. United States Jaycees, 468 U.S. 609, 82 L. Ed. 2d 462, 104 S. Ct. 3244 (1984)
Moore v. East Cleveland, 431 U.S. 494, 52 L. Ed. 2d 531, 97 S. Ct. 1932 (1977)
Zablocki v. Redhail, 434 U.S. 374, 54 L. Ed. 2d 618, 98 S. Ct. 673 (1978)
Carey Population Services International, 431 U.S. 678, 52 L. Ed. 2d 675, 97 S. Ct. 2010 (1977)
Pierce v. Society of Sisters, 268 U.S. 510, 69 L. Ed. 1020, 45 S. Ct. 571 (1925)
Runyon v. McCrary, 427 U.S. 160, 49 L. Ed. 2d 415, 96 S. Ct. 2586 (1976)
Clairborne Hardware, 458 U.S. 886, 73 L. Ed. 2d 1215, 102 S. Ct. 3409 (1982)
Hishon v. King & Spalding, 467 U.S. 69, 81 L. Ed. 2d 59, 104 S. Ct. 2229 (1984)
NAACP v. Button, 371 U.S. 415, 9 L. Ed. 2d 405, 83 S. Ct. 328 (1963)
NAACP v. Alabama ex rel. Patterson, 357 U.S. 449, 2 L. Ed. 2d 1488, 78 S. Ct. 1163 (1958)
Buckley v. Valeo, 424 U.S. 1, 46 L. Ed. 2d 659, 96 S. Ct. 612 (1976)
Webb v. Webb, 451 U.S. 493, 68 L. Ed. 2d 392, 101 S. Ct. 1889 (1981)
Exxon Corp. v. Eagerton, 462 U.S. 176, 76 L. Ed. 2d 497, 103 S. Ct. 2296 (1983)
Fuller v. Oregon, 417 U.S. 40, 40 L. Ed. 2d 642, 94 S. Ct. 2116 (1974)
Street v. New York, 394 U.S. 576, 22 L. Ed. 2d 572, 89 S. Ct. 1354 (1969)

Note—In July 1984, the Court (7–2) held that women must be admitted to membership in Jaycees (*Roberts* v. *Jaycees,* 82 L. Ed. 2d 462, 1984) the Court asserted that a Minnesota state law compelling Jaycees to accept women as members did not violate freedom of association and could cover the Jaycees since local chapters were not small, intimate, and selective. The Court uses essentially the same reasoning in opening up Rotary International to women. The state had a "compelling interest" in eradicating discrimination. With strong consistency the Court, voting 9–0 made a clean sweep in *New York State Club Ass'n* v. *New York City* (101 L. Ed. 2d 1, 1988) holding that women must be admitted to large social clubs traditionally restricted to men. The Court dismissed the argument that these rulings violate the "right of association."

Meritor Savings Bank v. Vinson, 477 U.S. 815; 91 L. Ed. 2d 49; 106 S. Ct. 2399 (1986)

Respondent, a former female employee, claimed that during her employment at the bank she had been subjected to sexual harassment. She worked at the bank for four years, was discharged in November 1978, and sued in the district court claiming that during her four years at the bank she had constantly been subjected to sexual harassment by her supervisor in violation of Title VII. There was a good deal of conflicting testimony before an eleven-day bench trial. The bank denied knowledge of any sexual harassment. The district court denied relief. The Court of Appeals for the District of Columbia reversed. It also denied that the bank was without liability merely because it did not know of the harassment. Supreme Court granted certiorari.

OPINION BY CHIEF JUSTICE REHNQUIST
(Vote: 9–0)

Question—Does sexual harassment without economic loss creating a hostile or abusive work environment violate Title VII of the 1964 Civil Rights Act.

Decision—No.

Reason—Respondent asserted and the court of appeals affirmed that unwelcome sexual advances create an offensive or hostile working environment in violation of Title VII. The Court rejects petitioner's view that Title VII is concerned only with "economic" or "tangible" discrimination. Not all workplace conduct—such as "mere utterance of an ethnic or racial epithet"—effects the term, condition or privilege of employment. But actions that are severe or persuasive enough to alter the conditions of the victim's employment create an abusive working environment. That conduct was "voluntary" in the sense that the complainant was not forced against her will "is not a defense to a sexual harassment suit under Title VII." We refuse to accept the court of appeals view that petitioner Taylor was covered by his employer, the Bank, even though the employer neither knew nor reasonably could have known of the alleged misconduct. We hold that a claim of "hostile environment" sex discrimination is actionable under Title VII. We reject petitioner's view that the existence of a grievance, a policy against discrimination "coupled with respondent's failure to invoke that procedure, must insulate petitioner from liability." The court of appeals affirmed the decision.

Corollary cases

Los Angeles Department of Water and Power v. Manhart, 435 U.S. 702, 55 L. Ed. 2d 657, 98 S. Ct. 1370 (1978)

Griggs v. Duke Power Co., 401 U.S. 424, 28 L. Ed. 2d 158, 91 S. Ct. 849 (1971)

General Electric Co. v. Gilbert, 429 U.S. 125, 50 L. Ed. 2d 343, 97 S. Ct. 401 (1976)

Skidmore v. Swift & Co., 323 U.S. 134, 89 L. Ed. 124, 65 S. Ct. 161 (1944)

Banta v. United States, 434 U.S. 819, 54 L. Ed. 2d 76, 98 S. Ct. 60 (1977)

Shapiro v. Thompson, 394 U.S. 618; 89 S. Ct. 1322; 22 L. Ed. 2d 600 (1969)

Statutory provisions in Connecticut, Pennsylvania, and the District of Columbia denied welfare assistance to persons who were residents and met all other eligibility requirements except that they had not resided within the jurisdiction for at least a year immediately preceding their applications for assistance.

OPINION BY MR. JUSTICE BRENNAN
(Vote: 6–3)

Question—Does this statutory provision create a classification that constitutes discrimination involving denial of equal protection of the laws?

Decision—Yes.

Reason—The purpose of inhibiting migration into a state by needy persons is constitutionally impermissible. Our constitutional concepts of personal liberty require that all citizens be free to travel throughout the country without unreasonable restrictions. Where the right of interstate movement is involved, the constitutionality of a statute must be judged by the stricter standard of whether the statute promotes a *compelling* state interest. In the current instance the waiting period requirement was held clearly to violate the equal protection clause. In the matter of the District of Columbia, since only states are bound by the equal protection clause, the one-year requirement was held to violate the due process clause of the Fifth Amendment.

Corollary cases

Passenger Cases, 7 Howard 283 (1849)
United States v. Guest, 383 U.S. 745 (1966)
Memorial Hospital v. Maricopa County, 415 U.S. 250 (1974)
Graham v. Richardson, 403 U.S. 365 (1971)
Zemel v. Rusk, 381 U.S. 1 (1965)
Bolling v. Sharpe, 347 U.S. 497 (1954)
Zablocki v. Redhail, 434 U.S. 374 (1978)
Dunn v. Blumstein, 405 U.S. 330 (1972)
Gladstone, Realtors v. Village of Bellwood, 441 U.S. 91; 60 L. Ed. 2d 66 (1979)
Hicklin v. Orbeck, 437 U.S. 475; 57 L. Ed. 2d 397 (1978)
McCarthy v. Philadelphia Civil Service Commission, 424 U.S. 645 (1976)

Note—Throughout the litany of the cases dealing with classification and equal protection is the basic concept of reasonableness. Any arbitrary classification is inherently bad. Thus, the residence requirement, under the Voting Rights Act of 1970, is thirty days in a presidential election, which the Court felt in *Dunn v. Blumstein* (1972), was enough.

Reed v. Reed, 404 U.S. 71; 30 L. Ed. 2d 225; 92 S. Ct. 251 (1971)

Sally, a mother, separated from her husband and on the death of her adopted son filed a petition in the Probate Court

of Ada County, Idaho. She sought to be named administra-
trix of her son's (Richard) estate. Meanwhile the father,
Cecil, similarly wanted to be named administrator. Although
the Idaho Probate Code favored neither one nor the other,
the probate court appointed the father exclusively on his
maleness as the administrator. The separated wife appealed.

OPINION BY MR. CHIEF JUSTICE BURGER
(Vote: 9–0)

Question—In the selection of an administrator or administra-
trix of the estate of a deceased adopted minor son, can the
state base its decision on sex gender?

Decision—No.

Reason—"We have concluded that the arbitrary preference
established in favor of males by . . . the Idaho code cannot
stand in the face of the Fourteenth Amendment's command
that no state deny the equal protection of the laws to any
person within its jurisdiction." The Fourteenth Amendment
does not deny to states the power to treat different classes of
persons in different ways. "The equal protection clause of that
amendment does, however, deny to States the power to legislate that different treatment be accorded to persons placed by
a statute into different classes on the basis of criteria wholly
unrelated to the objective of that statute." The equal protection clause cannot be abridged merely for administrative convenience as suggested by Idaho or to avoid family controversy.
". . . the choice in this context may not lawfully be mandated
solely on the basis of sex."

Corollary cases

Frontiero v. Richardson, 411 U.S. 677 (1973)
Kahn v. Shevin, 416 U.S. 351 (1974)
Schlesinger v. Ballard, 419 U.S. 498 (1975)
Stanton v. Stanton, 421 U.S. 7 (1975)
Orr v. Orr, 440 U.S. 268 (1979)
Pittsburgh Press Co. v. Pittsburgh Commission on Human Relations, 413
   U.S. 376 (1973)
Geduldig v. Aiello, 417 U.S. 484 (1974)
Stanley v. Illinois, 405 U.S. 645 (1972)
Cleveland Board of Education v. La Fleur, 414 U.S. 632 (1974)

Lalli v. Lalli, 439 U.S. 259 (1978)
Rostker v. Goldberg, 453 U.S. 57 (1981)
Michael M. v. Superior Court of Sonoma County, 450 U.S. 464; 67 L. Ed. 2d
437 (1981)
Caban v. Mohammed, 441 U.S. 380 (1979)
Vance v. Bradley, 440 U.S. 93 (1979)
Duren v. Missouri, 439 U.S. 357 (1979)
Personnel Administrator of Massachusetts v. Feeney, 442 U.S. 256 (1979)

Note—The Burger Court's first opinion declared a state law invalid because it discriminated against women. Although sex is not in the "suspect classification," as decided in *Michael M.* v. *Sonoma County Superior Court,* 67 L. Ed. 2d 437 (1981) at 442, it is in the higher level of Court scrutiny and thus shifts to the legislature or executive the responsibility to demonstrate its classification as a compelling state interest.

Weinberger v. Wiesenfeld, 420 U.S. 636; 43 L. Ed. 2d 514; 95 S. Ct. 1225 (1975)

Stephen C. Wiesenfeld and Paula Polatschek were married in November 1970. Paula worked as a teacher before her marriage and continued to do so after her marriage. Her earnings were the couple's principal source of support and far exceeded her husband's. Thus, in 1971 she earned $10,686 and he $2,188. On June 5, 1972, Paula died in child birth. Stephen, her husband, had the sole responsibility of an infant son, Jason Paul. Stephen sought survivor's benefits for himself and his son. He obtained benefits for his son but not for himself since he was not eligible for benefits that, under the social security law, were available only to women.

OPINION BY MR. JUSTICE BRENNAN
(Vote: 8–0)

Question—Is it a violation of the equal protection requirements under the Fifth Amendment's due process clause for the Social Security Act to allow survivor's benefits to widows with minor children but not to widowers in the same situation?

Decision—Yes.

Reason—Although the framers of the Social Security Act legislated on the generally accepted presumption that a man is responsible for the support of his wife and child, today "such a gender-based generalization cannot suffice to justify the denigration of the efforts of women who do work and whose earnings contribute significantly to their families' support." The statute operates to "deprive women of protection for their families which men receive as a result of their employment." Said the Court: ". . . the Constitution . . . forbids the gender-based differentiation that results in the efforts of women workers required to pay social security taxes producing less protection for their families than is produced by the efforts of men." This gender-based classification is entirely irrational. "The classification discriminates among surviving children solely on the basis of the sex of the surviving parent."

Corollary cases

Stanton v. Stanton, 421 U.S. 7 (1975)
Craig v. Boren, 429 U.S. 190 (1975)
Mathews v. de Castro, 429 U.S. 181 (1976)
General Electric Company v. Gilbert, 429 U.S. 125 (1976)
Frontiero v. Richardson, 411 U.S. 677 (1973)
Califano v. Goldfarb, 430 U.S. 199 (1977)
Califano v. Webster, 430 U.S. 313 (1977)
Kahn v. Shevin, 416 U.S. 351 (1974)
Stanley v. Illinois, 415 U.S. 645 (1972)
Quilloin v. Walcott, 434 U.S. 246 (1978)
U.S. Dept. of Transportation v. Paralyzed Veterans of America, 91 L. Ed. 2d 494 (1986)
Traynor v. Turnage, 99 L. Ed. 2d 618 (1988)

Note—When based on nothing more than mere sex roles, the Court, to be sure, will declare the statute or administrative ruling a violation of equal protection. An exception was reached in *Rostker* v. *Goldberg,* 69 L. Ed. 2d 478 (1981), which permits Congress to register only men for the draft. In addition, the Court has refused to put "sex" under a "suspect classification."

Regents of the University of California v. Bakke, 438 U.S. 265; 57 L. Ed. 2d 750; 98 S. Ct. 2733 (1978)

Allan Bakke, a white male, twice applied (1973–1974) to the medical school of the University of California at Davis.

Despite strong "bench marks" (interviewers' summaries, overall grade point average, science courses grade point, MCAT scores, letters of recommendation, extracurricular activities, and other biographical data) he was rejected. Davis had two admissions programs for its entering class of 100 students, the regular and the special admissions program. The special admissions program set aside 16 seats in each class for various minority groups ("Blacks," "Chicanos," "Asians," and "American Indians") who did not compete with the 84 other applicants (who competed against one another) and who were not required to meet the grade point average of regular (nonminority) applicants. Bakke's overall scores were significantly higher than the special applicants. He brought suit claiming that the Davis "quota system" violated the California Constitution, the equal protection clause of the Fourteenth Amendment, and Title VI of the Civil Rights Act of 1964. The Supreme Court of California agreed and the United States Supreme Court granted certiorari.

<u>OPINION BY MR. JUSTICE POWELL</u>
(Vote: 5–4)

Question—Is (a) the admissions program of the University of California (at Davis) which set aside 16 class positions for minority students unlawful? (b) Are considerations of race in admissions programs always unlawful?

Decision—(a) Yes. (b) No. Note: Justice Powell voted with one majority on question "a" and voted again with another majority on question "b".

Reason—"When a classification denies an individual opportunities or benefits enjoyed by others solely because of his race or ethnic background, it must be regarded as suspect. The Davis admissions program of explicit racial classification has never been countenanced by this court." It tells applicants who are not "minorities" that no matter how superior or strong their qualifications they will never be allowed the chance to compete for admission with all the other applicants. Racial and ethnic classifications are inherently suspect and call for exacting judicial scrutiny. The Davis program operated as a racial quota and is invalidated. But Title VI of the Civil

Rights Act of 1964 prescribes only those racial classifications that would violate the equal protection clause if employed by a state or its agencies. The California Supreme Court erred in holding that race can never be considered in evaluating an applicant for the "state has a substantial interest that legitimately may be served by a properly devised admissions program involving the competitive consideration of race and ethnic origin."

Corollary cases

Massachusetts Board of Retirement v. Murgia, 427 U.S. 307 (1976)
San Antonio Indep, School District v. Rodriguez, 411 U.S. 1 (1973)
Graham v. Richardson, 403 U.S. 365 (1971)
Lau v. Nichols, 414 U.S. 563 (1974)
Cort v. Ash, 422 U.S. 66 (1975)
Train v. Colorado Public Interest Research Group, 426 U.S. 1 (1976)
Missouri ex rel. Gaines v. Canada, 305 U.S. 337 (1938)
Sipuel v. Board of Regents, 332 U.S. 631 (1948)
Sweatt v. Painter, 339 U.S. 629 (1950)
McLaurin v. Oklahoma State Regents, 339 U.S. 637 (1950)
Hirabayashi v. United States, 320 U.S. 81 (1940)
Shelly v. Kraemer, 334 U.S. 1 (1948)
Skinner v. Oklahoma, 316 U.S. 535 (1942)
Rostker v. Goldberg, 453 U.S.—(1981)
Vance v. Bradley, 440 U.S. 93 (1979)
Reed v. Reed, 404 U.S. 71 (1971)
Orr v. Orr, 440 U.S. 268 (1979)

Note—*Bakke* is a landmark decision that has met criticism equal to that which came out of *Brown* v. *Board of Education,* 347 U.S. 483 (1954). The critics assert that *Brown* and *Bakke* contradict one another, with the former establishing reverse discrimination and the latter denouncing it; supporters agree that perhaps the California plan went too far, but a practical compromise is to utilize race among other factors to decrease past discrimination. What the Court did in *Bakke* was to move from deciding the issue on constitutional grounds to deciding the issue in light of the Civil Rights Act of 1964, indicating it was to be an active force in a continuous issue of our time—as it showed in *United Steel Workers of America* v. *Weber,* 443 U.S. 193 (1979) and in *Fullilove* v. *Klutznick,* 442 U.S. 448

(1980). In *Johnson* v. *Transportation Agency*, 94 L. Ed. 2d 615 (1987), the Court carried forward the constitutionality of classification based on sex largely on the bases of the promotion requirements of the *Weber* ruling.

Michael M. v. Superior Court of Sonoma County, 450 U.S. 464; 67 L. Ed. 2d 437; 101 S. Ct. 1200 (1981)

Michael M., a 17-year-old male, was charged with violating California's statutory rape law. The complaint, filed on behalf of the victim by her older sister, stated on June 3, 1978, petitioner and Sharon, the alleged victim of 16 years, met at a bus stop and soon moved away from their friends and began to kiss. Petitioner then made more sexual advances for which he was rebuffed. After being struck in the face, Sharon submitted to sexual intercourse. California's statutory rape law defines unlawful sexual intercourse as "an act of sexual intercourse accomplished with a female not the wife of the perpetrator, where the female is under the age of 18 years."

OPINION BY MR. JUSTICE REHNQUIST
(Vote: 5–4).

Question—Is California's statutory rape law a gender-based discriminatory law in violation of the equal protection clause of the Fourteenth Amendment since only females can be victims and only males can be violators?

Decision—No.

Reason—"We hold that the Equal Protection Clause does not demand that a statute necessarily apply equally to all persons or . . . things which are different in fact . . . to be treated as though they were the same. . . . We need not be medical doctors to discern that young men and women are not similarly situated with respect to the problems and risks of sexual intercourse. . . . All of the significant harmful and inescapably identifiable consequences of teenage pregnancy fall on the young female . . . pregnancy itself constitutes a substantial deterrence to young females. . . . A criminal sanction imposed solely on males thus serves roughly to equalize the deterrents on the sexes."

Corollary cases

Craig v. Boren, 429 U.S. 190 (1976)
Reed v. Reed, 404 U.S. 71 (1971)
Parham v. Hughes, 441 U.S. 347 (1979)
Rundlett v. Oliver, 607 F. 2d 495 (Cal 1979)
Carey v. Population Services International, 431 U.S. 678 (1977)
Frontiero v. Richardson, 411 U.S. 677 (1970)

Hishon v. King & Spalding, 467 U.S. 69; 81 L. Ed. 2d 59; 104 S. Ct. 2299 (1984)

Petitioner, a female lawyer, was employed in 1972 as an associate in a large law firm in Atlanta. Respondent law firm was established as a general partnership and in 1980 consisted of 50 partners and employed approximately 50 lawyers as associates. She alleged that her initial decision to join the firm was based on the possibility of ultimately becoming a partner "as a matter of course" after five or six years for associates who receive satisfactory evaluations. In May 1978 Hishon was considered and rejected for admission to partnership. She filed a charge with the Equal Employment Opportunity Commission that she was discriminated against because of her sex under Title VII of the Civil Rights Act 1964. The district court dismissed the complaint, a United States Court of Appeals affirmed the decision, the Supreme Court granted certiorari.

OPINION BY CHIEF JUSTICE BURGER
(Vote: 9–0)

Question—Did the respondent law firm deny petitioner a partnership on grounds of sex and did respondent's promise to consider her on a "fair and equal basis" create a binding employment contract?

Decision—Yes.

Reason—Title VII of the Civil Rights Act of 1964 defines an unlawful practice for an employer to fail, refuse to hire, or discharge an individual or discriminate against an individual, because of race, color, religion, sex, or national origin. Petitioner alleges that the law firm is an employer. "A benefit that is part and parcel of the employment relationship may not be doled out in a discriminatory fashion. . . ." The benefit of partnership consideration "was allegedly linked directly with an associate's status as an employee, and this linkage was far more than coincidental. . . ." Once a contractual employment relationship is established, the provisions of Title VII attach, forbidding unlawful discrimination as to the "terms, conditions, or privileges of employment," which clearly include benefits that are part of the employment contract." The benefit a plaintiff is denied need not be employment "to fall within Title VII's protection; it need only be a term, condition, or privilege of employment." The statute or its legislative history does not support an exemption of partnership decisions from scrutiny. Respondent has not shown that "the application of Title VII in this case would infringe its constitutional rights of expression or association."

Corollary cases

Allied Chemical & Alkali Workers v. Pittsburgh Plate Glass Co., 404 U.S. 157, 30 L. Ed. 341, 92 S. Ct. 383 (1971)

Franks v. Bowman, 424 U.S. 747, 47 L. Ed. 2d 444 (1976), 96 S. Ct. 1251 (1976)

Albemarle Paper Co. v. Moody, 422 U.S. 405, 45 L. Ed. 2d 280, 95 S. Ct. 2362 (1975)

NAACP v. Button, 371 U.S. 415, 9 L. Ed. 2d 405, 83 S. Ct. 328 (1963)

Norwood v. Harrison, 413 U.S. 455, 37 L. Ed. 2d 723, 93 S. Ct. 2804 (1973)

Runyon v. McCrary, 427 U.S. 160, 49 L. Ed. 2d 415, 96 S. Ct. 2586 (1976)

Railway Mail Association v. Corsi, 326 U.S. 88, 89 L. Ed. 2072, 65 S. Ct. 1483 (1945)

SEARCH AND SEIZURE

California v. Greenwood, 486 U.S. _____; 100 L. Ed. 2d 30; 108 S. Ct. 1625 (1988)

Acting on information that Greenwood might be in the narcotics trade, the Laguna Beach police department asked the neighborhood's regular trash collector to pick up the plastic garbage bags at the curb in front of Greenwood's home. Before doing so the trash collector cleaned his truck bin of other refuse, picked up the plastic bags, and turned them over to the police. Searching through the bags an officer found evidence of narcotic use, which was used for a warrant to search Greenwood's home, where the police discovered quantities of cocaine and hashish.

OPINION BY JUSTICE WHITE
(Vote: 6–2)

Question—Does the Fourth Amendment prohibit the warrantless search and seizure of garbage left for collection outside the curtilage of a home.

Decision—No.

Reason—"The warrantless search and seizure of the garbage bags left at the curb outside the Greenwood house would violate the Fourth Amendment only if respondents manifested a subjective expectation of privacy in their garbage that society accepts as objectively reasonable." We conclude that the defendants—in exposing their garbage to the public helped defeat their claim to Fourth Amendment protection. It is common knowledge that garbage in plastic bags left on or at the site of a public street is readily accessible to animals, children, scavengers, snoops, and others of the public. Respondents ". . . could have had no reasonable expectation of privacy in the culpatory items that they discarded." The police, furthermore, ". . . cannot reasonably be expected to avert their eyes from evidence of criminal activity that could have been observed by any member of the public. In *Smith* v. *Maryland* (1979) the police did not violate the Fourth Amendment by causing a pen register to be installed at the telephone company's office to record the telephone numbers dialed by a criminal suspect and in *California* v. *Ciraolo* (1986) the police were not "required by the Fourth Amendment to obtain a warrant before conducting surveillance of the respondent's fenced backyard from a private plane flying at an altitude of 1,000 feet."

Corollary cases

O'Connor v. Ortega, 480 U.S. _____, 94 L. Ed. 2d 714 107 S. Ct. 1492 (1987)
California v. Ciraolo, 476 U.S. 207, 90 L. Ed. 2d 210, 106 S. Ct. 1809 (1986)
Oliver v. United States, 466 U.S. 170, 80 L. Ed. 2d 214, 104 S. Ct. 1735 (1986)
Katz v. United States, 389 U.S. 347, 19 L. Ed. 2d 576, 88 S. Ct. 507 (1967)
Smith v. Maryland, 442 U.S. 735, 61 L. Ed 2d 220, 99 S. Ct. 2577 (1979)
Rakas v. Illinois, 439 U.S. 128, 58 L. Ed. 2d 387, 99 S. Ct. 421 (1978)
United States v. Leon, 468 U.S. 897, 82 L. Ed. 2d 677, 104 S. Ct. 3405 (1884)

Note—The holding in this case is predicated "common sense." Some cultural anthropologists regularly ransack the family garbage for scientific purposes. William Rathje, a Ph.D. from Harvard, is a "Garbologist" who studies garbage and its contents, which are logged in 185 categories. *Muncie Star* (Ind.), May 17, 1988.

Mapp v. Ohio, 367 U.S. 643; 81 S. Ct. 1684; 6 L. Ed. 2d 1081 (1961)

> Cleveland police officers requested admission to a home to seek a fugitive who was reportedly hiding there. They had also received information that a large amount of paraphernalia was hidden in the house. Without a warrant, the police forced their way into the house. There they found obscene materials. This evidence was used to convict Miss Mapp in the state courts.

OPINION BY MR. JUSTICE CLARK
(Vote: 6–3)

Question—Is evidence obtained in violation of the search and seizure provision of the Fourth Amendment admissible in a state court?

Decision—No.

Reason—Previous decisions have held that the security of one's privacy against arbitrary intrusion of the police is implicit in the concept of ordered liberty and as such enforceable against the states through the due process clause. However, the Court has previously refused to exclude evidence thus secured from state courts as "an essential ingredient of the right." Since the Fourth Amendment's right of privacy has been declared enforceable against the states through the due process clause of the Fourteenth Amendment, it is enforceable against them by the same sanction of exclusion as is used against the federal government. All evidence obtained by searches and seizures in violation of the Constitution is, by that same authority, inadmissible in a state court.

Corollary cases

Weeks v. United States, 232 U.S. 383 (1914)
Elkins v. United States, 364 U.S. 206 (1960)
Benanti v. United States, 355 U.S. 596 (1957)
Rea v. United States, 350 U.S. 214 (1956)
United States v. Rabinowitz, 339 U.S. 56 (1950)
United States v. Janis, 428 U.S. 433 (1976)
McNabb v. United States, 318 U.S. 332 (1943)
Rochin v. California, 342 U.S. 165 (1952)
Irvine v. California, 347 U.S. 128 (1954)
Breithaupt v. Abram, 352 U.S. 432 (1957)
Stefanelli v. Minard, 342 U.S. 117 (1951)
Ker v. California, 374 U.S. 23 (1963)
Linkletter v. Walker, 381 U.S. 618 (1965)
Washington v. Chrisman, 70 L. Ed. 2d 778 (1982)
Donovan v. Dewey, 69 L. Ed. 2d 262 (1981)
Steagald v. United States, 68 L. Ed. 2d 38 (1981)
Colorado v. Bannister, 449 U.S. 1 (1980)
New York v. Belton, 69 L. Ed. 2d 768 (1981)
Robbins v. California, 69 L. Ed. 2d 744 (1981)

Note—*Mapp,* which continues to be controversial, reversed *Wolf* v. *Colorado,* 338 U.S. 25 (1949). *Mapp* represents a still further extension of the "Gitlow doctrine," this time applying the Fourth Amendment to the states by means of the "liberty" and "due process" provision of the Fourteenth Amendment. It is worth noting that the protection one has under the Fourth Amendment does not cover the search of a motor home without a warrant. *California* v. *Carney,* 85 L. Ed. 2d 406, 1985.

Chimel v. California, 395 U.S. 752; 89 S. Ct. 2034; 23 L. Ed. 2d 685 (1969)

Three police officers searched the entire home of Chimel in Santa Ana, California. The officers had a warrant authorizing his arrest for the burglary of a coin shop but there was no search warrant. Chimel's wife admitted the officers to the house. Some items taken from the house at this time were admitted into Chimel's trial. He was convicted.

OPINION BY MR. JUSTICE STEWART
(Vote: 7–2).

Question—Can the warrantless search of an entire house be justified under the Fourth Amendment as incident to an arrest?

Decision—No.

Reason—Such a search is unreasonable and thus contrary to the Fourth Amendment. An arresting officer may search the person arrested in order to remove any weapons the prisoner might seek to use and to seize any evidence on the arrestee's person in order to prevent its concealment or destruction. Included here is the area from within which the prisoner might gain possession of a weapon or destructible evidence, the area under his immediate control. Stewart's opinion embodies an excellent survey of cases on search incident to arrest.

Corollary cases

Terry v. Ohio, 392 U.S. 1 (1968)
Sibron v. New York, 392 U.S. 40 (1968)
Weeks v. United States, 232 U.S. 383 (1914)
Marron v. United States, 275 U.S. 192 (1927)
Adams v. Williams, 407 U.S. 143 (1972)
United States v. Brignoni-Ponce, 422 U.S. 873 (1975)
Almeida-Sanchez v. United States, 413 U.S. 266 (1973)
Mapp v. Ohio, 367 U.S. 643 (1961)
Hill v. California, 401 U.S. 797 (1971)
United States v. Martinez-Fuerte, 428 U.S. 543 (1976)

United States v. Watson, 423 U.S. 411 (1976)
United States v. Santana, 427 U.S. 38 (1976)
Delaware v. Proust, 440 U.S. 686 (1979)
Mincey v. Arizona, 57 L. Ed. 2d 290 (1978)
Pennsylvania v. Mimms, 434 U.S. 106 (1977)
Steagald v. United States, 69 L. Ed. 2d 38 (1981)
Robbins v. California, 69 L. Ed. 2d 744 (1981)
Smith v. Maryland, 61 L. Ed. 2d 220 (1979)
Lo-Ji Sales, Inc. v. New York, 60 L. Ed. 2d 920 (1979)
Marshall v. Barlow's Inc., 436 U.S. 307 (1978)
United States v. Ramsey, 431 U.S. 607 (1977)
United States v. Miller, 425 U.S. 435 (1976)

Note—*Chimel* overrules *Harris* v. *United States,* 331 U.S. 145 (1947) and *United States* v. *Rabinowitz,* 339 U.S. 56 (1950).

Zurcher v. the Stanford Dailey, 436 U.S. 547; 56 L. Ed. 2d 525; 98 S. Ct. 1920 (1978)

On April 9, 1971, officers from the Palo Alto Police Department and the Santa Clara County Sheriff's Department were called to the Stanford University Hospital to remove demonstrators occupying administrative offices. They refused to leave peacefully and when nine policemen tried to force their way beyond the barricades they were attacked by clubs. All nine police were injured. The police could only identify two rioters but the student newspaper, the Stanford Dailey, on April 11, carried photos of the riot. The Santa Clara County prosecutor got a warrant to search the offices of the Stanford Dailey for negatives. The warrant contained no accusation against the newspaper and the search revealed only the photographs that had appeared. The district court held that since the newspaper was the innocent object of a search, the prosecutor should have sought a subpoena duces tecum rather than a search warrant. The court of appeals affirmed the decision.

OPINION BY MR. JUSTICE WHITE
(Vote: 5–3)

Question—Was a warrant, based on probable cause to search a newspaper office for evidence of crimes by third parties, a violation of the First and Fourth Amendments?

Decision—No.

Reason—A valid warrant may be "issued to search any property, whether or not occupied by a third party, at which there is probable cause to believe that fruits, instrumentalities, or evidence of a crime will be found." The Fourth Amendment speaks of search warrants issued on "probable cause" and particularly describing the place to be searched and the persons or things to be seized. As a ". . . constitutional matter they need not even name the person from whom the things will be seized." The critical element in a reasonable search is not that the owner of the property is suspected of crime, but that there is a reasonable cause that the "things" to be searched for are there. The issue is one of reasonableness and the Fourth Amendment does not forbid warrants where the press is involved. Properly administered the pre-conditions of a proper search warrant afford the press protection against alleged hazards—such as press confidentiality.

Corollary cases

Fisher v. United States, 425 U.S. 391 (1976)
United States v. Kahn, 41 U.S. 143 (1974)
Camara v. Municipal Court, 387 U.S. 523 (1967)
Carroll v. United States, 267 U.S. 132 (1925)
United States v. Ventresca, 380 U.S. 102 (1965)
Branzburg v. Hayes, 408 U.S. 665 (1972)
Michigan v. Summers, 69 L. Ed. 2d 340 (1981)
Donovan v. Dewey, 69 L. Ed. 2d 262 (1981)
Steagald v. United States, 68 L. Ed. 2d 38 (1981)

Note—The criticism and legislative fall-out after *Zurcher* was quick and widespread. A number of states have restricted police searches of newsrooms and require subpoenas, the issuance of which can be challenged in courts, and Congress itself has prohibited courts from issuing warrants to search "the products of news organizations and others engaged in First Amendment activities."

Marshall v. Barlow's, Inc., 436 U.S. 307; 56 L. Ed. 2d 305; 98 S. Ct. 1816 (1978)

On September 11, 1975, an inspector under the Occupational Safety and Health Act of 1970 (OSHA) entered Barlow's, Inc., an electrical and plumbing installation business, located in Pocatello, Idaho. No complaint had been made against Barlow, (Barlow's, Inc. had simply turned up in the agency's selection process) and the inspector demanded to conduct a search of the working areas but had no search warrant. Barlow refused on the basis of the Fourth Amendment. Despite a federal district court order, Barlow still refused to admit an inspector without a warrant. A three-judge court agreed with Barlow and the secretary of labor appealed.

OPINION BY MR. JUSTICE WHITE
(Vote 5–3)

Question—Is the statutory authorization for warrantless inspection under OSHA constitutional?

Decision—No.

Reason—"The warrant clause of the Fourth Amendment protects commercial buildings as well as private homes" and to hold otherwise would deny American colonial experience. The Fourth Amendment grew out of the experience with the writs of assistance. The Court has already held "that warrantless searches are generally unreasonable. . . ." The businessman, like the occupant of a residence, has a "constitutional right to go about his business free from unreasonable official entries upon his private commercial property." There are recognizable exceptions involving "pervasively regulated businesses," but they have a "history of government oversight that no reasonable expectation of privacy . . . could exist for a proprietor over the stock of such an enterprise," i.e., liquor and firearms. The authority to make warrantless searches settles unbridled discretion on administrative and field officers.

Corollary cases

United States v. Chadwick, 433 U.S. 1 (1977)
G. M. Leasing Corporation v. United States, 429 U.S. 338 (1977)
Camara v. Municipal Court, 387 U.S. 523 (1967)
See v. City of Seattle, 387 U.S. 541 (1967)
United States v. Biswell, 406 U.S. 311 (1972)
Colonnade Catering Corp. v. United States, 397 U.S. 72 (1970)
Katz v. United States, 389 U.S. 347 (1967)

Donovan v. Dewey, 69 L. Ed. 2d 262 (1981)
Steagald v. United States, 68 L. Ed. 2d 38 (1981)
Lo-Ji Sales v. New York, 60 L. Ed. 2d 920 (1979)

Note—Only this provision of OSHA (Occupational Safety and Health Act of 1970) was declared unconstitutional; the act itself was upheld in *Atlas Roofing, Inc.* v. *Occupational Safety and Health Review Commission,* 430 U.S. 442 (1977).

Ybarra v. Illinois, 444 U.S. 85; 62 L. Ed. 2d 238; 100 S. Ct. 338 (1979)

Police were issued a warrant to search a tavern and its bartender for possession of heroin. Upon entering they announced an intention to conduct a "cursory search for weapons," and proceeded to pat down the customers. One officer found on Ybarra "a cigarette pack with objects in it" that later was discovered to be heroin. He was then convicted of possession of heroin.

OPINION BY MR. JUSTICE STEWART
(Vote 6–3).

Question—Did the facts of the present case violate the Fourth and Fourteenth Amendments?

Decision—Yes.

Reason—The authorities had no reason to believe that anyone other than the bartender would be violating the law. Ybarra did not give the police any cause to believe that he had violated any law.

"Where the standard is probable cause, a search or seizure of a person must be supported by probable cause particularized with respect to that person. This requirement cannot be undercut or avoided by simply pointing to the fact that coincidentally there exists probable cause to search or seize another or to search the premises where the person may happen to be.

"Each patron who walked into the Aurora Tap Tavern . . . was clothed with constitutional protection against an unreasonable search or an unreasonable seizure.

"The initial frisk of Ybarra was simply not supported by a reasonable belief that he was armed and presently dangerous, a belief which this Court has invariably held must form the predicate to a pat-down of a person for weapons.''

Corollary cases

Sibron v. New York, 392 U.S. 40 (1968)
Rakas v. Illinois, 439 U.S. 128 (1978)
Katz v. United States, 389 U.S. 347 (1967)
Terry v. Ohio, 392 U.S. 1 (1967)
Lo-Ji Sales, Inc. v. New York, 60 L. Ed. 2d 920 (1979)
United States v. Di Re, 332 U.S. 581 (1948)
Marshall v. Barlow's, Inc., 436 U.S. 307 (1978)
United States v. Martinez Fuerte, 428 U.S. 543 (1976)
Camara v. Municipal Court, 387 U.S. 523 (1967)
Berger v. New York, 388 U.S. 41 (1967)
Michigan v. Summers, 69 L. Ed. 2d 340 (1981)
Steagald v. United States, 68 L. Ed. 2d 38 (1981)
Colorado v. Bannister, 449 U.S. 1 (1980)
Robbins v. California, 69 L. Ed. 2d 744 (1981)
New York v. Belton, 69 L. Ed. 2d 768 (1981)

Note—*Ybarra* turns on whether or not this search is the kind permitted in *Terry* v. *Ohio,* that is, a "pat down." The Court said no, but the dissent argued that since the police were executing a valid search warrant they were entitled to "pat down" the patrons in order to insure the officers' safety. The Constitution does not prohibit all searches or seizures, but only those that are "unreasonable." There is unhappily in this area no single line of cases evincing any logical development. See *Katz.* (1967)

Payton v. New York, 445 U.S. 573; 63 L. Ed. 2d 639; 100 S. Ct. 1371 (1980)

After detectives had assembled sufficient evidence to establish probable cause that Theodore Payton had murdered the manager of a gas station, six New York police officers went to Payton's apartment intending to arrest him. They had not obtained a warrant. After prying open the door and entering the apartment, the officers found no one home and proceeded to seize a .30 caliber shell casing that was in plain view. The casing was later admitted into evidence at Payton's murder trial. In due course, Payton surrendered to police, was indicted for murder, and moved to suppress the evidence taken from his apartment.

OPINION BY MR. JUSTICE STEVENS

(Vote: 6–3)

Question—Does the Fourth Amendment, made applicable to the states by the Fourteenth Amendment, prohibit the police from making a warrantless and nonconsensual entry into a suspect's home in order to make a routine felony arrest?

Decision—Yes.

Reason—Unreasonable searches or seizure the Court noted, conducted without any warrant at all are condemned by the plain language of the first clause of the Fourth Amendment. "The simple language of the Amendment applies equally to seizures of persons and to seizures of property. It is a 'basic principle of Fourth Amendment law' that searches and seizures inside a home without a warrant are presumptively unreasonable. Yet it is also well-settled that objects such as weapons or contraband found in a public place may be seized by the police without a warrant." Absent exigent circumstances, a warrantless entry of the home to search for weapons is unconstitutional even when a felony has been committed and there is probable cause to believe that incriminating evidence will be found within. Neither "history nor this nation's experience requires us to disregard the overriding respect for the sanctity of the home that has been embedded in our tradition since the origins of the Republic."

Corollary cases

United States v. Watson, 423 U.S. 411 (1976)
Mapp v. Ohio, 367 U.S. 643 (1961)
Wolf v. Colorado, 338 U.S. 25 (1949)
Boyd v. United States, 116 U.S. 616 (1886)
Beck v. Ohio, 379 U.S. 89 (1964)
G. M. Leasing Corp. v. U.S. 429 U.S. 338 (1977)

United States v. Ross, 456 U.S.—; 72 L. Ed. 2d 572; 102 S. Ct. 2157 (1982)

Acting on information supplied by a reliable informant, the police stopped a described automobile and individual, opened the car's trunk, and discovered heroin. The police then drove the car to the police station where a warrantless search revealed a zippered leather pouch containing over $3,000 dollars in cash. Ross was charged with possession with intent to distribute. He was convicted in the district court, but the verdict was reversed by a court of appeals.

OPINION BY MR. JUSTICE STEVENS
(Vote: 6–3)

Question—Can the police, who have legitimately stopped an automobile with probable cause to believe that contraband is concealed somewhere within it, conduct a probing search of compartments and containers within the vehicle whose contents are not in plain view?

Decision—Yes.

Reason—Since its earliest days, Congress has recognized the impracticability of securing a warrant in cases involving the transportation of contraband goods, and in *Carroll* v. *United States,* 267 U.S. 132 (1925), the Court has emphasized the importance of the requirement that officers have probable cause to believe that the vehicle contains contraband.

"Probable cause . . . must be based on objective facts that could justify the issuance of a warrant by a magistrate and not merely on the subjective good faith of the police officers." A lawful search of a fixed premise generally extends to the entire area in which the object of the search may be found and is not limited by the possibility that separate acts of entry or opening may be required to complete the search.

"A warrant to search a vehicle would support a search of every part of the vehicle that might contain the object of the search. When a legitimate search is under way, and when its purpose and its limits have been precisely defined, nice distinctions between closets, drawers, and containers, in the case of a home, or between glove compartments, upholstered seats, trunks, and wrapped packages, in the case of a vehicle, must give way to the interest in the prompt and efficient completion of the task at hand. . . . We hold that the scope of the warrantless search authorized . . . is no broader and no narrower than a magistrate could legitimately authorize by warrant. If probable cause justifies the search of a lawfully stopped vehicle, it justifies the search of every part of the vehicle and its contents that may conceal the object of the search."

Corollary cases

Carroll v. United States, 267 U.S. 132 (1925)
Chambers v. Maroney, 399 U.S. 42 (1970)
Robbins v. California, 453 U.S. 420 (1981)
Arkansas v. Sanders, 442 U.S. 753 (1979)
Brinegar v. United States, 338 U.S. 160 (1949)
Henry v. United States, 361 U.S. 98 (1958)
United States v. Chadwick, 433 U.S. 1 (1977)
Cady v. Dombrowski, 413 U.S. 433 (1973)
Ex Parte Jackson, 96 U.S. 727 (1878)
Mincey v. Arizona, 437 U.S. 385 (1978)

Note—*Ross* is sure to alter—if not stop—the kinds of search-and-seizure-of-contraband cases that have plagued the Court. The police have been allowed greater freedom under the probable cause doctrine. it is now virtually co-extensive with a warrant. *Ross* neatly ties together previous doctrines involving movable entities and the Fourth Amendment.

California v. Ciraolo, 476 U.S. _____; 90 L. Ed. 2d 210; 106 S. Ct. 1809 (1986)

> Policemen acted on a tip that Ciraolo was growing marijuana in his backyard. Because of an inner and outer high fence it was difficult to see anything. The police secured a private plane and at an altitude of 1,000 feet flew over the marijuana patch, made naked- eye observations, and on this basis got a search warrant. The defendant pleaded guilty, the California Court of Appeals reversed and on certiorari the Supreme Court heard the case.

OPINION BY CHIEF JUSTICE BURGER
(Vote: 5–4)

Question—Is a warrantless aerial observation of a marijuana patch a violation of the Fourth Amendment?

Decision—No.

Reason—The touchstone of the Fourth Amendment analysis is whether a person has a "constitutionally protected reasonable expectation of privacy." The Fourth Amendment protection of the home "has never been extended to require law enforcement officers to shield their eyes when passing by a home on public thoroughfares." The police observations "took place within public navigable airspace . . . any member of the public flying in this airspace who glanced down could have seen everything that these officers observed." Justice Harlan noted that one who enters a telephone booth is entitled to assume that his conversation is not being intercepted; but this does not translate into "a rule of constitutional dimensions that one who grows illicit drugs in his backyard is entitled to assume his unlawful conduct will not be observed by a passing aircraft or by a power company repair mechanic on a pole overlooking the yard." The Fourth Amendment does not require police flying in public space to obtain a warrant in order to observe what is visible to the naked eye. Reversed.

Corollary cases

Oliver v. United States, 466 U.S. 170, 80 L. Ed. 2d 214, 104 S. Ct. 1735 (1984)

Katz v. United States, 389 U.S. 347, 19 L. Ed. 2d 576, 88 S. Ct. 507 (1967)

Smith v. Maryland, 442 U.S. 735, 61 L. Ed. 2d 220, 99 S. Ct. 2577 (1979)

Rawlings v. Kentucky, 448 U.S. 98, 65 L. Ed. 2d 633, 100 S. Ct. 256 (1980)

Boyd v. United States, 116 U.S. 616, 29 L. Ed. 246, 6 S. Ct. 524 (1886)

United States v. Knotts, 460 U.S. 276, 75 L. Ed. 2d 55, 103 S. Ct. 1081 (1983)

United States v. United States District Court, 407 U.S. 297, 32 L. Ed. 2d 752, 92 S. Ct. 2125 (1972)

Dow Chemical Co. v. United States, _____U.S., 90 L. Ed. 2d 226, 106 S. Ct. _____(1986)

Note—*Ciraola* (1986) and *Greenwood* (100 L. Ed. 2d 30, 1988) touch on the degree of "privacy" one can expect. An element also found in the doctrine of "plain view" is that a policeman can seize evidence that is in "plain view" during the investigation. See *Texas* v. *Brown*, (75 L. Ed. 2d 502, 1983) in which policemen seized a balloon they believed contained narcotics during a routine driver's license checkup.

SELF-INCRIMINATION

Olmstead v. United States, 277 U.S. 438; 48 S. Ct. 564; 72 L. Ed. 944 (1928)

This was a conspiracy to violate the National Prohibition Act by unlawfully possessing, transporting, and importing intoxicating liquors and maintaining nuisances, and by selling intoxicating liquors. Olmstead was the leading conspirator and the general manager of the business. One of the chief men was always on duty at the main office to receive orders by telephone and to direct their filling by a corps of men stationed in another room. The information that led to the discovery of the conspiracy and its nature and intent was largely obtained by intercepting messages on the telephones of the conspirators by four federal prohibition officers. However, the wire tapping was done outside the residence, and not in the offices but in the basement of the building housing the offices. All conversations were recorded, and the evidence of the wiretapping was used in court against the conspirators.

OPINION BY MR. CHIEF JUSTICE TAFT
(Vote: 5–4)

Question—Does the use of evidence of private telephone conversations between the defendants and others, intercepted by means of wire tapping, amount to a violation of the Fourth and Fifth Amendments?

Decision—No.

Reason—The Court ruled that there is no room for applying the Fifth Amendment unless the Fourth Amendment was first violated. Therefore, the Court limited its consideration to the Fourth Amendment. The amendment does not forbid what was done in this case. There was no searching. There was no seizure. The evidence was secured by the use of the sense of hearing and that only. There was no entry of the houses or offices of the defendants. By invention of the telephone and its application for the purpose of extending communications, one can talk with another at a far distant place. The language of the amendment cannot be extended and expanded to include telephone wires, reaching to the whole world from the defendant's house or office any more than to the highways along which they are stretched.

"A standard which would forbid the reception of evidence if obtained by other than nice ethical conduct by government officials would make society suffer and give criminals greater immunity than has been known heretofore. In the absence of controlling legislation by Congress, those who realize the difficulties in bringing offenders to justice may well deem it wise that the exclusion of evidence should be confined to cases where rights under the Constitution would be violated by admitting it."

Corollary cases

Adams v. New York, 192 U.S. 585 (1904)
Gouled v. United States, 255 U.S. 298 (1921)
South Dakota v. Opperman, 428 U.S. 364 (1976)
Weeks v. United States, 232 U.S. 383 (1914)
Nardone v. United States, 302 U.S. 379 (1937)
Benanti v. United States, 355 U.S. 96 (1957)
Goldman v. United States, 316 U.S. 129 (1942)
Weiss v. United States, 308 U.S. 321 (1939)
Berger v. New York, 388 U.S. 41 (1967)
Lopez v. U.S., 373 U.S. 427 (1963)
On Lee v. U.S., 343 U.S. 747 (1952)
Silverman v. U.S., 365 U.S. 505 (1961)

Note—*Olmstead* was overruled by *Katz* v. *United States,* 389 U.S. 347 (1967).

Adamson v. California, 332 U.S. 46; 67 S. Ct. 1672; 91 L. Ed. 1903 (1947)

Adamson, a citizen of the United States, was convicted, without recommendation for mercy, by a jury in the Superior Court of the state of California of murder in the first degree. Sentence of death was affirmed by the supreme court of the state.

The provisions of California law that were challenged permit the failure of a defendant to explain or deny evidence to be commented upon by the court and by counsel, and to be considered by the court and by the jury. These were challenged as invalid under the Fourteenth and Fifth Amendments.

OPINION BY MR. JUSTICE REED
(Vote: 5–4)

Question—Do the provisions of the California state constitution and its penal law abridge the guarantee against self-incrimination and of due process?

Decision—No.

Reason—The clause of the Fifth Amendment is not made effective by the Fourteenth Amendment as a protection against state action. The clause in the Bill of Rights is for the protection of the individual from the federal government, and its provisions are not applicable to the states. As a matter of fact, the Fourteenth Amendment forbids a state from abridging privileges of citizens of the United States, leaving the state free, so to speak, to abridge, within the limits of due process, the privileges and immunities of state citizenship.

A right to a fair trial is undoubtedly guaranteed by the Fourteenth Amendment. However, the due process clause does not include all the rights of the federal Bill of Rights under its protection. The purpose of due process is not to protect the accused against a proper conviction, but against an unfair conviction. The Court held that the state may control such a situation as this, where the defendant remains silent, with its own ideas of efficient administration of criminal justice.

Corollary cases

Barron v. Baltimore, 7 Peters 243 (1833)
Griffin v. California, 380 U.S. 609 (1965)
Twining v. New Jersey, 211 U.S. 78 (1908)
Palko v. Connecticut, 302 U.S. 319 (1937)
Wolf v. Colorado, 338 U.S. 25 (1949)
Illinois v. Allen, 397 U.S. 337 (1970)
Powell v. Alabama, 287 U.S. 45 (1932)
Adams v. Maryland, 347 U.S. 179 (1954)
Chambers v. State of Florida, 309 U.S. 227 (1940)
Haley v. State of Ohio, 332 U.S. 596 (1948)

United States v. Murdock, 284 U.S. 141 (1931)
Feldman v. United States, 322 U.S. 487 (1944)
Knapp v. Schweitzer, 357 U.S. 371 (1958)
Corbitt v. New Jersey, 58 L. Ed. 2d 466 (1979)
Lakeside v. Oregon, 55 L. Ed. 2d 319 (1978)
New Jersey v. Potash, 59 L. Ed. 2d 501 (1979)
Milton v. Wainwright, 407 U.S. 371 (1972)
Kastigar v. United States, 406 U.S. 441 (1972)
United States v. Mara, 410 U.S. 19 (1973)
United States v. Henry, 447 U.S. 264 (1980)

Note—*Adamson* was reversed by *Malloy* v. *Hogan,* 378 U.S. 1 (1964) and *Murphy* v. *New York Waterfront Commission,* 378 U.S. 52 (1964). *Griffin* v. *California,* 380 U.S. 609 (1965), along with reversing *Twining* v. *New Jersey,* 211 U.S. 78 (1902), also reversed *Adamson. Adamson* contains Justice Black's ringing affirmation of the total incorporation of the Bill of Rights.

Schmerber v. California, 384 U.S. 757; 86 S. Ct. 1826; 16 L. Ed. 2d 908 (1966)

Armando Schmerber had been convicted of driving an automobile while under the influence of intoxicating liquor. He had been arrested at a hospital while receiving treatment for injuries suffered in an accident involving the automobile he had apparently been driving. Under police direction a blood sample was taken from Schmerber by a physician at the hospital. This was done despite Schmerber's protests. Analysis of the sample of blood indicated intoxication, and the report of this analysis was admitted in evidence at the trial.

Opinion by Mr. Justice Brennan
(Vote: 5–4)

Question—Does taking a blood sample under these circumstances (1) deny the accused due process of law, (2) abridge the privilege against self-incrimination, (3) deny the right to counsel, and (4) constitute unreasonable search and seizure?

Decision—No on all four contentions.

Reason—(1) The case of *Breithaupt* v. *Abram* (352 U.S. 432, 1957) is controlling here. There a similar blood sample was taken while the individual was unconscious. This did not constitute offense against a "sense of justice" and thus there was no denial of due process. (2) *Breithaupt* also controls the self-incrimination aspect of the case. The privilege protects an accused person only from being compelled to testify against himself or otherwise provide the state with evidence of a testimonial or communicative nature. The taking and use of the blood sample did not involve compulsion to these ends. (3) Here there was no issue presented of counsel's ability to assist Schmerber in respect of any rights he did possess. (4) As to the search and seizure claim, there was plainly probable cause for the officer to arrest the accused. Further, the officer "might reasonably have believed that he was confronted with an emergency, in which the delay necessary to obtain a warrant, under the circumstances, threatened 'the destruction of the evidence'. . . . We are told that the percentage of alcohol in the blood begins to diminish shortly after drinking stops, as the body functions to eliminate it from the system."

Finally the Court noted that the test was performed in a reasonable manner in a hospital environment according to accepted medical practices and emphasized that the judgment was only on the basis of the facts of the present case.

Corollary cases

Brown v. Walker, 161 U.S. 591 (1896)
Rochin v. California, 342 U.S. 165 (1952)
Escobedo v. Illinois, 378 U.S. 478 (1964)
Miranda v. Arizona, 384 U.S. 436 (1966)
Twining v. New Jersey, 211 U.S. 78 (1908)
Malloy v. Hogan, 378 U.S. 1 (1964)
Mapp v. Ohio, 367 U.S. 643 (1961)

Note—*Schmerber* (conscious) must be contrasted with *Breithaupt* v. *Abram* (unconscious) and *Rochin* v. *California* (protesting and "shock the conscience"). The differences seem razor thin. Can a robbery suspect be forced to undergo surgery in order to extract a bullet but in doing so run the risk of incriminating himself? The Court said "No" in *Winston* v. *Lee* (84 L. Ed. 2d 662, 1985).

Marchetti v. United States, 390 U.S. 39; 88 S. Ct. 697; 19 L. Ed. 2d 889 (1968)

James Marchetti was convicted in federal district court in Connecticut (where there are numerous criminal penalties for gambling) for violation of federal statutes requiring the payment of an annual gambling occupational stamp tax and for failing to register before accepting wagers. These requirements were part of an intricate system of federal taxation applying to wagering, and the registration requirement was designed to aid the collection of the taxes. The arrangement was challenged as being unconstitutional.

OPINION BY MR. JUSTICE HARLAN
(Vote: 7–1)

Question—Are the methods employed by Congress in the federal wagering tax statutes consistent with the guarantee against self-incrimination contained in the Fifth Amendment?

Decision—No.

Reason—The federal International Revenue Service makes available to state law enforcement agencies the names and addresses of those who have paid the wagering tax. This creates a real and appreciable hazard of self-incrimination. The likelihood that any past or present gambling offenses will be discovered is increased. The tax provisions obliges even a prospective gambler to accuse himself of conspiracy to violate laws. Further, the premise that the self-incrimination guarantee is entirely inapplicable to prospective acts is too narrow an application of the privilege. Not merely time or a chronological formula must be considered but also the substantiality of the risks of incrimination. Those persons who properly assert the constitutional privilege as to these wagering tax provisions may not be criminally punished for failure to comply with their requirements.

Corollary cases

License Tax Cases, 5 Wallace 462 (1867)
United States v. Doremus, 249 U.S. 86 (1919)
United States v. Sullivan, 274 U.S. 259 (1927)

Shapiro v. United States, 335 U.S. 1 (1948)
Murphy v. Waterfront Commission, 378 U.S. 52 (1964)
Bailey v. Drexel Furniture Co., 259 U.S. 20 (1922)
Ullmann v. United States, 350 U.S. 422 (1956)
Grosso v. United States, 390 U.S. 62 (1968)
Sonzinsky v. United States, 300 U.S. 506 (1937)
Andresen v. Maryland, 427 U.S. 463 (1976)
United States v. Miller, 425 U.S. 435 (1976)
Albertson v. Subversive Activities Control Board, 382 U.S. 70 (1965)
Mackey v. United States, 401 U.S. 667 (1971)
United States v. Euge, 444 U.S. 707 (1980)

Note—*Marchetti* overruled *United States* v. *Kahriger,* 345 U.S. 22 (1953) and *Lewis* v. *United States,* 348 U.S. 419 (1955).

Katz v. United States, 389 U.S. 347; 88 S. Ct. 507; 19 L. Ed. 2d 576 (1967)

Charles Katz was convicted in federal district court in California of violation of federal communication statutes by transmitting wagering information by telephone from Los Angeles to Miami and Boston. At the trial, evidence was introduced of Katz's telephone conversations at his end overheard by FBI agents who had attached an electronic listening and recording device to the outside of the public telephone booth from which Katz had placed his calls. The court of appeals had rejected the contention that the recordings had been obtained in violation of the Fourth Amendment because there was "no physical entrance into the area occupied" by the accused.

OPINION BY MR. JUSTICE STEWART
(Vote: 7–1)

Question—Was the search and seizure conducted in this case in compliance with constitutional standards?

Decision—No.

Reason—The Fourth Amendment protects people and not simply "areas" against unreasonable searches and seizures. The reach of that amendment cannot turn upon the presence or absence of a physical intrusion into any given enclosure. The protection does not extend only to tangible property and to incidents where there has been trespass. What a person seeks to preserve as private, even in an area accessible to the public, may be constitutionally protected.

In this case the surveillance was so narrowly circumscribed that a judge could have authorized the search and seizure. Omission of this authorization bypassed the safeguards provided by an objective predetermination of probable cause and substituted instead the far less reliable procedure of an after-the-event justification. This sort of bypassing leaves individuals secure from Fourth Amendment violations only in the discretion of the police.

Corollary cases

Berger v. New York, 388 U.S. 41 (1967)
Silverman v. United States, 365 U.S. 505 (1961)
Osborn v. United States, 385 U.S. 323 (1966)
Warden v. Hayden, 387 U.S. 294 (1967)
Rios v. United States, 364 U.S. 253 (1960)
On Lee v. United States, 343 U.S. 747 (1952)
Nardone v. United States, 302 U.S. 379 (1937); 308 U.S. 338 (1939)
Dalia v. United States, 60 L. Ed. 2d 177 (1979)
Rathbun v. United States, 355 U.S. 107 (1957)
Benanti v. United States, 355 U.S. 96 (1957)
Camara v. Municipal Court, 387 U.S. 523 (1967)
Olmstead v. United States, 277 U.S. 438 (1928)
Agnello v. United States, 269 U.S. 20 (1925)
Weeks v. United States, 232 U.S. 383 (1914)
United States v. United States District Court, 407 U.S. 297 (1972)
United States v. Caceres, 59 L. Ed. 2d 733 (1979)
Smith v. Maryland, 61 L. Ed. 2d 220 (1979)
Scott v. United States, 56 L. Ed. 2d 220 (1972)
United States v. New York Telephone Co. 434 U.S. 159 (1977)

Note—*Katz* overruled *Olmstead* and *Goldman* v. *United States,* 316 U.S. 129 (1942). The Court distinguished between domestic and foreign wiretapping in *United States* v. *United States District Court,* 407 U.S. 297 (1972).

SELF-INCRIMINATION—IMMUNITY

Ullmann v. United States, 350 U.S. 422; 76 S. Ct. 497; 100 L. Ed. 511 (1956)

Congress in 1954 passed the Immunity Act providing that whenever, in the judgment of a United States attorney, the testimony of any witness, or the production of books, papers, or other evidence by any witness, in any case or proceeding before any grand jury or court of the United States involving any interference with or endangering of national security (including certain specified federal statutes) is necessary to the public interest, the United States attorney, upon the approval of the attorney general, shall make application to the court for an order to the witness to testify. However, the witness cannot subsequently be prosecuted in any court on the basis of the testimony he then gives.

William L. Ullmann refused to answer questions regarding espionage activity before a grand jury of the Southern District of New York despite the statutory provision of immunity, and he was convicted of contempt.

OPINION BY MR. JUSTICE FRANKFURTER
(Vote: 7–2)

Question—Is the immunity provided by the act sufficiently broad to displace the protection afforded by the Constitutional privilege against self-incrimination?

Decision—Yes.

Reason—The Immunity Act protects a witness who is compelled to answer to the extent of his Constitutional immunity, that is, giving testimony that might possibly expose him to a criminal charge. The immunity thus granted by the statute is also effective as against state action. "We cannot say that Congress's paramount authority in safeguarding national security does not justify the restriction it has placed on the exercise of state power for the more effective exercise of conceded federal power." The Court noted that the sole concern of the privilege against self-incrimination "is, as its name indicates, with the danger to a witness forced to give testimony leading to the infliction of 'penalties affixed to the criminal acts. . . .' Immunity displaces the danger. Once the reason for the privilege ceases, the privilege ceases."

The Court also noted that the act does not impose a nonjudicial function on the district court since this court has no discretion to deny an application for an order requiring a witness to answer, assuming that the statutory requirements have been met.

Corollary cases

Brown v. Walker, 161 U.S. 591 (1896)
Hale v. Henkel, 201 U.S. 43 (1906)
Adams v. Maryland, 347 U.S. 179 (1954)
Boyd v. United States, 116 U.S. 616 (1886)
Slochower v. Board of Higher Education of New York City, 350 U.S. 551 (1956)
Kastigar v. United States, 406 U.S. 441 (1972)
Adamson v. California, 332 U.S. 46 (1947)
Beilan v. Board of Education, 357 U.S. 399 (1958)
Marchetti v. United States, 390 U.S. 39 (1968)
Grosso v. United States, 390 U.S. 62 (1968)
United States v. Euge, 444 U.S. 707 (1980)
See citations at Molloy v. Hogan, 378 U.S. 1 (1964)

Note—In *Kastigar* v. *United States,* 406 U.S. 441 (1972) the Court distinguished between "use immunity," co-extensive with the guarantee of the Fifth Amendment, and "transactional immunity," wider than the Fifth Amendment. The Court has said only the former immunity is required.

Murphy v. Waterfront Commission of New York Harbor, 378 U.S. 52; 84 S. Ct. 1594; 12 L. Ed. 2d 678 (1964)

A number of persons had been subpoenaed to testify at a hearing conducted by the Waterfront Commission concerning a work stoppage at the Hoboken, New Jersey, piers. Even though they were granted immunity from prosecution under the laws of New Jersey and New York, they refused to testify on the ground that the answers might tend to incriminate them "under *federal* law, to which the grant of immunity did not purport to extend."

OPINION BY MR. JUSTICE GOLDBERG
(Vote: 9–0)

Question—May a state compel a witness, whom it has immunized from prosecution under its laws, to give testimony that might then be used to convict him of a crime against the federal government?

Decision—No.

Reason—There is no continuing legal vitality to or historical justification for the rule that one jurisdiction within our federal structure may compel a witness to give testimony that could be used to convict him of a crime in another jurisdiction. "We hold that the constitutional privilege against self-incrimination protects a state witness against incrimination under federal as well as state law and a federal witness against incrimination under state as well as federal law . . . we hold the constitutional rule to be that a state witness may not be compelled to give testimony which may be incriminating under federal law unless the compelled testimony and its fruits cannot be used in any manner by federal officials in connection with a criminal prosecution against him."

Corollary cases

Malloy v. Hogan, 378 U.S. 1 (1964)
Adamson v. California, 332 U.S. 46 (1947)
Twining v. New Jersey, 211 U.S. 78 (1908)
Estelle v. Smith, 68 L. Ed. 2d 359 (1981)
Carter v. Kentucky, 67 L. Ed. 2d 241 (1981)
United States v. Apfelbaum, 445 U.S. 115 (1980)

Note—*Murphy* overruled *United States* v. *Murdock*, 284 U.S. 141 (1931) and *Feldman* v. *United States,* 332 U.S. 487 (1944). As in *Malloy,* there is now mutual immunity extended to witnesses in federal and state courts based on the Fifth Amendment's guarantee against self-incrimination.

Malloy v. Hogan, 378 U.S. 1; 84 S. Ct. 1489; 12 L. Ed. 2d 653 (1964)

William Malloy was arrested during a gambling raid in 1959 by Hartford, Connecticut, police. He was convicted and given a suspended sentence. Later he was held in contempt by a state court for refusal to answer questions on the basis of possible self-incrimination. The state court held that the Fifth Amendment was not applicable to state proceedings.

OPINION BY MR. JUSTICE BRENNAN
(Vote: 5–4)

Question—Is the Fifth Amendment privilege against self-incrimination safeguarded against state action by the Fourteenth Amendment?

Decision—Yes.

Reason—The same standards must determine whether the silence of an accused person in either a federal or a state proceeding is justified. "It would be incongruous to have different standards determine the validity of a claim of privilege based on the same feared prosecution, depending on whether the claim was asserted in a state or federal court."

Corollary cases

Murphy v. Waterfront Commission, 378 U.S. 52 (1964)
Barron v. Baltimore, 7 Peters 243 (1833)
Slaughterhouse Cases, 16 Wallace 36 (1873)
Maxwell v. Dow, 176 U.S. 581 (1900)
United States v. Cruikshank, 92 U.S. 542 (1876)
Adamson v. California, 332 U.S. 46 (1947)
Rochin v. California, 342 U.S. 165 (1952)
Breithaupt v. Abram, 352 U.S. 432 (1957)
Schmerber v. California, 384 U.S. 757 (1966)
Feldman v. United States, 322 U.S. 487 (1944)
Palko v. Connecticut, 302 U.S. 319 (1937)
Foster v. Illinois, 332 U.S. 134 (1947)
Louisiana v. Resweber, 329 U.S. 459 (1947)
Wolf v. Colorado, 338 U.S. 25 (1949)
Hoffman v. United States, 341 U.S. 479 (1951)
Murphy v. Waterfront Commission, 378 U.S. 52 (1964)
Griffin v. California, 380 U.S. 609 (1965)
Knapp v. Schweitzer, 357 U.S. 371 (1958)
United States v. Murdock, 284 U.S. 141 (1931)
Harris v. New York, 401 U.S. 22 (1971)
Ullmann v. United States, 350 U.S. 422 (1956)
Estelle v. Smith, 68 L. Ed. 2d 359 (1981)

Carter v. Kentucky, 67 L. Ed. 2d 241 (1981)
United States v. Apfelbaum, 445 U.S. 115 (1980)

Note—This decision reversed *Twining* v. *New Jersey,* 211 U.S. 78 (1908) and *Adamson* v. *California,* 332 U.S. 46 (1947). The due process clause of the Fourteenth Amendment extends the Fifth Amendment protection against self-incrimination to a state offender, as in *Murphy* v. *Waterfront Commission of New York Harbor,* 378 U.S. 52 (1964), and protects a state witness against self-incrimination under federal as well as state law.

JURIES

Hurtado v. California, 110 U.S. 516; 4 S. Ct. 111; 28 L. Ed. 232 (1884)

The plaintiff was charged by the district attorney with murder, by means of an information, in a California county court. Upon this alone and in the same court, the plaintiff was tried, the jury rendered a verdict of murder in the first degree, and the court sentenced him to death. The Supreme Court of California upheld the judgment. The plaintiff contended that under the due process clause of the Fourteenth Amendment he was entitled to a proper indictment by a grand jury before trial.

OPINION BY MR. JUSTICE MATTHEWS
(Vote: 7–1)

Question—In felony cases is an indictment by a grand jury a necessary part of "due process of law" guaranteed by the Fourteenth Amendment?

Decision—No.

Reason—The Court was of the opinion that the use of indictment by a grand jury was merely one process of the common law handed down to us from the courts of England. It is not a necessary part of the law but merely the way the law has been used. To hold that such a characteristic is essential to due process of law would be to render it incapable of progress or improvement. The information "is merely a preliminary proceeding, and can result in no final judgment, except as a consequence of a regular judicial trial, conducted precisely as in cases of indictments." Therefore the Court reasoned that mere usage of the law at the time the due process clause was added to the Constitution does not imply that that usage is the only means of due process of law.

New procedure does not deny due process. Due process of law must mean more than the actual existing law of the land. "It follows that any legal proceedings enforced by public authority, whether sanctioned by age and custom, or newly devised in the discretion of the legislative power, in furtherance of the general public good, which regards and preserves these principles of liberty and justice, must be held to be due process of law.''

Corollary cases

Munn v. Illinois, 94 U.S. 113 (1877)
Walker v. Savinet, 92 U.S. 90 (1876)
Davidson v. New Orleans, 96 U.S. 97 (1878)
Maxwell v. Dow, 176 U.S. 581 (1900)
Twining v. New Jersey, 211 U.S. 78 (1908)
Patton v. United States, 281 U.S. 276 (1930)

Note—The grand jury provision has not been incorporated. The grand jury is not widely used in the states although, of course, it is used in the federal courts. Largely on the basis of efficiency and economy the grand jury is giving way to "information" by which the prosecuting officer—under oath—charges a person with a crime. In *Hobby* v. *United States* (82 L. Ed. 2d 260, 1984) the Court held that racial or sexual discrimination in the selection of a grand jury foreman does not reverse a white male's conviction because the foreman's role is not so significant. The Court held that the deliberate use of peremptory challenges in order to exclude blacks from a jury may provide the defendant with an equal protection claim (*Batson* v. *Kentucky,* 90 L. Ed. 2d 69, 1986). In an interracial capital case (*Turner* v. *Murray,* 90 L. Ed. 2d 27, 1986) the defendant was entitled to have prospective jurors informed of the race of the person killed and questioned on racial bias.

Norris v. Alabama, 294 U.S. 587; 55 S. Ct. 579; 79 L. Ed. 1074 (1935)

Norris was one of nine Negro youths who were indicted in 1931 in Jackson County, Alabama, for the crime of rape. They were tried and convicted in Morgan County, Alabama, on change of venue. Norris claimed that his rights guaranteed to him by the Fourteenth Amendment had been violated because the juries that indicted and tried him were chosen in the exclusion of Negroes. The state contended that even if it were assumed that there was no name of a Negro on the jury roll, it was not established that race or color caused the omission. They said in this case the commission drawing up the jury did not take into consideration race or color, and that no one had been excluded because of race or color.

<u>OPINION BY MR. CHIEF JUSTICE HUGHES</u>
(Vote: 8–0)

Question—Was this a violation of the Fourteenth Amendment?

Decision—Yes.

Reason—The evidence produced disclosed that Negroes had never been called for jury duty in the two counties involved in this case. Furthermore, it was disclosed that there were some qualified Negroes in these counties. The Court reasoned that this was prima facie evidence that Negroes were denied jury duty because of their race or color, and this was therefore contrary to the Constitution.

Corollary cases

Powell v. Alabama, 287 U.S. 45 (1932)
Strauder v. West Virginia, 100 U.S. 303 (1880)
Neal v. Delaware, 103 U.S. 370 (1881)
Adkins v. Texas, 325 U.S. 398 (1945)
Virginia v. Rives, 100 U.S. 313 (1880)
Pierre v. Louisiana, 306 U.S. 354 (1939)
Johnson v. Louisiana, 406 U.S. 356 (1972)
Smith v. Texas, 311 U.S. 128 (1940)
Hill v. Texas, 316 U.S. 400 (1942)
Parker v. Gladden, 385 U.S. 363 (1966)
Duncan v. Louisiana, 391 U.S. 145 (1968)
United States v. Jackson, 390 U.S. 570 (1968)
Witherspoon v. Illinois, 391 U.S. 510 (1968)
Apodaca v. Oregon, 406 U.S. 404 (1972)
Duren v. Missouri, 439 U.S. 357 (1979)

Note—*Norris* is the second "Scottsboro case." The first was *Powell* v. *Alabama,* 287 U.S. 45 (1932), which applied to the states the guarantee of counsel provision of the Sixth Amendment if certain circumstances were present. At this time the Sixth Amendment had not been incorporated. The "Gitlow doctrine" did not incorporate the Sixth Amendment until *Gideon* v. *Wainwright,* 372 U.S. 335 (1963).

Patton v. State of Mississippi, 332 U.S. 463; 68 S. Ct. 184; 92 L. Ed. 76 (1948)

A Negro was indicted in the circuit court of Lauderdale County, Mississippi, by an all-white grand jury. He was charged with the murder of a white man. He was convicted by an all-white petit jury and sentenced to death by electrocution. The defendant Negro introduced evidence that in thirty years no Negro had served on a grand or petit jury in this county. He contended that this violated his rights under the Fourteenth Amendment.

OPINION BY MR. JUSTICE BLACK

(No evidence from the report that the decision was not unanimous.)

Question—Was there denial of equal protection in the selection of jurors?

Decision—Yes.

Reason—The Court recalled that, sixty-seven years before, the Court had held that the exclusion of Negroes from grand and petit juries solely because of their race denied Negro defendants in criminal cases equal protection of the laws required by the Fourteenth Amendment. The Court said there had been an unbroken line of decisions upholding the same principle, and held the facts to be the determining principle. The law provided that a juror must be a male citizen and a qualified elector in the state. The registration lists contained several hundred Negro electors. The circuit clerk of the county, charged with administrative duties, sent the names of eight Negroes to the jury commissioner. None was ever called, and the record showed that no Negro had served on a grand or petit jury for thirty years.

This was evidence that administrative practice was responsible, and that the state should have corrected the situation. This proved that there had been a systematic exclusion of Negroes from juries solely because of race, and such was a denial of the equal protection of the law for Negro defendants. Indictments and verdicts against Negroes under such circumstances cannot stand. The proper action of officials in such matters will have to be determined from the facts in cases as they arise.

Corollary cases

Strauder v. State of West Virginia, 100 U.S. 303 (1880)
Hill v. State of Texas, 316 U.S. 400 (1942)
Norris v. Alabama, 294 U.S. 587 (1935)
Alexander v. Louisiana, 405 U.S. 625 (1972)
Patton v. United States, 281 U.S. 276 (1930)
Akins v. Texas, 325 U.S. 398 (1945)
Cassell v. Texas, 339 U.S. 282 (1950)
Moore v. Dempsey, 261 U.S. 86 (1923)
Shepherd v. Florida, 341 U.S. 50 (1951)
Hernandez v. Texas, 347 U.S. 475 (1954)
Duren v. Missouri, 58 L. Ed. 2d 579 (1979)

Duncan v. Louisiana, 391 U.S. 145; 20 L. Ed. 491; 88 S. Ct. 1444 (1968)

Duncan, a black youth, was convicted of simple battery, a misdemeanor punishable by two years imprisonment and a $300 fine. He had slapped a white youth and was sentenced in a Louisiana parish court to sixty days and $150 fine. Duncan requested a jury trial and it was denied because the Louisiana constitution granted jury trials only in capital punishment cases or in cases of imprisonment at hard labor. He appealed the case to the Supreme Court contending that in sentences of two years or more the Sixth and Fourteenth Amendments secured citizens the right of a jury trial.

OPINION BY MR. JUSTICE WHITE
(Vote: 7–2)

Question—Is the state of Louisiana required to afford the accused a jury trial, under the Sixth and Fourteenth Amendments, in criminal prosecutions?

Decision—Yes.

Reason—The Fourteenth Amendment denies the states the power to "deprive any person of life, liberty, or property, without due process of law," and in determining the meaning of this language the Court looks for guidance to the Bill of Rights. Many of these rights already have been held to be protected against state action by the due process clause of the Fourteenth Amendment. Against the position of the state of Louisiana to the contrary, "we believe that trial by jury in criminal cases is fundamental to the American scheme of justice. We hold that the Fourteenth Amendment guarantees a right of jury trial in all criminal cases which—were they to be tried in a federal court—would come within the Sixth Amendment's guarantee. Since we consider the appeal before us to be such a case, we hold that the Constitution was violated when Duncan's demand for jury trial was refused. The nation has a deep commitment to the right of jury trial and is reluctant to entrust plenary powers over the life and liberty of the citizen to one judge or to a group of judges."

Corollary cases

Taylor v. Louisiana, 419 U.S. 522 (1975)
Ristaino v. Ross, 424 U.S. 589 (1976)
Test v. United States, 420 U.S. 42 (1975)
United States v. Calandra, 414 U.S. 338 (1974)
Parker v. Gladden, 385 U.S. 363 (1966)
Maxwell v. Dow, 176 U.S. 581 (1900)
Patton v. United States, 281 U.S. 276 (1930)
Singer v. United States, 380 U.S. 24 (1965)
Patton v. Mississippi, 332 U.S. 463 (1947)
Burch v. Louisiana, 441 U.S. 130 (1979)
Duren v. Missouri, 58 L. Ed. 2d 579 (1979)
Ballew v. Georgia, 435 U.S. 223 (1978)
Chandler and Granger v. Florida, 449 U.S. 560 (1981)
Rosales-Lopez v. United States, 69 L. Ed. 2d 22 (1981)
Smith v. Phillips, 71 L. Ed. 2d 78 (1982)
Brown v. Louisiana, 65 L. Ed. 2d 159 (1980)
Godfrey v. Georgia, 446 U.S. 420 (1980)
Prenell v. Georgia, 439 U.S. 14 (1978)
Rose v. Mitchell, 443 U.S. 76 (1979)

Note—Reversed *Jordan* v. *Massachusetts,* 225 U.S. 167 (1912) and *Maxwell* v. *Dow,* 176 U.S. 581 (1900).

Duren v. Missouri, 439 U.S. 357; 58 L. Ed. 2d 579, 99 S. Ct. 664 (1979)

In 1975 Duren was indicted in a circuit court of Jackson County, Mo., for first degree murder and first degree rob-

bery. He contended that his right to trial by jury from a fair
cross section of the community was denied by a provision of
the Missouri law that granted women who requested it an
automatic exemption from jury service. The jury selection
process in Jackson County randomly selected from the voter
registration list. In addition to several exempted categories,
the one on women stated:

Any woman who elects not to serve will fill out this
paragraph and mail this questionnaire to the jury commissioner at once.

Even those women who do not return the summons are
treated as having claimed exemption if they fail to appear
for jury service on the appointed day. Under this system
only about 15 percent of jurors were women.

OPINION BY MR. JUSTICE WHITE
(Vote: 8–1)

Question—Was Duren denied, under the Sixth Amendment, an
impartial jury (the Constitution's fair cross section requirement)?

Decision—Yes.

Reason—Petitioner Duren proved that the Jackson County,
Missouri, community has an adult population of whom over
half are women and that the jury venires containing approximately 15 percent women are not reasonably representative of
the community. This "gross discrepancy," requires "the conclusion that women were not fairly representative in the source
from which petit juries were drawn. . . ." Petitioner demonstrated that the underrepresentation of women was due to "the
operation of Missouri's exemption criteria—whether for the
automatic exemption for women or other statutory exemptions. . . ." States remain free to prescribe relevant qualifications for their jurors and provide reasonable exemptions "so
long as it may fairly be said that the jury lists or panels are
representative of the community." But exempting all women
because of "the preclusive domestic responsibilities of some
women is insufficient justification for their disproportionate
exclusion on jury venires." The constitutional guarantee to a
jury drawn from a fair cross section of the community "requires that states exercise proper caution."

Corollary cases

Taylor v. Louisiana, 419 U.S. 522 (1975)
Duncan v. Louisiana, 391 U.S. 145 (1968)
Burch v. Louisiana, 60 L. Ed. 2d (1979)
Ballew v. Georgia, 55 L. Ed. 2d 234 (1978)
Daniel v. Louisiana, 420 U.S. 31 (1975)
Murphy v. Florida, 421 U.S. 794 (1975)
Johnson v. Louisiana, 406 U.S. 356 (1972)
Apodaca v. Oregon, 406 U.S. 404 (1972)

CRUEL AND UNUSUAL PUNISHMENT

Thompson v. Oklahoma, 487 U.S. _____; 101 L. Ed. 2d 702; 108 S. Ct. 2687 (1988)

> William Wayne Thompson was tried and found guilty of murder and sentenced to death. At the time of the offense he was 15 years old. Under Oklahoma law a boy of that age is a "child". Under the law the "child" can be tried as an adult if the prosecution shows the prosecutive merit of the case and there are no reasonable prospects for rehabilitation within the juvenile system. Supreme Court granted certiorari.

OPINION BY JUSTICE STEVENS
(Vote: 5–3)

Question—Does capital punishment for a convicted murderer who was 15 years old at the time of the crime violate the cruel and unusual punishment provision of the Eighth Amendment.

Decision—Yes.

Reason—Contemporary standards of decency "confirm our judgment that such a young person is not capable of acting with the degree of culpability that can justify the ultimate penalty." The experience of mankind and the history of our law recognizes "that there are differences which must be accommodated in determining the rights and duties of children as compared with those of adults." Other than the special certification procedure (used in this instance by the prosecution) "apparently there are no Oklahoma statutes either civil or criminal that treat a person under 16 years of age as anything but a "child" . . . there is . . . complete or near unanimity among all 50 states and the District of Columbia in treating a person under 16 as a minor for several important purposes." The conclusion that it would "offend civilized standards of decency to execute a person who was less than 16 years old at the time of his or her offense" is consistent with the views expressed by respected professional organizations. A societal factor, moreover, involves American sensibility to jury behavior. The haphazard handing out of death sentences by capital juries was a prime factor in *Furman* v. *Georgia* (1972). Punishment should be related to culpability and "adolescents as a class are less mature and responsible than adults . . . (they) lack the experience, perspective, and judgment expected of adults. We conclude that the Eighth and Fourteenth Amendments prohibit the execution of a person who was under 16 years of age at the time of his or her offense."

Corollary cases

Bellotti v. Baird, 443 U.S. 622, 61 L. Ed. 2d 797, 99 S. Ct. 3035 (1979)
Weems v. United States, 217 U.S. 349, 54 L. Ed. 793, 30 S. Ct. 544, (1910)
Trop v. Dulles, 356 U.S. 86, 2 L. Ed. 2d 630, 78 S. Ct. 590 (1958)
Woodson v. North Carolina, 428 U.S. 280, 49 L. Ed. 2d 944, 96 S. Ct. 2978 (1978)
Coker v. Georgia, 433 U.S. 584, 53 L. Ed. 2d 982, 97 S. Ct. 2861 (1977)
Edmund v. Florida, 458 U.S. 782, 73 L. Ed. 2d 1140, 102 S. Ct. 3368 (1982)
Furman v. Georgia, 408 U.S. 238, 33 L. Ed. 2nd 346, 92 S. Ct. 2726 (1972)
Schall v. Martin, 467 U.S. 253, 81, L. Ed. 2d 207, 104 S. Ct. 2403 (1984)
May v. Anderson, 345 U.S. 528, 97 L. Ed. 1221, 73 S. Ct. 840 (1953)
Parham v. JR, 442 U.S. 584, 61 L. Ed. 2d 101, 99 S. Ct. 2493 (1979)
Williams v. New York, 337 U.S. 241, 93 L. Ed. 1337, 69 S. Ct. 1079 (1949)
California v. Brown, 479 U.S. 538, 93 L. Ed. 2d 934, 107 S. Ct. 837 (1987)
Greg v. Georgia, 428 U.S. 153, 49 L. Ed. 2d 859, 96 S. Ct. 2909 (1976)
Lockett v. Ohio, 438 U.S. 586, 57 L. Ed. 2d 973, 98 S. Ct. 2954 (1978)

Note—*Thompson* is a 5–4 case. Although the majority held that executing a defendant who was 15 years old at the time the offense was committed is "cruel and unusual" punishment and violates "standards of decency," the Court was unable to agree on a majority opinion. The three dissenters argued that there was no national consensus holding that no juveniles can possibly ever be mature and responsible enough to be punished.

State of Louisiana ex rel. Francis v. Resweber, 329 U.S. 459; 67 S. Ct. 374; 91 L. Ed. 422 (1947)

Willie Francis, a colored citizen of Louisiana, was duly convicted of murder in September 1945 and sentenced to be electrocuted for the crime. Upon a proper death warrant,

Francis was prepared for execution on May 3, 1946, and was placed in the electric chair of the state of Louisiana in the presence of the authorized witnesses. The executioner pulled the switch, but, because of mechanical difficulty, death did not result. A new death warrant was issued by the governor of Louisiana, fixing the execution for May 9, 1946. Because of this, an appeal was made and execution of the sentence was delayed.

OPINION BY MR. JUSTICE REED
(Vote: 5–4)

Question—Did the experience through which Francis passed violate the principles of the Fifth and Eighth Amendments as to double jeopardy and cruel and unusual punishment, as applied by the due process clause of the Fourteenth Amendment, and of equal protection?

Decision—No.

Reason—First, there was no case of double jeopardy. To quote the Court, "We see no difference from a constitutional point of view between a new trial for error of law at the instance of the state that results in a death sentence instead of imprisonment for life and an execution that follows a failure of equipment." Second, there was no unusual and cruel punishment involved in this case. The petitioner claimed that the psychological strain was cruel and unusual punishment. The cruelty against which the Constitution protects a convicted man is cruelty inherent in the method of punishment, not the necessary suffering involved in any method employed to extinguish life humanely. Just because of mechanical failure there was not unusual or cruel punishment. Third, there was no denial of equal protection of the laws. The state of Louisiana did not single out Francis for special treatment that would not be applied to others. Equal protection does not extend to accidents. The Supreme Court, after reviewing the records of the trial, said there was no evidence in any of the papers to show any violation of petitioner's constitutional rights.

Corollary cases

Lisenba v. California, 314 U.S. 219 (1941)
Carter v. Illinois, 329 U.S. 173 (1946)

Ex parte Lange, 18 Wallace 163 (1874)
Furman v. Georgia, 408 U.S. 238 (1972)
Adamson v. California, 332 U.S. 46 (1947)
Palko v. Connecticut, 302 U.S. 319 (1937)
Robinson v. California, 370 U.S. 660 (1962)
Bordenkircher v. Hayes, 434 U.S. 357 (1978)

Note—The Court virtually incorporated the cruel and unusual punishment provisions of the Eighth Amendment in the due process clause of the Fourteenth. The incorporation was definitely accomplished in *Robinson* v. *California* (1962). The Court ruled that it is cruel and unusual punishment to put a convicted criminal to death while he is insane (*Ford* v. *Wainwright,* 91 L. Ed. 2d 335, 1986) and to impose the death penalty on a person serving a life sentence without chance of parole violated the Eighth and Fourteenth amendments (*Sumner* v. *Shuman,* 97 L. Ed. 2d 56, 1987).

Gregg v. Georgia, 428 U.S. 153; 49 L. Ed. 2d 859; 96 S. Ct. 2909 (1976)

Troy Gregg was convicted in a Georgia trial court of robbery and murder. The trial was in two stages, a guilt stage and a sentencing stage. Fred Simons and Bob Moore gave two hitchhikers (Troy Gregg and Floyd Allen) a lift in their car. A short while later they offered a third hitchhiker, Dennis Weaver, a ride. He left the car in Atlanta. Subsequently, the remaining four stopped for a rest and at that point Allen testified that Gregg ambushed and killed the original occupants, Simons and Moore. Gregg claimed the killings were in self-defense.

OPINION BY MR. JUSTICE STEWART
(Vote: 7–2)

Question—Are the Georgia death penalty statutes a violation of the cruel and unusual punishment provisions under the Eighth and Fourteenth Amendments?

Decision—No.

Reason—"The punishment of death for the crime of murder does not," said the Court, "under all circumstances, violate the Eighth and Fourteenth Amendments." Though the legislature may not impose excessive punishment, it is not required to select the least severe penalty possible. Capital punishment is not invalid per se and was accepted by the framers of the Constitution. "Legislative measures adopted by the people's chosen representatives weigh heavily in ascertaining contemporary standards of decency" and in this connection the Court noted that, since *Furman* v. *Georgia* (1972) was struck down, thirty-five states have enacted new statutes providing for the death penalty. Moreover "retribution" and "deterrence" are not "impermissible considerations for a legislature to weigh in determining whether the death penalty should be imposed." The bifurcated proceedings in Georgia have met the concerns of arbitrariness and capriciousness condemned in *Furman*.

Corollary cases

Jurek v. Texas, 428 U.S. 262 (1976)
Proffit v. Florida, 428 U.S. 242 (1976)
Woodson v. North Carolina, 428 U.S. 280 (1976)
Roberts v. Louisiana, 428 U.S. 325 (1977)
Furman v. Georgia, 408 U.S. 238 (1972)
Louisiana v. Resweber, 329 U.S. 459 (1947)
Trop v. Dulles, 356 U.S. 86 (1958)
Witherspoon v. Illinois, 391 U.S. 510 (1968)
McGautha v. California, 402 U.S. 183 (1971)
Lockett v. Ohio, 438 U.S. 586 (1978)
Presnell v. Georgia, 439 U.S. 14 (1978)
Eddings v. Oklahoma, 71 L. Ed. 2d 11 (1982)
Bullington v. Missouri, 68 L. Ed. 2d 270 (1981)
Godfrey v. Georgia, 446 U.S. 420 (1980)
Adams v. Texas, 65 L. Ed. 2d 581 (1980)
Beck v. Alabama, 447 U.S. 625 (1980)

Note—The Court has outlawed jury sentences "wantonly and . . . freakishly imposed" in *Furman* v. *Georgia* (1972), as well as mandatory death sentences in *Woodson* v. *North Carolina* (1977), but not, as in *Gregg,* a two-part proceedings: one for determining guilt and the other for determining the sentence.

RIGHT TO COUNSEL

Powell v. Alabama, 287 U.S. 45; 53 S. Ct. 55; 77 L. Ed. 158 (1932)

Petitioners, nine Negro youths, were indicted for the rape of two white girls. They were tried by jury six days after the day upon which they were arrested, amidst an atmosphere of tense, hostile public sentiment. They were not represented by counsel, not asked if they desired counsel, the judge simply appointing "all members of the bar" to defend them. The jury returned the death penalty. This was affirmed on appeal although the chief justice of the state Supreme Court strongly dissented, claiming an unfair trial.

OPINION BY MR. JUSTICE SUTHERLAND
(Vote 7–2)

Question—Were the petitioners denied the right of counsel, and, if so, did such denial infringe the due process clause of the Fourteenth Amendment?

Decision—Yes.

Reason—The basic elements comprising due process of law according to the Constitution are notice and hearing (preliminary steps) together with a legally competent tribunal having jurisdiction of the case. A hearing includes, in our country at least, the right and aid of counsel when so desired. The ordinary layman, even the intelligent and educated layman, is not skilled in the science of law and needs the advice and direction of competent counsel. It is apparent from the settled facts that the Negroes were in effect denied the right to counsel. They were transients and all lived in other states, yet were given no chance to communicate with members of their families to obtain counsel. Further, the trial was carried out with such dispatch that they were accorded no time to prepare a defense employing a counsel of their own choice.

"In the light of the facts outlined in the forepart of this opinion—the ignorance and illiteracy of the defendants, their youth, the circumstances of public hostility, the imprisonment, and the close surveillance of the defendants by the military forces, the fact that their friends and families were all in other states and communications with them necessarily difficult, and above all that they stood in deadly peril of their lives—we think the failure of the trial courts to give them reasonable time and opportunity to secure counsel was a clear denial of due process."

This was the first of the famous "Scottsboro cases." The second was *North* v. *Alabama.* (287 U.S. 45, 1932)

Corollary cases

Betts v. Brady, 316 U.S. 455 (1942)
Bute v. Illinois, 333 U.S. 640 (1948)
Johnson v. Zerbst, 304 U.S. 458 (1938)
De Meerleer v. Michigan, 329 U.S. 663 (1947)
Carter v. Illinois, 329 U.S. 173 (1946)
Norris v. Alabama, 294 U.S. 587 (1935)
Smith v. O'Grady, 312 U.S. 329 (1941)
Gideon v. Wainwright, 372 U.S. 335 (1963)

Chambers v. Florida, 309 U.S. 227; 84 L. Ed. 716; 60 S. Ct. 472 (1940)

On May 13, 1933, Robert Darcy, white, was robbed and murdered in Pompano, Florida. The petitioners in this case were among the suspects rounded up for investigation. They were later removed to Dade County Jail at Miami as a measure of protection against mob violence. For a week's period the petitioners were continually questioned, and on the night of Saturday, May 20, the questioning routine became an all-night vigil. On Sunday, May 21, Woodward confessed. After one week of constant denial, all the petitioners "broke." These confessions were utilized by the state to obtain judgment. The petitioners were not, either in jail or in court, wholly removed from the constant observation, influence, custody, and control of those whose persistent pressure brought about the "sunrise" confessions.

Opinion by Mr. Justice Black
(Vote: 8–0)

Question—Was this an infringement of the due process of law guaranteed by the Fourteenth Amendment?

Decision—Yes.

Reason—The due process clause was intended to guarantee adequate and appropriate procedural standards and to protect, at all times, people charged with or suspected of crime. This determination comes from the knowledge of past history that the rights and liberties of people suspected of crime cannot safely be left to secret processes. Those who have suffered most from these secret and dictatorial processes have always been the poor, the ignorant, the weak, and the powerless.

The requirement of conforming to the fundamental standards of procedure was made operative against the states by the Fourteenth Amendment. Such law enforcement methods as those described in this case are not necessary to uphold our laws. The Constitution prohibits such lawless means regardless of the end in view.

Corollary cases

Powell v. Alabama, 287 U.S. 45 (1932)
Norris v. Alabama, 294 U.S. 587 (1935)
Moore v. Dempsey, 261 U.S. 86 (1923)
Bordenkircher v. Hayes, 434 U.S. 357 (1978)
Ashcraft v. Tennessee, 322 U.S. 143 (1944)
McNabb v. United States, 318 U.S. 332 (1943)
Rochin v. California, 342 U.S. 165 (1952)
Breithaupt v. Abram, 352 U.S. 432 (1957)
Mincey v. Arizona, 437 U.S. 385 (1978)

Note—The Court went beyond physical coercion and held that psychological coercion also violates the due process clause, which is binding on the states.

Gideon v. Wainwright, 372 U.S. 335; 83 S. Ct. 792; 9 L. Ed. 2d 799 (1963)

Clarence E. Gideon was charged in a Florida state court with having broken into and entered a poolroom with intent to commit a misdemeanor. Under Florida law such an offense is a noncapital felony. Gideon appeared in court without funds and without a lawyer. He asked the court to appoint counsel for him. This the court refused to do because Florida law permitted the appointment of counsel for indigent defendants in capital cases only. Gideon appealed his conviction claiming violation of the constitutional guarantee of counsel.

OPINION BY MR. JUSTICE BLACK
(Vote: 9–0)

Question—Must an indigent defendant be provided counsel in a noncapital case?

Decision—Yes.

Reason—A provision of the Bill of Rights that is "fundamental and essential to a fair trial" is made obligatory upon the states by the Fourteenth Amendment. The Court noted that "reason and reflection require us to recognize that in our adversary system of criminal justice, any person haled into court, who is too poor to hire a lawyer, cannot be assured a fair trial unless counsel is provided for him. This seems to be an obvious truth. . . . The right of one charged with crime to counsel may not be deemed fundamental and essential to fair trials in some countries, but it is in ours." Thus was the guarantee of counsel in the Sixth Amendment applied to all cases in the state courts, capital and noncapital. In so holding, the Court overruled *Betts* v. *Brady,* 316 U.S. 455 (1942).

Corollary cases

Powell v. Alabama, 287 U.S. 45 (1932)
Hurtado v. California, 110 U.S. 516 (1884)
Grosjean v. American Press Co., 297 U.S. 233 (1936)
Bute v. Illinois, 333 U.S. 640 (1948)
Loper v. Beto, 405 U.S. 473 (1972)
Argersinger v. Hamlin, 407 U.S. 25 (1972)
Faretta v. California, 422 U.S. 806 (1975)
Middendorf v. Henry, 425 U.S. 25 (1976)
Johnson v. Zerbst, 304 U.S. 458 (1938)
Adamson v. California, 332 U.S. 46 (1947)
Palko v. Connecticut, 302 U.S. 319 (1937)
Douglas v. California, 372 U.S. 353 (1963)
Illinois v. Allen, 397 U.S. 337 (1970)
Betts v. Brady, 316 U.S. 455 (1942)
Maxwell v. Dow, 176 U.S. 581 (1900)
Miranda v. Arizona, 384 U.S. 436 (1966)
Escobedo v. Illinois, 378 U.S. 478 (1964)

Note—*Gideon* extended the "Gitlow doctrine" and applied the guarantee of counsel in the Sixth Amendment to state courts in both capital and noncapital cases.

Escobedo v. Illinois, 378 U.S. 478; 84 S. Ct. 1758; 12 L. Ed. 2d 977 (1964)

> Danny Escobedo was convicted of fatally shooting his brother-in-law in Chicago. During the police questioning following his arrest he was not permitted to consult with the attorney he had retained and who was at police headquarters. In the course of this questioning Escobedo was not advised of his constitutional right to remain silent and made some incriminating statements.

OPINION BY MR. JUSTICE GOLDBERG
(Vote: 5–4)

Question—Was the refusal by the police under the circumstances to honor the request of the accused to consult with his lawyer a violation of the Sixth Amendment?

Decision—Yes.

Reason—When an investigation is no longer a general inquiry into an unsolved crime but has begun to focus on a particular suspect who has been taken into custody, is being interrogated, has requested and been denied counsel, and has not been advised of his constitutional rights, as was the case here, the accused has been denied "the assistance of counsel" guaranteed by the Sixth Amendment. This guarantee was held to be obligatory on the states under the terms of the Fourteenth Amendment in *Gideon* v. *Wainwright,* 372 U.S. 335 (1963). When the investigatory process becomes accusatory then our adversary system begins to operate and the accused must be permitted to consult with his attorney.

Corollary cases

Haynes v. Washington, 373 U.S. 503 (1963)
Massiah v. United States, 377 U.S. 201 (1964)
Crooker v. California, 357 U.S. 433 (1958)
Spano v. New York, 360 U.S. 315 (1959)
Miranda v. Arizona, 384 U.S. 436 (1966)

Johnson v. New Jersey, 384 U.S. 719 (1966)
Schmerber v. California, 384 U.S. 757 (1966)
Gideon v. Wainwright, 372 U.S. 335 (1963)
Jackson v. Denno, 378 U.S. 368 (1964)
United States v. Wade, 388 U.S. 218 (1967)
Gilbert v. California, 388 U.S. 263 (1967)
Edwards v. Arizona, 68 L. Ed. 2d 378 (1981)
California v. Prysock, 69 L. Ed. 2d 696 (1981)
Estelle v. Smith, 68 L. Ed. 2d 359 (1981)
United States v. Henry, 447 U.S. 264 (1980)
Moran v. Burbine, 89 L. Ed 2d 410 (1986)

Note—In overruling *Crooker* v. *California,* (1958) the Court incorporated the right to counsel under the Sixth Amendment.

Miranda v. Arizona, 384 U.S. 436; 86 S. Ct. 1602; 16 L. Ed. 2d 694 (1966)

Here four cases were decided by one opinion. They came from Arizona, New York, California, and the federal courts. In each of the cases the law enforcement officials had taken the defendant into custody and had interrogated him for the purpose of obtaining a confession. At no time did the police effectively advise a defendant of his right to remain silent or of his right to consult with his attorney. In the lead case, Ernesto Miranda had been arrested at his home and then taken to a Phoenix police station where he was questioned by two police officers. After two hours he made a written confession. He was subsequently convicted of kidnapping and rape. In the New York case the charge was first degree robbery, in the California case it was robbery and first degree murder, and in the federal case robbery of a savings and loan association and a bank in California.

OPINION BY MR. CHIEF JUSTICE WARREN
(Vote: 5–4)

Question—Are statements obtained from an individual subjected to custodial police interrogation under these circumstances admissible as evidence?

Decision—No.

Reason—An individual held for interrogation must be clearly informed that he has the right to consult counsel and to have his lawyer with him during interrogation. Financial inability of an accused person to furnish counsel is no excuse for the absence of counsel since in such an instance a lawyer must be appointed to represent the accused. If he answers some questions and gives some information on his own prior to invoking his right to remain silent this is not to warrant an assumption that the privilege has been waived.

The Court noted that "the prosecution may not use statements, whether exculpatory or inculpatory, stemming from custodial interrogation of the defendant unless it demonstrates the use of procedural safeguards effective to secure the privilege against self-incrimination. By custodial interrogation, we mean questioning initiated by law enforcement officers after a person has been taken into custody or otherwise deprived of his freedom of action in any significant way."

Corollary cases

Escobedo v. Illinois, 378 U.S. 478 (1964)
Johnson v. New Jersey, 384 U.S. 719 (1966)
Gideon v. Wainwright, 371 U.S. 335 (1963)
Betts v. Brady, 316 U.S. 455 (1942)
Mallory v. United States, 354 U.S. 449 (1957)
Michigan v. Tucker, 417 U.S. 433 (1974)
Schmerber v. California, 384 U.S. 757 (1966)
Chambers v. Florida, 309 U.S. 227 (1940)
McNabb v. United States, 318 U.S. 332 (1943)
Twining v. New Jersey, 211 U.S. 78 (1908)
Jackson v. Denno, 378 U.S. 368 (1964)
Orozco v. Texas, 294 U.S. 324 (1969)

OBSCENITY

Burstyn v. Wilson, 343 U.S. 495; 72 S. Ct. 777; 96 L. Ed. 1098 (1952)

A high controversial film, "The Miracle," produced in Italy and starring Anna Magnani, had at first been licensed for showing in New York and had been exhibited in the city for approximately eight weeks. Public reaction resulted in the license being withdrawn on the ground that the movie was "sacrilegious." The distributor of the motion picture brought action in the state courts and ultimately in the Supreme Court of the United States to attempt to force Wilson, New York State Commissioner of Education, to grant the license.

OPINION BY MR. JUSTICE CLARK
(Vote: 9–0)

Question—Is the New York statute that permits state authorities to ban films on the ground that they are "sacrilegious" contrary to the First and Fourteenth Amendments?

Decision—Yes.

Reason—Motion pictures are a significant medium for the communication of ideas. The importance of movies as an organ of public opinion is not lessened by the fact that they are designed to entertain as well as to inform. Also, their production, distribution, and exhibition for profit do not affect the application of the liberty guaranteed by the First Amendment any more than in the case of books, newspapers, and magazines. Expression by means of motion pictures is included within the free speech and free press guarantee of the First and Fourteenth Amendments. A state cannot ban a film on the basis of a censor's view that it is "sacrilegious." Such a standard is too vague. From the standpoint of freedom of speech and press, the state has no legitimate interest in protecting any or all religions from views sufficiently distasteful to them to justify prior restraint upon the expression of those views.

288

Corollary cases

Kingsley International Pictures Corp. v. Regents, 360 U.S. 684 (1959)
Times Film Corp. v. City of Chicago, 365 U.S. 43 (1957)
Roth v. United States, 354 U.S. 476 (1957)
Red Lion Broadcasting Co. v. FCC, 395 U.S. 367 (1969)
Erzoznik v. Jacksonville, 419 U.S. 822 (1975)
Young v. American Mini Theaters, Inc., 427 U.S. 50 (1976)
Jenkins v. Georgia, 418 U.S. 153 (1974)
Freedman v. Maryland, 380 U.S. 51 (1965)
Near v. Minnesota, 283 U.S. 697 (1931)
Mutual Film Corp. v. Industrial Commission of Ohio, 236 U.S. 230 (1915)
Rabe v. State of Washington, 405 U.S. 313 (1972)
Miller v. California, 413 U.S. 15 (1973)
Hamling v. United States, 418 U.S. 87 (1974)
California v. LaRue, 409 U.S. 109 (1972)
Vance v. Universal Amusement Co., 445 U.S. 308 (1980)

Note—*Burstyn* made "official" what *United States* v. *Paramount Pictures, Inc.*, 334 U.S. 131 (1948), said as dictum—that movies are part of the press in the First Amendment.

Roth v. United States (Alberts v. California), 354 U.S. 476; 77 S. Ct. 1304; 1 L. Ed. 2d 1498 (1957)

Samuel Roth conducted a business in New York in the publication and sale of books, photographs, and magazines. He was indicted and convicted of mailing obscene circulars and advertising and an obscene book in violation of the federal obscenity statute. Combined with this case was *Alberts* v. *California*, in which David Alberts had been convicted of publishing obscene matter in violation of the California penal code.

OPINION BY MR. JUSTICE BRENNAN
(Vote: 6–3 in *Roth;* 7–2 in *Alberts*)

Question—Do these statutes violate the provisions of the First Amendment?

Decision—No.

Reason—The guarantees of freedom of expression give no absolute protection for every utterance. The protection was fashioned to assure unfettered interchange of ideas for the bringing about of political and social changes by the people. All ideas having the slightest redeeming social importance have the full protection of the guarantees unless excludable because they encroach upon the limited area of more important interests. But obscenity is not within the area of constitutionally protected speech or press. The test of obscenity is "whether to the average person, applying contemporary community standards, the dominant theme of the material taken as a whole appeals to prurient interest." The Court held that these statutes, applied according to the proper standard for judging obscenity, did not offend constitutional safeguards against convictions based upon protected material. Both trial courts in these cases had sufficiently followed the proper standard.

Corollary cases

Beauharnais v. Illinois, 343 U.S. 250 (1952)
Kingsley International Pictures Corp. v. Regents, 360 U.S. 684 (1959)
Manual Enterprises, Inc. v. Day, 370 U.S. 478 (1962)
Jacobellis v. Ohio, 378 U.S. 184 (1964)
Burstyn v. Wilson, 343 U.S. 684 (1959)
Memoirs v. Massachusetts, 383 U.S. 413 (1966)
Young v. American Mini Theatres, Inc., 427 U.S. 50 (1976)
Ginzburg v. United States, 383 U.S. 463 (1966)
Mishkin v. New York, 383 U.S. 503 (1966)
Ginsberg v. New York, 390 U.S. 629 (1968)
Stanley v. Georgia, 394 U.S. 557 (1969)
California v. LaRue, 409 U.S. 109 (1972)
Miller v. California, 413 U.S. 15 (1973)
FCC v. Pacifica Foundation, 438 U.S. 726 (1978)

Note—The *Roth* guidelines have been altered by *Miller* v. *California,* 413 U.S. 15 (1973), the most important being that "utterly" in "utterly without redeeming social value" has been dropped and "contemporary community standards" has replaced "national standards."

Ginzburg v. United States, 383 U.S. 463; 86 S. Ct. 942; 16 L. Ed. 2d 31 (1966)

Ralph Ginzburg was convicted of violation of the federal obscenity statute by producing and selling obscene publications. The accusation was made that the advertising for the publications openly appealed to the erotic interest of potential customers. This case involved another application of what has come to be known as "the *Roth* test." This attempt to define obscenity was first set forth in *Roth* v. *United States,* 354 U.S. 476 (1957) and has been elaborated in subsequent cases. Under this test three elements must coalesce to constitute obscenity: (1) the dominant theme of the material in question must appeal to a prurient interest in sex, (2) it must affront contemporary community standards, and (3) the material must be utterly without redeeming social value.

OPINION BY MR. JUSTICE BRENNAN
(Vote: 5–4)

Question—Have the standards of "the *Roth* test" been correctly applied in this case?

Decision—Yes.

Reason—There was abundant evidence that pandering—the business of purveying textual or graphic matter openly advertised to appeal to the erotic interests of persons—was involved. The Court saw no threat to First Amendment guarantees in its holding but rather felt "the fact that each of these publications was created or exploited entirely on the basis of its appeal to prurient interests strengthens the conclusion that the transactions here were sales of illicit merchandise, not sales of constitutionally protected matter." The determination of the opinion is simply that questionable publications are obscene in a context—here the commercial exploitation of erotica solely for the sake of prurient appeal—which "brands them as obscene as the term is defined in *Roth*—a use inconsistent with any claim to the shelter of the First Amendment."

Corollary cases

Jacobellis v. Ohio, 378 U.S. 184 (1964)
Mishkin v. New York, 383 U.S. 502 (1966)
Near v. Minnesota, 283 U.S. 697 (1931)
Roth v. United States, 354 U.S. 476 (1957)
Kingsley Books v. Brown, 354 U.S. 436 (1957)
Bantam Books v. Sullivan, 372 U.S. 58 (1963)

A Quantity of Books v. Kansas, 378 U.S. 205 (1964)
Miller v. California, 413 U.S. 15 (1973)
FCC v. Pacifica Foundation, 438 U.S. 726 (1978)
Butler v. Michigan, 352 U.S. 380 (1957)
New York State Liquor Authority v. Bellanca, 69 L. Ed. 2d 357 (1981)
Schad v. Mount Ephraim, 68 L. Ed. 2d 671 (1981)
Walter v. United States, 65 L. Ed. 2d 410 (1980)
Cooper v. Michell Brothers, 70 L. Ed. 2d 262 (1981)

Note—Although the standard for obscenity was outlined in *Roth* and carefully altered in *Miller,* the Court treated *Ginzburg* differently and made their ruling on the basis of "pandering." This concept was reaffirmed in *Splawn* v. *California,* 431 U.S. 595 (1977).

Miller v. California, 413 U.S. 15; 93 S. Ct. 2607; 37 L. Ed. 2d 419 (1973)

Sexually explicit materials were sent through the mails to persons who had in no way indicated interest in receiving such materials. These were brochures advertising books and a movie. California attempted to apply its criminal obscenity statute to this situation.

OPINION BY MR. CHIEF JUSTICE BURGER
(Vote: 5–4)

Question—Under the First Amendment may a state enforce obscenity statutes against publications that offend local community standards as to what is prurient?

Decision—Yes.

Reason—States may regulate works that depict or describe sexual conduct, but such legislation must be carefully limited. The basic guidelines must be (a) whether the average person, applying contemporary community standards, would find the work as a whole appealing to the prurient interest; (b) whether the work depicts or describes in a patently offensive way sexual conduct specifically defined by the applicable state law; and (c) whether the work as a whole lacks serious literary, artistic, political, or scientific value. The "utterly without redeeming social value" test is rejected. Local standards rather than a national definition of obscenity may be used.

Corollary cases

Paris Adult Theater I v. Slaton, 413 U.S. 49 (1973)
Kaplan v. California, 413 U.S. 115 (1973)
United States v. Orito, 413 U.S. 139 (1973)
United States v. 12 200-ft. Reels of Super 8MM Film, 413 U.S. 123 (1973)
Roth v. United States, 354 U.S. 476 (1957)
Memoirs v. Massachusetts, 383 U.S. 413 (1966)
Jacobellis v. Ohio, 378 U.S. 184 (1964)
Mishkin v. New York, 383 U.S. 502 (1966)
Ginzburg v. United States, 383 U.S. 463 (1966)
Stanley v. Georgia, 394 U.S. 557 (1969)
Ginsberg v. New York, 390 U.S. 629 (1968)
Pinkus v. United States, 56 L. Ed. 2d 293 (1978)
FCC v. Pacifica Foundation, 438 U.S. 726 (1978)

ABORTION

Griswold v. Connecticut, 381 U.S. 479; 85 S. Ct. 1678; 14 L. Ed. 2d 510 (1965)

Here the constitutionality of Connecticut's birth control law was involved. The statute provided that "any person who uses any drug, medical article or instrument for the purpose of preventing conception" was to be subject to fine or imprisonment or both. The statute further specified that a person who assisted another in committing any offense could be prosecuted and punished as if he were the principal offender. Estelle Griswold, executive director of the Planned Parenthood League of Connecticut, was convicted of being an accessory.

OPINION BY MR. JUSTICE DOUGLAS
(Vote: 7–2)

Question—Is the Connecticut statute valid under the Constitution?

Decision—No.

Reason—First, the appellants were held to have standing to raise the constitutional issue because they were accessories to violation of the criminal statute inasmuch as they were advising married persons as to the means of preventing conception. The decision established a new constitutional "right of privacy" really using the Ninth Amendment as a basis. The Court noted that "specific guarantees in the Bill of Rights have penumbras, formed by emanations from those guarantees that help give them life and substance . . . the right of privacy which presses for recognition here is a legitimate one. The present case, then, concerns a relationship lying within the zone of privacy created by several constitutional guarantees. . . . We deal with a right of privacy older than the Bill of Rights." In the course of the opinion the Court referred favorably to the Ninth Amendment's provision that "The enumeration in the Constitution, of certain rights, shall not be construed to deny or disparage others retained by the people." A concurring opinion emphasized the Ninth Amendment.

294

Corollary Cases

Poe v. Ullman, 367 U.S. 497 (1961)
Tileston v. Ullman, 318 U.S. 44 (1943)
De Jonge v. Oregon, 299 U.S. 353 (1937)
Eisenstadt v. Baird, 405 U.S. 438 (1972)
Roe v. Wade, 410 U.S. 113 (1973)
Cantrell v. Forest City Publishing Co., 419 U.S. 245 (1974)
Pierce v. Society of Sisters, 268 U.S. 510 (1925)
Meyer v. Nebraska, 262 U.S. 390 (1923)
Mapp v. Ohio, 367 U.S. 643 (1962)
Palko v. Connecticut, 302 U.S. 319 (1937)
Doe v. Bolton, 410 U.S. 179 (1973)
Cox Broadcasting Corporation v. Cohn, 420 U.S. 469 (1975)
Skinner v. Oklahoma, 316 U.S. 535 (1942)
Carey v. Population Services International, 431 U.S. 678 (1977)
Zablocki v. Redhail, 434 U.S. 374 (1972)

Note—The Constitution does not mention any right of privacy, but the Court concluded it is one of the penumbras of the Bill of Rights. It virtually became the cornerstone of the abortion decision in *Roe* v. *Wade,* 410 U.S. 113 (1973).

Roe v. Wade, 410 U.S. 113; 93 S. Ct. 705; 35 L. Ed. 2d 147 (1973)

> Texas statutes prohibited abortions except by medical advice for the purpose of saving the life of the mother. Proceeding under the pseudonym of Jane Roe, a federal class action was instituted against the district attorney of Dallas County challenging the validity of the statutes. Her life did not appear to be threatened by a continuation of the pregnancy, so no legal abortion was possible in Texas.

OPINION BY MR. JUSTICE BLACKMUN
(Vote: 7–2)

Question—1. Does the term "person" as used in the Fourteenth Amendment include the unborn?

2. Does the right of privacy include a woman's decision on an abortion?

Decisions—1. No.
2. Yes.

Reason—1. The Constitution does not define "person" as such. However, the use of the word in the various instances where it is used in the Constitution is such that the word has application only postnatally. The unborn have never been recognized in the law as persons in the whole sense. "We need not resolve the difficult question of when life begins. When those trained in the respective disciplines of medicine, philosophy, and theology are unable to arrive at any consensus, the judiciary, at this point in the development of man's knowledge, is not in a position to speculate as to the answer."

2. The Constitution does not explicitly recognize any right of privacy. However, for years the Court has recognized that a right of personal privacy does exist under the Constitution. This has been primarily based upon the Fourteenth Amendment's concept of personal liberty and the Ninth Amendment's reservation of rights to the people. This right is not unqualified and is subject to state regulation when important interests intervene. The right of privacy is broad enough to cover the decision as to an abortion. The right is not absolute and is subject to state interests as to protection of health, medical standards, and prenatal life.

The period of pregnancy can be divided into three-month periods—trimesters. During the first period there is no agreement as to the fetus being a person, so the discretion rests with the woman and her physician. During the second and third trimesters agreement increases as to the fetus becoming a "person," and the interest of the state increases accordingly, along with its power to restrict the discretion of the woman. During the final trimester the state may even proscribe abortions, except when necessary to preserve the life or health of the mother.

Corollary cases

Griswold v. Connecticut, 381 U.S. 479 (1965)
Stanley v. Georgia, 394 U.S. 557 (1969)
Meyer v. Nebraska, 262 U.S. 390 (1923)
Loving v. Virginia, 388 U.S. 1 (1967)
Planned Parenthood of Central Missouri v. Danforth, 428 U.S. 52 (1976)
Skinner v. Oklahoma, 316 U.S. 535 (1942)

Eisenstadt v. Baird, 405 U.S. 438 (1972)
Jacobson v. Massachusetts, 197 U.S. 11 (1905)
Buck v. Bell, 274 U.S. 200 (1927)
Bigelow v. Virginia, 421 U.S. 809 (1975)
Colautti v. Franklin, 439 U.S. 379 (1979)
Harris v. McRae, 448 U.S. 297 (1980)
Williams v. Zbaraz, 448 U.S. 358 (1980)
H. L. v. Matheson, 450 U.S. 398 (1981)
Bellotti v. Baird, 443 U.S. 622 (1979)
Beel v. Doe, 432 U.S. 438 (1977)
Maher v. Roe, 432 U.S. 464 (1977)

Note—Fifteen years after *Roe* (1973) when the Court "federalized" the right of abortion under the "privacy" doctrine of the Ninth Amendment, legal, political, and social pressure continues unabated for a reversal. The issue of "pro-life" or "pro-choice" was raised in the campaigns of 1984 and 1988. The Supreme Court's "pro-choice" majority has weakened and was under siege. Among the liberal octogenarians who are "pro-choice" in 1989, Brennan will be 82, and Marshall and Blackmun will be 80. In 1973, *Roe* was decided by 7–2; in 1983, *Akron* by 6–3 (Justice O'Connor saying that *Roe* was on a collision course with the Roe framework) and in 1986 *Thornburgh* by 5–4. Dissenting in *Thornburgh,* Chief Justice Burger complained that if the majority holding meant what it appears to mean, then the Supreme Court should re-examine *Roe* v. *Wade*. Whatever the "politics" of decision-making, "We are under the Constitution," said Chief Justice Charles Evans Hughes, "but the Constitution is what the judges say it is." Hugo Black who served from 1937–1971 under five chief justices (Hughes, Stone, Vinson, Warren, and Burger) commented on a TV interview with Eric Sevareid who asked how the Constitution could mean one thing in 1896 and another in 1954 (referring to *Plessy* v. *Ferguson* (41 L. Ed. 256, and *Brown* v. *Board of Education,* 98 L. Ed. 873), "That's right, Mr. Sevareid, the Constitution hadn't changed—but the judges changed." Surprisingly for his candor, no less than Blackmun, the author of *Roe* recently told law students in Little Rock, Arkansas: "Will *Roe* go down the drain? I think there is a very distinct possibility that it will—this term. You can count the votes." If this were to happen, it would mean that the abortion issue would revert to the states. The Court refused to reverse *Roe*—saying that the facts of *Webster* differ from those in *Roe*—but did "modify and narrow" it. The leading case is *Webster* v. *Reproductive Health Services,* 106 L.Ed. 2d 410 (1989).

Harris v. McRae, 448 U.S. 297; 65 L. Ed. 2d 784; 100 S. Ct. 2671 (1980)

Title XIX of the Social Security Act established the Medicaid program in 1965 to provide federal financial assistance to states that choose to reimburse certain costs of medical treatment for needy persons. Since 1976, versions of the so-called Hyde Amendment have severely limited the use of any federal funds to reimburse the cost of abortions under the Medicaid program. The Hyde Amendment was attached on the grounds, inter alia, that it violates the due process clause of the Fifth Amendment and the religion clauses of the First Amendment and that, despite the Hyde Amendment, a participating state remains obligated under Title XIX to fund all medically necessary abortions. The district court agreed that the state was free from obligation to pay for elective abortions but that the Hyde Amendment violated the First, Fifth, and Fourteenth Amendments.

OPINION BY MR. JUSTICE STEWART
(Vote: 6–3)

Question—(1) Must a state pay for elective abortions when, under the Hyde Amendment, Congress has withdrawn its support; and (2) does the Hyde Amendment violate constitutional guarantees, especially the establishment clause of the First Amendment and the equal protection and liberty clauses of the Fourteenth Amendment?

Decision—1. No.
        2. No.

Reason—"Nothing in Title XIX as originally enacted, or in its legislative history, suggests that Congress intended to require a participating State to assume the full costs of providing any health services in its Medicaid plan . . . if Congress chooses to withdraw federal funding for a particular service, a state is not obliged to continue to pay for that service as a condition of continued federal financial support of other services." The state (*Maher* v. *Roe,* 432 U.S. 464) can make a value judgment favoring childbirth over abortion "but it has imposed no restriction on access to abortions that was not already there. . . . [I]t simply does not follow that a woman's freedom of choice carries with it a constitutional entitlement to the financial resources to avail herself of the full range of protected choices." To require this funding as a due process entitlement would mean that Congress was mandated "to subsidize the medically necessary abortion of an indigent woman even if Congress had not enacted a Medicaid program to subsidize other medically necessary services." Under the free exercise clause the parties lack standing and the Fifth Amendment is not a source of substantive rights on liberties, but rather a right to be free from invidious governmental discrimination.

Corollary cases

Roe v. Wade, 410 U.S. 168 (1973)
Maher v. Roe, 432 U.S. 464 (1977)
Beal v. Doe, 432 U.S. 438; 53 L. Ed. 2d 464 (1977)
Colautti v. Franklin, 439 U.S. 379 (1979)
Broadrick v. Oklahoma, 413 U.S. 601 (1973)
Loving v. Virginia, 388 U.S. 1 (1967)
Skinner v. Oklahoma, 316 U.S. 535 (1942)
Eisenstadt v. Baird, 405 U.S. 438 (1972)
Prince v. Massachusetts, 321 U.S. 158 (1944)
Meyer v. Nebraska, 262 U.S. 390 (1923)
Memorial Hospital v. Maricopa County, 415 U.S. 250 (1974)
Whalen v. Roe, 429 U.S. 589 (1977)
Committee for Public Education and Religious Liberty v. Regan, 444 U.S. 646 (1980)
San Antonio Independent School District v. Rodriguez, 411 U.S. 1 (1973)
Williamson v. Lee Optical Co., 348 U.S. 483 (1955)

H. L. v. Matheson, 450 U.S. 398; 67 L. Ed. 2d 388; 101 S. Ct. 1164 (1981)

A Utah statute required that a physician "notify if possible," the parents or guardian of a minor upon whom an abortion is to be performed. The appellant, an unmarried minor who lived with her parents, became pregnant. While a physician advised the girl that an abortion would be in her best medical interest, he refused to perform the abortion without first notifying her parents. The appellant brought suit in state court seeking a declaration that the statute is unconstitutional and an injunction against its enforcement.

OPINION BY MR. CHIEF JUSTICE BURGER
(Vote: 6–3)

Question—Does the Utah state statute that requires a physician to "notify if possible" the parents of a dependent, unmarried minor girl prior to performing an abortion on the girl violate federal constitutional guarantees?

Decision—No.

Reason—"Although we have held that a state may not constitutionally legislate a blanket, unreviewable power of parents to veto their daughter's abortion, a statute setting out a 'mere requirement of parental notice' does not violate the constitutional rights of an immature, dependent minor. . . . The Utah statute gives neither parents nor judges a veto power over the minor's abortion decision." The statute plainly serves the important considerations of family integrity and protecting adolescents. "The medical, emotional, and psychological consequences of an abortion are serious and can be lasting. . . ." An adequate medical and psychological case history is important to the physician. "Parents can provide medical and psychological data, refer the physician to other sources of medical history, such as family physicians and authorize family physicians to give relevant data. . . . The . . . statute is reasonably calculated to protect minors in appellant's class by enhancing the potential for parental consultation concerning a decision that has potentially traumatic and permanent consequences. . . . The Constitution does not compel a state to fine tune its statutes so as to encourage or facilitate abortions. . . . State action 'encouraging childbirth except in the most urgent circumstances' [is] rationally related to the legitimate governmental objective of protecting potential life.''

Corollary cases

Bellotti v. Baird, 443 U.S. 622 (1979)
Planned Parenthood v. Danforth, 428 U.S. 52 (1976)
Doe v. Bolton, 410 U.S. 179 (1973)
Harris v. McRae, 448 U.S. 297 (1980)
Thornburgh v. American College of Obstetricians and Gynecologists, 90 L.
 Ed. 2d 779 (1986)
Planned Parenthood Association v. Ashcraft, 76 L. Ed. 2d 733 (1983)

Akron v. Akron Ctr. for Reproductive Health, 462 U.S. 416; 76 L. Ed. 2d 687; 103 S. Ct. 2481 (1983)

An Akron ordinance, required that after the first trimester of pregnancy an abortion must be performed in a hospital; that a minor under age 15 required parental (or court) consent; the attending physician inform his patient of the possibility of emotional consequences; prohibits a physician from performing an abortion until 24 hours after the pregnant woman signed a consent form; and requires that the fetal remains be disposed of in a "human and sanitary manner." The district court invalidated the ordinance for the most part and the court of appeals affirmed the decision. The Supreme Court granted certiorari.

OPINION BY JUSTICE POWELL
(Vote: 6–3)

Question—Are the provisions of the Akron abortion ordinance constitutional?

Decision—No.

Reason—"The decision in *Roe* was based firmly "on a long recognized and essential element of personal liberty." Although the state has a legitimate concern with the health of women undergoing an abortion, this interest does not become a compelling state interest until the end of the first trimester of pregnancy. Examples of state interest are requirements as to the qualifications of the abortionist, the licensure of that person, the facility within which the abortion will take place, and the kind of hospital or clinic. The Court recognizes the state's legitimacy authority in legitimate health interests but it will not uphold obstacles to the constitutional right of privacy.

Akron has unreasonably placed obstacles on the attending physician and pregnant women. Accordingly, "we affirm the judgment of the court of appeals invalidating those sections of Akron's "Regulations of Abortions" ordinance that deal with parental consent, informed consent, a 24-hour waiting period, and the disposal of fetal remains. The remaining portion of the judgment, sustaining Akron's requirement that all second trimester abortions be performed in a hospital, is reversed.

Corollary cases

Roe v. Wade, 410 U.S. 113, 35 L. Ed. 2d 147, 93 S. Ct. 705 (1973)
Connecticut v. Menillo, 423 U.S. 9, 46 L. Ed. 2d 152, 96 S. Ct. 170 (1975)
Planned Parenthood of Central Mo. v. Danforth, 428 U.S. 52, 49 L. Ed. 2d 788, 96 S. Ct.
Beal v. Doe, 432 U.S. 438, 53 L. Ed. 2d 464, 97 S. Ct. 2366 (1977)
Maher v. Roe, 432 U.S. 464, 53 L. Ed. 2d 484, 97 S. Ct. 2376 (1977)
Colavtti v. Franklin, 439 U.S. 379, 58 L. Ed. 2d 596, 99 S. Ct. 675 (1979)
Bellotti v. Baird, 443 U.S. 622, 61 L. Ed. 2d 797, 99 S. Ct. 3035 (1979)
Harris v. McRae, 448 U.S. 297, 65 L. Ed. 2d 784, 100 S. Ct. 2671 (1980)
H. L. Matheson, 450 U.S. 398, 67 L. Ed. 2d 388, 101 S. Ct. 1164 (1981)
Griswold v. Connecticut, 381 U.S. 479, 14 L. Ed. 2d 510, 85 S. Ct. 1678 (1965)
Eisenstadt v. Baird, 405 U.S. 438, 31 L. Ed. 2d 349, 92 S. Ct. 1029 (1972)
Carey v. Population Services International, 431 U.S. 678, 52 L. Ed. 2d 675, 97 S. Ct. 2010 (1977)

Note—Between *Akron* (1983) in which Justice O'Connor, White and Rehnquist strongly dissented, and *Thornburgh* (1986) in which Chief Justice Burger repudiated his previous support of *Roe* v.*Wade* (1973) and Justices White and Rehnquist openly called for overruling *Roe,* the "pro-choice" majority steadily diminished. In *Akron* (note #1) Justice Powell, speaks of "compelling reasons for adhering to *stare decisis* and in *Thornburgh,* Justice Stevens says that while *stare decisis* is not an absolute bar to the re-examination of past interpretation, it does not mean that the values underlying the doctrine can be so easily rejected. The record indicates, however, that when convinced of former error, the Court has never felt constrained to follow precedent. Moreover, as Justice O'Connor points out, the practice is not to apply *stare decisis* as rigidly in constitutional as in nonconstitutional cases. Justice Hugo Black said it best: "When precedent and precedent alone is all the argument that can be made to support a court-fashioned rule, it is time for the rule's creator to destroy it." (dissenting in *Francis* v. *Southern Pacific Co.*, 92 L. Ed. 798, 1948).

SCHOOLS

Meyer v. Nebraska, 262 U.S. 390; 43 S. Ct. 625; 67 L. Ed. 1042 (1923)

In 1919 Nebraska passed a statute that prohibited the teaching of any subject in any other language except English. Languages could be taught only after the child has successfully passed the eighth grade. Meyer taught in a parochial school and used a German bible history as a text for reading. The use of the text served a double purpose, teaching the German language and religious instruction.

OPINION BY MR. JUSTICE MCREYNOLDS
(Vote: 7–2)

Question—Is the statute in question a violation of the "liberty" protected by the Fourteenth Amendment?

Decision—Yes.

Reason—The Court has never attempted to define, with exactness, the liberty guaranteed by the Fourteenth Amendment. Certainly education and the pursuit of knowledge should be encouraged. Mere knowledge of the German language cannot be looked upon as harmful. Meyer's right to teach and the right of parents to hire him so to teach were within the liberty of this amendment.

The statute also forbade the teaching below the eighth grade of any other language except English. The state Supreme Court had ruled that "ancient or dead languages" did not come within the meaning of this statute. This evidently interfered with the modern language teachers, with the opportunities of children to acquire knowledge, and with the power of parents to control the education of their children.

The state may go very far to improve the quality of its citizens, but certain fundamental rights of the individual must be respected, since the protection of the Constitution also extends to those who speak a language other than English. There are advantages to a ready knowledge of ordinary speech, but "a desirable end cannot be promoted by prohibited means."

304

No emergency has arisen that would render knowledge of another language so harmful as to justify its promotion. Nor is this prohibition justified as a protection for mental health, since it is well known that a foreign language is more easily acquired at an early age. The Court cannot but conclude that this statute is arbitrary and without a reasonable relation to any end within the competency of the state.

Corollary cases

Pierce v. Society of Sisters, 268 U.S. 510 (1925)
Minersville School District v. Gobitis, 310 U.S. 586 (1940)
West Virginia State Board of Education v. Barnette, 319 U.S. 624 (1943)
Everson v. Board of Education of Ewing Township, 330 U.S. 1 (1947)
McCollum v. Board of Education, 333 U.S. 203 (1948)
Zorach v. Clauson, 343 U.S. 307 (1952)
Swann v. Charlotte-Mecklenburg Board of Education, 402 U.S. 1 (1971)
Engel v. Vitale, 370 U.S. 421 (1962)
Lemon v. Kurtzman, 403 U.S. 602 (1971)
Epperson v. Arkansas, 393 U.S. 97 (1968)
Meek v. Pittinger, 421 U.S. 349 (1975)
Wolman v. Walter, 433 U.S. 229 (1977)

Note—*Meyer* is often linked with *Pierce* v. *Society of Sisters* (1925), which safeguarded the freedom of parents, in the area of personal liberty, to choose public or private education for their children.

Pierce v. Society of Sisters of the Holy Names of Jesus and Mary, 268 U.S. 510; 45 S. Ct. 571; 69 L. Ed. 1070 (1925)

In November 1922, the state of Oregon passed a Compulsory Education Act requiring every child from the ages of eight to sixteen to attend public school. Parents or guardians who refused would be guilty of a misdemeanor. The plaintiff corporation conducted a group of private schools, according to the tenets of the Roman Catholic Church. They brought suit challenging that the statute conflicted with the right of parents to choose schools where their children would receive appropriate moral and religious training, and the right of schools and teachers to engage in a useful business or profession.

OPINION BY MR. JUSTICE MCREYNOLDS
(No evidence from the report that the decision was not unanimous.)

Question—Can a state require children to attend public schools?

Decision—No.

Reason—Rights guaranteed by the Constitution may not be abridged by state legislation that has no reasonable relation to some purpose within the competency of the state. The liberty of the Constitution forbids the standardization of children by compelling them to attend public school instruction only. "The child is not the mere creature of the state; those who nurture him and direct his destiny have the right, coupled with the high duty, to recognize and prepare him for additional obligations.

"We think it entirely plain that the act of 1922 unreasonably interferes with the liberty of parents and guardians to direct the upbringing and education of children under their control." (1943)

Also, the corporations or schools involved had business and property for which they had a claim to protection under the Fourteenth Amendment. These rights, the Court held, were threatened with destruction through this unwarranted compulsion.

Corollary cases

Meyer v. Nebraska, 262 U.S. 390 (1923)
Minersville School District v. Gobitis, 310 U.S. 586 (1940)
West Virginia State Board of Education v. Barnette, 319 U.S. 624 (1943)
Cochran v. Louisiana State Board of Education, 281 U.S. 370 (1930)
Wisconsin v. Yoder, 406 U.S. 205 (1972)

Note—Although *Pierce* and *Cochran* v. *Louisiana State Board of Education* (1930) are linked with church-state cases, the former concerned the liberty and property provisions of the Fourteenth Amendment; in the latter the question of religion was not raised.

San Antonio Independent School District v. Rodriguez, 411 U.S. 1; 93 S. Ct. 1278; 36 L. Ed. 2d 16 (1973)

Mexican-American parents whose children attended elementary and secondary schools in a school district in San

Antonio that had a low property-tax base brought suit attacking the Texas system of financing public education. The growing disparities between districts in population and taxable property were responsible in part for the increasingly notable differences in levels of local expenditure for education.

OPINION BY MR. JUSTICE POWELL
(Vote: 5–4)

Question—Does the state's system of financing public education infringe on a fundamental right explicitly or implicitly protected by the Constitution?

Decision—No.

Reason—There is no real evidence that the financing system discriminates against any definable category of "poor" people or that it results in the absolute deprivation of education. As a result, the disadvantaged class is not susceptible to identification in traditional terms. At least where wealth is involved, the equal protection clause does not require absolute equality or precisely equal advantages. "Education, of course, is not among the rights afforded explicit protection under our federal Constitution. Nor do we find any basis for saying it is implicitly so protected." Insofar as the system of financing schools results in disparities, it cannot be said that the arrangement is so irrational as to be individually discriminatory. There is need for reform in tax systems, but the challenged state action certainly furthers a legitimate state purpose or interest. The ultimate solutions must come from the lawmakers and from the democratic pressures of those who elect them.

Corollary cases

Brown v. Board of Education, 347 U.S. 483 (1954)
McLaughlin v. Florida, 379 U.S. 184 (1964)
McGinnis v. Royster, 410 U.S. 263 (1973)
Wright v. Council of the City of Emporia, 407 U.S. 451 (1972)
Jefferson v. Hackney, 406 U.S. 535 (1972)
Katzenbach v. Morgan, 384 U.S. 641 (1966)
Milliken v. Bradley, 418 U.S. 717 (1971)

Note—*San Antonio* makes two very important points: (1) that education is not a fundamental right, and (2) that wealth is not a suspect classification. Critics often see *San Antonio* as a defeat for poor people, while supporters, including the Court itself, see it as coming under federalism and local control.

Goss v. Lopez, 419 U.S. 565; 42 L. Ed. 2d 725; 95 S. Ct. 729 (1975)

> Ohio law empowers the principal of a public school to suspend a pupil for misconduct for up to ten days or to expel him. When a student is expelled, the student or his parent can appeal the decision. No similar procedure is provided for a suspended student. Nine suspended students at the Marion-Franklin High School, Columbus, Ohio, charged the Columbus Board of Education and school administrators with depriving them of their rights to an education without a hearing of any kind (following student unrest, March 1971) in violation of the procedural due process component of the Fourteenth Amendment.

OPINION BY MR. JUSTICE WHITE
(Vote: 5–4)

Question—Is the due process clause of the Fourteenth Amendment violated when, without notice and hearing, public school students are suspended for up to ten days?

Decision—Yes.

Reason—The school authorities misconceive the nature of the issue when they hold that there is no constitutional right to an education at public expense or that the due process clause does not protect against expulsions from the public school systems. Said the Court: ". . . the state is constrained to recognize a student's legitimate entitlements to a public education as a property interest which is protected by the Due Process Clause and which may not be taken away for misconduct without adherence to the minimum procedures required by the clause. Neither the property interest in educational benefits temporarily denied nor the liberty interest in reputation is so insubstantial that suspensions—however arbitrary—can be ignored." School authorities are not "free from notice and hearing requirements." The Court stops short of construing the due process clause as requiring an opportunity for counsel, cross examination of witnesses, or calling one's own witnesses. But however informal a hearing, a student must be allowed to state his version "as a hedge against erroneous action."

Corollary cases

In re Gault, 387 U.S. 1 (1969)
Breed v. Jones, 421 U.S. 519 (1975)
McKiever v. Pennsylvania, 403 U.S. 528 (1971)
Tinker v. Des Moines School District, 393 U.S. 503 (1969)
Southeastern Community College v. Davis, 442 U.S. 397; 60 L. Ed. 2d 980 (1979)
Cannon v. University of Chicago, 60 L. Ed. 2d 560 (1979)
Harrah Independent School District v. Martin, 440 U.S. 194 (1979)
Board of Curators, University of Missouri v. Horowitz, 435 U.S. 78 (1978)

New Jersey v. T.L.O., 469 U.S. 325; 83 L. Ed. 2d 720; 105 S. Ct. 733 (1985)

A 14-year-old high school freshman in New Jersey (and a companion) were discovered smoking in the school lavatory in violation of school rules, in addition, her purse (which she was made to open) contained cigarette paper commonly used with marijuana, a substantial amount of money, and a list of students who owed T.L.O. money. The lower court found the student delinquent and sentenced her to one year's probation. The Appellate Division affirmed but the Supreme Court of New Jersey reversed the decision. On certiorari it went to the Supreme Court.

OPINION BY JUSTICE WHITE
(Vote: 5–3)

Question—Is the reasonableness standard a proper standard for determining the legality of searches by school officials?

Decision—Yes.

Reason—The Fourteenth Amendment prohibits unreasonable searches and seizures by state officers and protects the rights of students against encroachment by public school officials. Moreover, the Court has held the Fourth Amendment applicable to the activities of civil as well as criminal authorities.

The Fourth Amendment requires searches be reasonable and requires balancing the need to search against the invasion that the search entails. The Fourth Amendment "does not protect subjective expectations of privacy that are unreasonable or otherwise illegitimate." Factors against the right to privacy are the substantial interest of school authorities to maintain order and discipline. This requires a certain degree of flexibility and school disciplinary procedures. In striking a balance between expectations of privacy and maintaining a learning environment, it is obvious there is an easing of restrictions to which public authorities are ordinarily subject. "The warrant requirement, in particular, is unsuited." Nor is "probable cause" an irreducible requirement for the Fourth Amendment demands that searches and seizures be "reasonable." Evidence to be relevant need not conclusively prove the ultimate fact in issue. Reasonable suspicion is not a requirement of absolute certainty. "Sufficient probability, not certainty, is the touchstone of reasonableness . . ." The judgment of the Supreme Court of New Jersey is reversed."

Corollary cases

Elkins v. United States, 364 U.S. 206, 4 L. Ed. 2d 1669, 80 S. Ct. 1437 (1960)
Mapp v. Ohio, 367 U.S. 643, 6 L. Ed. 2d 1081, 81 S. Ct. 1684 (1961)
Wolf v. Colorado, 338 U.S. 25, 93 L. Ed. 1782, 69 S. Ct. 1359 (1949)
West Virginia State Board of Education v. Barnette, 319 U.S. 624, 87 L. Ed. 1628, 63 S. Ct. 1178 (1943)
United States v. Chadwick, 433 U.S. 1, 53 L. Ed. 2d 538, 97 S. Ct. 2476 (1977)
Boyd v. United States, 116 U.S. 616, 29 L. Ed. 746, 6 S. Ct. 524 (1886)
Burdeau v. McDowell, 256 U.S. 465, 65 L. Ed. 1048, 41 S. Ct. 574 (1921)
Marshall v. Barlow's Inc., 436 U.S. 307, 56 L. Ed. 2d 305, 98 S. Ct. 1816 (1978)
Michigan v. Tyler, 436 U.S. 499, 56 L. Ed. 2d 486, 98 S. Ct. 1942 (1978)
Camara v. Municipal Court, 387 U.S. 523, 18 L. Ed. 2d 930, 87 S. Ct. 1727 (1967)
Tinker v. Des Moines Independent Community School District, 393 U.S. 503, 21 L. Ed. 2d 731, 89 S. Ct. 733 (1967)
Goss v. Lopez, 419 U.S. 565, 42 L. Ed. 2d 725, 95 S. Ct. 729 (1975)
Ingraham v. Wright, 430 U.S. 651, 51 L. Ed. 2d 711, 97 S. Ct. 1401 (1977)
Terry v. Ohio, 392 U.S. 1, 20 L. Ed. 889, 88 S. Ct. 1868 (1968)
United States v. Ross, 456 U.S. 798, 72 L. Ed. 2d 572, 102 S. Ct. 2157 (1982)
Hudson v. Palmer, 468 U.S. _____, 82 L. Ed. 2d 393, 104 S. Ct. 3194 (1984)

Rawlings v. Kentucky, 448 U.S. 98, 65 L. Ed. 2d 633, 100 S. Ct. 2556 (1980)
Almeida-Sanchez v. United States, 413 U.S. 266, 37 L. Ed. 2d 596, 93 S. Ct. 2535 (1973)
Sibron v. New York, 392 U.S. 40, 20 L. Ed. 2d 917, 88 S. Ct. 1889 (1968)
United States v. Brignoni, 442 U.S. 873, 45 L. Ed. 2d 607, 95 S. Ct. 2574 (1975)
Delaware v. Prouse, 440 U.S. 648, 59 L. Ed. 2d 660, 99 S. Ct. 1391 (1979)
United States v. Martinez-Feurte, 428 U.S. 543, 49 L. Ed. 2d 1116, 96 S. Ct. 3074 (1976)

Hazelwood School District v. Kuhlmeier, 484 U.S.; 98 L. Ed. 2d 592; 108 S. Ct. 562 (1988)

Staff members of *Spectrum,* a high school newspaper, filed a suit against the school district and school officials alleging that their First Amendment rights were violated when the school principal deleted two pages he found offensive which dealt with pregnancy and divorce. One of the articles dealt with teenage and school pregnancies. The principal felt that the articles did not adequately protect the anonymity of the pregnant students, friends, and parents. The other article dealt with the impact of divorce on students and, in particular, a student identified by name (later deleted) who was critical of her father's culpability in the divorce. The father did not have an opportunity to respond. The principal also objected to sexual references as inappropriate for some younger children in school. The United States District Court held that the school authorities were wrong in censoring *Spectrum*, the Court of Appeals reversed, the Supreme Court granted certiorari.

OPINION BY JUSTICE WHITE
(Vote: 5–3)

Question—Was *Spectrum* appropriately characterized as a forum for public expression?

Decision—No.

Reason—"The public schools do not possess all of the attributes of streets, parks, and other traditional public forums." School facilities are considered public forums if by policy or practice, they were open "for indiscriminate use by the general public." The government does not create a public forum "by inaction or by permitting limited discourse, but only by inten-

tionally opening a nontraditional forum." Student editors felt
that *Spectrum* could publish "practically anything" but school
officials retained ultimate control over what constituted responsible journalism in a school sponsored newspaper. "A
decision to teach leadership skills in the context of a classroom activity hardly implies a decision to relinquish school
control over that activity."

Corollary cases

Tinker v. Des Moines Independent Community School District, 393 U.S. 503,
 (1969)
Bethel School District No 403 v. Fraser, 478 U.S. 92 L. Ed. 2d 549, 106 S.
 Ct. 3159 (1986)
New Jersey v. T.L.O., 469 U.S. 325, 83 L. Ed. 2d 720, 105 S. Ct. 733 (1985)
Widmar v. Vincent, 454 U.S. 263, 70 L. Ed. 2d 440, 102 S. Ct. 269 (1981)
Perry Educational Association v. Perry Local Educators Association, 460
 U.S. 37, 74 L. Ed. 2d 794, 103 S. Ct. 948 (1983)
Cornelius v. NAACP Legal Defense & Educational Fund, Inc., 473 U.S. 788,
 87 L. Ed. 2d 567, 105 S. Ct. 3439 (1985)
Papish v. Board of Curators, 410 U.S. 667, 35 L. Ed. 2d 618, 93 S. Ct. 1197
 (1973)
Board of Education of Hendrick Hudson Central School District v. Rowley,
 458 U.S. 176, 73 L. Ed. 2d 690, 102 S. Ct. 3034 (1982)
Wood v. Strickland, 420 U.S. 308, 43 L. Ed. 2d 214, 95 S. Ct. 992 (1975)

Note—*Hazelwood* is best contrasted with *Tinker* v. *Des Moines*
(1969) in which the Court upheld "symbolic" speech as well
as "oral" speech and *Bethel School District* v. *Frazer* (1986)
in which the Court supported school officials who suspended
a student from class for two days for a sexually suggestive
speech at a school assembly. In *Tinker* the students were
protesting the Vietnam war by wearing black armbands to
class. Justice Black, dissented vigorously saying: "It is a myth
to say any person has a constitutional right to say what he
pleases, where he pleases, and when he pleases." It is worth
noting that Justice Brennan, voted with the majority in *Hazelwood*.

Edwards v. Aguillard, 482 U.S. _____; 96 L. Ed. 2d 510; 107 S. Ct. 2573 (1987)

Unless accompanied by a discussion of "creation science," "a Louisiana Act forbad the teaching of the theory

of evolution. The Act did not require the teaching of one or the other, but if either was taught, the other must be also. The point of the statute required the public schools to give "balanced treatment" to "creation science" and "evolution science." School boards were forbidden to discriminate against anyone who chose to be a creation scientist or teach creationism. The statute was challenged as a violation of the establishment clause of the First Amendment and the Constitution of Louisiana. In Louisiana, the State Supreme Court upheld the statute but it was declared invalid in the United States District Court. The Fifth Circuit affirmed in turn.

OPINION BY JUSTICE BRENNAN
(Vote: 7–2)

Question—Is the Louisiana statute requiring public schools that teach evolution to also teach "creation science" a violation of the First Amendment's establishment clause?

Decision—Yes.

Reason—The act violates the first part in the three prong test in *Lemon* v. *Kurtzman* (1971) in that the statute must have a secular purpose. The second part requires that the statute neither advances nor inhibits religion. The third part requires the law must not result in an excessive entanglement of government with religion. "A governmental intention to promote religion is clear when the state enacts a law to serve a religious purpose."

If the law was enacted for the purpose of endorsing religion, "no consideration of the second or third criteria (of *Lemon*) is necessary." It is clear "that requiring schools to teach creation science with evolution does not advance academic freedom." There can be no legitimate state interest in protecting particular religions from scientific views distasteful to them. "The preeminent purpose of Louisiana legislature was clearly to advance the religious viewpoint." The Louisiana act violates the First Amendment and seeks "to employ the symbolic and financial support of government to achieve a religious purpose." The appeal is affirmed.

Corollary cases

Epperson v. Arkansas, 393 U.S. 97, 21 L. Ed. 2d 228, 89 S. Ct. 266 (1968)

Lemon v. Kurtzman, 403 U.S. 602, 29 L. Ed. 2d 745, 91 S. Ct. 2105 (1971)

Bethel School District No. 403 v. Fraser, 478 U.S. _____ , 92 L. Ed. 2d 549, 106 S. Ct. 3159 (1986)

Board of Education v. Pico, 457 U.S. 853, 73 L. Ed. 2d 435, 102 S. Ct. 2799 (1982)

Marsh v. Chambers, 463 U.S. 783, 77 L. Ed. 2d 1019, 103 S. Ct. 3330 (1983)

Wallace v. Jaffree, 472 U.S. 38, 86 L. Ed. 2d 29, 105 S. Ct. 2479 (1985)

Tinker v. Des Moines, 393 U.S. 503, 21 L. Ed. 2d 731, S. Ct. 733 (1969)

Abington School Dist. v. Schempp, 374 U.S. 203, 10 L. Ed. 2d 844, 83 S. Ct. 1560 (1963)

Grand Rapids School District v. Ball, 473 U.S. 373, 87 L. Ed. 2d 267, 105 S. Ct. 2479 (1985)

Meek v. Pittenger, 421 U.S. 349, 44 L. Ed. 2d 217, 95 S. Ct. 1753 (1975)

Illinois Ex rel. McCollum v. Board of Education, 333 U.S. 203, 92 L. Ed. 649, 68 S. Ct. 461 (1948)

Widmar v. Vincent, 454 U.S. 263, 70 L. Ed. 2d 440, 102 S. Ct. 269 (1981)

Stone v. Graham, 449 U.S. 39, 66 L. Ed. 2d 199, 101 S. Ct. 191 (1980)

Lynch v. Donnelly, 465 U.S. 668, 79 L. Ed. 2d 604, 104 S. Ct. 1355 (1984)

DISCRIMINATION

Scott v. Sandford, 19 Howard 393; 15 L. Ed. 691 (1857)

In 1834, Dred Scott, a Negro slave belonging to Dr. Emerson, a surgeon in the United States Army, was taken by his master to Rock Island, Illinois, where slavery was prohibited by statute. Later he was taken, in 1836, to Fort Snelling, in the territory of Louisiana, which was north of the line of 36° 30', and consequently an area in which slavery had been forbidden by the Missouri Compromise. In 1838, he was brought back to Missouri, and in 1847 brought suit in the Missouri Circuit Court to recover his freedom, basing his action on previous decisions that residence in free territory conferred freedom. Before the commencement of this suit, Scott was sold to Sandford, a citizen of New York.

OPINION BY MR. CHIEF JUSTICE TANEY
(Vote: 7–2)

Question—Can a Negro slave become a member of the political community formed and brought into existence by the Constitution of the United States and as such become entitled to all the rights and privileges guaranteed by the Constitution to the citizen?

Decision—No.

Reason—The Court held that the Negro was not included, and not intended to be included under the word "citizen" in the Constitution, and therefore could claim none of the rights and privileges secured to citizens of the United States.

This did not prevent a state from bestowing the right of state citizenship upon any person it thought proper. However, no state could by a law of its own, make a person a member of the United States by making him a member in its own territory. Nor could a state clothe an individual with the rights and privileges of the United States, or of any other state.

The history of our country and the language of the Declaration of Independence, as well as the legislation of the colonies, point to the fact that the Negro had no rights that the white man was bound to respect, and that he might justly and lawfully be reduced to slavery. The Constitution shows that public opinion had undergone no change, and pledged the states to maintain the property of the master by returning any escaped slaves.

The next question involved asked was he, together with his family, free in Missouri by reason of the stay in the territory of the United States? The plaintiff here relied on the act of Congress prohibiting involuntary servitude north of Missouri (36° 30′). The difficulty here was whether Congress was authorized to pass such a law, according to the Constitution.

The power of Congress over the person or property of an individual can never be a mere discretionary power, but must be regulated by the Constitution. Rights of property are identified with the rights of a person who may not be deprived of them without due process of law. Therefore, an act of Congress that deprives a man of his property because he came into a particular territory can hardly be called the process of law. It was, therefore, the opinion of the Court that the act of Congress (The Missouri Compromise) that prohibited a citizen from holding property of this kind north of the line mentioned was not warranted in the Constitution, and was therefore void. Dred Scott and his family were not free by reason of being taken there.

The plaintiff also contended that he was free, by reason of being taken to Rock Island, in the State of Illinois, and that, being free, he was not again reduced to a state of slavery when brought back to Missouri. On the basis of the decision in *Strader* v. *Graham*, the Court held that the status of the slaves depended on the law of the state of residence. Therefore, Scott's status, free or slave, depended on the law of Missouri, not of Illinois.

In the light of these considerations, the plaintiff was not a citizen in the sense of the Constitution and the courts had no jurisdiction in this case.

Corollary cases

Strader et al. v. Graham, 10 Howard 82
United States v. Wong Kim Ark, 169 U.S. 649 (1898)
American Insurance Co. v. Canter, 1 Peters 511 (1828)

Bailey v. Alabama, 219 U.S. 219 (1911)
Pollock v. Williams, 322 U.S. 4 (1944)

Note—As a sign of the times, it is noteworthy that all nine justices wrote opinions in *Scott* and in *Brown* v. *Board of Education of Topeka,* 347 U.S. 483 (1954), just short of 100 years later in which the vote was a resounding 9 to 0. *Scott,* of course, had been reversed by the Fourteenth Amendment, Section I, which reads: "All persons born or naturalized in the United States, and subject to the jurisdiction thereof, are citizens of the United States and of the state wherein they reside."

The Civil Rights Cases, 109 U.S. 3; 3 S. Ct. 18; 27 L. Ed. 835 (1883)

> Various colored persons had been denied by the proprietors of hotels, theaters, and railway companies, the full enjoyment of the accommodations thereof, contrary to the act of Congress requiring no discrimination. Those proprietors had been indicted or sued for the penalty prescribed by the act.

OPINION BY MR. JUSTICE BRADLEY
(Vote: 8–1)

Question—Does the Fourteenth Amendment compel a private citizen to refrain from the practice of discrimination?

Decision—No.

Reason—The law was founded on the Fourteenth Amendment. This is concerned only with the state practicing discrimination. It makes no mention of individual persons infringing on individual rights. If the state does not assist the discrimination of an individual against another individual, it is purely a matter as between the two individuals. "In fine, the legislation which Congress is authorized to adopt in this behalf is not general legislation upon the rights of the citizen, but corrective legislation; that is, such as may be necessary and proper for counteracting such laws as the states may adopt or enforce, and which by the amendment they are prohibited from making or enforcing, or such acts and proceedings as the states may commit or take, and which by the amendment they are prohibited from committing or taking.''

Corollary cases

Virginia v. Rives, 100 U.S. 313 (1880)
United States v. Cruikshank, 92 U.S. 542 (1876)
United States v. Harris, 106 U.S. 629 (1883)
Screws v. United States, 325 U.S. 91 (1945)
Hamilton v. Regents of University of California, 293 U.S. 245 (1934)
Shelley v. Kraemer, 334 U.S. 1 (1948)
Home Telegraph and Telephone Co. v. City of Los Angeles, 227 U.S. 278 (1913)
Heart of Atlanta Hotel, Inc. v. U.S., 379 U.S. 241 (1965)
Katzenbach v. McClung, 379 U.S. 294 (1966)
Jones v. Mayer Co., 392 U.S. 409 (1968)
Rostker v. Goldberg, 453 U.S. _____; 69 L. Ed. 2d 478 (1981)
Rosales-Lopez v. United States, 451 U.S. _____; L. Ed. 2d 22 (1981)
Thomas v. Review Board of Indiana Employment Security Division, 57 L. Ed. 2d 624 (1981)
Fullilove v. Klutznick, 448 U.S. 448 (1980)
United States v. Weber, 443 U.S. 193 (1979)
Regents of the University of California v. Bakke, 438 U.S. 265 (1978)

Note—This was reversed in *Heart of Atlanta Motel* v. *United States,* 379 U.S. 241 (1965). Although used interchangeably, civil rights and civil liberties are slightly different, the former meaning rights belonging to someone by virtue of his status as a citizen and the Civil War amendments guarantee of racial equality, and the latter guaranteeing an individual the rights of thought, speech, and action.

Plessy v. Ferguson, 163 U.S. 537; 16 S. Ct. 1138; 41 L. Ed. 256 (1896)

In 1892, Plessy, a citizen of Louisiana, having seven-eighths Caucasian and one-eighth African blood, boarded a train from New Orleans to Covington in the same state. The conductor ordered him out of the car for white passengers and to sit in the Negro car. When Plessy refused to obey the order he was forcibly jailed by a policeman and convicted of violating a state statute of July 10, 1890, which required separate accommodations for white and colored passengers on railroads. An information was filed against him for the violation, and Plessy filed a demurrer against Ferguson, judge of the Criminal District Court. Plessy appealed on a writ of error when relief was denied him in the state court.

OPINION BY MR. JUSTICE BROWN
(Vote: 7–1)

Question—Does the Louisiana statute providing "equal but separate" railway carriages for the whites and colored violate the Thirteenth and Fourteenth Amendments?

Decision—No.

Reason—The object of the law is to ensure absolute equality of both races before the law. However, this is a political equality, not a social equality. The case hinges itself on the question of whether or not this is a reasonable regulation. Thus established usages, customs, and traditions, as well as the preservation of public peace and good order must be considered. Gauged by this standard, separate public conveyances are not unreasonable nor contrary to the Fourteenth Amendment.

If the colored race assumes that this separation makes them inferior, it is not by reason of the act. If the civil and political rights of both races be equal, that is sufficient. The Constitution cannot put them on the same plane socially.

Corollary cases

McCabe v. Atchison, Topeka and Santa Fe Ry. Co., 235 U.S. 151 (1914)
Shelley v. Kraemer, 334 U.S. 1 (1948)
Missouri ex rel. Gaines v. Canada, 305 U.S. 337 (1938)
Gayle v. Browder, 352 U.S. 903 (1956)
Sipuel v. Board of Regents of the University of Oklahoma, 332 U.S. 631 (1948)
Sweatt v. Painter, 338 U.S. 865 (1950)
Morgan v. Virginia, 328 U.S. 373 (1946)
Hall v. De Cuir, 95 U.S. 485 (1872)

Note—Despite the famous dissent by Justice Harlan, who said, "our Constitution is color-blind, and neither knows nor tolerates classes among citizens," the Court upheld the doctrine of "separate but equal," which continued until it was reversed in *Brown* v. *Board of Education of Topeka,* 347 U.S. 483 (1954).

Missouri ex rel. Gaines v. Canada, 305 U.S. 337; 59 S. Ct. 232; 83 L. Ed. 208 (1938)

> Lloyd Gaines, a Negro, was refused admittance to the Law School of the University of Missouri on the ground that he was colored. He had completed his undergraduate training at Lincoln University, an all-Negro school. It had been the practice of the state of Missouri to separate the white students from the colored students all through the school system, but as yet the state had not added a law school to the course of study at Lincoln University. If a Negro student wanted to go to law school, the state would pay his tuition in an out-of-state school that accepted Negroes.

OPINION BY MR. JUSTICE ROBERTS
(Vote: 7–2)

Question—Was the equal protection guarantee of the Fourteenth Amendment violated by this practice?

Decision—Yes.

Reason—The actions of the curators of the university must be considered equivalent to the official actions of the state itself. State policy is that Negroes attend Lincoln University while whites attend the University of Missouri. Meanwhile Negroes are granted the opportunity of studying, tuition paid, at any nearby state university pending the full development of Lincoln University to the level of the University of Missouri. While such an arrangement is praiseworthy, the fact that Lincoln University actually does not have a law school at present is a deprivation of equal privileges, since Gaines is denied an advantage extended to white students. The advantages of an alternate program allowing study in a nearby state and the relative excellence of that program with that offered by Missouri are beside the point since the whole consideration is whether or not Missouri had given equal privileges to both white and colored students within the state. This has not been done; therefore the state statute violates the Fourteenth Amendment by discrimination.

It was as an individual that he was entitled to the equal protection of the laws, and the state was bound to furnish him within its borders facilities for a legal education substantially equal to those that the state afforded for persons of the white race, even though he was the only Negro who wanted to study there.

Corollary cases

Yick Wo v. Hopkins, 118 U.S. 356 (1886)
McCabe v. Atchison, Topeka and Santa Fe R. R., 235 U.S. 151 (1914)
Sipuel v. Regents of University of Oklahoma, 332 U.S. 631 (1948)
Fisher v. Hurst, 333 U.S. 147 (1948)
Berea College v. Kentucky, 211 U.S. 45 (1908)
Cumming v. County Board of Education, 175 U.S. 528 (1899)
Gong Lum v. Rice, 275 U.S. 78 (1927)
McLaurin v. Oklahoma State Regents, 339 U.S. 637 (1950)
Sweatt v. Painter, 339 U.S. 629 (1950)
San Antonio Independent School District v. Rodriguez, 411 U.S. 1 (1973)
Richmond School Board v. Virginia State Board of Education, 412 U.S. 92 (1973)
Lau v. Nichols, 414 U.S. 563 (1974)
Runyon v. McCrary, 427 U.S. 160 (1976)
Dougherty County, Georgia, Board of Education v. White, 439 U.S. 32 (1978)

Note—One of the first of the cases challenging and ultimately reversing the "separate but equal" doctrine is *Plessy* v. *Ferguson,* 163 U.S. 537 (1896).

Morgan v. Commonwealth of Virginia, 328 U.S. 373; 66 S. Ct. 1050; 90 L. Ed. 1317 (1946)

This case involved a bus trip from Virginia, through the District of Columbia, to Baltimore. A state statute of Virginia required the assigning of separate seats or other space to white and colored persons, respectively. In this case the appellant, a Negro, was traveling on this bus. Upon her refusal to give up her seat to a white passenger and move to the rear of the bus, she was arrested, tried, and convicted under the Virginia statute.

OPINION BY MR. JUSTICE REED
(Vote: 7–1)

Question—Is the Virginia statute constitutional?

Decision—No.

Reason—As there was no federal act dealing with the separation of races in interstate transportation, the Court reasoned that they must decide the validity of this Virginia statute on the challenge that it interfered with commerce, as a matter of balance between the exercise of the local police power and the need for national uniformity in the regulations for interstate travel. It seemed clear to the Court that seating arrangements for the different races in interstate motor travel required a single, uniform rule to promote and protect national travel. Consequently, the Court held the Virginia statute in controversy invalid.

Corollary cases

Hall v. DeCuir, 95 U.S. 485 (1878)
Bob-Lo Excursion Co. v. Michigan, 333 U.S. 28 (1948)
Plessy v. Ferguson, 163 U.S. 537 (1896)
McCabe v. Atchison, Topeka and Santa Fe Ry. Co., 235 U.S. 151 (1914)
Henderson v. United States, 339 U.S. 816 (1950)

Note—The Court has been willing to permit state "police power" even in areas of interstate commerce if justified by local interests, but this does not cover a Jim Crow law to interstate bus passengers. It was under the Civil Rights Act of 1964—upheld in *Heart of Atlanta Motel* v. *United States,* 377 U.S. 218 (1964) that Congress, under the interstate commerce clause, ended discrimination in privately owned public accommodations.

Shelley v. Kraemer, 334 U.S. 1; 68 S. Ct. 836; 92 L. Ed. 1161 (1948)

This case involves two instances of enforcement by state courts of private agreements, known as restrictive covenants, that barred Negroes from holding real property in certain sections of St. Louis and Detroit. Shelley, a Negro, purchased some property in a section of St. Louis covered by a restrictive covenant that barred such Negro ownership. Other owners of property in the same area requested relief, but a Missouri trial court refused it. However, the Supreme Court of Missouri reversed the ruling of the lower court and ordered the Negroes to vacate their newly occupied property. The Detroit case was similar. Negroes acquired property in a privately restricted zone and were ordered out by a state court. The Supreme Court of Michigan upheld the lower court.

OPINION BY MR. CHIEF JUSTICE VINSON
(Vote: 6–0)

Question—Are orders by state courts enforcing private restrictive covenants based on race and color a violation of the equal protection clause of the Fourteenth Amendment?

Decision—Yes.

Reason—Restrictive covenants drawn up by private individuals are not in themselves a violation of the Fourteenth Amendment. As long as they are completely private and voluntary they are within the law. Here, however, there was more. The state, through its courts, aided in the enforcement of the covenants. Indeed, if it were not for the courts, the purpose of the agreements would not be fulfilled. The fact that the state merely carries out something started by private individuals does not free the state from a part in the original intent; nor does the fact that it is the judicial branch of the government that carries out the discrimination. The Court has consistently held that the judicial branch of the government is subject to the Constitution as much as are the executive and legislative branches. Thus the states here involved were playing, through their judiciaries, an integral part in a policy of discrimination in clear violation of the Fourteenth Amendment, which prohibits the states from denying equal protection of the laws.

Corollary cases

Civil Rights Cases, 109 U.S. 3 (1883)
Buchanan v. Warley, 245 U.S. 60 (1917)
Corrigan v. Buckley, 271 U.S. 323 (1926)
Hurd v. Hodge, 334 U.S. 24 (1948)
Slaughter-House Cases, 16 Wallace 36 (1873)
Barrows v. Jackson, 346 U.S. 249 (1953)
Jones v. Alfred H. Mayer Co., 392 U.S. 409 (1968)
Hunter v. Erickson, 393 U.S. 385 (1969)
Heart of Atlanta Motel v. United States, 379 U.S. 241 (1964)
Daniel v. Paul, 395 U.S. 298 (1969)
Tillman v. Wheaton-Haven Recreational Association, 410 U.S. 431 (1973)

Heart of Atlanta Motel, Inc. v. United States, 379 U.S. 241 (1965)

Note—*Shelley* does not invalidate private restrictive covenants but only state enforcement. It is worth noting, though, that *Jones* v. *Alfred H. Mayer Co.*, 392 U.S. 409 (1968) casts some doubt even on this view—if seen as a "conspiracy"—since the Civil Rights Act of 1866, enacted by Congress to enforce the Thirteenth Amendment, bars all racial discrimination, private as well as public, in the sale or rental of property.

Sweatt v. Painter, 339 U.S. 629; 70 S. Ct. 848; 94 L. Ed. 1114 (1950)

Sweatt was denied admission to the University of Texas Law School solely because he was colored and Negroes by state law were prohibited from admission to the school. The state of Texas then established a Law School for Negroes that was not on an academic par with the Law School of the University of Texas.

OPINION BY MR. CHIEF JUSTICE VINSON
(No evidence from the report that the decision was not unanimous.)

Question—Was there denial of equal protection?

Decision—Yes.

Reason—As an individual Sweatt was entitled to the equal protection of the laws, and the state was bound to furnish facilities for legal education substantially equal to those the state afforded to persons of the white race. Such education was not available to him in a separate law school as offered by the state.

Corollary cases

Shelley v. Kraemer, 334 U.S. 1 (1948)
Missouri ex rel. Gaines v. Canada, 305 U.S. 337 (1938)
Sipuel v. Board of Regents, 332 U.S. 631 (1948)
Fisher v. Hurst, 333 U.S. 147 (1948)
McLaurin v. Oklahoma State Regents, 339 U.S. 637 (1950)
Craig v. Boren, 429 U.S. 190 (1977)
Stanton v. Stanton, 421 U.S. 7 (1975)
Heart of Atlanta Motel, 379 U.S. 241 (1964)
Katzenbach v. McClung, 379 U.S. 294 (1964)

Note—*Sweatt* is a pre-*Brown* case, during the "separate but equal" era that had been established in *Plessy* v. *Ferguson,* 163 U.S. 537 (1896).

Brown v. Board of Education of Topeka, 347 U.S. 483; 74 S. Ct. 686; 98 L. Ed. 873 (1954)

A series of cases went to the Supreme Court from the states of Kansas, South Carolina, Virginia, and Delaware. Since all of the cases involved the same basic problem— Negro minors, through their legal representatives, seeking the aid of the courts in obtaining admission to the public schools of their respective communities on a nonsegregated basis—all were determined by one decision of the Court. The Kansas case is taken as the nominal leading case. In the various states, the Negro children were of elementary or high school age or both. Segregation requirements were on a statutory and state constitutional basis except in Kansas where only statutory provisions were involved.

Opinion by Mr. Chief Justice Warren
(Vote: 9–0)

Question—Does segregation of children in public schools solely on the basis of race, even though the physical facilities and other "tangible" factors may be equal, deprive the children of the minority group of equal educational opportunities?

Decision—Yes.

Reason—Intangible factors involved in the separation of students of similar age and qualifications solely because of their race need very serious consideration. Such segregation of white and colored children in public schools has a detrimental effect upon the colored children, an impact that is greater when it has the sanction of law. It "generates a feeling of inferiority as to their status in the community that may affect their hearts and minds in a way unlikely ever to be undone. . . . We conclude that in the field of public education the doctrine of 'separate but equal' has no place. Separate educational facilities are inherently unequal. Therefore, we hold that the plaintiffs and others similarly situated for whom the actions have been brought are, by reason of the segregation complained of, deprived of the equal protection of the laws guaranteed by the Fourteenth Amendment.''

Corollary cases

Plessy v. Ferguson, 163 U.S. 537 (1896)
McCabe v. Atchison, Topeka and Santa Fe Ry. Co., 235 U.S. 151 (1914)
Henderson v. U.S., 339 U.S. 816 (1950)
Shelley v. Kraemer, 334 U.S. 1 (1948)
Morgan v. Virginia, 328 U.S. 373 (1946)
Sweatt v. Painter, 339 U.S. 629 (1950)
Bolling v. Sharp, 347 U.S. 497 (1954)
McLaurin v. Oklahoma State Regents, 339 U.S. 637 (1950)
Wright v. Council of the City of Emporia, 407 U.S. 451 (1972)
United States v. Scotland Neck City Board of Education, 407 U.S. 484 (1972)
Gong Lum v. Rice, 275 U.S. 78 (1927)
State of Missouri ex rel. Gaines v. Canada, 305 U.S. 337 (1938)
Sipuel v. Board of Regents, 332 U.S. 631 (1948)
Berea College v. Kentucky, 211 U.S. 45 (1908)
Buchanan v. Warley, 245 U.S. 60 (1917)
Cooper v. Aaron, 358 U.S. 1 (1958)
Shuttleworth v. Birmingham Board of Education, 358 U.S. 101 (1958)
Green v. County School Board, 391 U.S. 430 (1968)
Swann v. Charlotte-Mecklenburg Board of Education, 402 U.S. 1 (1971)
San Antonio Independent School District v. Rodriguez, 411 U.S. 1 (1973)
Regents of the University of California v. Bakke, 438 U.S. 265 (1978)

Note—This was the historic school desegregation case that reversed the "separate but equal" doctrine of *Plessy* v. *Ferguson,* 163 U.S. 537 (1896).

Loving v. Virginia, 388 U.S. 1; 87 S. Ct. 1817; 18 L. Ed. 2d 1010 (1967)

Two residents of Virginia, a Negro woman and a white man, Richard Loving, were married in the District of Columbia. They then returned to Caroline County, Virginia. There they were indicted for violation of Virginia's ban on interracial marriages. Their conviction was upheld by the Supreme Court of Appeals of Virginia. The central provision of the state's Racial Integrity Act was the absolute prohibition of a "white person" marrying other than another "white person." The term "white person" was defined in the statute.

OPINION BY MR. CHIEF JUSTICE WARREN
(Vote: 9–0)

Question—Does the statutory scheme of Virginia to prevent marriages between persons solely on the basis of racial classification violate the Fourteenth Amendment?

Decision—Yes.

Reason—The statutes violate both the equal protection and due process clauses of the Fourteenth Amendment. "There can be no question but that Virginia's miscegenation statutes rest solely upon distinctions drawn according to race. . . . There can be no doubt that restricting the freedom to marry solely because of racial classifications violates the central meaning of the equal protection clause. . . . The freedom to marry has long been recognized as one of the vital personal rights essential to the orderly pursuit of happiness by free men. Marriage is one of the 'basic civil rights of man,' fundamental to our very existence and survival. . . . Under our Constitution, the freedom to marry or not marry, a person of another race resides with the individual and cannot be infringed by the state."

Corollary cases

Pace v. Alabama, 106 U.S. 583 (1882)
McLaughlin v. Florida, 379 U.S. 184 (1964)
Brown v. Board of Education, 347 U.S. 483 (1954)
Strauder v. West Virginia, 100 U.S. 303 (1880)
Skinner v. Oklahoma, 316 U.S. 535 (1942)
Maynard v. Hill, 125 U.S. 190 (1888)
Zablocki v. Redhail, 434 U.S. 324 (1978)
Orr v. Orr, 440 U.S. 268 (1979)
Griswold v. Connecticut, 381 U.S. 479 (1965)
Roe v. Wade, 410 U.S. 113 (1973)
Missouri v. Danforth, 428 U.S. 52 (1976)
Dandridge v. Williams, 397 U.S. 471 (1970)

Note—This is the first case in which the Court explicitly noted that classification by race was "inherently suspect" and only under compelling state reasons justifiable. Along with *Virginia*, antimiscegenation laws in some fifteen states were invalidated.

McLaurin v. Oklahoma State Regents, 339 U.S. 637; 70 S. Ct. 851; 96 L. Ed. 1149 (1950)

Mr. G. W. McLaurin, a Negro, applied to the University of Oklahoma to pursue studies leading to a doctorate in education. His application was denied solely because of his race. McLaurin filed complaint, alleging that the action of the school authorities and the statutes upon which their action was based were unconstitutional and deprived him of equal protection of the laws. A three-judge district court held that the state had a constitutional duty to provide him with the education he sought as soon as it had provided that education for applicants of any other group. It held void the Oklahoma statutes that denied him admission.

The Oklahoma legislature amended its laws to permit admission of Negroes to institutions of higher learning, provided such courses were not available in Negro schools. Such instruction, however, was to be given on a segregated basis. McLaurin was required to sit at a desk in an anteroom adjoining the classroom, to sit at a designated desk on the mezzanine floor of the library, not to use the desks in the regular reading room, and to eat at a different time in the school cafeteria. McLaurin filed a motion to have these conditions removed, which the lower court rejected, holding that the Fourteenth Amendment was not violated. McLaurin then appealed to the United States Supreme Court.

Opinion by Mr. Chief Justice Vinson
(No evidence from the report that the decision was not unanimous.)

Question—Can a state, in its state university, after admitting a student to graduate instruction, afford him different treatment from the other students solely because of his race?

Decision—No.

Reason—It was argued that the separations imposed were merely nominal, in order to comply with the statutory laws of Oklahoma, but it was significant that the state set McLaurin apart from the other students, thus hindering his pursuit of effective graduate study. "There is a vast difference—a Constitutional difference—between restrictions imposed by the state which prohibit the intellectual commingling of students and the refusal of individuals to commingle where the state presents no such bar." The conditions under which this appellant was forced to study deprived him of his personal and present right to equal protection of the laws.

Corollary cases

Missouri ex rel. Gaines v. Canada, 305 U.S. 337 (1938)
Sipuel v. Board of Regents, 332 U.S. 631 (1948)
Shelley v. Kraemer, 334 U.S. 1 (1948)
Sweatt v. Painter, 339 U.S. 629 (1950)
Palmer v. Thompson, 403 U.S. 217 (1971)
Moose Lodge No. 107 v. Irvis, 407 U.S. 163 (1972)
Brown v. Board of Education, 347 U.S. 483 (1954)
Plessy v. Ferguson, 163 U.S. 537 (1896)
United States v. Scotland Neck Board of Education, 407 U.S. 484 (1972)
Runyon v. McCrary, Fairfax-Brewster School v. Gonzalez, 427 U.S. 160
  (1976)
Lau v. Nichols, 414 U.S. 563 (1974)

Note—*McLaurin* and *Sweatt* v. *Painter,* 339 U.S. 629 (1950) were handed down the same day. Both cases helped corrode the "separate but equal" doctrine of *Plessy* v. *Ferguson.*

Jones v. Alfred H. Mayer Co., 392 U.S. 409; 88 S. Ct. 2186; 20 L. Ed. 2d 1189 (1968)

Jones claimed that the Mayer Company had refused to sell him a house in a particular section of St. Louis County solely because of his race, Negro. A federal statute enacted in 1866 under the power granted to Congress to enforce the Thirteenth Amendment places all citizens on the same level as white citizens to receive, hold, and dispose of real and personal property.

Opinion by Mr. Justice Stewart
(Vote: 7–2)

Question—Does the statute apply to private as well as public sale or rental of property?

Decision—Yes.

Reason—Congress has the power under the Thirteenth Amendment rationally to determine what are the "badges and the incidents of slavery" and the authority to translate that determination into legislation. Such badges of slavery include restraints on the right to inherit, purchase, lease, sell, and convey property. The statute prohibits all discrimination against Negroes in matters of property by private owners as well as by public authorities.

Corollary cases

Hurd v. Hodge, 334 U.S. 24 (1948)
Shelley v. Kraemer, 334 U.S. 1 (1948)
Civil Rights Cases, 109 U.S. 3 (1883)
Buchanan v. Warley, 245 U.S. 60 (1917)
Hunter v. Erickson, 393 U.S. 385 (1969)
Reitman v. Mulkey, 387 U.S. 369 (1967)

Note—*Mayer* shored up the Thirteenth Amendment's purpose of preventing racial discrimination and supported minorities in fighting racial discrimination in housing. *Mayer* also supported the open housing provisions of the Civil Rights Act of 1968.

Moose Lodge No. 107 v. Irvis, 407 U.S. 163; 92 S. Ct. 1965; 32 L. Ed. 2d 627 (1972)

Leroy Irvis, a Negro, was refused service by the Moose Lodge of Harrisburg, Pennsylvania, while he was the guest of a member. Irvis claimed that since the state liquor board had issued the lodge a private club liquor license, the refusal of service to him was a "state action" in violation of the equal protection clause of the Fourteenth Amendment.

OPINION BY MR. JUSTICE REHNQUIST
(Vote: 6–3)

Question—Was this discrimination by the lodge in effect state action because of the state's part in granting a liquor license?

Decision—No.

Reason—The Moose Lodge is a private club in the ordinary meaning of that term. It is not publicly funded. Only members and guests are permitted in any lodge of the order. The Court has never held that a private entity that discriminates involves the state because of some benefit or service furnished by the state. Since state-furnished services include all manner of things, such as police and fire protection, such a holding would utterly emasculate the distinction between private as distinguished from state conduct. The state must have significantly involved itself with invidious discriminations in order for the discriminatory action to fall within the ambit of the constitutional prohibition.

Corollary cases

Daniel v. Paul, 395 U.S. 298 (1969)
Burton v. Wilmington Parking Authority, 365 U.S. 715 (1951)
Peterson v. City of Greenville, 373 U.S. 244 (1963)
Reitman v. Mulkey, 387 U.S. 369 (1967)
Civil Rights Cases, 109 U.S. 3 (1883)
Tillman v. Wheaton-Haven Recreation Association Inc., 410 U.S. 431 (1973)
Evans v. Newton, 382 U.S. 296 (1966)

Note—"State action" involves an official act by the state or an officer in violation of the Fourteenth Amendment. Thus a discriminatory act by a private official unconnected with governmental power is exempt. A twist in *Moose Lodge* occurred when the Pennsylvania Civil Rights Commission went to Court claiming that the Moose Lodge, however, violated a state statute. Moose Lodge appealed on the basis of *Moose Lodge* v. *Irvis,* but the Supreme Court denied certiorari, letting the state statute stand.

Although not involving "state action" but touching "compelling state interest" constitutional development is narrowing—if not abolishing—the difference between "private" and "public" the "right of association" or the right of the people to "peaceably to assemble." Thus in *Roberts v. United States Jaycees* (82 L. Ed. 2d 462, 1984) the Court held that a state law mandating that the Jaycees accept women as members did not violate the "right of association." *In the Board of Directors of Rotary International* v. *Rotary Club of Duarte* (95 L. Ed. 2d 474, 1987), Rotary like the Jaycees was told to admit women to membership because it was not a small intimate club that needed constitutional protection. New York City law indicates how a law can be narrowed to meet the requirements of those favoring "right of privacy" and those favoring the "right of association." In *New York State Club Association* v.

City of New York (101 L. Ed. 2d 1, 1988) the Court upheld in a 9–0 decision New York City's antidiscrimination law (religious associations and benevolent orders).

Milliken v. Bradley, 418 U.S. 717; 94 S. Ct. 3112; 41 L. Ed. 2d 1069 (1974)

> Both the federal district court and the court of appeals had held that to bring about the desegregation of the Detroit city schools there needed to be mandatory busing of children across boundary lines between the Detroit school district and adjacent or nearby school districts, specially to Wayne, Oakland, and Macomb counties. The lower courts agreed on an order for such busing.

OPINION BY MR. CHIEF JUSTICE BURGER
(Vote: 5–4, Marshall, White, Douglas and Brennan dissenting.)

Question—Does the equal protection clause, which prohibits segregated education, require busing between independent school districts to bring about desegregation?

Decision—No.

Reason—School district lines cannot be casually ignored or treated as a mere administrative convenience. Such would be contrary to the history and tradition of public education. In this country local autonomy for school districts has long been thought essential. However, school district lines are not sacrosanct if they conflict with the Fourteenth Amendment. Here the Court held that there was no inter-district violation and so no basis for an inter-district remedy. Even if the state might be derivatively responsible for Detroit's segregated conditions, there was no constitutional justification for an inter-district remedy since there was no evidence of activity by the state or outlying districts that had a cross-district effect. The constitutional right of Negroes residing in Detroit is to attend a unitary school system in that district. Cross-district busing would involve an expansion of that right without any support in either constitutional principle or precedent.

Corollary cases

Brown v. Board of Education, 347 U.S. 483 (1954)
Swann v. Charlotte-Mecklenburg Board of Education, 402 U.S. 1 (1971)

San Antonio Independent School District v. Rodriguez, 411 U.S. 1 (1973)
Runyon v. McRary, 427 U.S. 160 (1976)
Pasadena City Board of Education v. Spangler, 427 U.S. 424 (1976)
Green v. County School Board, 391 U.S. 430 (1968)
Wright v. Council of the City of Emporia, 407 U.S. 451 (1972)
United States v. Scotland Neck City Board of Education, 407 U.S. 484 (1972)
Memphis v. Greene, 67 L. Ed. 2d 769 (1981)
Keyes v. School District #1, Denver, 413 U.S. 189 (1973)
Dayton (Ohio) Board of Education v. Brinkman, 433 U.S. 406 (1977)

Note—By contrast, though, the Court held, in a case involving public housing, *Hills* v. *Gautreaux,* 425 U.S. 284 (1976), that intergovernmental remedies are permissible for an areawide solution to segregation in public housing in Chicago.

Village of Arlington Heights v. Metropolitan Housing Development Corporation, 429 U.S. 252; 50 L. Ed. 2d 450; 97 S. Ct. 555 (1977)

In 1971 the Metropolitan Housing Development Corporation petitioned the Village of Arlington Heights, Illinois, to rezone a fifteen-acre parcel of land from a single family to a multiple family classification. Arlington Heights is located twenty-six miles northwest of Chicago. A series of three public hearings were held and following the last one the Village Plan Commission denied the rezoning by a 6–1 vote. The United States District Court concluded that the denial would not have a racially discriminatory effect but on appeal to the court of appeals, the district court was reversed holding that the denial of the proposed Lincoln Green would have a racially discriminatory effect. The Supreme Court granted the Village's petition for certiorari.

OPINION BY MR. JUSTICE POWELL
(Vote: 7–1)

Question—Is the refusal of the Village of Arlington Heights to rezone land from a single family to multiple family classification, at the request of a nonprofit developer, racially discriminatory and does it violate, *inter alia,* the equal protection clause of the Fourteenth Amendment?

Decision—No.

Reason—The Court admits that not to rezone would have racial effects given the small percentage of minorities in the village and given the further fact that, if the proposed Lincoln Green were built, that at least 40 percent of the income groups eligible to live there were members of a minority. Citing *Washington v. Davis,* 426 U.S. 229, however, the Court said: "Disproportionate impact is not irrelevant, but it is not the sole touchstone of an invidious racial discrimination." After setting out some examples of discriminatory purpose, the Court said as regards the village: "But there is little about the sequence of events leading up to the decision that would spark suspicion. Discrimination was not a motivating factor in the village's decision. This conclusion ends the constitutional inquiry."

Corollary cases

Washington v. Davis, 426 U.S. 229 (1976)
Brown v. General Services Administration, 425 U.S. 820 (1977)
Kelly v. Johnson, 425 U.S. 238 (1976)
Hills v. Gautreaux, 425 U.S. 284 (1976)
Massachusetts Board of Retirement v. Murgia, 427 U.S. 307 (1976)
City of Eastlake v. Forest City Enterprises, Inc., 426 U.S. 668 (1976)
Warth v. Seldin, 422 U.S. 490 (1975)
Schad v. Mt. Ephraim, 68 L. Ed. 2d 671 (1981)
Memphis v. Green, 67 L. Ed. 2d 769 (1981)
Agins v. Tiburon, 65 L. Ed. 2d 106 (1980)
County Board of Arlington County v. Richard, 434 U.S. 5 (1977)
Moore v. East Cleveland, 437 U.S. 494 (1977)

Note—Since the leading case of *Euclid* v. *Ambler Realty Co.,* 272 U.S. 365 (1926), the Court has hesitated to reject state zoning laws unless they impinge on the equal protection clause of the Fourteenth Amendment. Thus, in *Village of Belle Terre* v. *Boraas,* 416 U.S. 1 (1974), the Court rejected a challenge on equal protection grounds to an ordinance that prohibited more than two unrelated persons from sharing a single family residence.

United Steel Workers of America v. Weber, Kaiser Aluminum v. Weber, United States v. Weber, 443 U.S. 193; 61 L. Ed. 2d 480; 99 S. Ct. 2721 (1979)

In 1974 petitioner United Steel Workers of America (USWA) and petitioner Kaiser Aluminum and Chemical Corporation (Kaiser) entered into a master collective-bargaining agreement covering terms and conditions of employment. It included an affirmative action plan designed to eliminate racial imbalances in Kaiser's then almost exclusively white craftwork forces by reserving for black employees 50 percent of the openings in in-plant craft-training programs until the percentage of black craftworkers were equal to the percentage of blacks in the local labor force. Selection of craft trainees was made on the basis of seniority. At the Kaiser plant in Gramercy, La., a black was selected with less seniority than several white production workers whose bids for admission were rejected. Thereafter, Brian Weber instituted a class action in the U.S. district court alleging that the manner of filling craft trainee positions discriminated against him in violation of Title VII of the Civil Rights Act of 1964.

OPINION BY MR. JUSTICE BRENNAN
(Vote: 5–2)

Question—Does Title VII prohibit all private, voluntary race-conscious affirmative action plans?

Decision—No.

Reason—"Given . . . legislative history, we cannot agree with respondent that Congress intended to prohibit the private sector from taking effective steps to accomplish the goal that Congress designed Title VII to achieve . . . in view of Congress's desire to avoid undue federal regulation of private businesses, use of the word 'require' rather than the phrase 'require or permit' (in Sec. 703 j) fortifies the conclusion that Congress did not intend to limit traditional business freedom to such a degree as to prohibit all voluntary, race-conscious affirmative action. We need not today define in detail the line of demarcation between permissible and impermissible affirmative action plans. It suffices to hold that the challenged Kaiser-USWA affirmative action plan falls on the permissible side of the line. The purposes of the plan mirror those of the statute. Both were designed to break down old patterns of racial segregation and hierarchy. Both were structured to 'open employment opportunities for Negroes in occupations which have been traditionally closed to them.' At the same time the plan does not unnecessarily trammel the interests of the white employees. The plan does not require the discharge of white workers and their replacement with new black hires. Nor does the plan create an absolute bar to the advance of white employees; half of those trained in the program will be white. Moreover, the plan is a temporary measure; it is not intended to maintain racial balance, but simply to eliminate a manifest racial imbalance. We conclude, therefore, that the adoption of the Kaiser-USWA plan for the Gramercy plant falls within the area of discretion left by Title VII to the private sector voluntarily to adopt affirmative action plans designed to eliminate conspicuous racial imbalance in traditionally segregated job categories.''

Corollary cases

McDonald v. Santa Fe Trail Trans. Co., 427 U.S. 273 (1976)
Albemark v. Moody, 422 U.S. 405 (1975)
Train v. Colorado Public Interest Research Group, 426 U.S. 1 (1976)
Woodworkers v. N.L.R.B., 386 U.S. 612 (1967)
United States v. American Trucking Associations, 310 U.S. 534 (1940)
United States v. Public Utilities Commission, 345 U.S. 295 (1953)
Alexander v. Gardner-Denver Co., 415 U.S. 36 (1974)
Thomas v. Review Board of Indiana Employment Security Division, 67 L. Ed. 2d 624 (1981)
County of Washington v. Gunther, 68 L. Ed. 2d 751 (1981)
California Brewers Association v. Bryant, 444 U.S. 598 (1980)
Fullilove v. Klutznick, 448 U.S. 448 (1980)

Note—To quote a widely used phrase by Harold W. Chase and Craig R. Ducat, *Bakke* seemed to take the word "quota" out of "benign quota," and *Weber* seemed to put it back again. The Court emphasized that *Weber* was a narrow decision since the plan was voluntary and did not involve state action, and thus was not a violation of the equal protection clause of the Fourteenth Amendment.

Fullilove v. Klutznick, 448 U.S. 448; 65 L. Ed. 2d 902; 100 S. Ct. 2758 (1980)

In 1977 Congress passed the Public Works Employment Act, which provides that "at least 10 percent of federal funds for local public works projects must be used by the state or local grantee to procure services or supplies from businesses owned by minority group members, defined as United States citizens," who are Negroes, Spanish-speaking, Orientals, Indians, Eskimos and Aleuts. The "minority business enterprise" (MBE) section of the act also requires the government to seek out all available, qualified MBEs, lower or waive bonding requirements where feasible, help in getting working capital, and award contracts to MBEs even though they are not the lowest bidders. Several associations of construction contractors and subcontractors filed suit alleging they suffered economic injury under MBE requirements and on its face violated, *inter alia,* the equal protection clause of the Fourteenth Amendment. The district court upheld the MBE program and the court of appeals affirmed.

OPINION BY MR. CHIEF JUSTICE BURGER
(Vote: 6–3)

Question—Does the "minority business enterprise" (MBE) requirement of the Public Works Employment Act of 1977 violate the equal protection clause of the Fourteenth Amendment?

Decision—No.

Reason—"This Court has recognized that the power to provide for the . . . general welfare" is an independent grant of legislative authority distinct from other broad congressional powers ". . . Congress has frequently employed the spending power to further broad policy objectives by conditioning receipt of federal monies upon compliance by the recipient with federal statutory and administrative directives. . . . The reach of the spending power, within its sphere, is at least as broad as the regulatory powers of Congress. If, pursuant to its regulatory powers, Congress could have achieved the objectives of the MBE program, then it may do so under the spending power." Congress ". . . could have drawn on the Commerce clause to regulate the practices of prime contractors on federally funded public works projects." Moreover a ". . . review of our cases persuades us that the objectives of the MBE program are within the power of Congress under (Section) 5 'to enforce by appropriate legislation' the equal protection guarantees of the Fourteenth Amendment. . . . We reject the contention that in the remedial context the Congress must act in a wholly 'color-blind' fashion. Where federal anti-discrimination laws have been violated, an equitable remedy may in the appropriate case include a racial or ethnic factor. . . . Congress, not the Courts, has the heavy burden of dealing with a host of intractable economic and social problems.''

Corollary cases

Swann v. Charlotte-Mecklenberg Board of Education, 402 U.S. 1 (1971)
McDaniel v. Barresi, 402 U.S. 39 (1971)
North Carolina Board of Education v. Swann, 402 U.S. 43 (1971)
Blodgett v. Holden, 275 U.S. 142 (1927)
CBS v. Democratic National Committee, 412 U.S. 94 (1973)
Cleveland v. National College of Business, 435 U.S. 213 (1978)
Buckley v. Valeo, 424 U.S. 1 (1976)
United States v. Butler, 297 U.S. 1 (1936)
California Bankers Association v. Shultz, 416 U.S. 21 (1974)
Oklahoma v. U.S. Civil Service Commission, 330 U.S. 127 (1947)
Helvering v. Davis, 301 U.S. 619 (1937)
Steward Machine Co. v. Davis, 301 U.S. 548 (1937)
Heart of Atlanta Motel v. United States, 379 U.S. 241 (1964)
Franks v. Bowman Transportation Co., 424 U.S. 747 (1976)
International Brotherhood of Teamsters v. United States, 431 U.S. 324 (1977)
Katzenbach v. Morgan, 384 U.S. 641 (1966)
Lau v. Nichols, 414 U.S. 563 (1974)

McCleskey v. Kemp, 481 U.S. _____; 95 L. Ed. 2d 262; 107 S. Ct. 1756 (1987)

McCleskey, a black man, was convicted in a Georgia Court for armed robbery and the murder of a police officer. The jury recommended the death penalty. After unsuccessfully seeking relief in state courts, he sought a writ of habeas corpus in the federal district court on the grounds, inter alia, that the sentencing process was administered in a radically biased manner. He offered a statistical study (Baldus Study) of some 2,000 murder cases that occurred in Georgia during the 1970s that "indicates that black defendants who killed white victims have the greatest likelihood of receiving the death penalty." The district court dismissed the petition, which was affirmed by the court of appeals. The Supreme Court granted certiorari.

Opinion by Justice Powell
(Vote: 5–4)

Question—Does a complex statistical study that indicates that racial discrimination affects capital sentencing determination prove that McCleskey's capital sentence is unconstitutional under Eighth and Fourteenth Amendments?

Decision—No.

Reason—The federal district and court of appeals found the Baldus Study flawed; data was incomplete, did not take into account to catch the full degree of the aggravating or mitigating circumstances, researchers could not discover whether penalty trials were held in many of the cases, there was no preponderance of evidence that the study data was trustworthy, the methodology was infirm, the various models instable, and correlations between race and nonracial variables unpersuasive. The basic principle is not only that the defendant has to prove the existence of purposeful discrimination but that the decisionmakers in *his* case acted with discriminatory purpose. He offers no evidence specific to his own case that would support an inference that racial considerations played a part in his sentence." The Court has accepted statistics showing a violation of equal protection (as in selection of a jury) and to prove statutory violations. The Baldus Study is insufficient to support an inference of discrimination. We find, in fact, that the "Georgia capital sentencing system could operate in a fair and neutral manner." On this issue objective indicia which reflects the public attitude toward this sanction is firm. Judgment of the court of appeals affirmed the decision.

Corollary cases

Whitus v. Georgia, 385 U.S. 545, 17 L. Ed. 2d 599, 87 S. Ct. 643 (1967)
Wayte v. United States, 470 U.S. 598, 84 L. Ed. 2d 547, 105 S. Ct. 1524 (1985)
Arlington Heights v. Metropolitan Housing Dev. Corp., 49 U.S. 252, 50 L. Ed. 2d 450, 97 S. Ct. 555 (1977)
Gomillion v. Lightfoot, 364 U.S. 339, 5 L. Ed. 2d 110, 81 S. Ct. 125 (1960)
Yo Wick v. Hopkins, 118 U.S. 356, 30 L. Ed. 220, 6 S. Ct. 1064 (1886)
Castaneda v. Partida, 430 U.S. 482, 51 L. Ed. 2d 498, 97 S. Ct. 1272 (1977)

Texas Dept. of Community Affairs v. Burdine, 450 U.S. 248, 67 L. Ed. 2d 207, 101 S. Ct. 1089 (1981)

McDonnel Douglas Corp. v. Green, 411 U.S. 792, 36 L. Ed. 2d 668, 93 S. Ct. 1817 (1973)

Borden Kircher v. Hayes, 434 U.S. 357, 54 L. Ed. 2d 604, 98 S. Ct. 663 (1978)

McDonald v. Pless, 238 U.S. 264, 59 L. Ed. 1300, 35 S. Ct. 783 (1915)

Gregg v. Georgia, 428 U.S. 226, 49 L. Ed. 2d 859, 96 S. Ct. 2909 (1976)

Batson v. Kentucky, 476 U.S. _____, 90 L. Ed. 2d 69, 106 S. Ct. 1712 (1986)

Personnel Admin. of Mass. v. Feeney, 442 U.S. 256, 60 L. Ed. 2d 870, 99 S. Ct. 2282 (1979)

In rem Kemmler, 136 U.S. 436, 34 L. Ed. 519, 10 S. Ct. 930 (1890)

Weems v. United States, 217 U.S. 349, 54 L. Ed. 793, 30 S. Ct. 544 (1910)

Trop v. Dulles, 356 U.S. 86, 2 L. Ed. 2d 630, 78 S. Ct. 590 (1958)

Emmund v. Florida, 458 U.S. 782, 73 L. Ed. 2d 1140, 102 S. Ct. 3368 (1977)

Coker v. Georgia, 433 U.S. 584, 53 L. Ed. 2d 982, 97 S. Ct. 2861 (1977)

Note—In addition to the majority rationale, a factor very much in the mind of the Court is the uneasiness except in carefully defined areas such as racial discrimination in the public schools, work place, or racial exclusion on juries of imperiling the criminal justice system mired in social science statistics. Thus, through a "process of regressive analysis" statistics could be utilized in disparities among races, attorneys, judges, gender, geography, social classes and the like.

RELIGION

West Virginia State Board of Education v. Barnette, 319 U.S. 624; 63 S. Ct. 1178, 87 L. Ed. 1628 (1943)

Following the decision of the Supreme Court in *Minersville School District* v. *Gobitis,* 310 U.S. 586, the West Virginia legislature amended its statutes to require all schools to conduct courses in history, civics, and the Constitution. The Board of Education went further and required a salute and a pledge of allegiance to the flag. Failure to conform was insubordination, dealt with by expulsion. Readmission was denied by statute until compliance. Meanwhile the expelled child was unlawfully absent and the parents were subject to a fine. The appellees, who were Jehovah's Witnesses, sought to restrain the enforcement of this statute.

OPINION BY MR. JUSTICE JACKSON
(Vote: 6–3)

Question—Is the statute contrary to the First and Fourteenth Amendments?

Decision—Yes.

Reason—Denial of the freedoms guaranteed by the Constitution can only be due to present grave and immediate danger to interests that the state can lawfully protect. The limitations of the Constitution are applied with no fear that freedom to be intellectually and spiritually diverse or even contrary will disintegrate social organization. Freedom of religion and expression cannot be hampered when the expressions and the religious practices dealt with are harmless to others and to the state, as is here the case. "If there is any fixed star in our constitutional constellation, it is that no official, high or petty, can prescribe what shall be orthodox in politics, nationalism, religion, or other matters of opinion or force citizens to confess by word or act their faith therein. If there are any circumstances which permit an exception, they do not now occur to us."

The Court felt that the action of the local authorities in compelling the flag salute and pledge transcended constitutional limitations on their power and invaded the sphere of intellect and spirit that the First Amendment to our Constitution reserves from all official control. Therefore, the Court overruled the *Minersville School District* v. *Gobitis* decision and affirmed the order restraining the West Virginia regulations.

Corollary cases

Stromberg v. California, 283 U.S. 359 (1931)
Minersville School District v. Gobitis, 310 U.S. 586 (1940)
Meyer v. Nebraska, 262 U.S. 390 (1923)
Cochran v. Louisiana State Board of Education, 281 U.S. 370 (1930)
Everson v. Board of Education of Ewing Township, 330 U.S. 1 (1947)
McCollum v. Board of Education, 333 U.S. 203 (1948)
Zorach v. Clauson, 343 U.S. 307 (1952)
Doremus v. Board of Education, 342 U.S. 429 (1952)
Welsh v. United States, 398 U.S. 333 (1970)

Note—*Barnette* reversed *Minersville School District* v. *Gobitis,* 310 U.S. 586 (1940), the first "flag salute" case. Handed down almost three years later to the day, the reversal, though, was not based on the religious argument of Stone's dissent, but on the "clear and present danger" test to show the legislation was not needed. The Court also spoke of the freedom not to speak, later emphasized in *Watkins* v. *United States,* 354 U.S. 178 (1957).

**Everson v. Board of Education of Ewing Township, 330 U.S. 1;
67 S. Ct. 504; 91 L. Ed. 711 (1947)**

> A New Jersey statute authorized local school districts to make rules and contracts for the transportation of children to schools. In this case, Ewing Township authorized a reimbursement to taxpayers using the public bus system in the township to transport their children. The reimbursement was also made to the parents of Catholic school children going to and from parochial schools. The appellant, a taxpayer, challenged the right of the board to reimburse parents of parochial school students.

OPINION BY MR. JUSTICE BLACK
(Vote: 5–4)

Question—Does the statute violate the Fourteenth Amendment and the First Amendment?

Decision—No.

Reason—The Court reasoned that the transportation of children to their schools is considered in the same category as the provision of police protection near school crossings, the availability of fire protection, sanitary sewer facilities, public highways, and sidewalks. To cut off these facilities would make it far more difficult for the parochial schools to operate. The Court held that such was not the intention of the First Amendment, and that under the First Amendment the state power is no more to be used so as to handicap religions than it is to favor them. Here the children attending Catholic schools were receiving no more than the benefits of public welfare legislation and therefore the New Jersey statute was not contrary to the constitution. It did not, as contended, run contrary to the concept of separation of church and state.

Corollary cases

Pierce v. Society of Sisters, 268 U.S. 510 (1925)
Cochran v. Louisiana State Board of Education, 281 U.S. 370 (1930)
Zorach v. Clauson, 343 U.S. 307 (1952)
Doremus v. Board of Education, 342 U.S. 429 (1952)
McCollum v. Board of Education, 333 U.S. 203 (1948)
Lemon v. Kurtzman, 403 U.S. 602 (1971); 411 U.S. 192 (1973)
Sloan v. Lemon, 413 U.S. 825 (1973)
McGowan v. Maryland, 366 U.S. 420 (1961)
Torcaso v. Watkins, 367 U.S. 488 (1961)
Engel v. Vitale, 370 U.S. 421 (1962)
School District of Abington Twp. v. Schempp, 374 U.S. 203 (1963)
Walz v. New York City Tax Commission, 397 U.S. 664 (1970)
Committee for Public Education and Religious Liberty v. Nyquist, 413 U.S. 756 (1973)

Note—Justice Black's famous "wall between church and state" (actually a Jeffersonian metaphor) surfaced for the first time and has since helped to confuse the establishment and free exercise clauses. Dallin H. Oaks, in his book *The Wall Between Church and State* (Chicago: University of Chicago Press, 1963), writes: "The metaphor is not an aid to thought and it can be a positive barrier to communication."

People of State of Illinois ex rel. McCollum v. Board of Education of School District No. 71, Champaign County, Illinois, 333 U.S. 203; 68 S. Ct. 461; 92 L. Ed. 648 (1948)

In the schools of Champaign County, Illinois, religious teachers were allowed to come into tax-supported public schools and give weekly religious instruction to the children who were attending school in these buildings. School authorities provided a thirty or forty-five minute religious period taken from the time of the regular school day. If the children did not attend the religious instruction, they were given something else to do in this time. The instructors were not paid by the school board and the children were required to have parental consent to attend these classes.

OPINION BY MR. JUSTICE BLACK
(Vote: 8–1)

Question—Is this use of the school building and school time a violation of the First and Fourteenth Amendments?

Decision—Yes.

Reason—The facts show there was a close cooperation between the secular and religious authorities in promoting religious education. Classes were conducted in the regular classrooms of the school building. The operation of the state's compulsory education system assisted in and was integrated with the program of religious education carried on by the separate sects. Pupils compelled by law to attend school for a secular education were released in part from their duty if they went to these religious classes. This was beyond all question a utilization of the tax-supported public system to aid religious groups to spread their faith, and it fell squarely under the ban of the First Amendment (as made applicable to the states by the Fourteenth Amendment).

Corollary cases

Everson v. Board of Education of Ewing Township, 330 U.S. 1 (1947)
Cochran v. Louisiana State Board of Education, 281 U.S. 370 (1930)
Sloan v. Lemon, 413 U.S. 825 (1973)
Zorach v. Clauson, 343 U.S. 307 (1952)
Doremus v. Board of Education, 342 U.S. 429 (1952)

Committee for Public Education and Religious Liberty v. Nyquist, 413 U.S.
756 (1973)

Note—The church-state cases are likely to be unending now
that the Court operates as a national school board. The school
utilized the state's compulsory education system impermissibly; contrast the circumstances in *McCollum* with those in
Zorach v. *Clauson,* 343 U.S. 307 (1952), in which the same
compulsory machinery is utilized, but for "release time," that
is, leaving the school premises. See also the citations under
Nyquist.

Zorach v. Clauson, 343 U.S. 306; 72 S. Ct. 679; 96 L. Ed. 954 (1952)

> New York City arranged a program permitting its public
> schools to release students during the school day so that
> they might go to religious centers for religious instruction or
> devotional exercises. A student was released on the written
> request of his parents. The churches made a weekly list of
> the children released from the public school, but who had
> not reported for religious instruction. This "released time"
> program involved neither the use of the public school class-
> rooms nor the expenditure of any public funds. All costs
> were paid by the religious organizations.

OPINION BY MR. JUSTICE DOUGLAS
(Vote: 6–3)

Question—Does the New York City statute violate the First
Amendment, which, by reason of the Fourteenth Amendment, prohibits the states from establishing religion or prohibiting its free exercise?

Decision—No.

Reason—There was no issue concerned here with the prohibition of the "free exercise" of religion. No one was forced to
attend the religious instruction, nor was the religious training
brought into the classrooms of the public schools.

The First Amendment does reflect the philosophy of separation of Church and State, but does not say that in every and
all respects there must be separation. It rather defines ways in

which there shall be no dependency, one on the other. This is only common sense.

The concept of separation of church and state would have to be pressed to extreme views to condemn the present law on a constitutional basis. We are a religious people with a belief in a Supreme Being. Our government shows no partiality to any one group, but lets each flourish. The state follows the best of our traditions when it schedules its events so as to encourage religious instruction. The government may not finance religious instruction. The government may not finance religious groups, undertake religious instruction, blend secular and sectarian education, nor use secular institutions to force some religion on any person. However, there is no constitutional requirement for government to be hostile to religion. The *McCollum* case cannot be expanded to cover this case, unless separation of church and state means that public institutions cannot accommodate the religious needs of the people. "We cannot read into the Bill of Rights such a philosophy of hostility to religion."

Corollary cases

McCollum v. Board of Education, 333 U.S. 203 (1948)
Everson v. Board of Education, 330 U.S. 1 (1947)
Committee for Public Education and Religious Liberty v. Nyquist, 413 U.S. 756 (1973)
Levitt v. Committee for Public Education and Religious Liberty, 413 U.S. 742 (1973)
Sloan v. Lemon, 413 U.S. 825 (1973)
Cochran v. Louisiana State Board of Education, 281 U.S. 370 (1930)
Doremus v. Board of Education, 342 U.S. 429 (1952)
Lemon v. Kurtzman, 403 U.S. 602 (1971)
Tilton v. Richardson, 403 U.S. 672 (1971)
Norwood v. Harrison, 413 U.S. 455 (1973)
Hunt v. McNair, 413 U.S. 734 (1973)
Lemon v. Kurtzman, 411 U.S. 192 (1973)

Note—Despite the formula for determining church-state issues in *Committee for Public Education and Religious Liberty* v. *Nyquist* (1973), the Court engages in much "balancing." It is difficult otherwise to see any real difference between *Zorach* (religious education outside the school) and *McCollum* (religious education inside the school) considering that in each instance it was the state's compulsory school machinery that congregated the children.

Steven I. Engel et al. v. William J. Vitale, Jr. et al., 370 U.S. 421; 82 S. Ct. 1261; 8 L. Ed. 2d 601 (1962)

The New York State Board of Regents had recommended, and the local school board had directed the school district's principal, that the following prayer be said aloud by each class in the presence of the teacher at the beginning of each school day:

"Almighty God, we acknowledge our dependence upon Thee, and we beg Thy blessings upon us, our parents, our teachers, and our country."

The parents of ten pupils brought action challenging the use of the prayer.

OPINION BY MR. JUSTICE BLACK
(Vote: 6–1)

Question—Does the use of the prayer violate the establishment clause of the First Amendment made applicable to the states by the Fourteenth Amendment?

Decision—Yes.

Reason—Using the public school system to encourage recitation of the prayer is inconsistent with the establishment clause since this is a religious activity and the prayer was composed by governmental officials as a part of a governmental program to further religious beliefs. The fact that the prayer may be denominationally neutral and the fact that its observance on the part of the students is voluntary cannot change the application of the establishment clause. The establishment clause is violated by the enactment of laws that establish an official religion regardless of whether those laws coerce nonobserving individuals or not. It is an historical fact that governmentally-established religions and religious persecutions go hand in hand. "When the power, prestige, and financial support of government is placed behind a particular religious belief, the indirect coercive pressure upon religious minorities to conform to the prevailing officially-approved religion is plain."

Under the First Amendment's "prohibition against governmental establishment of religion, as reinforced by the provisions of the Fourteenth Amendment, government in this country, be it state or federal, is without power to prescribe by law any particular form of prayer which is to be used as an official prayer in carrying on any program of governmentally-sponsored religious activity."

Corollary cases

Everson v. Board of Education, 330 U.S. 1 (1947)
McCollum v. Board of Education, 333 U.S. 203 (1948)
Zorach v. Clauson, 343 U.S. 306 (1952)
West Virginia State Board of Education v. Barnette, 319 U.S. 624 (1943)
School District of Abington Twp. v. Schempp, 374 U.S. 203 (1963)

Note—In *Engel,* there was no cost to the school system or taxpayers and participation was voluntary, and thus the Court might have dodged it on the grounds of standing. There was no interference with the "free exercise clause." *Engel* and *Stone* v. *Graham,* 449 U.S. 39 (1980), which barred the recital of the Ten Commandments in public school classrooms, has engendered a good deal of public debate.

School District of Abington Township, Pa. v. Schempp, 374 U.S. 203; 83 S. Ct. 1560; 10 L. Ed. 2d 844 (1963)

> Pennsylvania by statute required that at least ten verses from the Bible should be read, without comment, at the opening of each public school on each school day. Any child could be excused from attending the Bible reading upon written request of his parent or guardian. The Schempp family, members of the Unitarian church, brought suit to enjoin enforcement of the statute. In a companion case *(Murray* v. *Curlett)* Mrs. Murray and her son, professed atheists, brought similar action against a similar situation in Baltimore.

OPINION BY MR. JUSTICE CLARK
(Vote: 8–1)

Question—Does the requirement of Bible reading in public schools violate the establishment clause of the First Amendment made applicable to the states by the Fourteenth Amendment?

Decision—Yes.

Reason—The Court noted that the establishment clause withdrew all legislative power respecting religious belief or the expression thereof. "The test may be stated as follows: What are the purpose and the primary effect of the enactment? If either is the advancement of inhibition of religion then the enactment exceeds the scope of legislative power as circumscribed by the Constitution. . . . The conclusion follows that in both cases the laws require religious exercises and such exercises are being conducted in direct violation of the rights of the appellees and petitioners. Nor are these required exercises mitigated by the fact that individual students may absent themselves upon parental request, for that fact furnishes no defense to a claim of unconstitutionality under the establishment clause."

Corollary cases

Engel v. Vitale, 370 U.S. 421 (1962)
Everson v. Board of Education, 330 U.S. 1 (1947)
McCollum v. Board of Education, 333 U.S. 203 (1948)
Lemon v. Kurtzman, 403 U.S. 602 (1971); 411 U.S. 192 (1973)
Zorach v. Clauson, 343 U.S. 306 (1952)
McGowan v. Maryland, 366 U.S. 420 (1961)
Torcaso v. Watkins, 367 U.S. 488 (1961)
Stone v. Graham, 449 U.S. 39 (1980)
Widmar v. Vincent, 454 U.S. 440 (1981)

Note—*Murray* v. *Curlett,* 374 U.S. 203 (1963) reached the same conclusion as *Abington.* The Court has continued its balancing act, as seen in *Stone* v. *Graham,* 449 U.S. 39 (1980), in which the Court banned posting the Ten Commandments in classrooms, and *Widmar* v. *Vincent,* 70 L. Ed. 2d 440 (1981), which opened up state university classrooms on First Amendment grounds for student religious groups.

Swann v. Charlotte-Mecklenburg Board of Education, 402 U.S. 1, 91 S. Ct. 1267; 28 L. Ed. 2d 554 (1971)

The Charlotte-Mecklenburg school system encompasses the city of Charlotte and surrounding Mecklenburg County,

North Carolina. Two-thirds of the Negro students in the system attended schools that were either totally Negro or more than 99 percent Negro. The federal district court ordered the school authorities to carry out a plan for desegregation of the schools that involved bus transportation of pupils in order to bring about integration.

OPINION BY MR. CHIEF JUSTICE BURGER
(Vote: 9–0)

Question—Does the district court have the power to order that such a plan be carried out?

Decision—Yes.

Reason—The Court had previously held that school authorities have the duty to take affirmative action to bring about integration. When the school authorities do not carry out this obligation to remedy violations of the equal protection guarantee, the district court has broad equitable power to fashion a remedy that will assure a unitary school system. School authorities may be required to employ bus transportation as one tool of school desegregation. There is no requirement that every school in every community reflect the racial composition of the school system as a whole, but a district court, again as part of its equitable remedial discretion, may make use of mathematical ratios. The burden is on the school authorities to satisfy the court that their racial composition is not the result of present or past discriminatory action.

Corollary cases

Green v. County School Board, 391 U.S. 430 (1968)
United States v. Montgomery Board of Education, 395 U.S. 225 (1969)
Davis v. Board of School Commissioners of Mobile County, 402 U.S. 33 (1971)
North Carolina State Board of Education v. Swann, 402 U.S. 43 (1971)
McDaniel v. Barresi, 402 U.S. 39 (1971)
Alexander v. Holmes County Board of Education, 396 U.S. 19 (1969)
Northcross v. Board of Education of Memphis, 397 U.S. 232 (1970)
Griffin v. County School Board, 377 U.S. 218 (1964)
Brown v. Board of Education, 374 U.S. 483 (1954)
San Antonio Independent School District v. Rodriguez, 411 U.S. 1 (1973)
Regents of the University of California v. Bakke, 438 U.S. 265 (1978)

Note—*Swann* is more concerned with state-imposed segregation in a dual system and not de facto segregation. In *Keyes* v. *School District, No. 1, Denver, Colorado,* 413 U.S. 189 (1973), the Court defined de jure segregation and de facto segregation in terms of purpose or intent to segregate. A year later, now less sure of itself, the Court pulled back in *Milliken* v. *Bradley,* 418 U.S. 717 (1974), saying that a multi-district remedy can only be ordered when all the districts have been responsible for the segregation.

Wisconsin v. Yoder, 406 U.S. 205; 92 S. Ct. 1526; 32 L. Ed. 2d 15 (1972)

Suit was brought by Wisconsin against members of the Amish church to force them to abide by the state's compulsory school attendance law, which requires children to attend public or private school until the age of sixteen. The Amish parents refused to send their children to school beyond the eighth grade. Their objection to higher education generally is that the values it teaches are in marked variance with the Amish values and way of life. They agree that elementary education is necessary since their children must have the basic skills "in order to read the Bible, to be good farmers and citizens and to be able to deal with non-Amish people when necessary in the course of daily affairs."

OPINION BY MR. CHIEF JUSTICE BURGER
(Vote: 6–1)

Question—Does the Wisconsin compulsory attendance law infringe on the free exercise clause of the First Amendment?

Decision—Yes.

Reason—However strong a state's interest in universal compulsory education, it is by no means absolute to the exclusion or subordination of all other interests. The traditional way of life of the Amish is not merely a matter of personal preference but one of deep religious conviction, shared by an organized group, and intimately related to daily living. "A way of life that is odd or even erratic but interferes with no rights or interests of others is not to be condemned because it is different." The First and Fourteenth Amendments prevent the state from enforcing this law in the case of the Amish.

Corollary cases

Meyer v. Nebraska, 262 U.S. 390 (1923)
Pierce v. Society of Sisters, 268 U.S. 510 (1925)
Sherbert v. Verner, 374 U.S. 398 (1963)
Tinker v. Des Moines Independent Community School District, 393 U.S. 503 (1969)
West Virginia State Board of Education v. Barnette, 319 U.S. 624 (1943)
Reynolds v. United States, 98 U.S. 145 (1879)
Prince v. Massachusetts, 321 U.S. 158 (1944)
Braunfield v. Brown, 366 U.S. 599 (1961)
Tilton v. Richardson, 403 U.S. 672 (1971)
Lemon v. Kurtzman, 403 U.S. 602 (1971)
United States v. Lee, 71 L. Ed. 127 (1982)
Thomas v. Review Board of the Indiana Employment Security Division, 450 U.S. 707 (1981)
Widmar v. Vincent, 70 L. Ed. 2d 440 (1981)
Hobbie v. Unemployment Appeals Commission, 94 L. Ed. 2d 190 (1987)

Note—In *Cantwell* v. *Connecticut,* 310 U.S. 296 (1940), the Court notes a distinction between religious beliefs and acts. Thus, in *Reynolds* v. *United States,* 98 U.S. 145 (1897), Mormons were penalized for practicing polygamy; Jehovah's Witnesses for allowing their children in violation of child welfare law to distribute religious tracts at night, *Prince* v. *Massachusetts,* 321 U.S. 158 (1944); and Jewish merchants who suffered under a Sunday closing law, *Braunfield* v. *Brown,* 366 U.S. 599 (1961). Is the Court "establishing" a particular religion in Wisconsin in making an exception for the Amish? In a recent case, *United States* v. *Lee,* 71 L. Ed. 2d 127 (1982), the Court held that while an individual Amish is exempt from Social Security taxes, his employees are not. Although concurring, Justice Stevens noted that the attempt to distinguish *Lee* from *Yoder* was "unconvincing."

Committee for Public Education and Religious Liberty v. Nyquist, 413 U.S. 756; 93 S. Ct. 2955; 37 L. Ed. 2d 948 (1973)

New York state laws provided funds for nonpublic schools for repairs and maintenance, including utilities, as well as a program of direct payments to reimburse parents for up to 50 percent of tuition at nonpublic schools provided that this did not exceed $50 for a grade-school child and $100 for each high-school student. To qualify, the parents had to have an annual taxable income of less than $5,000. Also, the law provided for a state income tax deduction according to a set table on taxable income for each child attending a nonpublic school. This deduction was to be computed without relation to actual tuition paid, but no deduction was permitted if the gross income exceeded $25,000. Recipients were not required to spend the money on education.

Opinion by Mr. Justice Powell
(Vote: 6–3)

Question—Does this program violate the establishment provision of the First Amendment?

Decision—Yes.

Reason—Government must remain neutral toward religion and must avoid excessive entanglement with religious institutions. This program has the effect of advancing religion by providing indirectly for financial support of nonpublic sectarian institutions. The arrangements set up by the law do not alter the effect of the law to provide financial support for sectarian institutions. "Our examination of New York's aid provisions, in light of all relevant considerations, compels the judgment that each, as written, has a 'primary effect that advances religion' and offends the constitutional prohibition against laws 'respecting the establishment of religion.'"

Corollary cases

Levitt v. Committee for Public Education and Religious Liberty, 413 U.S. 472 (1973)
Hunt v. McNair, 413 U.S. 734 (1973)
Zorach v. Clauson, 343 U.S. 306 (1952)
Everson v. Board of Education, 330 U.S. 1 (1973)
Cochran v. Louisiana State Board of Education, 281 U.S. 370 (1930)
Roemer v. Board of Public Works of Maryland, 426 U.S. 736 (1976)
McCollum v. Board of Education, 333 U.S. 203 (1948)
Lemon v. Kurtzman, 403 U.S. 602 (1971)
Tilton v. Richardson, 403 U.S. 672 (1971)
Board of Education v. Allen, 392 U.S. 236 (1968)

Walz v. Tax Commission, 397 U.S. 664 (1970)
Servian Eastern Orthodox Diocese v. Milivojevich, 426 U.S. 696 (1976)
Meek v. Pittenger, 412 U.S. 349 (1975)
Sloan v. Lemon, 413 U.S. 825 (1973)
Valley Forge Christian College v. Americans United for Separation of Church and State, 70 L. Ed. 2d 700 (1982)
Heffron v. International Society for Krishna Consciousness, 69 L. Ed. 2d 298 (1981)
Stone v. Graham, 449 U.S. 39 (1980)
St. Martin Evangelical Lutheran Church v. South Dakota, 68 L. Ed. 2d 612 (1981)
Committee for Public Education and Religious Liberty v. Regan, 444 U.S. 646 (1980)
Widmar v. Vinson, 70 L. Ed. 2d 440 (1981)
NLRB v. Catholic Bishop of Chicago, 440 U.S. 490 (1979)

Note—*Nyquist* lays down the controlling formula for a church-state issue to be upheld: (1) it must have a secular legislative purpose; (2) it neither advances nor impedes religion; and (3) it must avoid excessive entanglement with religion.

National Labor Relations Board v. Catholic Bishop of Chicago, 440 U.S. 490; 59 L. Ed. 2d 533; 99 S. Ct. 1313 (1979)

The National Labor Relations Board certified unions as the collective bargaining agents for lay teachers in certain Catholic high schools in Illinois and Indiana. Because the schools refused to bargain, the unions filed unfair labor practices. The NLRB issued a cease-and-desist order and claimed that it refused jurisdiction only when a school was "completely religious" and not, as here, merely "religiously associated." The court of appeals denied enforcement.

OPINION BY MR. CHIEF JUSTICE BURGER
(Vote: 5–4)

Question—Are (a) teachers in church-operated schools that teach religion as well as secular subjects under the jurisdiction of the National Labor Relations Board and, if so, (b) does the act that authorizes such jurisdiction violate the guarantees of the religion clauses of the First Amendment?

Decision—(a) No. (b) Yes.

Reason—Religious authority, said the Court, necessarily pervades the church-operated school. The teacher is intimately connected with the subject matter and, while a textbook's content is ascertainable, a teacher's handling of a subject is not. The NLRB claims it can avoid excessive entanglement since it will involve only factual issues, but the board's actions will infringe the First Amendment. In deciding what are "terms" and "conditions of employment" the board will implicate sensitive issues that open the door to conflicts between clergy-administrators and the board or conflicts with negotiators for unions. "There is no clear expression of an affirmative intention of Congress that teachers in church-operated schools would be covered by the act."

Corollary cases

Wisconsin v. Yoder, 406 U.S. 205 (1972)
Lemon v. Kurtzman, 403 U.S. 602 (1971)
Wolman v. Walters, 433 U.S. 229 (1977)
Meek v. Pittenger, 421 U.S. 349 (1975)
Associated Press v. NLRB, 30 U.S. 103 (1937)
Thomas v. Review Board of Indiana Employment Security Division, 450 U.S. 707 (1981)
Sherbert v. Verner, 374 U.S. 398 (1963)
United States v. Lee, 455 U.S. _____; 71 L. Ed. 2d 127 (1982)

Note—The Court steered clear of this issue, perhaps mindful of its words in *Committee for Public Education* v. *Nyquist,* 413 U.S. 756 (1973), that, in order to pass muster under the establishment clause, the law "must avoid excessive government entanglement with religion."

Committee for Public Education and Religious Liberty v. Regan, 444 U.S. 646; 63 L. Ed. 94; 100 S. Ct. 840 (1980)

In 1973, a New York statute that appropriated public funds to reimburse both secular nonpublic and church-sponsored schools for performing various state-mandated services, including both state-prepared and teacher-prepared examinations, was held in violation of the establishment of religion clause of the First Amendment. In 1974, a new statute was enacted directing New York's Commissioner of Education to apportion and to pay nonpublic schools the actual costs incurred as a result of compliance with certain state-mandated requirements, including state-prepared examinations and reporting procedures. Unlike the 1970 version, the 1974 statute provided a means by which state funds were to be audited, and no reimbursement was made to nonpublic schools for the preparation, administration, or grading of teacher-prepared tests.

OPINION BY MR. JUSTICE WHITE
(Vote: 5–4)

Question—Does the 1974 New York statute violate the establishment of religion clause of the First Amendment, which is made applicable to the states by virtue of the Fourteenth Amendment?

Decision—No.

Reason—"Under the precedents of this court, a legislative enactment does not contravene the establishment clause if it has a secular legislative purpose, if its principal or primary effect neither advances nor inhibits religion, and if it does not foster an excessive government entanglement with religion . . . we note . . . that there is clearly a secular purpose behind the legislative enactment. The nonpublic school thus has no control whatsoever over the content of the tests. . . . Each . . . test addresses a secular academic subject; none deals with religious subject matter." Reimbursement to the nonpublic school for administering the state-prescribed examinations "does not invalidate the New York statute." The services for which the private schools would be reimbursed are discrete and clearly identifiable. "The reimbursement process . . . is straight forward and susceptible to the routinization that characterizes most reimbursement schemes."

Corollary cases

Lemon v. Kurtzman, 403 U.S. 602 (1971)
Everson v. Board of Education, 330 U.S. 1 (1947)
Meek v. Pittenger, 421 U.S. 349 (1975)
Wolman v. Walter, 433 U.S. 229 (1977)
Roemer v. Maryland Public Works, 426 U.S. 736 (1976)

Stone v. Graham, 449 U.S. 39; 66 L. Ed. 2d 199; 101 S. Ct. 690 (1980)

A Kentucky statute required that a copy of the Ten Commandments be posted on the wall of each public school classroom in the state. The copies were to be purchased by private contributors. The petitioners claimed that the statute violated the establishment and free exercise clauses of the First Amendment.

OPINION: PER CURIAM

(Vote: 5–4)

Question—Does the Kentucky statute violate the establishment and free exercise clauses of the First Amendment?

Decision—Yes.

Reason—This Court has already announced a three-part test for determining whether a challenged state statute is permissible under the First Amendment: "First, the statute must have a secular legislative purpose; second, its principal or primary effect must be one that neither advances nor inhibits religion . . . ; finally, the statute must not foster 'an excessive government entanglement with religion,' " If a statute violates any of these three principles, it must be struck down under the establishment clause. . . . The pre-eminent purpose for posting the Ten Commandments on schoolroom walls is plainly religious in nature. The Ten Commandments is undeniably a sacred text . . . and no legislative recitation of a supposed secular purpose can blind us to that fact. . . . It does not matter that the posted copies of the Ten Commandments are financed by voluntary private contributions for the mere posting of the copies under the auspices of the legislature provides the 'official support of the state . . . Government' that the establishment clause prohibits."

Corollary cases

Lemon v. Kurtzman, 403 U.S. 602 (1971)
School District of Abington Township v. Schempp, 374 U.S. 203 (1963)
Engel v. Vitale, 370 U.S. 421 (1962)
Public Education v. Nyquist, 413 U.S. 756 (1975)

Widmar v. Vincent, 454 U.S. _____; 70 L. Ed. 2d 440; 102 S. Ct. 269 (1981)

The facilities at the University of Missouri at Kansas City, a state university, are generally made available for the activities of registered student groups. While a registered religious group named Cornerstone originally sought and received permission to conduct its meetings in university facilities, the university subsequently informed the organization that Cornerstone's meetings could no longer be held in university buildings. The exclusion was based on a regulation adopted by the Board of Curators that prohibits the use of university buildings or grounds "for purposes of religious worship or religious teaching." Members of Cornerstone brought suit, alleging that the university's discrimination against religious activity and discussion violated their rights of free exercise of religion, equal protection, and freedom of speech under the First and Fourteenth Amendments to the Constitution.

OPINION BY MR. JUSTICE POWELL
(Vote: 8–1)

Question—Can a state university, which makes its facilities generally available for the activities of registered student groups, close its facilities to a registered group desiring to use the facilities for religious worship and religious discussion?

Decision—No.

Reason—"With respect to persons entitled to be there, our cases leave no doubt that the First Amendment rights of speech and association extend to the campuses of state universities." It is possible—perhaps even forseeable—that religious groups will benefit from access to university facilities. "But this court has explained that a religious organization's enjoyment of merely 'incidental' benefits does not violate the prohibition against the 'primary advancement' of religion. . . . We are satisfied that any religious benefits of an open forum at UMKC would be 'incidental' within the meaning of our cases . . . an open forum in a public university does not confer any imprimatur of state approval on religious sects or practices. . . . The forum is available to a broad class of non-religious as well as religious speakers; there are over 100 recognized student groups at UMKC. The provision of benefits to so broad a spectrum of groups is an important index of secular effect. . . .

In the absence of empirical evidence that religious groups will dominate UMKC's open forum, . . . the advancement of religion would not be the forum's 'primary effect'. . . . The basis for our decision is narrow. Having created a forum generally open to student groups, the university seeks to enforce a content-based exclusion of religious speech. Its exclusionary policy violates the fundamental principle that a state regulation of speech should be content-neutral, and the university is unable to justify this violation under applicable constitutional standards.''

Corollary cases

Tilton v. Richardson, 403 U.S. 672 (1971)
Healy v. James, 408 U.S. 169 (1972)
Tinker v. Des Moines Independent School District, 393 U.S. 503 (1969)
Lemon v. Kurtzman, 403 U.S. 602 (1971)
Committee for Public Education v. Nyquist, 413 U.S. 756 (1973)
Roemer v. Maryland, 426 U.S. 736 (1976)

United States v. Lee, 455 U.S. _____; 71 L. Ed. 2d 127; 102 S. Ct. 1051 (1982)

Lee, a member of the Old Order Amish, is a farmer and carpenter who, between 1970 and 1977, employed other Amish. He paid no Social Security Taxes and filed no Social Security Tax returns. The Internal Revenue Service assessed Lee in excess of $27,000, of which he only paid $91.00, and then sued for a refund claiming, *inter alia,* that the imposition of the Social Security tax violated his First Amendment Free Exercise Rights and those of his Amish employees. Congress had previously accommodated self-employed Amish and self-employed members of other religious groups with similar beliefs by providing exemptions from Social Security taxes. The district court agreed with Amish Lee.

OPINION BY MR. CHIEF JUSTICE BURGER
(Vote: 9–0)

Question—Does the Social Security taxes interfere with the Free Exercise Rights of the Amish?

Decision—No.

Reason—"Not all burdens on religion are unconstitutional. Because the Social Security system is nationwide, the governmental interest is apparent. The design of the system requires support by mandatory contributions from covered employers and employees. This mandatory participation is indispensable to the fiscal vitality of the Social Security System. The government's interest . . . to the Social Security System is very high. The difficulty in attempting to accommodate religious beliefs in the area of taxation is that 'we are a cosmopolitan nation made up of people of almost every conceivable religious preference.' To maintain an organized society that guarantees religious freedom to a great variety of faiths requires that some religious practices yield to the common good. The tax system could not function if denominations were allowed to challenge the tax system because tax payments were spent in a manner that violates their religious belief. When followers of a particular sect enter into commercial activity as a matter of choice, the limits they accept on their own conduct as a matter of conscience and faith are not to be superimposed on the statutory schemes which are binding on others in that activity."

Corollary cases

Thomas v. Review Board of Indiana Employment Security Division, 450 U.S. 707 (1981)
Prince v. Massachusetts, 321 U.S. 158 (1944)
Reynolds v. United States, 98 U.S. 145 (1878)
Wisconsin v. Yoder, 406 U.S. 205 (1972)
Gillette v. United States, 401 U.S. 437 (1971)
Sherbert v. Verner, 374 U.S. 398 (1963)
Braunfeld v. Brown, 366 U.S. 599 (1961)
Follett v. Town of McCormick, 321 U.S. 573 (1944)
Murdock v. Pennsylvania, 319 U.S. 105 (1943)

Note—The Court by and large has been sympathetic to small religious groups—one is tempted to say that the "preferred freedoms" doctrine, at least to some Court critics, has become the preferred religious sect doctrine by treating minor religious groups, e.g., the Amish or Jehovah's Witnesses, differently than mainline religious groups. See *Yoder* v. *Wisconsin,* 406 U.S. 205 (1972), *Sherbert* v. *Verner,* 374 U.S. 398 (1963), and

Thomas v. *Review Board of Indiana Employment Security Division,* 450 U.S. 708 (1981).

Wallace v. Jaffree, 472 U.S. _____, 86 L. Ed. 2d 29, 105 S. Ct. 2479 (1985)

Ismael Jaffree, a resident of Mobile County, Alabama, filed a complaint on behalf on his minor children against the Mobile County School Board, various school officials, and several teachers. He sought a declaratory judgment and an injunction restraining the defendants from allowing the maintenance of regular religious services or other forms of religious expression. An Alabama statute permitted one minute of silence for "meditation or voluntary prayer" each day in the public schools. A United States District Court found the statute permissible on the grounds that a state could establish a state religion if it chose, and the court of appeals reversed the decision.

OPINION BY JUSTICE STEVENS
(Vote: 6–3)

Question—Is a state statute that permits a moment of silence for "meditation and voluntary prayer" for the express purpose of introducing prayer into the school a violation of the establishment clause?

Decision—Yes.

Reason—The Court's unanimous affirmance of the court of appeals reversal "makes it unnecessary to comment at length on the district court's remarkable conclusion that the federal constitution imposes no obstacle to Alabama's establishment of a state religion." It is firmly embedded in our constitutional jurisprudence "that the several states have no greater power to restrain the individual freedoms protected by the First Amendment than does the Congress." The First Amendment was adopted to curtail Congress and the Fourteenth Amendment "imposed the same substantive limitations on the states' power to legislate that the First Amendment had always imposed on Congress's power." Here, as in *Barnette,* "we are faced with a state measure which forces an individual, as part of his daily life . . . to be an instrument for fostering public adherence to an ideological point of view he finds unacceptable." The Court has concluded that the First Amendment embraces "the right to select any religious faith or none at all." It was held previously in *Lemon* v. *Kurtzman* (403 U.S. 602) that in construing the establishment clause (1) a statute must have a secular legislative purpose, (2) must neither advance nor inhibit the practice of religion and (3) must not foster an excessive government entanglement with religion. It "is the first of these three criteria that is most plainly implicated." and the second and third criteria will not be considered "if a statute does not have a clearly secular purpose." The Alabama statute has "no secular purpose."

Corollary cases

Lemon v. Kurtzman, 403 U.S. 602, 29 L. Ed. 2d 745, 91 S. Ct. 2105 (1971)
Abington School District v. Schempp, 374 U.S. 203, 10 L. Ed. 2d 844, 83 S. Ct. 1560 (1963)
Engle v. Vitale, 370 U.S. 421, 8 L. Ed. 2d 601, 82 S. Ct. 1261 (1962)
Cantwell v. Connecticut, 310 U.S. 296, 84 L. Ed. 1213, 60 S. Ct. 900 (1940)
Wooley v. Maynard, 430 U.S. 705, 51 L. Ed. 2d 752, 97 S. Ct. 1428 (1977)
Terminiello v. Chicago, 337 U.S. 1, 93 L. Ed. 1131, 69 S. Ct. 894 (1949)
West Virginia State Board of Education v. Barnette, 319 U.S. 624, 87 L. Ed. 1628, 63 S. Ct. 1178 (1943)
Mear v. Minnesota Expel. Olson, 283 U.S. 697, 75 L. Ed. 1357, 51 S. Ct. 625 (1931)
Gitlow v. New York, 268 U.S. 652, 69 L. Ed. 1138, 45 S. Ct. 625 (1925)
Torcaso v. Watkins, 367 U.S. 488, 6 L. Ed. 2d 982, 81 S. Ct. 1680 (1961)
Lynch v. Donnelly, 465 U.S. _____, 79 L. Ed. 2d 604, 104 S. Ct. 1355 (1984)
Stone v. Graham, 449 U.S. 39, 66 L. Ed. 2d 199, 101 S. Ct. 192 (1980)
Committee for Public Education v. Nyquist, 413 U.S. 756, 37 L. Ed. 2d 948, 93 S. Ct. 2955 (1973)
Epperson v. Arkansas, 393 U.S. 97, 21 L. Ed. 2d 228, 89 S. Ct. 266 (1968)
Illinois ex rel. McCollum v. Board of Education, 333 U.S. 203, 92 L. Ed. 649, 65 S. Ct. 461 (1948)
Everson v. Board of Education, 330 U.S. 1, 91 L. Ed. 711, 67 S. Ct. 504 (1947)

Note—The Court makes the point that inasmuch as it concurs with the appeals court, it is unnecessary to discuss other issues such as "the remarkable conclusion" that Alabama can have a "state religion" if it desires. The district court here is reviving and supporting the view that the Fourteenth Amendment was not meant to incorporate the First Amendment and did so in *Gitlow* v. *New York* only in 1925.

TAXING/SPENDING REGULATORY POWERS

Veazie Bank v. Fenno, 8 Wallace 533; 19 L. Ed. 482 (1869)

In 1866, Congress passed an act imposing a tax of 10 percent on notes of private persons, state banks, and state banking associations. The Veazie Bank paid the tax under protest, alleging Congress had no power to pass such an act. This was a suit by the bank against the collector, Fenno, for reimbursement.

OPINION BY MR. CHIEF JUSTICE CHASE
(Vote: 5–2)

Question—Is this an unauthorized use of the taxing power of Congress?

Decision—No.

Reason—Congress had just undertaken to provide for a uniform currency for the country. To protect the newly established national bank from undue competition from the state banks, Congress was using its power indirectly when it could have used a direct method. Congress had to protect the newly established bank notes and restrain the notes of the state banks as money. Under its power to regulate the circulation of coin it was able to do this. "It cannot be doubted that under the Constitution the power to provide a circulation of coin is given to Congress. And it is settled by the uniform practice of the government and by repeated decisions, that Congress may, constitutionally authorize the emission of bills of credit. . . . Having thus, in the exercise of undisputed constitutional powers, undertaken to provide a currency for the whole country, it cannot be questioned that Congress may, constitutionally, secure the benefits of it to the people by appropriate legislation. To this end, Congress has denied the quality of legal tender to foreign coins, and has provided by law against the imposition of counterfeit and base coin on the community. To the same end, Congress may restrain, by suitable enactments, the circulation as money of any notes not issued under its own authority. Without this power, indeed, its attempts to secure a sound and uniform currency for the country must be futile."

Corollary cases

McCray v. United States, 195 U.S. 27 (1904)
Sonzinsky v. United States, 300 U.S. 506 (1937)
Helvering v. Davis, 301 U.S. 619 (1937)
Bailey v. Drexel Furniture Co., 259 U.S. 20 (1922)
United States v. Butler, 297 U.S. 1 (1936)
United States v. Constantine, 296 U.S. 287 (1935)
United States v. Doremus, 249 U.S. 86 (1919)
License Tax Cases, 5 Wallace 462 (1867)
Nigro v. United States, 276 U.S. 332 (1928)
Carter v. Carter Coal Co., 298 U.S. 238 (1936)

Collector v. Day (Buffington v. Day), 11 Wallace 113; 20 L. Ed. 122 (1871)

Judge Day of the Probate Court for Barnstable County, Massachusetts, brought a suit against Buffington, collector of internal revenue, to recover federal income tax assessments upon his salary during the years 1866 and 1867, as judge of the Court of Probate and Insolvency, Barnstable County, Mass. Judge Day, having paid the tax under protest, brought suit to recover the amount paid and obtained judgment. The collector then sued for a writ of error.

OPINION BY MR. JUSTICE NELSON
(Vote: 8–1)

Question—Can Congress constitutionally impose a tax upon the salary of a judicial officer of a state?

Decision—No.

Reason—The work that a judge does is a vital function of the state. It is one of the reserved rights of the state coupled with the passing of laws and the administration of them. The federal government has only the delegated power that the states gave it, and since this is a part that the states reserved for themselves, these governmental actions are not properly subject to the taxing power of Congress.

The means and instrumentalities employed for carrying on the operations of state governments should not be liable to be crippled or defeated by the taxing power of another government. One of these means and instrumentalities is the judicial department of the state, and in its establishment the states are independent of the general government.

Although there is no express provision in the Constitution that prohibits the general government from taxing the means and instrumentalities of the states, the exemption rests upon necessary implication and is upheld by the law of self-preservation.

Corollary cases

McCulloch v. Maryland, 4 Wheaton 316 (1819)
Lane County v. Oregon, 7 Wallace 71 (1869)
Veazie Bank v. Fenno, 8 Wallace 533 (1869)
Helvering v. Gerhardt, 304 U.S. 405 (1938)
Graves v. New York ex rel. O'Keefe, 306 U.S. 466 (1939)
New York ex rel. Rogers v. Graves, 299 U.S. 401 (1937)
South Carolina v. United States, 199 U.S. 437 (1905)
Dobbins v. Commissioners of Erie County, 16 Peters 435 (1842)
Carson v. Roane-Anderson Co., 342 U.S. 232 (1952)

Note—This case was reversed by *Graves et al., Tax Commissioners* v. *New York ex rel. O'Keefe,* 306 U.S. 466 (1939), but the power of Congress to apply the "supremacy rule" to federal agencies remains.

Legal Tender Cases (Knox v. Lee; Parker v. Davis), 12 Wallace 457; 20 L. Ed. 287 (1871)

Congress provided for the issuance of paper money by the United States and made such money legal tender for the payment of private debts. Knox had purchased a number of sheep that had been confiscated under the Confederacy in Texas during the Civil War. Lee, after the war, brought suit to recover the value of the sheep and won. The payment was to be made in United States Treasury certificates called "greenbacks," which were of less value than gold or silver. When Knox was about to pay the debt in greenbacks, Lee appealed the case to secure payment in gold or silver. In the second case, Davis asked for a writ of specific performance to compel Parker to transfer real estate upon payment of a set sum of money that Davis had previously offered to pay in legal tender notes.

OPINION BY MR. JUSTICE STRONG
(Vote: 5-4)

Question—Does Congress have the power to make the treasury notes legal tender applicable to both previous and subsequent contracts.

Decision—Yes.

Reason—"And here it is to be observed it is not indispensable to the existence of any power claimed for the federal government that it can be found specified in the words of the Constitution, or clearly and directly traceable to some one of the specified powers. Its existence may be deduced fairly from more than one of the substantive powers expressly defined, or from them all combined. . . . And it is of importance to observe that Congress has often exercised, without question, powers that are not expressly given nor ancillary to any single enumerated power. Powers thus exercised are what are called by Judge Story, in his *Commentaries on the Constitution,* resulting powers, arising from the aggregate powers of the government."

The statute here was passed as a war measure to obtain credit for the equipment of armies and the employment of money to an extent beyond the capacity of all ordinary sources of supply. If nothing else would have supplied the necessaries of the Treasury, these acts would be valid. To say that some other means might have been chosen is mere conjecture, and if it be conceded, it proves nothing more than that Congress had the choice of means for a legitimate end, each appropriate and adapted to that end. The Court could not say that Congress ought to have adopted one rather than the other.

Corollary cases

Hepburn v. Griswold, 8 Wallace 603 (1870)
Juilliard v. Greenman, 110 U.S. 421 (1884)
Perry v. United States, 294 U.S. 330 (1935)
McCulloch v. Maryland, 4 Wheaton 316 (1819)
Lane County v. Oregon, 7 Wallace 71 (1869)
Norman v. B. and O. R. R. Co., 294 U.S. 240 (1935)

Note—This case reverses the first legal tender case, *Hepburn* v. *Griswold,* 8 Wallace 603 (1870), one of the earliest uses of substantive due process. The *Legal Tender Cases* were tinged by politics and charges of Court-packing by President Grant.

Juilliard v. Greenman, 110 U.S. 421; 4 S. Ct. 122; 28 L. Ed. 204 (1884)

Juilliard, the plaintiff, sued for the balance of $5,100 due on a cotton shipment to defendant. The balance had been paid in the form of two United States notes for $5,000 and $100 each, which plaintiff refused to accept as "legal tender."

OPINION BY MR. JUSTICE GRAY
(Vote: 8–1)

Question—Are notes of the United States legal tender in the payment of private debts in time of peace?

Decision—Yes.

Reason—The power, as incident to the power of borrowing money and issuing bills or notes of the government for money borrowed, and of impressing upon these bills or notes the quality of being legal tender for the payment of private debts, was a power universally understood to belong to sovereignty, in Europe and America, at the time of the framing and adoption of the Constitution of the United States. This power is not defeated or restricted by the fact that its exercise may affect the value of private contracts. Under the power to coin money and to regulate its value, Congress may issue coins of the same denominations as those already current by law, but of less intrinsic value, and thereby enable debtors to discharge their debts. A contract to pay a certain sum in money, without any stipulation as to the kind of money in which it shall be paid, may always be satisfied by payment of that sum in any currency that is lawful money at the place and time at which payment is to be made.

Corollary cases

Craig v. Missouri, 4 Peters 435 (1830)
Briscoe v. Bank of Kentucky, 11 Peters 257 (1837)

Legal Tender Cases, 12 Wallace 557 (1871)
Norman v. Baltimore and Ohio R. R. Co., 294 U.S. 240 (1935)
Darrington v. Bank of Alabama, 13 Howard 12 (1851)

Note—Only fifteen months earlier, the *Legal Tender Cases*
(1871) reversed *Hepburn* v. *Griswold,* 8 Wallace 603 (1870) and
permitted paper money to be legal tender (under a wartime
act). *Juilliard* v. *Greenman* (1884) allowed the legality of paper
money in times of peace. In the *Legal Tender Cases* and in
Juilliard the implied powers doctrine of *McCulloch* v. *Maryland,* 4 Wheaton 316 (1819), was supplemented by the development of the doctrine of 'resulting' (or resultant) powers.

Pollock v. Farmers' Loan and Trust Co., 158 U.S. 601; 15 S. Ct. 912; 39 L. Ed. 1108 (1895)

A bill was filed by Charles Pollock, a citizen of the state
of Massachusetts, on behalf of himself and all other stockholders of the company against the Farmers' Loan and Trust
Co., a corporation of the state of New York. The bill alleged
that the defendant claimed authority under the provisions of
the act of August 1894 (a statute providing for the imposition
of a tax on incomes in excess of $4,000 received by individ-
uals, associations, or corporations) to pay to the United
States a tax of 2 percent on the net profits of money in
question including income derived from real estate and
bonds of municipal corporations owned by it. Moreover, the
bill alleged that such a tax was unconstitutional, in that the
income from stocks and bonds of the states of the United
States, counties, and municipalities therein is not subject to
taxation.

OPINION BY MR. CHIEF JUSTICE FULLER
(Vote: 5–4)

Question—Is this a direct tax? Did any partial unconstitutionality of the 1894 income tax law render it void in its entirety?

Decision—Yes (to both questions).

Reason—"If the revenue derived from municipal bonds cannot
be taxed because the source cannot be, the same rule applies
to revenue from any other source not subject to the tax; and
the lack of power to levy any but an apportioned tax on real

estate and personal property equally exists as to the revenue therefrom.''

The same statute may be in part constitutional and unconstitutional, and if the parts are wholly independent of each other, that which is constitutional may stand and that which is unconstitutional will be rejected. If they are dependent on each other for the outcome or purpose of the legislation then both parts or all of the statute is to be declared unconstitutional.

Here the income from realty formed a vital part of this scheme for taxation embodied therein. If that were to be stricken out and also all income from invested property, the largest part of the anticipated revenue would be eliminated and this would leave the burden of the tax to be borne by the professions, trades, and labor. In that way what was intended as a tax on capital would have remained in substance a tax on occupations and labor. This was not the intention of Congress and the whole law had to be declared unconstitutional.

Corollary cases

Springer v. United States, 102 U.S. 588 (1881)
Frost v. Corporation Commission, 278 U.S. 515 (1929)
Nicol v. Amer, 173 U.S. 509 (1899)
Pollock v. Trust Co., 157 U.S. 429 (1895)
Bromley v. McCaughn, 280 U.S. 124 (1929)
Knowlton v. Moore, 178 U.S. 41 (1900)
Flint v. Stone Tracy Co., 220 U.S. 107 (1911)
Patton v. Brady, 184 U.S. 608 (1902)
Hylton v. United States, 3 Dallas 171 (1796)
Brushaber v. Union Pacific R. R. Co., 240 U.S. 1 (1916)

Note—During the Civil War, Congress had levied an income tax to finance the war. It was upheld in *Spring* v. *United States,* 102 U.S. 586 (1881). *Pollock* reversed this view and it, in turn, was reversed by the Sixteenth Amendment. The tax power is utilized as federal police power.

McCray v. United States, 195 U.S. 27; 24 S. Ct. 769; 49 L. Ed. 78 (1904)

McCray was sued by the United States for a statutory penalty of $50. He purchased for resale a fifty-pound package of oleomargarine artificially colored to look like butter, to which were affixed internal revenue stamps of one-fourth of a cent per pound, upon which the law required stamps at the rate of ten cents per pound. The excise McCray paid was that imposed upon oleomargarine free from artificial coloration.

OPINION BY MR. JUSTICE WHITE
(Vote: 6–3)

Question—Was the tax upon the colored oleomargarine one which was in conflict with the Constitution as an attempt to use the federal taxing power so as to regulate a matter reserved to the states?

Decision—No.

Reason—"Undoubtedly, in determining whether a particular act is within a granted power, its scope and effect are to be considered. Applying this rule to the acts assailed, it is self-evident that on their face they levy an excise tax. That being their necessary scope and operation, it follows that the acts are within the grant of power." Therefore, the Supreme Court refused to go behind the appearance of a revenue act and inquire into the motives of indirect regulation that might have inspired Congress.

Corollary cases

McCulloch v. Maryland, 4 Wheaton 431 (1819)
Veazie Bank v. Fenno, 8 Wallace 533 (1869)
License Tax Cases, 5 Wallace 462 (1867)
Sonzinsky v. United States, 300 U.S. 506 (1937)
Bailey v. Drexel Furniture Co., 259 U.S. 20 (1922)
Hill v. Wallace, 259 U.S. 44 (1922)
Carter v. Carter Coal Co., 298 U.S. 239 (1936)
United States v. Butler, 297 U.S. 1 (1936)
Helvering v. Davis, 301 U.S. 619 (1937)
United States v. Constantine, 296 U.S. 287 (1935)
United States v. Doremus, 249 U.S. 86 (1919)
Steward Machine Co. v. Davis, 301 U.S. 548 (1937)
Marchetti v. United States, 390 U.S. 39 (1962)

Note—While not entirely consistent, the Court will, in general, not examine the motives of Congress in taxing. The rule seems to be that where Congress can regulate, it can tax in order to do so. While general police power is a state function, a limited federal power has developed from the commerce, postal, and taxing power.

South Carolina v. United States, 199 U.S. 437; 26 S. Ct. 110; 50 L. Ed. 261 (1905)

South Carolina was the sole dispenser of wholesale and retail liquor within the state. All profits went to the state treasury. Prior to 1901, the state paid the United States tax, but on April 14, 1901 the state authorities refused further payments.

OPINION BY MR. JUSTICE BREWER
(Vote: 6–3)

Question—Should this state agency be granted immunity from taxation by the federal government because they were exercising the sovereign power of a state?

Decision—No.

Reason—The necessity of regulation may induce the states to the possession of other fields such as tobacco and other objects of internal revenue tax. But "if one state finds it thus profitable, other states may follow, and the whole body of internal revenue tax be thus striken down." The national government would be crippled. If all the states exercised such power the efficiency of the national government could be destroyed. The exemption of state agencies and instrumentalities from national taxation is limited to those which are strictly governmental in character and does not extend to those which are used by the state in the carrying on of ordinary business. Thus "whenever a state engages in business which is of a private nature, that business is not withdrawn from the taxing power of the nation."

Corollary cases

Veazie Bank v. Fenno, 8 Wallace 533 (1869)
United States v. Perkins, 163 U.S. 625 (1886)
Ambrosini v. United States, 187 U.S. 1 (1902)

Ohio v. Helvering, 292 U.S. 360 (1934)
Helvering v. Powers, 293 U.S. 214 (1934)
New York v. United States, 326 U.S. 572 (1946)

United States v. Doremus, 249 U.S. 86; 39 S. Ct. 214; 63 L. Ed. 493 (1919)

Doremus, a physician, was indicted for violating Section 2 of the Harrison Narcotic Drug Act. It forbade any person to dispose of narcotic drugs except by a written order on a form issued by the Commissioner of Internal Revenue. It was not to apply to physicians who used drugs to treat patients. Section I of the act stated that all persons who would have contact with this type of drug in a commercial way must pay a special tax of one dollar per annum. Doremus was convicted of selling to one Ameris five hundred one-sixth grain heroin tablets without an order of the official type, and of selling not in porfessional practice but to relieve the appetite of a known drug addict. The lower court had held Section 2 of the act unconstitutional as not a revenue measure but an invasion of state police power.

OPINION BY MR. JUSTICE DAY
(Vote: 5–4)

Question—Have the provisions in question any relation to the raising of revenue?

Decision—Yes.

Reason—That Congress might levy an excise tax upon such dealers and others named is not disputed. The provision in Section 2 aims to confine sales to registered dealers and to those dispensing the drugs as physicians. Congress, with full power over the subject, short of arbitrary and unreasonable treatment that is not to be assumed, inserted these provisions into the act specifically to provide revenue. These provisions tend to keep traffic aboveboard and subject to inspection by those authorized to collect the revenue. They tend to restrain unauthorized persons from selling the drug and not paying the tax. Ameris might not have used all the drug himself and he then may have sold the remainder to others without paying the tax. At least Congress may have deemed it wise to prevent such possible dealings because of their effect on the collection of revenue. "The fact that other motives may impel the exercise of Federal taxing power does not authorize the courts to inquire into the subject. If the legislation enacted has some reasonable relation to the exercise of the taxing authority conferred by the Constitution, it cannot be invalidated because of the supposed motives which induced it."

Corollary cases

License Tax Cases, 5 Wallace 462 (1867)
Veazie Bank v. Fenno, 8 Wallace 533 (1869)
McCray v. United States, 195 U.S. 27 (1904)
Nigro v. United States, 276 U.S. 332 (1928)
Bailey v. Drexel Furniture Co., 259 U.S. 20 (1922)
Sonzinsky v. United States, 300 U.S. 506 (1937)
Hill v. Wallace, 259 U.S. 44 (1922)
Carter v. Carter Coal Co., 298 U.S. 238 (1936)

Note—*Doremus* follows the tax-regulatory principle shown in *Veazie Bank* v. *Fenno,* 8 Wallace 533 (1869) and *McCray* v. *United States,* 195 U.S. 27 (1904), in which the Court would not look into the motives or intent of Congress. At other times, however, it has looked into the motives, as was the case of *Marchetti* v. *United States,* 390 U.S. 39 (1968) that, on self-incrimination grounds, reversed *United States* v. *Kahriger,* 345 U.S. 22 (1953) and *Lewis* v. *United States,* 348 U.S. 419 (1955).

Evans v. Gore, 253 U.S. 245; 40 S. Ct. 550; 64 L. Ed. 887 (1920)

This was a suit by Judge Walter Evans of the United States District Court for the Western District of Kentucky against J. R. Gore, acting collector of internal revenue, to recover the amount of a tax paid by him under protest on his salary as a judge. The tax was collected by the authority of the Revenue Act of 1919, whereas Judge Evans had been appointed in 1899. The Constitution in Article III, Section I provides that judges "shall, at stated times, receive for their services a compensation which shall not be diminished during their continuance in office."

Opinion by Mr. Justice Van Devanter
(Vote: 7–2)

Question—Is the tax imposed in this case an unconstitutional diminution of compensation?

Decision—Yes.

Reason—The Constitution provides that judges of both supreme and inferior courts shall hold office ''during good behavior'' and that their compensation ''shall not be diminished during their continuance in office.'' The meaning of this phrase has to be determined. 1. Is it to benefit the judges and promote the public welfare by giving them the independence necessary for the impartial and courageous discharge of their office? 2. Does it not only forbid direct reduction but also indirect reduction in the form of a tax? 3. Does it mean that the judge shall have no fears for his support while he remains in office?

The Constitution provides for three separate departments of government with definite checks and balances to ensure their independence of each other. Of the three, the judiciary is the weakest, possessing only the power of judgment. However, it is the balance wheel of the entire system, preserving an adjustment between individual rights and governmental powers.

It is not without a set purpose that tenure during good behavior and an undiminishable compensation were coupled together. The prohibition was included, not to benefit the judges, but to attract good, competent men to the bench and to promote independence of action without respect to persons. The words of the prohibition in the Constitution are not qualified and therefore are taken by the Court to prohibit diminution in salaries.

The Sixteenth Amendment does not justify the taxation of persons or things previously immune. It was intended only to remove all occasion for any appointment of income taxes among the states. Therefore the tax in question was not supported by the Sixteenth Amendment. This tax was a diminution of salary, and therefore invalid. (This case was, in effect, overruled by *O'Malley* v. *Woodrough,* 307 U.S. 277,

1939. There the Court held that to subject judges to a nondiscriminatory general income tax is merely to recognize that judges are also citizens and that their particular function in government does not generate an immunity from sharing with their fellow citizens the material burden of the government whose Constitution and laws they are charged with administering.)

Corollary cases

Miles v. Graham, 268 U.S. 501 (1925)
O'Malley v. Woodrough, 307 U.S. 277 (1939)
United States v. Will, 449 U.S. 200 (1980)

Note—In an interesting "rule of necessity" case involving a problem of "impropriety" and political fallout, the Court ruled that federal cost of living increases for 1976 and 1979 (but not 1977 and 1978) for federal judges violated the Constitution's prohibition against diminishing a judge's pay.

Commonwealth of Massachusetts v. Mellon (Frothingham v. Mellon), 262 U.S. 447, 43 S. Ct. 597, 67 L. Ed. 1078 (1923)

The Maternity Act of November 23, 1921 provided for annual federal appropriations to be apportioned among the states that might cooperate to reduce maternal and infant mortality and protect the health of mothers and infants. The state of Massachusetts, in an original suit against the secretary of the treasury, Andrew Mellon, stated that the act of November 23, 1921, "The Maternity Act," was unconstitutional on the ground that the federal government usurped reserve powers of the states as guaranteed by the Constitution in the Tenth Amendment, since this act invaded local powers and therefore should be enjoined by the Supreme Court.

Mrs. Frothingham appealed from a decision of the Circuit Court of Appeals of Washington, D.C., contesting the same act and endeavoring to have the Supreme Court enjoin the enforcement of the act on the ground that the provisions of this act would take her property under the guise of taxation.

OPINION BY MR. JUSTICE SUTHERLAND
(No evidence from the report that the decision was not unanimous.)

Question—1. Can the Supreme Court issue an enjoining order on a federal appropriation act in a suit brought by the state?

2. Can a taxpayer invoke the power of the court to enjoin a federal appropriation act on the ground that it is invalid because it imposes hardship?

Decision—1. No. Case dismissed.
　　　　　2. No. Decision of lower court upheld.

Reason—The state cannot institute judicial proceedings to protect citizens of the United States who are also its citizens from the operation of statutes of the United States. Further, the Supreme Court has no jurisdiction to enjoin the enforcement of an act of Congress, which is to become operative in any state only upon acceptance by it, on the grounds that Congress is legislating outside its power and into the reserved powers of the states, since this is a political question and not judicial in character. "His [the taxpayer's] interest in the moneys of the treasury—partly realized from taxation and partly from other sources—is shared with millions of others, is comparatively minute and indeterminable, and the effect upon future taxation, of any payment out of the funds, so remote, fluctuating, and uncertain, that no basis is afforded for an appeal to the preventive powers of a court of equity." A party invoking judicial action to hold a law of appropriation unconstitutional must show direct injury sustained or threatened, not merely that the individual is suffering in an indefinite way with the general public.

Corollary cases

Millard v. Roberts, 202 U.S. 429 (1906)
Bradfield v. Roberts, 175 U.S. 291 (1899)
Luther v. Borden, 7 Howard 1 (1849)
United States v. Butler, 297 U.S. 1 (1936)
Ex parte Levitt, 302 U.S. 633 (1937)
Florida v. Mellon, 273 U.S. 12 (1927)
Fairchild v. Hughes, 258 U.S. 126 (1922)
New Jersey v. Sargent, 269 U.S. 328 (1926)
Doremus v. Board of Education, 342 U.S. 420 (1952)
Everson v. Board of Education, 330 U.S. 1 (1952)
Flast v. Cohen, 392 U.S. 83 (1968)
Harris v. McRae, 448 U.S. 297 (1980)
Williams v. Zbaraz, 448 U.S. 358 (1980)

Beal v. Doe, 432 U.S. 438 (1977)
United States v. Lee, 71 L. Ed. 2d 127 (1982)

Note—While the *Mellon* principle is still strong, *Flast* v. *Cohen,* 392 U.S. 83 (1968), prohibits spending public funds in violation of the establishment clause in the First Amendment.

United States v. Butler, 297 U.S. 1; 56 S. Ct. 312; 80 L. Ed. 477 (1936)

> In accordance with the Agricultural Adjustment Act of 1933, the secretary of agriculture ordered the payment of crop reduction benefits on cotton. To meet these, processing taxes were levied on the processors. The act provided also for the levying of floor taxes upon the existent stocks of floor goods that would have been subject to processing taxes had the law been effective earlier. The receiver for a Massachusetts cotton mill, the Hoosac Mills Corporation, attacked the constitutionality of the processing and floor taxes assessed against it.

OPINION BY MR. JUSTICE ROBERTS
(Vote: 6–3)

Question—Is this act a proper exercise of the federal taxing power?

Decision—No.

Reason—It was an act that invaded the rights reserved to the states. It was a statutory plan to regulate and control agricultural production, a matter beyond the power delegated to the federal government. "Resort to the taxing power to effectuate an end which is not legitimate, not within the scope of the constitution, is obviously inadmissible."

The tax was based on the general welfare clause of the Constitution. This is a limitation on the power to tax, not an enlargement of it. The law took money from one group for the benefit of another group. This was not a tax.

It was claimed that the act was voluntary, but it was not. It forced the farmer to comply with it under threat of financial ruin. Congress cannot invade state jurisdiction to compel individual action. "At best it is a scheme for purchasing with federal funds submission to federal regulation of a subject reserved to the states."

Corollary cases

Mulford v. Smith, 307 U.S. 38 (1939)
Bailey v. Drexel Furniture Co., 259 U.S. 20 (1922)
Sonzinsky v. United States, 300 U.S. 506 (1937)
McCray v. United States, 195 U.S. 27 (1904)
Veazie Bank v. Fenno, 8 Wallace 533 (1869)
Steward Machine Co. v. Davis, 301 U.S. 548 (1937)

Note—*Butler* declared the "triple A," the Agricultural Adjustment Act, null and void; but in the second "triple A" case involving the Agriculture Act of 1938, *Mulford* v. *Smith,* 307 U.S. 38 (1939), the Court practically, if not formally, overruled *Butler.*

Sonzinsky v. United States, 300 U.S. 506; 57 S. Ct. 554; 81 L. Ed. 772 (1937)

The National Firearms Act of 1934 imposed a $200 annual license tax on dealers in firearms. The petitioner was convicted on two counts: (1) for failure to pay the firearms tax set down by Congress, and (2) for failure to register as a dealer in firearms as required by the National Firearms Act. The petitioner contended that the tax was for the purpose of suppressing the sale of certain types of firearms.

OPINION BY MR. JUSTICE STONE
(No evidence from the report that the decision was not unanimous.)

Question—Can Congress use a tax for the purpose of regulation?

Decision—Yes.

Reason—"Every tax is in some measure regulatory. To some extent it interposes an economic impediment to the activity taxed as compared with others not taxed. But a tax is not any the less a tax because it has a regulatory effect . . . and it has long been established that an act of Congress which on its face purports to be an exercise of the taxing power is not any the less so because the tax is burdensome or tends to restrict or suppress the thing taxed." The Court called attention to the fact that the tax "is productive of some revenue" and added, "we are not free to speculate as to the motives which moved Congress to impose it or as to the extent to which it may operate to restrict the activities taxed. As it is not attended by an offensive regulation and since it operates as a tax, it is within the national taxing power."

Corollary cases

Weller v. New York, 268 U.S. 319 (1925)
Field v. Clark, 143 U.S. 649 (1892)
Hill v. Wallace, 259 U.S. 44 (1922)
United States v. Doremus, 249 U.S. 86 (1919)
McCray v. United States, 195 U.S. 27 (1904)
Alaska Fish Co. v. Smith, 255 U.S. 44 (1921)
Alston v. United States, 274 U.S. 289
Hampton & Co. v. United States, 276 U.S. 394 (1928)
Carter v. Carter Coal Co., 298 U.S. 238 (1936)
United States v. Butler, 297 U.S. 1 (1936)
Bailey v. Drexel Furniture Co., 259 U.S. 20 (1922)
Helvering v. Davis, 301 U.S. 619 (1937)
United States v. Kahriger, 345 U.S. 22 (1953)
Haynes v. United States, 390 U.S. 85 (1968)
Marchetti v. United States, 390 U.S. 39 (1968)
Gorsso v. United States, 390 U.S. 62 (1968)

Note—*Haynes* v. *United States,* 390 U.S. 85 (1968), cast doubt on the continuing validity of *Sonzinsky.* In *Haynes* the Court held that the hazards of incrimination created by the registration requirements are real and appreciable. The principle that Congress can tax what it can regulate is easier stated than followed. *Marchetti* v. *United States,* 390 U.S. 39 (1968) reversed *Lewis* v. *United States,* 348 U.S. 419 (1955) and *United States* v. *Kahriger* because of the self-incriminating tax provisions.

Helvering v. Davis, 301 U.S. 619; 57 S. Ct. 904; 81 L. Ed. 1307 (1937)

Suits were brought by George P. Davis, a shareholder, of the Edison Illuminating Company of Boston, to restrain the corporation from making the payments and deductions called for by the Social Security Act under Titles VIII and II. The district court held that the tax on employees was not the issue, and that the tax on employers was constitutional.

The court of appeals reversed the decision, holding that Title II was an invasion of powers reserved by the Tenth Amendment to the states, or to the people. The tax on employers was considered invalid for the additional reason that it was not the type of excise understood when the Constitution was adopted.

OPINION BY MR. JUSTICE CARDOZO
(Vote: 7–2)

Question—Two questions were included in a petition for a writ of certiorari (1) is the tax imposed upon employers contrary to the Tenth Amendment because of an invasion of powers reserved to the states, (2) and are the purposes of expenditure legal?

Decision—1. No.
2. Yes.

Reason—Under the Constitution, Congress can spend money for the general welfare; however, difficulties are left when the power is conceded. The line must be drawn between one welfare and another: general and particular. There is a middle ground. The discretion is not confided to the courts. The discretion belongs to the Congress, unless the choice is clearly wrong. The spreading from state to state of unemployment is an ill not particular but general, which may be checked, if Congress so determines, by the resources of the nation. The ill is all one, or at least not greatly different, whether men are thrown out of work because there is no longer work to do or because the disabilities of age make them incapable of doing it. Consequently, when money is spent to promote the general welfare, the concept of welfare is shaped by Congress and not by the states.

Corollary cases

Charles C. Steward Machine Company v. Davis, 301 U.S. 548 (1937)
United States v. Butler, 297 U.S. 1 (1936)
Alabama Power Co. v. Ickes, 302 U.S. 464 (1938)

Califano v. Aznavorian, 58 L. Ed. 2d 435 (1978)

Note—*Helvering* was handed down the same day as *Charles C. Steward Machine Co.* v. *Davis,* 301 U.S. 548 (1937), and greatly relied on it.

Charles C. Steward Machine Co. v. Davis, 301 U.S. 548; 57 S. Ct. 883; 81 L. Ed. 1279 (1937)

> The petitioner, an Alabama corporation, paid a tax in compliance with the Social Security Act. It filed claim for refund with the Commissioner of Internal Revenue to recover the payment ($46.14) asserting a conflict between the statute and the Constitution. Funds realized are used to aid the states in the administration of their unemployment compensation laws.

OPINION BY MR. JUSTICE CARDOZO
(Vote: 5–4)

Question—Is the tax a valid exercise of federal power?

Decision—Yes.

Reason—It was contended that it is not lawful to tax a right, and that, as such, employment is not open to taxation. However, employment is a business relation, and business is a legitimate object of the taxing power.

There was also the contention that an ulterior motive was contained in the structure of the act, and that the motive was essentially contrary to the Tenth Amendment. However, neither the taxpayer nor the state was coerced in this matter. The taxpayer fulfilled the mandate of his local legislature. The state chose to administer unemployment relief under laws of her own making. Nor did the statute call for a surrender by the state of powers essential to their quasi-sovereign existence. The state did not bind itself to keep the law in force. The state might repeal the statute; the state was not forced.

Corollary cases

Knowlton v. Moore, 178 U.S. 41 (1900)
Cincinnati Soap Co. v. United States, 301 U.S. 308 (1937)
Sonzinsky v. United States, 300 U.S. 506 (1937)

Carmichael v. Southern Coal and Coke Co., 301 U.S. 495 (1937)
State of Oklahoma v. U.S. Civil Service Commission, 330 U.S. 127 (1947)
Massachusetts v. Mellon, 262 U.S. 447 (1923)
Helvering v. Davis, 301 U.S. 619 (1937)
United States v. Butler, 297 U.S. 1 (1936)
Harris v. McRae, 448 U.S. 297 (1980)
O'Bannon v. Town Court Nursing Center, 65 L. Ed. 2d 506 (1980)
Califano v. Boles, 61 L. Ed. 2d 541 (1979)
California v. Aznavorian, 439 U.S. 170 (1978)

Note—*Standard Machine* and *Helvering* v. *Davis* decided the same day, are the Social Security Cases. The former dealt with a payroll tax and unemployment compensation laws, and the latter upheld the Social Security Act of 1935, which placed a tax on employers and employees to pay benefits to retired employees. Both cases leaned heavily on the loose and generous construction of the general welfare clause in Article I, Section 8 that allows Congress to tax and spend liberally in behalf of general welfare.

Graves v. New York ex rel. O'Keefe, 306 U.S. 466; 59 Sup. Ct. 595; 83 L. Ed. 927 (1939)

O'Keefe, a resident of New York, was employed by the Home Owners' Loan Corporation, a federal government corporation. He contended that the New York Tax Commission had taxed him illegally because, as a federal employee, his salary was exempted from state income tax. The HOLC, as designed by Congress, was completely a federal government project, but nowhere in the act was there even intimated any congressional purpose to grant immunity from state taxation of employee salaries. In his income tax return, O'Keefe included his salary as subject to the New York state income tax and sought a tax refund on the basis of his federal employment.

OPINION BY MR. JUSTICE STONE
(Vote: 7–2)

Question—Does the tax laid by the state upon the salary of the respondent, employed by a corporate instrumentality of the federal government, impose an unconstitutional burden upon that government?

Decision—No.

Reason—The Court ruled that the state income tax is a nondiscriminatory tax on income applied to salaries at a specified rate. It is not in form or substance a tax upon the Home Owners' Loan Corporation or its property or income, nor is it paid by the corporation or the government from their funds. It was laid directly on the income of the respondent that he received as compensation for his services. These funds were his private funds and not the funds of the government. The only possible basis for implying a constitutional immunity from state income tax of the salary of an employee of the national government or of a governmental agency is that the economic burden of the tax is in some way passed on so as to impose a burden on the national government. Private funds received as compensation for services to the federal government constitute in no way a burden on the federal government when such funds are taxed by the state.

Tax immunity evolves from the premise that there is an implied immunity between the state and federal taxing powers as a limitation to prevent interference each by the other in the exercise of that power where the other government's activities are concerned. There is no implied restriction, therefore, no burden, on the federal government because the theory that a tax on income is legally a tax on its source is not tenable. The tax here is nondiscriminatory. Any burden that would exist here is one that the Constitution presupposes in a system of dual governments, such as our federal system, and cannot be held to be within the implied taxing restrictions of the state. If such an immunity were implied it would impose too greatly on the taxing power confirmed to the state.

Corollary cases

McCulloch v. Maryland, 4 Wheaton 435 (1819)
Helvering v. Gerhardt, 304 U.S. 412 (1938)
Collector v. Day, 11 Wallace 113 (1871)
Metcalf & Eddy v. Mitchell, 269 U.S. 514 (1926)
Dobbins v. Commissioners of Erie County, 16 Peters 435 (1842)
New York v. United States, 326 U.S. 572 (1946)
Ohio v. Helvering, 290 U.S. 360 (1934)

Alabama v. King and Boozer, 314 U.S. 1 (1941)
Federal Land Bank v. Bismark Lumber Co., 314 U.S. 95 (1941)
Howard v. Commissioners of Sinking Fund, 344 U.S. 624 (1953)

Note—*Graves* overruled *Dobbins* v. *Erie County,* 16 Peters 435 (1842) and *Collector* v. *Day,* 11 Wallace 113 (1871). Since *McCulloch* v. *Maryland,* 4 Wheaton 316 (1819), the Court moved from reciprocal immunity to reciprocal taxation, subject, though, to the "supremacy clause" of the Constitution (Article VI, Clause 2).

Mulford v. Smith, 307 U.S. 38; 59 S. Ct. 648; 83 L. Ed. 1092 (1939)

The Agriculture Act of 1938, based upon the commerce power of the Constitution, regulated the marketing of various farm products. Congress set detailed limits in the act and left it to the secretary of agriculture to put the act into effect. The purpose of the act was "to regulate interstate and foreign commerce in cotton, wheat, corn, tobacco, and rice to the extent necessary to provide an orderly, adequate, and balanced flow of such commodities in interstate and foreign commerce through storage of reserve supplies, loans, marketing, quotas, assisting farmers to obtain, in so far as practicable, parity prices for such commodities and parity of income, and assisting consumers to obtain an adequate and steady supply of such commodities at fair prices." The appellants brought suit under the portion of the act dealing with marketing quotas for flue-cured tobacco.

OPINION BY MR. JUSTICE ROBERTS
(Vote: 7–2)

Question—1. Is the act beyond the powers delegated to Congress?

2. Does it result in an unconstitutional delegation of legislative power to the secretary of agriculture?

3. Does it deprive farmers of their property without due process of law?

Decision—1. No.

2. No.

3. No.

Reasons—1. The tobacco produced was for interstate commerce. The law did not limit the amount of the crop grown, but limited only what might be sold. It was a regulation of commerce granted to Congress in the Constitution. "The motive of Congress in exerting the power is irrelevant to the validity of the legislation."

2. There was no improper delegation of legislative power since definite standards were set down in the act in both the fixing of quotas and in their allotment among states and farms.

3. The act dealt only with the marketing and not with the growing of crops. The farmers could hold over their tobacco until a late year if they saw fit.

Corollary cases

Wickard v. Filburn, 317 U.S. 111 (1942)
United States v. Butler, 297 U.S. 1 (1936)
United States v. Darby, 312 U.S. 100 (1941)
United States v. Rock Royal Cooperative, 307 U.S. 533 (1939)
Currin v. Wallace, 306 U.S. 1 (1939)
Kentucky Whip and Collar Co. v. Illinois Central R. R. Co., 299 U.S. 334 (1937)

Pittman v. Home Owners' Loan Corporation, 308 U.S. 21, 60 S. Ct. 15, 84 L. Ed. 11 (1939)

The Home Owners' Loan Corporation brought this proceeding in Baltimore for a writ of mandamus requiring the clerk of the Superior Court of Baltimore to record a mortgage executed to the corporation upon the payment of the ordinary recording charge and without affixing stamps for the state recording tax. Since the Home Owners' Loan Corporation was expressly an instrumentality of the United States, it was contended that the tax as thus applied was invalid. The act of Congress setting up this corporation stated that it should be exempt from all state or municipal taxes.

OPINION BY MR. CHIEF JUSTICE HUGHES
(Vote: 8–0)

Question—Did Congress grant a tax immunity of a greater extent than was within its constitutional power?

Decision—No.

Reason—Congress has not only the power to create a corporation to facilitate the performance of governmental functions
but also to protect the operations thus validly authorized. This
power to preserve necessarily comes within the range of the
express power conferred upon Congress to make all laws that
shall be necessary and proper for carrying into execution all
powers vested by the Constitution in the government of the
United States. In this case, Congress had undertaken to safeguard the operations of the Home Owners' Loan Corporation
by providing the described immunity. The Court construed
this provision as embracing and prohibiting the tax in question.
Since Congress had the constitutional authority to enact this
provision, it was binding upon the Supreme Court as the
supreme law of the land.

Corollary cases

Graves v. New York ex rel. O'Keefe, 306 U.S. 466 (1939)
McCulloch v. Maryland, 4 Wheaton 316 (1819)
Smith v. Kansas City Title Co., 255 U.S. 180 (1921)
The Shreveport Case, 234 U.S. 342 (1914)
New York v. United States, 326 U.S. 572 (1946)
Federal Land Bank of St. Paul v. Bismarck Lumber Co., 314 U.S. 95 (1941)
Standard Oil Co. v. Johnson, 316 U.S. 418 (1942)
Alabama v. King and Boozer, 314 U.S. 1 (1941)
Oklahoma Tax Commission v. Texas Co., 336 U.S. 342 (1942)
Carson v. Roane-Anderson Co., 342 U.S. 232 (1952)
Massachusetts v. United States, 55 L. Ed. 2d 403 (1981)

New York and Saratoga Springs Commission v. United States, 326 U.S. 572; 66 S. Ct. 310; 90 L. Ed. 326 (1946)

The issue was the validity of a federal tax on the sale of
mineral waters, as applied to sales by the state of New York
of water taken from Saratoga Springs. New York claimed
the sales were immune from the tax on the ground that the
state was engaged in the exercise of a usual, traditional, and
essential governmental function.

OPINION BY MR. JUSTICE FRANKFURTER
(Vote: 6–2)

Question—Is the tax valid?

Decision—Yes.

Reason—The federal government is a government of all the states, and all the states share in the legislative process by which a tax of general application is levied. We have moved away from the notion of immunity of functionaries of one government from taxation by the other. "So long as Congress generally taps a source of revenue by whomsoever earned and not uniquely capable of being earned only by a state, the Constitution of the United States does not forbid it merely because its incidence falls also on a State."

Corollary cases

South Carolina v. United States, 199 U.S. 437 (1905)
Helvering v. Gerhardt, 304 U.S. 405 (1938)
Graves v. New York, ex rel. O'Keefe, 306 U.S. 240 (1939)
Ohio v. Helvering, 292 U.S. 360 (1934)
University of Illinois v. United States, 289 U.S. 48 (1933)
Helvering v. Powers, 293 U.S. 214 (1934)
Wilmette Park District v. Campbell, 338 U.S. 411 (1949)

Note—The Court made a distinction between a *propriety* function—one that could be conducted by a private person, legal or natural—and a *governmental* function that only a government can undertake. In *Garcia* v. *San Antonio Metropolitan Transit Authority,* 83 L. Ed. 2d 1016 (1985). Quoting *New York* v. *United States,* 90 L. Ed. 326, 1946, Blackmun said that the distinction between "propriety" and "governmental" are untenable and must be abandoned. Even in its heyday "the Court never explained the constitutional basis for that distinction."

LABOR

National Labor Relations Board v. Jones & Laughlin Steel Corporation, 301 U.S. 1; 57. Ct. 615; 81 L. Ed. 893 (1937)

In a proceeding under the National Labor Relations Act of 1935, the National Labor Relations Board found that the Jones and Laughlin Steel Corporation had violated the act by engaging in unfair labor practices. The unfair labor practices charged were that the corporation was discriminating against the members of the union with regard to hiring and tenure of employment, and was coercing and intimidating its employees in order to interfere with their self-organization. The National Labor Relations Board tried to enforce the provisions of the act, and the corporation failed to comply. The circuit court of appeals refused to enforce the order of the board, holding that the order lay beyond the range of federal power. The Supreme Court granted certiorari.

OPINION BY MR. CHIEF JUSTICE HUGHES
(Vote: 5–4)

Question—Can Congress regulate labor relations under its interstate commerce power?

Decision—Yes.

Reason—"The fundamental principle is that the power to regulate commerce is the power to enact 'all appropriate legislation' for its protection or advancement; . . . to adopt measures 'to promote its growth and insure its safety' . . . 'to foster, protect, control and restrain.' . . . That power is plenary and may be exerted to protect interstate commerce 'no matter what the source of the dangers which threaten it.' . . . Although activities may be intrastate in character when separately considered, if they have such a close and substantial relation to interstate commerce that their control is essential or appropriate to protect that commerce from burdens and obstructions, Congress cannot be denied the power to exercise that control. . . . The fact remains that the stoppage of those operations by industrial strife would have a most serious effect upon interstate commerce. In view of respondent's far-flung activities, it is idle to say that the effect would be indirect or

389

remote. It is obvious that it would be immediate and might be catastrophic. We are asked to shut our eyes to the plainest facts of our national life and to deal with the question of direct and indirect effects in an intellectual vacuum.''

The Court stated that the cardinal principle of statutory construction is to save and not to destroy. The Court has repeatedly held that as between two possible interpretations of a statute, by one of which it would be unconstitutional and by the other valid, their plain duty is to adopt that which will save the act. After reviewing the evidence in the case, it was determined that the main purpose of the act was to obstruct interference with the flow of interstate commerce.

The Court said that the steel industry is one of the great basic industries of the United States, affecting interstate commerce at every point. The Court referred to the steel strike of 1919–1920 with its far-reaching consequences. The fact that there appeared to have been no major disturbance in this case, did not dispose of the possibilities of the future. Therefore, the Court had no doubt that Congress had constitutional authority to safeguard the right of the employees to self-organization and freedom in the choice of representatives for collective bargaining.

Corollary cases

Schechter Corp. v. United States, 295 U.S. 495 (1935)
FTC v. American Tobacco Co., 264 U.S. 298 (1924)
Panama R. R. Co. v. Johnson, 264 U.S. 375 (1924)
Blodgett v. Holden, 275 U.S. 142 (1927)
Texas & N. O. R. R. Co. v. Brotherhood of Railway & S. S. Clerks, 281 U.S. 538 (1930)
American Steel Foundries v. Tri-City Central Trade Council, 257 U.S. 184 (1921)
Baltimore & Ohio R. R. Co. v. ICC, 221 U.S. 612 (1911)
Second Employers' Liability Cases, 223 U.S. 1 (1912)
United States v. E. C. Knight Co., 156 U.S. (1895)
NLRB v. Fruehauf Trailer Co., 301 U.S. 49 (1937)
NLRB v. Friedman-Harry Marks Clothing Co., 301 U.S. 58 (1937)
Santa Cruz Fruit Packing Co. v. NLRB, 303 U.S. 453 (1938)
Consolidated Edison Co., v. NLRB, 305 U.S. 197 (1938)
Kirschbaum v. Walling, 316 U.S. 517 (1942)
NLRB v. Catholic Bishop of Chicago, 440 U.S. 490 (1979)

NLRB v. Hendricks County Rural Electric Corporation, 70 L. Ed. 2d 323
   (1981)

Note—*Jones and Laughlin Steel* pointed to a shift to a more governmentally regulated industrial economy. The underpinnings of *Carter v. Carter Coal Co.*, 298 U.S. 238 (1936), were reversed.

Thornhill v. Alabama, 310 U.S. 88; 60 S. Ct. 736; 84 L. Ed. 1093 (1940)

> Thornhill was convicted in Alabama of violating an Alabama statute that forbade loitering or picketing around a place of business for the purpose of inducing others not to trade with or work for the place of business. He was arrested for picketing the plant of the Brown Wood Preserving Co.

OPINION BY MR. JUSTICE MURPHY
(Vote: 8–1)

Question—Did the Alabama statute violate the First Amendment to the Constitution?

Decision—Yes.

Reason—The Court reasoned that the freedom of speech and of the press guaranteed by the Constitution embraces at the least the liberty to discuss publicly and truthfully all matters of public concern without previous restraint or fear of subsequent punishment. The Court stated that in the circumstances of our times the dissemination of information concerning the facts of a labor dispute must be regarded as within the area of free discussion that is guaranteed by the Constitution. The Court held that free discussion concerning the conditions in industry and the causes of labor disputes are indispensable to the effective and intelligent use of the processes of popular government to shape the destiny of modern industrial society. The Court further stated that the streets are natural and proper places for the dissemination of information and opinion, and one is not to have the exercise of his liberty of expression in appropriate places abridged on the plea that it may be exercised in some other place.

Corollary cases

United States v. Carolene Products, 404 U.S. 144 (1938)
De Jonge v. Oregon, 299 U.S. 353 (1937)
Stromberg v. California, 283 U.S. 359 (1931)
Lanzetta v. New Jersey, 306 U.S. 451 (1939)
Schneider v. State, 308 U.S. 147 (1939)
Police Department of the City of Chicago v. Mosley, 408 U.S. 92 (1972)
Hudgens v. NLRB, 424 U.S. 507 (1976)
Hague v. CIO, 307 U.S. 496 (1939)
Lovell v. Griffin, 303 U.S. 444 (1938)
Carlson v. California, 310 U.S. 106 (1940)
Youngdahl v. Rainfair, 355 U.S. 131 (1957)
Amalgamated Food Employees Union Local 590 v. Logan Valley Plaza, 391
    U.S. 308 (1968)

Note—The Court first developed the "speech plus" concept in its picketing decisions. In a series of cases beginning with *Giboney v. Empire Storage and Ice Co.,* 336 U.S. 490 (1949), involving unionized peddlers picketing nonunionized peddlers, the Court effectively reversed *Thornhill*. While there can be no blanket prohibition on picketing, it can be subject to state police power.

Lincoln Federal Labor Union No. 19129, American Federation of Labor, et al., v. Northwestern Iron and Metal Co., et al., 335 U.S. 525; 69 S. Ct. 251; 93 L. Ed. 212 (1949)

A North Carolina statute made it unlawful for an employer to refuse employment to or to discharge anyone because of membership or nonmembership in a labor union, or for a labor organization and an employer to enter into a contract for a closed or union shop. In North Carolina an employer and officers of a labor union were convicted of a misdemeanor for entering into such a contract.

Opinion by Mr. Justice Black
(No evidence from the report that the decision was not unanimous.)

Question—Do these state laws violate rights guaranteed employers, unions, and their members by the United States Constitution?

Decision—No.

Reason—Neither the due process clause nor the equal protection clause prohibits the states from outlawing closed or union shop agreements. The constitutional right of workers to assemble to discuss and formulate plans for the furthering of their own interest in jobs cannot be construed as a constitutional guarantee that none shall get and hold jobs except those who join in such plans. Where conduct affects the interest of others and the general public, the legality of that conduct must be measured by whether the conduct conforms to valid laws.

The liberty of contracts protected by the Fourteenth Amendment is not unqualified. Due process does not forbid a state to pass laws designed to safeguard the opportunity of nonunion members to get and hold jobs, free from discrimination because they are not members of a union. The Court rejected the earlier due process philosophy of the cases and returned to the even earlier philosophy that the states have the power to legislate against what are found to be injurious practices in their internal commercial and business affairs, so long as their laws do not run afoul of some specific federal Constitutional prohibition or some valid federal law. "Under this constitutional doctrine the due process clause is no longer to be so broadly construed that the Congress and state legislatures are put in a strait jacket when they attempt to suppress business and industrial conditions which they regard as offensive to the public welfare. Just as we have held that the due process clause erects no obstacle to block legislative protection of union members, we now hold that legislative protection can be afforded non-union workers."

Corollary cases

A. F. of L. v. American Sash Co., 335 U.S. 538 (1949)
Daniel v. Family Security Life Insurance Co., 336 U.S. 220 (1949)
West Coast Hotel Co. v. Parrish, 300 U.S. 379 (1937)
Coppage v. Kansas, 236 U.S. 1 (1915)
Adair v. United States, 208 U.S. 161 (1908)
Phelps Dodge Corp, v. NLRB, 313 U.S. 177 (1941)
NLRB v. Scribner, 405 U.S, 117 (1972)
NLRB v. Burns International Security Services, 406 U.S. 272 (1972)
First National Maintenance Corporation v. NLRB, 69 L. Ed. 2d 318 (1981)

Note—The Court here supports the principle of the "right to work" or the "open shop." Some twenty states have different kinds of right-to-work statutes, but these states are generally nonindustrial. In one important decision involving labor and food stamps, the Court held that a federal statute which provided a household of strikers with food stamps would no longer do so and this would not violate the First and Fifth Amendments (*Lyng v. International Union, United Automobile Aerospace and Agricultural Implement Workers of America Law* 99 L. Ed. 2d 380, 1988). In still another important decision affecting labor, the Court held that a union is not permitted to solicit and extract dues from non-union members for activities not related to labor-management bargaining. (*Communication Workers v. Beck,* 101 L. Ed. 2d 634, 1988).

Giboney v. Empire Storage & Ice Co., 336 U.S, 490; 69 S. Ct. 684; 93 L. Ed. 834 (1949)

In this case the ice peddlers' union of Kansas City, Mo. sought to unionize all ice peddlers in Kansas City. The means used involved making an agreement with the ice wholesalers to refuse the sale of ice to nonunion peddlers. All agreed except the Empire Ice Company. The union proceeded to set up picket lines around the Empire Company's place of business and threatened the union members with the loss of their cards if they crossed the picket line. The avowed purpose of the picketing was to compel the Empire Company to stop selling ice to nonunion peddlers. There was a Missouri statute prohibiting competing dealers and their aiders and abettors from combining to restrain the freedom of trade.

Opinion by Mr. Justice Black
(No evidence from the report that the decision was not unanimous.)

Question—Does Missouri have paramount constitutional power over a labor union to regulate and govern the manner in which certain trade practices shall be carried on within the state of Missouri?

Decision—Yes.

Reason—The Court ruled that the Missouri statute regulated trade one way, and the union adopted a program to regulate trade another way. The state had provided for enforcement of its statutory rule by imposing civil and criminal sanctions. The union had provided for enforcement of its rule by sanctions against union members who crossed picket lines. The purpose of the statute was to prevent trust combinations such as the union sought to compel the Empire Company to enter. The Court ruled that the constitutional power to prevent such combinations by a state is beyond question.

"The conditions developed in industry may be such that those engaged in it cannot continue their struggle without danger to the community. But it is not for judges to determine whether such conditions exist, nor is it their function to set the limits of permissible contest and to declare the duties which the new situation demands. This is the function of the legislature which, while limiting individual and group rights of aggression and defense, may substitute processes of justice for the more primitive method of trial by combat."

Therefore the Court held that the state's power to govern in this field is paramount, and that nothing in the constitutional guarantees of speech or press compels a state to apply or not to apply its antitrade restraint law to groups of workers, businessmen, or others.

Corollary cases

International Harvester Co. v. Missouri, 234 U.S. 199 (1914)
Grenada Lumber Co. v. Mississippi, 217 U.S. 433 (1910)
Allen Bradley Co. v. Union, 325 U.S. 797 (1945)
Thornhill v. Alabama, 310 U.S. 88 (1940)
Bridges v. California, 314 U.S. 252 (1941)
Schneider v. State, 308 U.S. 147 (1939)
Associated Press v. United States, 326 U.S. 1 (1947)
Thomas v. Collins, 323 U.S. 516 (1945)
Carlson v. California, 310 U.S. 106 (1940)

Carey v. Brown, 447 U.S. 455; 65 L. Ed. 2d 263; 100 S. Ct. 2286 (1980)

In 1972, Brown and several other members of a civil rights organization entitled The Committee Against Racism participated in a peaceful demonstration in front of the home of Michael Bilandic, then mayor of Chicago, protesting his alleged failure to support the busing of school children to achieve racial integration. They were arrested and charged with a violation of an Illinois statute that prohibited picketing before or about a residence that is not used as a place of business. Appellees brought suit in the United States District Court for the Northern District of Illinois contending that the residential picketing statute violated the First and Fourteenth Amendments as being overbroad and vague, and contained an impermissible content-based restriction on protected expression.

OPINION BY MR. JUSTICE BRENNAN
(Vote: 6–3)

Question—Is the Illinois residential picketing statute in violation of the equal protection clause of the Fourteenth Amendment

Decision—Yes.

Reason—"In *Police Department of Chicago v. Mosley,* 92 S. Ct. 2268, we held a Chicago ordinance that prohibited picketing in front of any school other than one involved in a labor dispute in violation of the equal protection clause because it impermissibly distinguished between labor picketing and all other peaceful picketing without any showing that the latter was clearly more disruptive than the former. We find the Illinois Residential Picketing statute at issue in the present case constitutionally indistinguishable from the ordinance invalidated in *Mosley.* . . . There can be no doubt that in prohibiting peaceful picketing on the public streets and sidewalks in residential neighborhoods, the Illinois statute regulates expressive conduct that falls within the First Amendment's pressure. . . . Nor can it be seriously disputed that in exempting from its general prohibition only the peaceful picketing of a place of employment involved in a labor dispute . . . the Illinois statute discriminates between lawful and unlawful conduct based upon the content of the demonstrator's communication. On its face, the act accords preferential treatment to the expression of views on one particular subject. Information about labor disputes may be freely disseminated but discussion of all other issues is restricted. . . . As we explained in *Mosley,* 'Chicago may not vindicate its interest in preventing disruption by the wholesome exclusion of picketing on all but one preferred subject. Yet here under the guise of preserving residential privacy, Illinois has flatly prohibited all nonlabor picketing that is equally likely to intrude on the tranquility of the home. . . . The state's interest in protecting the well-being, tranquility, and privacy of the home is certainly of the highest order in a free and civilized society. The crucial question, however, is whether Illinois's statute advances that objective in a manner consistent with the command of the Equal Protection Clause. . . . Because the statute discriminates among pickets based on the subject matter of their expression, the answer must be no.''

Corollary cases

Police Department of Chicago v. Mosley, 92 S. Ct. 2286 (1972)
Erzoznik v. City of Jacksonville, 95 S. Ct. 2268 (1975)
Adderly v. Florida, 87 S. Ct. 242 (1966)
Thornhill v. Alabama, 60 S. Ct. 736 (1940)
Gregory v. Chicago, 89 S. Ct. 946 (1969)
Hudgens v. NLRB, 96 S. Ct. 1029 (1976)

Note—Is picketing and leafletting of the Supreme Court sidewalks permitted? The Court said "yes" and declared an all-embracing anti-picketing law in violation of the First Amendment (*United States* v. *Grace,* 75 L. Ed. 2d 236, 1983). Anti-abortionists picketing the home of doctors who perform abortions violated a Brockfield, Wisconsin ordinance that banned such picketing "before and about" any residence. In upholding the ordinance the Court held the ordinance was content-neutral, narrowly tailored to meet government objectives, and there were other channels of communication (*Frisby* v. *Schultz,* 101 L. Ed. 2d 420, 1988).

NLRB v. Yeshiva University, 444 U.S. 672; 63 L. Ed 2d 115; 100 S. Ct. 856 (1980)

Yeshiva, a private university in New York City, conducts a wide variety of arts and sciences programs at its under-

graduate and graduate schools. The University Faculty Association (union) filed a petition with the NLRB seeking
certification as bargaining agent for the full-time faculty
members at ten of the thirteen schools. The university
opposed the petition contending that all of its faculty members are managerial or supervisory personnel and are not
considered employees within the meaning of the National
Labor Relations Act.

OPINION BY MR. JUSTICE POWELL
(Vote: 5–4)

Question—Are the full-time faculty members of Yeshiva University excluded from the categories of employees entitled
to collectively bargain under the National Labor Relations
Act?

Decision—Yes.

Reason—"There is no evidence that Congress has considered
whether a university faculty may organize for collective bargaining under the act. The act was intended to accommodate
the type of management-employee relations that prevail in the
pyramidal hierarchies of private industy. The authority [of
Yeshiva University's faculty] is absolute. They decide what
courses will be offered, when they will be scheduled, and to
whom they will be taught. They debate and determine teaching
methods, grading policies, and matriculation standards. . . . It
is difficult to imagine decisions more managerial than these. In
arguing that a faculty member exercising independent judgement acts primarily in his own interest and therefore does not
represent the interest of his employer, the board assumes that
the professional interests of the faculty and the interests of the
institution are distinct, separable entities with which a faculty
member could not simultaneously be aligned, we perceive no
justification for this. The faculty's professional interests . . .
cannot be separated from those of the institution."

Corollary cases

NLRB v. Catholic Bishop of Chicago, 440 U.S. 490 (1979)
NLRB v. Hearst Publications, 322 U.S. 111 (1944)

Beasley v. Food Fair of North Carolina, 416 U.S. 653 (1974)
NLRB v. Bell Aerospace, 416 U.S. 267 (1974)

American Tobacco Co. v. Patterson, 456 U.S.—; 71 L. Ed. 2d 748; 102 S. Ct. 1534 (1982)

Patterson and two other black employees filed charges with the Equal Employment Opportunity Commission alleging tht American Tobacco Co. had discriminated against them on the basis of race. They alleged that American Tobacco's seniority, wage, and job classification practices violated Title VII of the Civil Rights Act of 1964. The district court agreed that the challenged seniority system was not justified and the court of appeal affirmed. The Supreme Court granted petition for cetiorari.

OPINION BY MR. JUSTICE WHITE
(Vote: 5–4)

Question—Does a bona fide seniority system that has a discriminatory impact—in the absence of discriminatory intent—violate Title VII of the Civil Rights Act of 1964?

Decision—No.

Reason—"The starting point must be the language employed by Congress, the legislative intent, and the meaning of words which then must be regarded as conclusive. On its face the act makes no distinction between pre- and post-act merit systems of pre- and post-act ability tests. . . . To be cognizable, a claim that a seniority system has a discriminatory impact must be accompanied by proof of a discriminatory purpose. . . . We have not been informed of and have not found a single statement anywhere in the legislative history that (Title VII) does not protect seniority systems adopted or modified after the effective date of Title VII. A Department of Justice memorandum stated that Title VII would not have any affect on seniority rights lasting at the time it takes effect and the legislative intent that the bill would not affect seniority systems adopted before its effective date and those adopted after its effective date. Consistent with our prior decisions, we decline the invitation to read such a distinction into the statute."

Corollary cases

Griggs v. Duke Power Co., 401 U.S. 424 (1971)
Teamsters v. United States, 431 U.S. 324 (1977)
Reiter v. Sonotone Corp, 442 U.S. 330 (1979)
Richards v. United States, 369 U.S. 1 (1962)
Consumer Product Safety Commission v. GTE Sylvania Inc., 447 U.S. 102 (1980)
Franks v. Bowman Transportation Co., 424 U.S. 747 (1976)
Piper v. Chris-Craft Industries, Inc., 430 U.S. 1 (1977)
Trans World Airlines v. Hardison, 432 U.S. 63 (1977)
United Air Lines, Inc. v. Evans, 431 U.S. 553 (1977)
Humphrey v. Moore, 375 U.S. 335 (1964)

Note—*Patterson* illustrates the sharp contrast that can occur—in this case, between equal opportunity, including affirmative action, and the time-honored seniority system.

MINIMUM WAGE AND CHILD LABOR LAWS

Holden v. Hardy, 169 U.S. 366, 18 S. Ct. 383, 42 L. Ed. 780 (1898)

The legislature of the state of Utah enacted an eight-hour day for workmen in underground mines, smelters, and similar places for the reduction of ore and metals, except in the event of an emergency. Violation of the statute was made a misdemeanor. Plaintiff in error was convicted of employing men contrary to the terms of the statute. He challenged the validity of the statute upon the ground of an alleged violation of the Fourteenth Amendment, in that it abridged the privileges or immunities of citizens of the United States, deprived both the employer and the laborer of his property without due process of law, and denied to them the equal protection of the laws.

OPINION BY MR. JUSTICE BROWN
(Vote: 7–2)

Question—Is the Utah law constitutional?

Decision—No.

Reason—The Court reasoned that the act was a valid exercise of the police power of the state. The enactment did not profess to limit the hours of all workmen, but merely those who are employed in underground mines, or in the smelting, reduction, or refining of ores and metals. These employments, when too long pursued, the legislature has judged to be detrimental to the health of the employees, and so long as there are reasonable grounds for believing that this is so, its decision upon this subject cannot be set aside by the federal courts.

Corollary cases

Allgeyer v. Louisiana, 165 U.S. 578 (1897)
Lochner v. New York, 198 U.S. 45 (1905)
Muller v. Oregon, 208 U.S. 412 (1908)
West Coast Hotel Co. v. Parrish, 300 U.S. 379 (1937)
Bunting v. Oregon, 243 U.S. 426 (1937)
Morehead v. Tipaldo, 298 U.S. 587 (1936)
Adkins v. Children's Hospital, 261 U.S. 525 (1923)

Note—Despite *Holden* and *Muller* v. *Oregon,* (1908) upholding a ten-hour workday law applying to women in industry, and *Munn* v. *Illinois,* 94 U.S. 113 (1877), fixing rates in Chicago grain elevators, the Court generally followed the principles of substantive due process well into the 1930s.

Lochner v. New York, 198 U.S. 45; 25 S. Ct. 539; 49 L. Ed. 937 (1905)

A New York statute forbade any employee in a bakery of confectionery establishment to be permitted to work over sixty hours in any one week, or an average of over ten hours a day. Lochner was convicted in Utica of requiring and permitting an employee to work more than sixty hours in one week.

OPINION BY MR. JUSTICE PECKHAM
(Vote: 5–4)

Question—Does this statute violate the Fourteenth Amendment?

Decision—Yes.

Reason—The right of an individual to make a contract with regard to his labor is part of the liberty of the individual protected by the Fourteenth Amendment. The right to purchase or sell labor is also part of this liberty, unless there are circumstances that exclude the right. Against these rights we have the police powers of the states, which under certain conditions may impose restrictions on the exercise of those rights. At times it is of great importance to determine which shall prevail—the right of the individual to labor for such a time as he may choose, or the right of the state to prevent an individual from laboring beyond a certain time prescribed by the state.

If this is a valid exercise of state police power, it involves the question of health. The Court held that there was no reasonable foundation for holding that this statute was necessary to safeguard the public health, or the health of bakers in general. The trade of a baker, while not the healthiest of occupations, does not affect health to such a degree that the legislature is warranted in interfering. At that rate, no trade or occupation would be able to escape acts of the legislature restricting the hours of labor.

The statute in question, the Court held, was an illegal interference in the rights of individuals, both employers and employees, for reasons entirely arbitrary. The Court was of the opinion that the only purpose of the act was to regulate the hours of labor in an occupation that is not dangerous in any degree to morals, nor in any substantial way injurious to health. This freedom to contract in relation to employment cannot be interfered with except by violating the Constitution.

Corollary cases

Allgeyer v. Louisiana, 165 U.S. 578 (1897)
Holden v. Hardy, 169 U.S. 366 (1898)
Atkin v. Kansas, 191 U.S. 207 (1903)
Jacobson v. Massachusetts, 197 U.S. 11 (1905)
Nebbia v. New York, 291 U.S. 502 (1934)
West Coast Hotel Co. v. Parrish, 300 U.S. 379 (1937)
Olsen v. Nebraska, 313 U.S. 236 (1941)
Phelps Dodge Corp, v. NLRB, 313 U.S. 177 (1941)

Note—In upholding a state statute that required a ten-hour day in certain industries, in *Bunting* v. *Oregon,* 243 U.S. 426 (1917), the Court overruled sub silento *Lochner,* which was a high-water mark of social Darwinism. The Court used the liberty of the contract clause to invalidate a New York state law. The case is also known for Justice Holmes's dissent.

Muller v. Oregon, 208 U.S. 412; 28 S. Ct. 324; 52 L. Ed. 551 (1908)

> An Oregon statute made illegal the employment of women in any mechanical establishment, factory, or laundry for more than ten hours during the day. Muller was convicted and fined for violating this statute in his laundry.

Opinion by Mr. Justice Brewer

(No evidence from the report that the decision was not unanimous.)

Question—Is the Oregon statute constitutional?

Decision—Yes.

Reason—In *Lochner* v. *New York,* the Court held that a law prohibiting a man from working more than ten hours a day was an unreasonable and arbitrary interference with his liberty to contract in relation to labor. A woman's physical well-being "becomes an object of public interest and care in order to preserve the strength and vigor of the race" and thus justifies the "special legislation restricting or qualifying the conditions under which she should be permitted to toil." The two sexes differ. This difference justifies a difference in legislation.

Corollary cases

Lochner v. New York, 198 U.S. 45 (1905)
Bunting v. Oregon, 243 U.S. 426 (1917)
West Coast Hotel Co. v. Parrish, 300 U.S. 379 (1937)
Morehead v. Tipaldo, 298 U.S. 587 (1936)
Adkins v. Children's Hospital, 261 U.S. 525 (1923)
Holden v. Hardy, 169 U.S. 366 (1898)

Note—The Court took "judicial cognizance" of women as the "weaker sex," an argument today hotly debated under equal protection cases and the rejected Equal Rights Amendment. In *Muller* also, Louis D. Brandeis, counsel for Oregon, introduced what came to be known as the "Brandeis Brief"—a brief-preparing style that emphasized economics and sociology rather than precedent.

Bunting v. State of Oregon, 243 U.S. 426; 37 S. Ct. 435; 61 L. Ed. 830 (1917)

> A statute of Oregon required that any person employed in a mill, factory, or manufacturing establishment should not work more than ten hours a day, except for necessary repairs, or in an emergency. However, an additional three hours could be spent, but with payment of time and one-half for the overtime period. Bunting employed a man named Hammersly for thirteen hours one day, with no payment for overtime.

OPINION BY MR. JUSTICE McKENNA
(Vote: 5–3)

Question—Does this statute violate the Fourteenth Amendment?

Decision—No.

Reason—The Court held that this was a valid extension of state police power. The state found that it was injurious to men to work longer than ten hours in the types of establishments mentioned. This was not a wage law (which would have been in violation of the state constitution), since no attempt was made to fix standard wages, which were left to the contracting parties. The provision for overtime was simply for the purpose of giving an additional reason for not working overtime. This was adequate reasoning for the legislative judgment in this case.

"But we need not cast about for reasons for the legislative judgment. We are not required to be sure of the precise reasons for its exercise, or be convinced of the wisdom of its exercise. It is enough for our decision if the legislation under review was passed in the exercise of an admitted power of government."

Corollary cases

Coppage v. Kansas, 236 U.S. 1 (1915)
West Coast Hotel Co. v. Parrish, 300 U.S. 379 (1937)
Morehead v. Tipaldo, 298 U.S. 587 (1936)
Adkins v. Children's Hospital 261 U.S. 525 (1923)
Muller v. Oregon, 208 U.S. 412 (1908)
United States v. Darby, 312 U.S. 100 (1941)

Hammer v. Dagenhart, 247 U.S. 251; 38 S. Ct. 529; 62 L. Ed. 1101 (1918)

In 1916 the Keating-Owen Act was passed. This provided that commodities produced under conditions in factories where children under fourteen years of age were employed or in mines where children under sixteen years of age were employed should be excluded from shipment in interstate or foreign commerce. Hours of employment were also specified for children between fourteen and sixteen years of age. Dagenhart, the father of two children, one under fourteen and the other between fourteen and sixteen, both of whom were employed in a mill in North Carolina, brought suit to enjoin Hammer, United States District Attorney, from enforcing the law against the employment of his two children. He got this injunction and Hammer took an appeal to the

Supreme Court. The penalties connected with the act made it financially impossible to employ children under the age of sixteen because any establishment producing goods with the aid of underaged children could not ship its products in interstate commerce until thirty days after cessation of the practice.

OPINION BY MR. JUSTICE DAY
(Vote: 5–4)

Question—Can Congress exclude from interstate commerce all goods manufactured by child labor?

Decision—No.

Reason—The making of goods and the mining of products is not commerce, nor does the fact that those things are to go afterwards into interstate commerce make them in their production interstate commerce *per se*. Congress has the power to regulate and deny to interstate commerce such products as impure foods, liquors, drugs, and others having possible harmful effects. However, there is nothing harmful, in themselves, in goods produced by child labor; therefore, this power does not apply. Child labor may be regulated only under the police power of the states, and therefore, Congress may not violate this state right. Thus the act "not only transcends the authority delegated to Congress over commerce, but also exerts a power as to a purely local matter to which the federal authority does not extend." (This latter notion—that Congress may not use its delegated powers to perform functions that are reserved to the states by the Tenth Amendment—came to be known as "dual federalism.")

Corollary cases

Gibbons v. Ogden, 9 Wheaton 1 (1824)
United States v. Darby, 312 U.S. 100 (1941)
In re Rahrer, 140 U.S. 545 (1891)
Clark Distilling Co. v. Western Maryland R. R. Co., 242 U.S. 311 (1917)
Whitfield v. Ohio, 297 U.S. 431 (1936)
Kentucky Whip and Collar Co. v. ICRR Co., 299 U.S. 334 (1937)
Mulford v. Smith, 307 U.S. 38 (1939)
NLRB v. Jones and Laughlin Steel Corp., 301 U.S. 1 (1937)

Note—*Hammer* was reversed by *United States* v. *Darby,* 312 U.S. 100 (1941), which upheld the Fair Labor Standards Act of 1938. An offshoot of *Darby* was the virtual dousing of the proposed child labor amendment submitted to the states in 1924. It has never been ratified.

Bailey v. Drexel Furniture Co., 259 U.S. 20; 42 S. Ct. 449; 66 L. Ed. 817 (1922)

> The Child Labor Tax Law of 1919 passed by Congress required that those employing children under the age of fourteen must pay a tax amounting to 10 percent of their net profits. In this case the Drexel Furniture Co. hired a boy under the age of fourteen and was assessed the tax by Bailey, collector of internal revenue. The company paid the tax under protest. Seeking a refund, they contended that the Child Labor Tax Law violated the states' powers under the Tenth Amendment. The defendants contended the law was passed under the federal government's power of taxation.

OPINION BY MR. CHIEF JUSTICE TAFT
(Vote: 8–1)

Question—Did Congress exercise constitutional power in passing the Child Labor Tax Law?

Decision—No.

Reason—The Court was of the opinion that the tax required in the Child Labor Tax Law was passed by Congress for the purpose of enforcing police power legislation. Although the Child Labor Law did not declare the employment of children illegal, the same purpose was accomplished by imposing the tax. The Court did not deny the power of Congress to tax. The tax in this law, however, seemed to accomplish the purpose of a penalty for not obeying the employment standards set down by Congress. The employment standard within a state is clearly a state power. Therefore, the Court ruled that the power to tax by Congress must be reasonably adapted to the collecting of a tax and not solely to the achievement of some other purpose plainly within the power of the states.

Corollary cases

Hammer v. Dagenhart, 247 U.S. 251 (1918)
McCray v. United States, 195 U.S. 27 (1904)
Flint v. Stone Tracy Co, 220 U.S. 107 (1911)
United States v. Darby, 312 U.S. 100 (1941)
United States v. Kahriger, 345 U.S. 22 (1953)
Marchetti v. United States, 390 U.S. 38 (1968)
Grosso v. United States, 389 U.S. 62 (1968)

Note—*Bailey* and *Hammer* v. *Dagenhart* (1918), decided under the influence of "dual federalism," were reversed in *United States* v. *Darby* (1941).

Adkins v. Children's Hospital, 261 U.S. 525; 43 S. Ct. 394; 67 L. Ed. 785 (1923)

The Minimum Wage Act of 1918 provided for the creation in the District of Columbia of a Minimum Wage Board. The board was authorized to investigate and ascertain the wages of women and minors and to set up standard minimum wages, which employers were forbidden to lower. The Children's Hospital employed several women at less than the minimum wage fixed by the board. Through the action of the Minimum Wage Board, these women lost their jobs. They were satisfied with their pay and working conditions. A suit was brought by the women seeking to enjoin the enforcement of the minimum wage law and to permit the taking of whatever jobs they desired.

OPINION BY MR. JUSTICE SUTHERLAND
(Vote: 5–3)

Question—Is the Minimum Wage Act a violation of the due process clause of the Fifth Amendment?

Decision—Yes.

Reason—The right to contract about one's affairs is part of the liberty of the individual protected by the Fifth Amendment. There is no such thing as absolute freedom of contract, but freedom is the rule and restraint is the exception. The statute in question is simply a price-fixing law forbidding two parties to contract in respect to the price for which one shall render service to the other.

The price fixed by the board has no relation to the capacity and earning power of the employee, the number of hours worked, the character of the place or the circumstances or surroundings involved, but is based solely on the presumption of what is necessary to provide a living for a woman and preserve her health and morals.

The law considers the necessities of one party only. It ignores the necessities of the employer by not considering whether the employee is capable of earning the sum. If the police power of a state may justify the fixing of a minimum wage, it may later be invoked to justify a maximum wage, which is power widened to a dangerous degree. To uphold individual freedom is not to strike down the common good, but to further it by the prevention of arbitrary restraint upon the liberty of its members.

Corollary cases

Lochner v. New York, 198 U.S. 45 (1905)
Holden v. Hardy, 169 U.S. 366 (1898)
Bunting v. Oregon, 243 U.S. 426 (1917)
Morehead v. Tipaldo, 298 U.S. 587 (1936)
Stettler v. O'Hara, 243 U.S. 629 (1917)
Muller v. Oregon, 208 U.S. 412 (1908)
McLean v. Arkansas, 211 U.S. 539 (1909)
West Coast Hotel Co. v. Parrish, 300 U.S. 379 (1937)
United States v. Darby, 312 U.S. 100 (1941)
National League of Cities v. Usery, 426 U.S. 833 (1976)

Note—*Adkins* was reversed by *West Coast Hotel Co.* v. *Parrish* (1937).

Nebbia v. New York, 291 U.S. 502; 54 S. Ct. 505; 78 L. Ed. 940 (1934)

Nebbia, the proprietor of a grocery store in Rochester, New York, was convicted of violating an order of the New York Milk Control Board fixing the selling price of milk by selling two quarts of milk and a loaf of bread for 18¢, whereas the board had fixed the price of a quart of milk at 9¢. Nebbia, after losing the appeal to the New York Court of Appeals, appealed to the Supreme Court on grounds that the order and the statute authorizing the order contravene the equal protection clause and due process clause of the Fourteenth Amendment.

OPINION BY MR. JUSTICE ROBERTS
(Vote: 5–4)

Question—Does a state violate the Fourteenth Amendment when it fixes the minimum and maximum prices of articles such as milk?

Decision—No.

Reason—The milk industry in New York has been the subject of long standing and drastic regulation in the public interest. Unrestricted competition in this industry aggravated existing evils, and the normal law of supply and demand was inadequate to correct maladjustments detrimental to the community. An inquiry disclosed the trade practices that resulted in retail price cutting, which reduced the income of the farmer below the cost of production. In light of this, the price fixing of the Control Board appeared not to be unreasonable, arbitrary, or without relation to the purpose of preventing ruthless competition from destroying the wholesale price structure on which the farmer depends for his livelihood and the community for an assured supply of milk.

The milk industry is of vital public interest since milk is a basic food in our diet, and the legislature of New York, realizing this, passed this law to safeguard the public interest. The Constitution does not secure to anyone the liberty to conduct his business in such a fashion as to inflict injury upon the public at large or a substantial group of the public.

"The phrase 'affected with a public interest' can, in the nature of things, mean no more than that an industry, for adequate reason, is subject to control for the public good. . . . So far as the requirement of due process is concerned, and in the absence of other constitutional restriction, a state is free to adopt whatever economic policy may reasonably be deemed to promote public welfare, and to enforce that policy by legislation adapted to its purpose. If the laws passed are seen to have a reasonable relation to a proper legislative purpose, and are neither arbitrary nor discriminatory, the requirements of due process are satisfied. . . . Times without number we have said that the Legislature is primarily the judge of the necessity of such an enactment, that every possible presumption is in favor of its validity, and that though the court may hold views inconsistent with the wisdom of the law, it may not be annulled unless palpably in excess of legislative power."

Corollary cases

Wolff Packing Co. v. Court of Industrial Relations, 262 U.S. 522 (1923)
Munn v. Illinois, 94 U.S. 113 (1877)
Olsen v. Nebraska, 313 U.S. 236 (1941)
Ribnik v. McBride, 277 U.S. 350 (1928)
West Coast Hotel Co. v. Parrish, 300 U.S. 379 (1937)
Tyson and Brothers v. Banton, 273 U.S. 418 (1927)

Note—*Nebbia* discarded the formula "affected with a public interest" that looms in *Munn* v. *Illinois* (1877). It ushered in the philosophy of the New Deal era and is often considered a watershed case.

Morehead v. New York ex rel. Tipaldo, 298 U.S. 587; 56 S. Ct. 918; 80 L. Ed. 1347 (1936)

Tipaldo was sent to jail upon the charge that, as manager of a laundry, he failed to obey the mandatory order of the state industrial commissioner of New York, prescribing minimum wages for women employees. Some of the employees were receiving less than the minimum wages established by the state industrial commissioner operating under the state minimum wage law.

OPINION BY MR. JUSTICE BUTLER
(Vote: 5–4)

Question—Can a state fix minimum wages for women?

Decision—No.

Reason—It was claimed that this case differed from the *Adkins* case in which such legislation was declared unconstitutional, in that here the minimum wage was prescribed in cases where the given wage was less than the fair and reasonable value of the services rendered and insufficient to meet the minimum cost of living necessary for health. This did not, however, change the principle of the case, namely, the exercise of legislative power to fix wages. The act left employers and men employees free to agree upon wages, but deprived employers and adult women of the same freedom. Likewise, women were restrained by the minimum wage in competition with men and were arbitrarily deprived of employment and a fair chance to find work. State legislation fixing wages for women is repugnant to the due process clause of the Fourteenth Amendment.

Corollary cases

Adkins v. Children's Hospital, 261 U.S. 525 (1923)
West Coast Hotel Co. v. Parrish, 300 U.S. 379 (1937)
Stettler v. O'Hara, 243 U.S. 629 (1917)
Muller v. Oregon, 208 U.S. 412 (1908)
Bunting v. Oregon, 243 U.S. 426 (1917)
McLean v. Arkansas, 211 U.S. 539 (1909)

Note—*Morehead* was reversed by *West Coast Hotel Co.* v. *Parrish* (1937), a year later, when Justice Roberts switched positions, "the switch in time that saved nine," and took the starch out of President Roosevelt's "court packing" attempt to increase the number of justices to fifteen and appoint new judges who were more sympathetic to his policies.

West Coast Hotel Co. v. Parrish, 300 U.S. 379; 57 S. Ct. 578; 81 L. Ed. 703 (1937)

Washington state laws prohibited wages below a living wage and conditions of labor detrimental to the health and morals of women and minors. Such wages were established by the state's Industrial Welfare Commission composed of members of management, labor, and the government. Elsie Parrish brought suit to recover the difference between her wages and those established by the Industrial Welfare Commission over a period of years during which she was employed by the West Coast Hotel Company.

OPINION BY MR. CHIEF JUSTICE HUGHES
(Vote: 5–4)

Question—Is the statute contrary to the due process clause of the Fourteenth Amendment?

Decision—No.

Reason—The principle controlling the decision—the Fourteenth Amendment—was not in doubt. Those attacking minimum wage regulation alleged that they were being deprived of freedom of contract. "What is this freedom? The Constitution does not speak of freedom of contract. It speaks of liberty and prohibits the deprivation of liberty without due process of law. In prohibiting that deprivation, the Constitution does not recognize an absolute, an uncontrollable liberty. Liberty in each of its phases has its history and connotation. But the liberty safeguarded is liberty in a social organization which requires the protection of law against the evils which menace the health, safety, morals and welfare of the people. Liberty under the Constitution is thus necessarily subject to the restraints of due process, and regulation which is reasonable in relation to its subject and is adopted in the interests of the community is due process."

The minimum wage requirement of the state of Washington did not seem to the Court to have gone beyond the boundary of its broad protective power. The wage was fixed after full consideration by representatives of employers, employees, and the public. No one was forced to pay anything, it simply forbade employment at rates fixed below the minimum requirement for health and right living. This the Court held was a valid exercise of state police power, and it was the conclusion of the Court that "the case of *Adkins* v. *Children's Hospital* should be, and it is overruled." (This decision also had the effect of reversing *Morehead* v. *New York ex rel. Tipaldo,* 298.)

Corollary cases

Adkins v. Children's Hospital, 261 U.S. 525 (1923)
Morehead v. Tipaldo, 298 U.S. 587 (1936)
Chicago, B. & Q. R. R. Co. v. McGuire, 219 U.S. 549 (1911)
United States v. Darby, 312 U.S. 100 (1941)
Atkin v. Kansas, 191 U.S. 207 (1903)
Perkins v. Lukens Steel Co., 310 U.S. 113 (1940)

ANTITRUST LAWS AND THE SHERMAN ACT

Northern Securities Co. v. United States, 193 U.S. 197, 24 S. Ct. 436, 48 L. Ed. 679 (1904)

The Northern Pacific and Great Northern Railroad Companies purchased most of the stock of the Burlington Railroad. The first two companies ran parallel lines and the Burlington was a connecting line. The Northern Pacific and Great Northern entered into a combination to form a New Jersey corporation, which came to be known as the Northern Securities Company. This company held three-fourths of the stock of the two companies. The United States charged them with violation of the antitrust laws.

OPINION BY MR. JUSTICE HARLAN
(Vote: 5–4)

Question—Does this railroad combination restrain trade among the several states and therefore violate the antitrust laws?

Decision—Yes.

Reason—The Court reasoned that this combination was, within the meaning of the act, a "trust," but, even if not, it was a combination in restraint of interstate and international commerce and that was enough to bring it under the condemnation of the act. The mere existence of such a combination and the power acquired by the holding company as its trustee constituted a meance to, and a restraint upon, that freedom of commerce which Congress intended to recognize and protect, and which the public was entitled to have protected. Even if the state allowed consolidation, it would not follow that the stockholders of two or more state railroad corporations, having competing lines and engaged in interstate commerce, could lawfully combine and form a distinct corporation to hold the stock of the constituent corporations, and by destroying competition between them in violation of the act, restrain commerce among the states and with foreign nations.

414

Corollary cases

Gibbons v. Ogden, 9 Wheaton 197 (1824)
United States v. Southeastern Underwriters Association, 332 U.S. 533 (1944)
Swift and Co. v. United States, 196 U.S. 375 (1905)
United States v. E. C. Knight Co., 156 U.S. 1 (1895)
Times Picayune Publishing Co. v. United States, 345 U.S. 594 (1974)
Pfizer, Inc. v. Government of India, 54 L. Ed. 2d 506 (1978)
Reiter v. Sonotone Corporation, 442 U.S. 330; 60 L. Ed. 2d 931 (1979)
McLain v. Real Estate Board, 444 U.S. 232 (1980)
National Society of Professional Engineers v. United States, 55 L. Ed. 2d 637
    (1978)

Note—In dissenting, Justice Holmes launched a memorable phrase, "Great cases, like hard cases, make bad law." President Theodore Roosevelt, who appointed Holmes as a liberal only to see him vote as a conservative, stormed, "I could carve out of a banana a judge with more backbone than that."

Swift and Co. v. United States, 196 U.S. 375; 25 S. Ct. 276; 49 L. Ed. 518 (1905)

This suit was brought against a number of corporations, firms, and individuals of different states, and charged, in summary, a combination of a dominant proportion of the dealers in fresh meat throughout the United States not to bid against each other in the livestock markets or the different states, to bid up prices to induce cattlemen to send their stocks to the yards, to fix selling prices, and to that end to restrict shipments of meat when necessary, to establish a uniform rule of credit to dealers, to keep a blacklist, and to make uniform and improper charges for cartage, and finally, to get less than lawful rates from the railroads to the exclusion of competitors.

OPINION BY MR. JUSTICE HOLMES

(No evidence from the report that the decision was not unanimous.)

Question—Is this an illegal monopoly in violation of the Sherman Antitrust Act?

Decision—Yes.

Reason—Although the combination alleged embraces restraint and monopoly of trade within a single state, its effect upon commerce among the states was not accidental, but rather the commerce was an object of attack. The commerce intended to be monopolized was undoubtedly interstate commerce protected from restraint by the act of 1890, since the meat shipments and sales involved were between citizens of diverse states. Thus, any attempt to monopolize this commerce would be a violation of the Sherman Act. The actions in this case were directed to this purpose and thus violated the act.

"It is said that this charge was too vague and that it does not set forth a case of commerce among the states. Taking up the latter objection first, commerce among the states is not a technical legal conception, but a practical one, drawn from the course of business. When cattle are sent for sale from a place in one state, with the expectation that they will end their transit, after purchase, in another, and when in effect they do so, with only the interruption necessary to find a purchaser at the stock yards, and when this is a typical, constantly recurring course, the current thus existing is a current of commerce among the states, and the purchase of the cattle is a part and incident of such commerce. . . . It is immaterial if the section also embraces domestic transactions.

"It should be added that the cattle in the stock yard are not at rest."

Corollary cases

American Steel and Wire Co. v. Speed,, 192 U.S. 500 (1904)
Hopkins v. United States, 171 U.S. 578 (1898)
Kidd v. Pearson, 128 U.S. 1 (1880)
Broadcast Music, Inc. v. CBS, 60 L. Ed. 2d 1 (1979)
United States v. E. C. Knight Co., 156 U.S. 1 (1895)
Addyston Pipe and Steel Co. v. United States, 175 U.S. 211 (1899)
Minnesota v. Blasius, 290 U.S. 1 (1933)
Stafford v. Wallace, 258 U.S. 495 (1922)
Pfizer, Inc. v. Government of India, 438 U.S. 308 (1978)

Standard Oil Co. of New Jersey v. United States, 221 U.S. 1; 31 S. Ct. 502; 55 L. Ed. 619 (1910)

John D. Rockefeller and associates were convicted of violating the Sherman Antitrust Act. The specific charge of violation involved a combining of the stocks of a number of companies in the hands of Standard of New Jersey. The decree of the lower court enjoined the company from voting the stocks or exerting control over the various subsidiary companies, some thirty-seven in number. These companies, in turn, were ordered not to pay dividends to Standard Oil Co. of New Jersey or to cooperate in any way in making effective the combination. With this background the case went to the Supreme Court.

OPINION BY MR. CHIEF JUSTICE WHITE

(No evidence from the report that the decision was not unanimous.)

Question—Was this combination contrary to the Sherman Act?

Decision—Yes.

Reason—This was a combination that would result in the control of interstate and foreign commerce by this group rather than the only one authorized to do so, the Congress of the United States. Hence this was an illegal operation and it had to be abolished. The Court then proceeded to set forth what has come to be known as the "rule of reason." This, briefly, simply provides that the restraint of trade outlawed by the Sherman Act is not to apply to every contract or combination in restraint of trade, but only to those that do so unreasonably. "Undoubtedly, the words 'to monopolize' and 'monopolize,' as used in the section, reach every act bringing about the prohibited results. The ambiguity, if any, is involved in determining what is intended by monopolize. But this ambiguity is readily dispelled in the light of the previous history of the law of restraint of trade to which we have referred and the indication which it gives of the practical evolution by which monopoly and the acts which produce the same result as monopoly, that is, an undue restraint of the course of trade, all came to be spoken of as, and to be indeed synonymous with, restraint of trade. . . . It becomes obvious that the criteria to be resorted to in any given case for the purpose of ascertaining whether violations of the section have been committed is the rule of reason guided by the established law and by the plain duty to enforce the prohibitions of the act, and thus the public policy which its restrictions were obviously enacted to observe."

Corollary cases

Swift and Co. v. United States, 196 U.S. 375 (1905)
United States v. Northern Securities Co., 193 U.S. 197 (1904)
United States v. American Tobacco Co., 221 U.S. 106 (1911)
NLRB v. Jones and Laughlin Steel Corp., 301 U.S. 1 (1937)
United States v. E. C. Knight Co., 156 U.S. 1 (1895)

Note—The "rule of reason" in *Standard Oil* came to mean only monopolies on restraints of trade that were "unreasonably" so. This doctrine, added to the view that manufacturing trusts were not involved in interstate commerce, greatly weakened the Sherman Act. Congress reinforced it in 1914 with the Clayton Act and the Federal Trade Commission Act. See *Northern Securities* (1904).

Reiter v. Sonotone Corp., 442 U.S. 330; 60 L. Ed. 2d 931; 99 S. Ct. 2326 (1979)

> Reiter brought a class action on behalf of herself and all persons in the United States who purchased hearing aids manufactured by five corporations. Her complaint alleges that respondents committed a variety of antitrust violations, including vertical and horizontal price fixing. She sought treble damages under Section 4 of the Clayton Act, which authorizes such damage actions by "any person who shall be injured in his business or property by reason of anything forbidden in the antitrust laws." Because of the violations, she alleged that she and the persons she seeks to represent have been forced to pay illegally fixed higher prices for the hearing aids.

OPINION BY MR. CHIEF JUSTICE BURGER
(Vote: 8–0)

Question—May consumers sustain injury to "property" and be entitled to sue for treble damages under the Clayton Act?

Decision—Yes.

Reason—"A consumer whose money has been diminished by reason of an anti-trust violation has been injured 'in his . . . property' within the meaning of Section Four." Furthermore, "We have often referred to 'consumers' as parties entitled to seek damages under Section Four without intimating that consumers of goods and services purchased for personal rather than commercial use were in any way foreclosed by the statutory language from asserting an injury in their 'property.' Thus, to the extent that the legislative history is relevant, "it supports our holding that a consumer deprived of money by reason of allegedly anticompetitive conduct is injured in 'property' within the meaning of Section Four. . . . Recognition of the plain meaning of the statutory language 'business property' need not result in administrative chaos, class action harassment, or 'windfall' settlements if the district courts exercise sound discretion and use the tools available."

Corollary cases

Chattanooga Foundry and Pipe Works v. City of Atlanta, 203 U.S. 390 (1906)
Brunswick Corp. v. Pueblo Bowl-O-Mat, Inc., 429 U.S. 477 (1977)
Pfizer, Inc. v. Government of India, 434 U.S. 308 (1978)
Mandeville Island Farms, Inc. v. American Crystal Sugar Co., 334 U.S. 219 (1948)
Goldfarb v. Virginia State Bar, 421 U.S. 773 (1975)
McLain v. Real Estate Board, 444 U.S. 232 (1980)
National Society of Professional Engineers v. United States, 55 L. Ed. 2d 637 (1978)

NCAA v. Board of Regents of University of Oklahoma, 468 U. S. _____; 82 L. Ed. 2d 70; 104 S. Ct. 2948 (1984)

In 1981 the National Collegiate Ass'n (NCAA) adopted a plan for televising football games of member institutions. The plan proposed to reduce the adverse effect of live television upon game attendance. The plan limits the total number of football games and the number that any one college may televise. The NCAA had separate agreements with ABC and CBS that allowed each network to telecast the live "exposures." The College Football Ass'n (CFA) wanted a voice in the formulation of television policy and contracted with NBC. The NCAA threatened to retaliate against any member that complied with the CFA-NBC contract. The district court said NCAA had violated the Sherman Act. The court of appeals affirmed the decision.

OPINION BY MR. JUSTICE STEVENS
(Vote: 7–2)

Question—Does the telecasting plan of NCAA violate the Sherman Antitrust Act?

Decision—Yes.

Reason—"There can be no doubt that the challenged practices of the NCAA constitute a restraint of trade in the sense that they limit members freedom to negotiate and enter into their own television contracts." Because it places a ceiling on the number of games member institutions may televise, "the horizontal agreement places an artificial limit on the quantity of televised football that is available to broadcasters and consumers . . . the challenged practices create a limitation on output; our cases have held that such limitations are unreasonable restraints of trade." "Under the Sherman Act the criterion to be used in judging the validity of a restraint on trade is its impact on competition . . . because it restrains price and output, the NCAA's television plan has a significant potential for anticompetitive effects." The Court found that by "fixing a price for television rights to all games, the NCAA creates a price structure that is unresponsive to viewer demand and unrelated to the prices that would prevail in a competitive market." In addition many telecasts that would occur in a competitive market are foreclosed by the NCAA's plan. The judgment of the court of appeals is affirmed.

Corollary cases

Broadcast Music, Inc. v. CBS, 441 U.S. 1, 60 L. Ed. 2d 1, 99 S. Ct. 1551 (1979)

Continental T.V. Inc. v. GTE Sylvania Inc., 433 U.S. 36, 53 L. Ed. 2d 568, 97 S. Ct. 2549 (1977)

Standard Oil Co., v. United States, 221 U.S. 1, 55 L. Ed. 619, 31 S. Ct. 502 (1911)

International Boxing Club v. United States, 358 U.S. 242, 3 L. Ed. 2d 270, 79 S. Ct. 245 (1959)

Times-Picayune Pub. Co., v. United States, 345 U.S. 594, 97 L. Ed. 1277, 73 S. Ct. 872 (1953)

United States v. E. I. Du Pont de Nemours & Co., 351 U.S. 371, 100 L. Ed. 1264, 76 S. Ct. 994 (1956)

Arizona v. Maricopa County Medical Society, 457 U.S. 332, 73 L. Ed. 2d 48, 102 S. Ct. 2466 (1982)

Brunswick Corp. v. Pueblo Bowl-O-Mat, 429 U.S. 427, 50 L. Ed. 2d 701, 97 S. Ct. 690 (1977)

National Society of Professional Engineers v. United States, 435 U.S. 629, 55 L. Ed. 2d 637, 98 S. Ct. 1355 (1978)

United States v. Topco Associates, 405 U.S. 596, 31 L. Ed. 2d 515, 92 S. Ct. 1126 (1972)

United States v. Sealy, 388 U.S. 350, 18 L. Ed. 2d, 1238, 82 S. Ct. 1847 (1967)

Catalano Inc., v. Target Sales, 446 U.S. 643, 64 L. Ed. 2d 580, 100 S. Ct. 1925 (1980)

White Motor Co., v. United States, 372 U.S. 253, 71 L. Ed. 700, 47 S. Ct. 377 (1963)

American Society of Mechanical Engineers, Inc. v. Hydrolevel Corp., 456 U.S. 556, 72 L. Ed. 2d 330, 102 S. Ct. 1935 (1982)

ALIENS

United States v. Wong Kim Ark, 169 U.S. 649; 18 S. Ct. 456; 42 L. Ed. 890 (1898)

The collector of the port of San Francisco denied admission into the United States to Wong Kim Ark, a Chinese person who was admitted to have been born in California and was returning from a temporary visit to China. His parents were subjects of the emperor of China, but had a permanent domicile and residence in the United States and were carrying on business here. They were not employed in any official diplomatic capacity for the emperor of China.

OPINION BY MR. JUSTICE GRAY
(Vote: 7–2)

Question—Does a child in such circumstances become a citizen of the United States at birth?

Decision—Yes.

Reason—Wong Kim Ark became a citizen at birth by virtue of the first clause of the Fourteenth Amendment, "All persons born or naturalized in the United States, and subject to the jurisdiction thereof, are citizens of the United States and of the state wherein they reside." The Constitution nowhere defines the meaning of the word "citizen" or "natural-born citizen" either by way of inclusion or exclusion. The meaning of the phrase must therefore be interpreted in the light of the common law.

The fundamental principle of the common law was birth within the allegiance of the king. Children of aliens born in England were natural-born subjects, as were children of ambassadors representing England, although born on foreign soil. Children of foreign ambassadors or diplomats or of alien enemies were not natural-born subjects since they were born outside the obedience of the king. This was the rule in all the English colonies up to the Declaration of Independence.

Roman law, which considered the citizenship of the child to be that of the parents, was not a principle of international law since there was no settled and definite rule at the time the Fourteenth Amendment was adopted.

Corollary cases

Dred Scott v. Sanford, 19 Howard 393 (1857)
Slaughterhouse Cases, 16 Wallace 36 (1873)
Elk v. Wilkins, 112 U.S. 94 (1884)
Chirac v. Chirac, 2 Wheaton 259 (1877)
Fong Yue Ting v. United States, 149 U.S. 698 (1893)
United States v. Schwimmer, 279 U.S. 644 (1929)
Kleindienst v. Mandel, 408 U.S. 753 (1972)
Girouard v. United States, 328 U.S. 61 (1946)
Keller v. United States, 213 U.S. 138 (1909)
Harisiades v. Shaughnessy, 342 U.S. 580 (1952)
Kennedy v. Mendoza-Martinez, 372 U.S. 144 (1963)
Afroyim v. Rusk, 387 U.S. 253 (1967)
Minor v. Happersett, 21 Wallace 162 (1875)
Immigration and Naturalization Service v. Wang, 67 L. Ed. 2d 123 (1981)
Haig v. Agee, 69 L. Ed. 2d 686 (1981)
Fedorenko v. United States, 229 U.S. 490 (1981)
Vance v. Terrazas, 444 U.S. 252 (1980)

Note—*Wong Kim Ark* is the first instance in which the Court interpreted the citizens clause of the Fourteenth Amendment. The two rules of citizenship used universally are *jus solis* and *jus sanguinis*. Both rules are used by the United States, with *Wong* emphasizing *jus solis,* as does the Fourteenth Amendment.

Truax v. Raich, 239 U.S. 33; 36 S. Ct. 7; 60 L. Ed. 131 (1915)

The state of Arizona passed a law to the effect that when any company, corporation, partnership, association, or individual employs more than five workers at any one time, not less than 80 percent must be qualified electors or native born citizens of the United States or some subdivision thereof. Raich, a native of Austria, but living in Arizona, lost his job as a result of this legislation since his employer feared the penalty that might be incurred. Raich filed his suit, asserting that the act denied equal protection of the laws to him.

<u>OPINION BY MR. JUSTICE HUGHES</u>
(Vote: 8–1)

Question—Is the Arizona act repugnant to the Fourteenth Amendment of the Constitution.

Decision—Yes.

Reason—The Court reasoned that Raich had been admitted to the United States under federal law. He was thus admitted with the privilege of entering and living anywhere in the United States. Being lawfully an inhabitant of Arizona, the complainant was entitled under the Fourteenth Amendment to the equal protection of its laws. The Fourteenth Amendment states that all persons within the territorial jurisdiction of the United States are entitled to the due process and equal protection clauses of the amendment. It has been frequently held that this includes aliens. Although this law did not totally exclude aliens from equal rights by setting down a percentage, it did, however, if this law were to be declared valid, give the state power to exclude aliens totally from equal protection within their borders. Thus the Arizona act was against aliens as such in competition with citizens of a defined category, and in the opinion of the Court it clearly fell under the condemnation of the Constitution. The use of the state's police power does not permit the state to deny to lawful inhabitants the ordinary means of earning a livelihood.

Corollary cases

McCabe v. Atchison, Topeka & Santa Fe Ry., 235 U.S. 151 (1914)
Yick Wo v. Hopkins, 118 U.S. 356 (1886)
Wong Wing v. United States, 163 U.S. 228 (1896)
United States v. Wong Kim Ark, 169 U.S. 649 (1898)
McCready v. Virginia, 94 U.S. 391 (1977)
Patsone v. Pennsylvania, 232 U.S. 138 (1914)
Mathews v. Diaz, 426 U.S. 67 (1976)
Ambach v. Norwich, 441 U.S. 68 (1978)
Fong Yue Ting v. United States, 149 U.S. 698 (1893)
Takahashi v. Fish and Game Commission, 334 U.S. 410 (1948)
Oyama v. State of California, 332 U.S. 633 (1948)
Terrace v. Thompson, 263 U.S. 197 (1923)
De Canas v. BICA, Inc., 424 U.S. 351 (1976)

Foley v. Connelie, 435 U.S. 291 (1978)
Toll v. Moreno, 60 L. Ed. 2d 354 (1979)
Graham v. Richardson, 403 U.S. 365 (1971)
Rosales-Lopez v. United States, 62 L. Ed. 2d 22 (1981)
Fedorenko v. United States, 449 U.S. 490 (1981)
Hampton v. Mow Sung Wong, 426 U.S. 88 (1976)

Note—In an earlier case, *Yick Wo* v. *Hopkins*, 118 U.S. 356 (1886), the Court held that the Fourteenth Amendment protected persons, not just citizens. *Truax* amplified this decision. Eighty-five years after *Yick Wo*, in *Graham* v. *Richardson*, 403 U.S. 365 (1971), the Court ruled that classifications based on alienage, like those based on nationality and race, are inherently suspect.

Girouard v. United States, 328 U.S. 61; 66 S. Ct. 826; 90 L. Ed. 1084 (1946)

In 1943 Girouard filed a petition for naturalization in the district court of Massachusetts. He stated in his application that he understood the principles of the United States government and that he was willing to take the oath of allegiance required of all citizens-to-be. However, he said that he would not bear arms in the defense of the country, but that he would serve as a noncombatant. He was a Seventh Day Adventist and his religious views did not permit him to bear arms. He was admitted to citizenship by the district court, but this decision was reversed by the court of appeals.

Question—Does the fact that an alien refuses to bear arms deny him citizenship?

Decision—No.

Reason—The oath required of aliens does not in terms require that they promise to bear arms, nor has Congress expressly made any such finding a prerequisite to citizenship. To hold that it is required is to read it into the act by unreasonable implication. The Court could not assume that Congress intended to make such an abrupt and radical departure from our traditions unless it spoke in unequivocal terms.

Religious scruples against bearing arms have been recognized by Congress in the various draft laws. This is evidence that one can support and defend our government even though his religious convictions prevent him from bearing arms. "We cannot believe that the oath was designed to exact something more from one person than from another."

Corollary cases

United States v. Schwimmer, 279 U.S. 644 (1929)
United States v. Macintosh, 283 U.S. 605 (1931)
United States v. Bland, 283 U.S. 636 (1931)
Fedorenko v. United States, 449 U.S. 490 (1981)
Haig v. Agee, 69 L. Ed. 2d 640 (1981)
Agosto v. Immigration & Naturalization Service, 53 L. Ed. 2d 63 (1977)
Nyquist v. Mauclet, 432 U.S. 1 (1977)

Note—*Girouard* reversed *U.S.* v. *Schwimmer,* 279 U.S. 644 (1929) and *United States* v. *Macintosh,* 283 U.S. 605 (1931).

Oyama v. California, 332 U.S. 633; 68 S. Ct. 269; 92 L. Ed. 249 (1948)

The California Alien Land Law forbade aliens ineligible for citizenship to acquire, own, occupy, lease, or transfer agricultural land. The father, Kajiro Oyama, was a Japanese citizen not eligible for citizenship. He bought six acres of land in 1934, and the seller executed the deed to Fred Oyama, then six years old, and an American citizen. Some six months later, the father petitioned the court to be Fred's guardian, which was ordered, and the father posted the necessary bond. In 1937, two adjoining acres were acquired. In 1942, Fred and his family were evacuated from the Pacific Coast. In 1944 when he was sixteen and still forbidden to return home, the state filed a petition to escheat the two parcels of land on the contention that there was an intent to violate and evade the Alien Land Law.

OPINION BY MR. CHIEF JUSTICE VINSON
(Vote: 6–3)

Question—Does this statute deprive Fred Oyama of equal protection of the laws and of his privileges as an American citizen?

Decision—Yes.

Reason—The state of California had discriminated against Fred Oyama, and this discrimination was based solely on his parents' country of origin. By the Fourteenth Amendment, and a federal statute, all states must accord to all citizens the right to take and hold real property. Under California law, infancy does not incapacitate a minor from holding real property. A minor citizen holding such property may have his father appointed his guardian, whether he be a citizen, an eligible alien, or an ineligible alien. At this point, the laws differ, pointing in one direction for minors whose parents cannot be naturalized, and in another direction for all other children.

Only the most exceptional circumstances can excuse such discrimination in the face of the equal protection clause and a federal statute giving all citizens the right to own land. In this case, the conflict was between a state's right to form a policy of landholding within its boundaries, and the right of American citizens to own land anywhere in the United States. When these two rights clash, the country of the father's origin may not be used as a pretense for subordinating the rights of the citizen.

Corollary cases

Hirabayashi v. United States, 320 U.S. 81 (1940)
Truax v. Raich, 239 U.S. 33 (1915)
Terrace v. Thompson, 263 U.S. 197 (1923)
Cockrill v. California, 268 U.S. 258 (1925)
Takahashi v. Fish and Game Commission, 334 U.S. 410 (1948)
Frick v. Webb, 263 U.S. 326 (1923)
Palmer v. Thompson, 403 U.S. 217 (1971)
Douglas v. Seacoast Products, 431 U.S. 265; 52 L. Ed. 2d 304 (1977)

Takahashi v. Fish & Game Commission, 334 U.S. 410; 68 S. Ct. 1138; 92 L. Ed. 1478 (1948)

Takahashi, a Japanese alien ineligible for citizenship, brought suit for mandamus in the California Superior Court to compel issuance to him of a commercial fishing license. The commission denied him the license on the ground that a California law forbade giving a commercial fishing license to a person ineligible for citizenship. Holding this provision violative of the equal protection clause of the federal Constitution, the Superior Court granted the petition. The California Supreme Court reversed. In presenting the case to the United States Supreme Court, the Fish and Game Commission contended that the California law was a conservation measure and that the fishing waters belonged to the state. Takahashi contended that the law was the outgrowth of racial antagonism.

OPINION BY MR. JUSTICE BLACK
(Vote: 7–2)

Question—Can California use the federally-created racial ineligibility to citizenship as a basis for barring Takahashi from a commercial fishing license?

Decision—No.

Reason—The power to regulate immigration and naturalization is a constitutional power given to the federal government. Furthermore, the Fourteenth Amendment embodies the "general policy that all persons lawfully in this country shall abide 'in any state' on an equality of legal privilege with all citizens under non-discriminatory laws."

Whatever special public interest there may be, due to ownership of fish by California citizens, are inadequate to justify this legislation. The barring of aliens from landownership rests solely upon the power of the states to control the devolution and ownership of land within their borders, but cannot be extended to cover this case.

Corollary cases

Hines v. Davidowitz, 312 U.S. 53 (1941)
Hurd v. Hodge, 334 U.S. 24 (1948)
Truax v. Raich, 239 U.S. 33 (1915)
Oyama v. California, 332 U.S. 633 (1948)
Terrace v. Thompson, 233 U.S. 107 (1923)
Heim v. McCall, 239 U.S. 175 (1915)
Bayside Fish Co. v. Gentry, 297 U.S. 422 (1936)
Palmer v. Thompson, 403 U.S. 217 (1971)
Douglas v. Seacoast Products, 431 U.S. 265 (1977)

Note—Six months after *Oyama* v. *California* voided California's alien land law and cast doubt on the validity of other alien land legislation, the Court said that a state is not free to use in its statutes a formula of classification used by the federal government in immigration and naturalization statutes.

Hampton v. Mow Sun Wong, 426 U.S. 88; 48 L. Ed. 2d 495; 96 S. Ct 1895 (1976)

> Five aliens, lawfully and permanently residing in the United States, brought this litigation to challenge the validity of a policy adopted and enforced by the Civil Service Commission and certain other agencies that excluded all persons except American citizens and natives of Samoa from employment in most positions subject to their jurisdictions. Each of the five aliens was denied federal employment solely because of his or her alienage. They were all Chinese residents of San Francisco, each was qualified for an available job, and two of the five had filed declarations of intent to become citizens.

OPINION BY MR. JUSTICE STEVENS
(Vote: 5–4)

Question—Is the regulation of the United States Civil Service Commission barring resident aliens from employment in the federal competitive civil service constitutional?

Decision—No.

Reason—The Court agrees that the national interest might provide a justification for a citizenship requirement in the federal service but it does not agree that the federal power is so plenary that any agent of the national government may "arbitrarily subject all resident aliens to different substantive rules than those applied to citizens." The Civil Service rule "is of sufficient significance to be characterized as a deprivation of an interest in liberty" and by reason of the Fifth Amendment "such deprivation must be accompanied by due process." *Mow Sun Wong et al.* have identified several interests which Congress or the president might deem sufficient to justify the exclusion of noncitizens from federal service. The present exclusion is not one in the national interest. Neither the president nor Congress had ever required the Civil Service to adopt its exclusion policy. An admitted convenience in establishing one single rule excluding all noncitizens from federal employment does not provide a rational basis for the exclusion.

Corollary cases

Elrod v. Burns, 427 U.S. 347 (1976)
Grahan v. Richardson, 403 U.S. 365 (1971)
Sugarman v. Dougall, 413 U.S. 634 (1973)
In re Griffiths, 413 U.S. 717 (1973)
Truax v. Raich, 239 U.S. 33 (1915)
Arnett v. Kennedy, 416 U.S. 134 (1974)
Cafeteria Workers v. McElroy, 367 U.S. 886 (1961)
Harisiades v. Schaughnessy, 342 U.S. 580 (1952)
Galvan v. Press, 347 U.S. 522 (1954)
Kleindienst v. Mandel, 408 U.S. 753 (1972)
Roger v. Bellei, 401 U.S. 815 (1971)
Toll v. Moreno, 60 L. Ed. 2d 354 (1979)
Ambach v. Norwick, 441 U.S. 68 (1978)
Foley v. Connelie, 435 U.S. 291 (1978)
Cabel v. Chavez-Salido, 70 L. Ed. 2d 677 (1982)

Note—Following an invitation to the Congress and the president to state clearly its determination to exclude all noncitizens from federal service, President Ford, by executive order, banned aliens from federal service, and when the issue returned to federal district court, it was upheld.

Vance v. Terrazas, 444 U.S. 252; 62 L. Ed. 2d 461; 100 S. Ct. 540 (1980)

Terrazas, 22, who was a citizen of both the United States and Mexico at birth, executed an application for a certificate of Mexican nationality. The certificate recited that Terrazas had sworn allegiance to Mexico, thus renouncing all rights inherent to any other nationality. After a certificate of loss of nationality was issued to Terrazas by the U.S. Department of State, stating that he had voluntarily renounced his citizenship, Terrazas brought suit for a declaration of his United States nationality.

OPINION BY MR. JUSTICE WHITE
(Vote: 5–4)

Question—1. In establishing loss of citizenship, must the government prove intent to surrender United States citizenship?

2. Can Congress prescribe the standard of proof in expatriation proceedings?

Decision—1. Yes

2. Yes.

Reason—The intent of the Fourteenth Amendment, among other things, was to define citizenship and that definition, said the Court, cannot coexist with a congressional power to specify acts that work a renunciation of citizenship even absent an intent to renounce. "But the trier of fact must in the end conclude that the citizen not only voluntarily committed the expatriating act prescribed in the statute, but also intended to relinquish his citizenship. . . . We are unable to conclude that the specific evidentiary standard provided by Congress . . . is invalid under either the Citizenship Clause or the Due Process Clause of the Fifth Amendment." Thus, "we hold that in proving expatriation, an expatriating act and an intent must be proved by a preponderance of the evidence. We also hold that when one of the statutory expatriating acts is proved, it is constitutional to presume it to have been a voluntary act until and unless proved otherwise by the actor. If he succeeds, there can be no expatriation. If he fails, the question remains whether on all the evidence the government has satisfied its burden of proof that the expatriating act was performed with the necessary intent to relinquish citizenship."

Corollary cases

Afroyim v. Rusk, 387 U.S. 253 (1967)
Perez v. Brownell, 356 U.S. (1958)

Plyler v. Doe, 457 U.S. _____; 72 L. Ed. 2d 786; 102 S. Ct. 2382 (1982)

In May 1975, the Texas legislature revised its educational laws to withhold from school districts any state funds for the education of children who were not "legally admitted" into the United States. Local school districts were authorized to deny enrollment to children not "legally admitted" to the country. A class action was filed in the district court on behalf of certain school-age children of Mexican origin. The

district court enjoined the school corporations from excluding the undocumented children, holding the Texas law violated the equal protection clause. The court of appeals
affirmed.

OPINION BY MR. JUSTICE BRENNAN
(Vote: 5–4)

Question—May Texas deny to undocumented school-age children the free public education that it provides to children
who are citizens of the United States or legally admitted
aliens?

Decision—No.

Reason—''Whatever his status under the immigration laws, an
alien is surely a 'person' in any ordinary sense of that term.
Aliens, whose presence in this country is unlawful, have long
been recognized as 'persons' guaranteed due process of law
by the Fifth and Fourteenth Amendments. We have clearly
held that the Fifth Amendment protects aliens whose presence
in this country is unlawful from invidious discrimination by
the federal government. . . . Neither our cases nor the logic of
the Fourteenth Amendment supports the construction of the
phrase 'within its jurisdiction' to mean that illegal aliens are
not within a state's jurisdiction. . . . The Equal Protection
Clause was intended to work nothing less than the abolition of
all caste and invidious class based legislation. . . . Use of the
phrase 'within its jurisdiction' thus does not detract from, but
rather confirms, the understanding that the protection of the
Fourteenth Amendment extends to anyone, citizen or
stranger, who is subject to the laws of a state, and reaches into
every corner of a state's territory. That a person's initial entry
into a state, or into the United States, was unlawful, and that
he may for that reason be expelled, cannot negate the simple
fact of his presence within the state's territorial perimeter.
Given such presence, he is subject to the full range of obligations imposed by the state's civil and criminal laws. And until
he leaves the jurisdiction—either voluntarily, or involuntarily

in accordance with the Constitution and laws of the United States—he is entitled to the equal protection of the laws that a state may choose to establish."

Corollary cases

DeCanas v. Bica, 424 U.S. 351 (1976)
United States v. Wong Kim Ark, 169 U.S. 649 (1898)
Shaughnessy v. Mezei, 345 U.S. 206 (1953)
Wong Wing v. United States, 163 U.S. 228 (1896)
Yick Wo v. Hopkins, 118 U.S. 356 (1886)
Mathews v. Diaz, 426 U.S. 67 (1976)
Leng May-Ma v. Barber, 357 U.S. 185 (1958)
Missouri ex rel. Gaines v. Canada, 305 U.S. 337 (1938)
F. S. Royster Guano Co. v. Virginia, 253 U.S. 412 (1920)
Tigner v. Texas, 310 U.S. 141 (1940)
San Antonio School District v. Rodriguez, 411 U.S. 1 (1973)
Graham v. Richardson, 403 U.S. 365 (1971)
United States v. Carolene Products Co., 304 U.S. 144 (1938)

Note—*Plyler* is sure to attract a good deal of comment. The dissent begins: "Were it our business to set the nation's social policy . . ." and continues: "However, the constitution does not constitute us as 'platonic guardians' nor does it vest in this Court the authority to strike down laws because they do not meet our standards of desirable social policy, 'wisdom,' or 'common snese.' " Although Brennan admits that education is not a "fundamental right" or that undocumented resident aliens cannot be treated as a "suspect class," yet there is no national policy perceived that might justify the state in denying alien children—not accountable for their undocumented status and unable to alter it—from an elementary education.

ELECTIONS AND POLITICS

Ex parte Yarbrough, 110 U.S. 651; 4 S. Ct. 152; 28 L. Ed. 274 (1884)

> Yarbrough and others were convicted in a federal court for having conspired to intimidate a colored person from voting for a member of Congress, in violation of the federal statutes. Since, under the law in question in this case, Congress was aiming at activities of the Ku Klux Klan and similar organizations specializing in intimidation, this is sometimes called the "Ku Klux Klan case."

OPINION BY MR. JUSTICE MILLER
(No evidence from the report that the decision was not unanimous.)

Question—Does Congress have the power to punish violations of election laws under the Constitution?

Decision—Yes.

Reason—"That a government whose essential character is republican, whose executive head and legislative body are both elective, whose most numerous and powerful branch of the legislature is elected by the people directly, has no power to appropriate laws to secure this election from the influence of violence, of corruption, and of fraud, is a proposition so startling as to arrest attention and demand the gravest consideration." If this government "is anything more than a mere aggregation of delegated agents of other states and governments, each of which is superior to the general government, it must have the power to protect the elections on which its existence depends from violence and corruption." The proposition that every power of Congress must be expressly granted has never been held by the Court. The right to vote in a congressional election is not dependent upon each state . . . for the office is one 'created by the Constitution and by that alone.' It also declares how it shall be filled, namely: by elections. . . . If the Government of the United States has within its constitutional domain no authority to provide against these evils . . . it will be at the mercy of the combinations of those who respect no right but brute force, on the one hand, and unprincipled corruptionists on the other.''

Corollary cases

Minor v. Happersett, 21 Wallace 162 (1875)
United States v. Reese, 92 U.S. 214 (1876)
Ex parte Siebold, 100 U.S. 371 (1880)
Guinn v. United States, 238 U.S. 347 (1915)
Burroughs v. United States, 290 U.S. 534 (1934)
Barry v. United States ex rel. Cunningham, 279 U.S. 597 (1929)
United States v. Classic, 313 U.S. 299 (1941)
Smith v. Allwright, 321 U.S. 649 (1944)
Screws v. United States, 325 U.S. 91 (1945)

Note—While it appeared that the right to vote was not one of the privileges and immunities of citizenship, *Yarbrough,* however, indicates that in a certain sense Congress has the right to protect the privilege to vote for congressmen since this is a right that flows from Article I of the Constitution for those who meet the qualifications of ''the most numerous branch of the state legislature.'' This is a federal right, but exercised on a state level.

Guinn v. United States, 238 U.S. 347; 35 S. Ct. 926; 59 L. Ed. 1340 (1915)

In 1910 Oklahoma amended its constitution to read as follows: ''No person shall be registered as an elector of this state or be allowed to vote in any election held therein, unless he be able to read and write any section of the constitution of the state of Oklahoma, but no person who was, on January 1, 1866, or at any time prior thereto, entitled to vote under any form of government, or who at that time resided in some foreign nation, and no lineal descendant of such person, shall be denied the right to register and vote because of his inability to so read and write sections of such constitution.'' In 1910, when certain Negro citizens of Oklahoma were denied the right to vote, the charge was made that the Oklahoma amendment was contrary to the Fifteenth Amendment.

OPINION BY MR. CHIEF JUSTICE WHITE
(Vote: 8–0)

Question—Does the Oklahoma amendment violate the Fifteenth Amendment?

Decision—Yes.

Reason—The Court reasoned that the Oklahoma amendment was designed to by-pass the provisions of the Fifteenth Amendment by setting the date of voting eligibility for those that could not read or write prior to the adoption of the Fifteenth Amendment. Since Negroes had no eligibility before that date, the Court reasoned that this amendment was an attempt to deny voting because of color or race.

"We say this because we are unable to discover how, unless the prohibitions of the Fifteenth Amendment were considered, the slightest reason was afforded for basing the classification upon a period of time prior to the Fifteenth Amendment. Certainly it cannot be said that there was any peculiar necromancy in the time named which engendered attributes affecting the qualification to vote which would not exist at another and different period unless the Fifteenth Amendment was in view."

Corollary cases

Ex parte Yarbrough, 110 U.S. 651 (1884)
Neal v. Delaware, 103 U.S. 370 (1881)
Lane v. Wilson, 307 U.S. 268 (1939)
Grovey v. Townsend, 295 U.S. 45 (1935)
United States v. Classic, 313 U.S. 299 (1941)
Smith v. Allwright, 321 U.S. 649 (1944)
South Carolina v. Katzenbach, 383 U.S. 301 (1966)
Katzenbach v. Morgan, 384 U.S. 641 (1966)
Burns v. Fortson, 410 U.S. 686 (1973)
Hill v. Stone, 421 U.S. 289 (1975)
United Jewish Organization of Williamsburgh v. Carey, 430 U.S. 144 (1977)
Harper v. Virginia Board of Education, 383 U.S. 663 (1966)
Dunn v. Blumstein, 403 U.S. 330 (1972)
Green v. New York City Board of Elections, 389 U.S. 1048 (1962)
Richardson v. Ramirez, 418 U.S. 24 (1974)
Marston v. Lewis, 410 U.S. 679 (1973)

Note—*Guinn* invalidated the infamous "grandfather clause."

Nixon v. Condon, 286 U.S. 73; 52 S. Ct. 484; 76 L. Ed. 984 (1932)

The petitioner, a Negro, brought this action against judges of a primary election in Texas for their refusal to allow him to vote by reason of his race or color. This was the second time Nixon had been denied the opportunity to vote. The first time the Supreme Court ruled a Texas statute denying the right of a Negro to vote in a party primary, was void. (See *Nixon* v. *Herndon,* 273, U.S. 536.) Texas then passed a new statute stating that the state executive committee of each party should determine who can vote in primaries. Under this statute, the Democratic party executive committee adopted a resolution allowing only white persons to vote in its party primary.

OPINION BY MR. JUSTICE CARDOZO
(Vote: 5–4)

Question—Was the new Texas statute in effect a violation of the Fourteenth Amendment, allowing for inequalities at the election polls for reasons of race and color?

Decision—Yes.

Reason—"The test is not whether the members of the executive committee are the representatives of the state in the strict sense in which an agent is the representative of his principal. The test is whether they are to be classified as representatives of the state to such an extent and in such a sense that the great restraints of the Constitution set limits to their action." The new statute placed the power in an executive committee, and thus the action was really state action and not private action, and was therefore subject to the limitations of the Fourteenth Amendment.

Corollary cases

Newberry v. United States, 256 U.S. 232 (1921)
Grovery v. Townsend, 295 U.S. 45 (1935)
United States v. Classic, 313 U.S. 299 (1941)
Smith v. Allwright, 321 U.S. 649 (1944)
Williams v. Mississippi, 170 U.S. 213 (1898)
Guinn v. United States, 238 U.S. 347 (1915)
Lane v. Wilson, 307 U.S. 268 (1939)
Schnell v. Davis, 336 U.S. 933 (1949)
Rice v. Elmore, 333 U.S. 875 (1948)
Ex parte Siebold, 100 U.S. 371 (1880)
Ex parte Yarbrough, 110 U.S. 651 (1884)

United States v. Mosley, 238 U.S. 383 (1915)
Minor v. Happersett, 21 Wallace 162 (1875)

Note—One of the Texas "white primary" cases. See the note at *Smith* v. *Allwright.*

United States v. Classic, 313 U.S. 299; 61 S. Ct. 1031; 85 L. Ed. 1368 (1941)

In Louisiana, a primary election to nominate a party candidate for representative in Congress was conducted at public expense and regulated by state statute. Candidates to be voted on in the general election were restricted to primary nominees, to persons, not candidates in the primary, who filed nomination papers with the requisite number of signatures, and to persons whose names might lawfully be written on the ballot by the electors. Some of the votes of qualified voters were deliberately changed for the benefit of a different candidate. Classic, a commissioner of elections, was convicted under the Federal Criminal Code, which prohibits interference with constitutional rights.

Opinion by Mr. Justice Stone
(Vote: 5–3)

Question—Has Congress the right to see that primary elections are carried on in accordance with the right of the people to vote?

Decision—Yes.

Reason—Although the state government has the power to regulate these primary elections, Congress still has the duty to see that the integrity of these elections is maintained. The state had made these primary elections an integral part of the act of choosing one's representative. Thus it would fall under the meaning of elections of Article I, Sections 2 and 4 of the Constitution. "The right to participate in the choice of representatives for Congress includes, as we have said, the right to cast a ballot and to have it counted at the general election whether for the successful candidate or not. Where the state law has made the primary an integral part of the procedure of choice or where in fact the primary effectively controls the choice, the right of the elector to have his ballot counted at the primary, is likewise included in the right protected by Article I, Section 2."

Corollary cases

Newberry v. United States, 256 U.S. 232 (1921)
Nixon v. Herndon, 273 U.S. 536 (1927)
Ex parte Yarbrough, 110 U.S. 651 (1884)
Ex parte Siebold, 100 U.S. 371 (1880)
Screws v. United States, 325 U.S. 91 (1945)
Oregon v. Mitchell, 400 U.S. 112 (1970)
Roudebush v. Hartke, 405 U.S. 15 (1972)
Grovey v. Townsend, 294 U.S. 699 (1935)
United States v. Mosley, 238 U.S. 383 (1915)
Minor v. Happersett, 21 Wallace 162 (1875)
Nixon v. Condon, 286 U.S. 73 (1932)
Smith v. Allwright, 321 U.S. 649 (1944)
United States v. Raines, 362 U.S. 17 (1960)
Bullock v. Carter, 405 U.S. 134 (1972)

Note—See the note at *Smith* v. *Allwright*, 321 U.S. 649 (1944).

Smith v. Allwright, 321 U.S. 649; 64 S. Ct. 757; 88 L. Ed. 987 (1944)

Lonnie E. Smith, a Negro citizen of Texas, sued for damages for the refusal of election and associate election judges to give him a ballot to vote in the primary election of July 27, 1940 for the nomination of Democratic candidates for the United States Senate and House of Representatives, and other state officers. This refusal was based solely on race and color. He fulfilled all other requirements for voting. It was argued by those representing the election officials that those officials were acting under a state of Texas Democratic party convention resolution that limited membership in the Democratic party to white persons.

OPINION BY MR. JUSTICE REED
(Vote: 8–1)

Question—Is the action of the Democratic convention a state action?

Decision—Yes.

Reason—The privilege of membership in a political party is of no concern to the state. However, when the privilege of membership in the party is an essential qualification for voting in the primary and selecting candidates for a general election, the action of the party is the action of the state. "When primaries become a part of the machinery for choosing officials, state and national, as they have here, the same tests to determine the character of discrimination or abridgement should be applied to the primary as are applied to the general election. If the state requires a certain electoral procedure, prescribes a general election ballot made up of party nominees so chosen and limits the choice of the electorate in general elections for state officers, practically speaking, to those whose names appear on such a ballot, it endorses, adopts and enforces the discrimination against Negroes practiced by a party entrusted by Texas law with the determination of the qualifications of participants in the primary. This is state action within the meaning of the Fifteenth Amendment."

Corollary cases

Grovey v. Townsend, 295 U.S. 45 (1935)
United States v. Classic, 313 U.S. 299 (1941)
Nixon v. Herndon, 273 U.S. 536 (1927)
Newberry v. United States, 256 U.S. 232 (1921)
Bullock v. Carter, 405 U.S. 134 (1972)
Guinn v. United States, 238 U.S. 347 (1915)
Williams v. Mississippi, 170 U.S. 213 (1892)
Lane v. Wilson, 307 U.S. 268 (1939)
Rice v. Elmore, 333 U.S. 875 (1948)
Terry v. Adams, 345 U.S. 461 (1953)
Minor v. Happersett, 21 Wallace 162 (1875)
California Medical Association v. Federal Election Commission, 69 L. Ed. 2d (1981)
Democratic Party of the United States v. La Follette, 67 L. Ed. 2d (1981)
Mobile v. Bolden, 446 U.S. 55 (1980)
State Board of Elections v. Socialist Workers Party, 440 U.S. 172 (1979)
Marchioro v. Chaney, 67 L. Ed. 2d 816 (1979)

Note—One of the Texas "white primary cases." In *Newberry* v. *United States,* 256 U.S. 232 (1921) the Court said that Congress could not regulate primaries; in *Nixon* v. *Herndon,* 273 U.S. 536 (1927) that the state Democratic Party could not exclude Negroes from voting; and in *Nixon* v. *Condon,* 286

U.S. 73 (1932) that the state Democratic party committee could not discriminate. In *Grovey* v. *Townsend,* 295 U.S. 45 (1935), however, the Court held a state convention to be a private organization and its discrimination licit. When *United States* v. *Classic,* 313 U.S. 299 (1941) overruled *Grovey,* saying that a primary was an integral part of the election process, it was a short step for *Smith* v. *Allwright* to overrule *Grovey,* declaring the party's discrimination to be state action.

Screws v. United States, 325 U.S. 91; 65 S. Ct. 1031; 89 L. Ed. 1495 (1945)

> Screws was a county sheriff who enlisted the assistance of a policeman and a deputy to assist in an arrest. They arrested a Negro late at night on a warrant charging him with the theft of a tire. They placed handcuffs on the Negro. When they arrived at the court house square, the petitioners immediately started to beat the Negro. They claimed he had reached for a gun. The Negro was beaten into unconsciousness and died at a hospital within an hour. An indictment returned against the petitioners charged violation of Section 20 of the Federal Criminal Code. This section makes it a criminal offense willfully to deprive one under color of law, of rights, privileges, or immunities secured to him by the Constitution and laws of the United States.

OPINION BY MR. JUSTICE DOUGLAS
(Vote: 5–4)

Question—Can Congress apply the Fourteenth Amendment to individual state officers when they act "under color of law?"

Decision—Yes.

Reason—Here the officers had deprived the accused of various rights guaranteed of the Fourteenth Amendment, "the right not to be deprived of life without due process of law; the right to be tried upon the charge on which he was arrested, by due process of law and if found guilty to be punished in accordance with the laws of Georgia." The Court stated that history shows that the word "willfully" was not added to the act until 1909. The Court reasoned that the word "willfully" makes the act less severe by requiring proof of purposeful discriminatory action. The Court therefore required a specific intent to deprive a person of a federal right, leaving no possibility for charging the act unconstitutional on grounds of vagueness.

The Court held that the petitioners acted "under color of law" in making the arrest since they were officers of the law. By their own admissions they assaulted the Negro in order to protect themselves. It was their duty under Georgia law to make the arrest effective. Therefore, their conduct came within the statute.

The Court further reasoned that the problem is not whether state law has been violated, but whether an inhabitant of the state has been deprived of a federal right by one who acts under "color of any law." The fact that it is also a violation of state law does not make it any the less a federal offense punishable as such. Nor does its punishment by federal authority encroach on state authority or relieve the state from its responsibility for punishing state offenses.

Corollary cases

Logan v United States, 144 U.S. 263 (1892)
United States v. Harris, 106 U.S. 629 (1883)
Jerome v United States, 318 U.S. 101 (1943)
United States v. Cruikshank, 92 U.S. 542 (1976)
United States v. Classic, 313 U.S. 299 (1941)
Commonwealth of Virginia v. Rives, 100 U.S. 313 (1880)
Mahnick v. Souther S. S. Co., 321 U.S. 96 (1944)
Civil Rights Cases, 109 U.S. 3 (1883)
Shelley v. Kraemer, 334 U.S. 1 (1948)
Monroe v. Pape, 365 U.S. 167 (1961)
United States v. Williams, 341 U.S. 70 (1951)

Note—*Screws* and *Benanti* v. *United States,* 355 U.S. 96 (1957), which held illegal wire tapping by state officers would not be permitted in federal courts, and *United States* v. *Classic,* 313 U.S. 299 (1941), involving primaries selecting candidates for federal office, are examples of the application to state officials of federal law. The Court has made "under color of law" and "under pretense of" state law mutually interchangeable.

United Public Workers of America v. Mitchell, 330 U.S. 75; 91 L. Ed. 754; 67 S. Ct. 556 (1947)

> The Hatch Act, enacted in 1940, makes it unlawful for federal employees to engage in certain specified political activities. The appellants, with the exception of George Poole, asked for a declaration of the legally permissible limits of regulation. The Court held that this would be an advisory opinion and refused to take jurisdiction. However, Poole was a ward executive committeeman of a political party and was politically active on election day as a worker at the polls and paymaster for other party workers. He had violated the Hatch Act.

OPINION BY MR. JUSTICE REED
(Vote: 4–3)

Question—Does the Hatch Act violate the political rights reserved to the people under the Ninth and Tenth Amendments?

Decision—No.

Reason—The practice of excluding classified employees from party offices and personal political activities at the polls is an old one. In *Ex parte Curtis* the decision was confirmed that prohibited employees from giving or receiving money for political purposes to or from other employees of the government because this was not a right protected by the Constitution, but one that was subject to regulation.

The prohibitions under discussion were not dissimilar, since they involved contributions of energy instead of money. Congress and the president are responsible for efficiency in the public service, and if they think prohibiting active political service will best obtain the objective, there is no constitutional objection. If Congress oversteps reasonable limits, the courts will interfere, but only when congressional interference passes beyond the general existing conception of government power.

Corollary cases

Ex parte Curtis, 106 U.S. 371 (1882)
United States v. Wurzbach, 280 U.S. 396 (1930)
Broadrick v. Oklahoma, 413 U.S. 601 (1973)

U.S. Civil Service Commission v. National Association of Letter Carriers,
413 U.S. 548 (1973)
Branti v. Finkel, 445 U.S. 507 (1980)
Elrod v. Burns, 427 U.S. 347 (1976)
Buckley v. Valeo, 424 U.S. 1 (1976)
Democratic Party of the United States v. LaFollette, 67 L. Ed. 2d 82 (1981)

Note—The Court reaffirmed the *Mitchell* rule in *United States Civil Service Commission* v. *National Association of Letter Carriers,* 413 U.S. 548 (1973). In both cases the Court followed the policy judgement of Congress that there is danger in government employees engaging in partisan political activity.

Wesberry v. Sanders, 376 U.S. 1; 84 S. Ct. 526; 11 L. Ed. 2d 481 (1964)

Action was brought by qualified voters of Georgia's Fifth Congressional District to have set aside a Georgia statute establishing congressional districts. The population of the Fifth District was two to three times greater than that of some other congressional districts in the state. Since there is only one congressman for each district, it was claimed that there resulted a debasement of the people's right to vote because their congressman represented two to three times as many people as did congressmen from some other Georgia districts.

OPINION BY MR. JUSTICE BLACK
(Vote: 6–3)

Question—Does the districting statute abridge the requirement of Article I, Section 2 of the Constitution of the United States?

Decision—Yes.

Reason—The statute contracts the value of some votes and expands the value of others. In its historical context the command of Article I, Section 2 that representatives be chosen "by the people of the several states" means that as nearly as practicable one man's vote in a congressional election is to be worth as much as another's. "While it may not be possible to draw congressional districts with mathematical precision, that is no excuse for ignoring our Constitution's plain objective of

making equal representation for equal numbers of people with
the fundamental goal for the House of Representatives. That
is the high standard of justice and common sense which the
founders set for us.''

Corollary cases

Colegrove v. Green, 328 U.S. 549 (1946)
Baker v. Carr, 369 U.S. 186 (1962)
Gray v. Sanders, 372 U.S. 368 (1963)
Wright v. Rockefeller, 376 U.S. 52 (1964)
Reynolds v. Sims, 377 U.S. 533 (1964)
McDaniel v. Sanchez, 68 L. Ed. 2d 724 (1981)
Mobile v. Bolden, 446 U.S. 55 (1980)
Wise v. Lipscomb, 57 L. Ed. 2d 411 (1978)

Note—*Baker* v. *Carr,* 369 U.S. 186 (1962) did not set any
formula for apportionment other than it be "fair," and in
Sanders, the Court held that one man's vote in a congressional
election is to be worth as much as another's. *Sanders, Reynolds* v. *Sims,* 377 U.S. 533 (1964), and the Voting Rights Act
of 1965—as amended in 1970 and 1975—have eliminated many
voting restrictions.

**Reynolds v. Sims, 377 U.S. 533; 84 S. Ct. 1362; 11 L. E. 2d 506
(1964)**

A complaint was filed by a group of residents, taxpayers,
and voters of Jefferson County, Alabama, challenging the
apportionment of the Alabama legislature. The most recent
apportionment of the Alabama legislature was based on the
1900 federal census despite the requirement of the state
constitution that the legislature be apportioned decennially.
As a result of population growth, Jefferson County and
others were alleged to have suffered serious discrimination
with respect to the allocation of legislative representation.

Also, there were two plans for appointment pending. One
was a proposed amendment to the state constitution. The
other was a statute enacted as standby legislation to take
effect if the proposed constitutional amendment should fail
of adoption or be declared void by the courts. In neither of
these plans was there provision for apportionment of either
of the houses of the Alabama legislature on a population
basis.

OPINION BY MR. JUSTICE WARREN
(Vote: 8–1)

Question—Had there been violation of the equal protection clause of the Fourteenth Amendment?

Decision—Yes.

Reason—A predominant consideration in determining whether a state legislative apportionment scheme constitutes an invidious discrimination violative of rights asserted under the equal protection clause is that the rights allegedly impaired are individual and personal in nature. Legislators represent people, not trees or acres. The right to elect legislators in a free and unimpaired fashion is a bedrock of our political system. Overweighting and overvaluing the votes of persons living in one place has the certain effect of dilution and undervaluing the votes of those living elsewhere. Full and effective participation by all citizens in state government requires that each citizen have an equally effective voice in the election of members of his state legislature.

As a basic constitutional standard the equal protection clause requires that the seats in both houses of a bicameral state legislature must be apportioned on a population basis. An individual's right to vote for state legislators is unconstitutionally impaired when its weight is in a substantial fashion diluted when compared with the votes of citizens living in other parts of the state. This applies to both houses of the legislature.

Attempted reliance on the federal analogy to state legislative apportionment arrangements "appears often to be little more than an after-the-fact rationalization offered in defense of maladjusted state apportionment arrangements." By apportionment on a population basis is meant an honest and good faith effort to set up districts on a practical basis. Mathematical exactness or precision is hardly a workable constitutional requirement.

Corollary cases

Colegrove v. Green, 328 U.S. 549 (1946)
Baker v. Carr, 369 U.S. 186 (1962)

Gary v. Sanders, 372 U.S. 368 (1963)
Wesberry v. Sanders, 376 U.S. 1 (1964)
WMCA, Inc. v. Lowenzo, 377 U.S. 633 (1964)
Avery v. Midland County, Texas, 390 U.S. 474 (1968)
City of Richmond v. United States, 422 U.S. 358 (1975)
East Carroll Parish School Board v. Marshall, 424 U.S. 636 (1976)
United Jewish Organization of Williamsburgh v. Carey, 430 U.S. 145 (1977)
Mahan v. Howell, 410 U.S. 315 (1973)
Lucas v. Forty-Fourth General Assembly of Colorado, 377 U.S. 713 (1964)
Maryland Committee for Fair Representation v. Tawes, 377 U.S. 656 (1964)
Davis v. Mann, 377 U.S. 678 (1964)
Roman v. Sincock, 377 U.S. 695 (1964)
Swann v. Adams, 378 U.S. 533 (1964)
Beer v. United States, 425 U.S. 130 (1976)
Lockport v. Citizens for Community Action, 430 U.S. 259 (1977)

Note—Rejecting the "federal analogy" that one of the houses of the state legislature is based on something other than population, the Court handed down the now-famous electoral yardstick of "one man, one vote." *Reynolds* is the progeny of *Baker* v. *Carr,* 369 U.S. 186 (1962).

Oregon v. Mitchell, 400 U.S. 112; 91 S. Ct. 260; 27 L. Ed. 2d 272 (1970)

The states of Oregon, Arizona, Texas, and Idaho resisted compliance with the Voting Rights Act Amendments of 1970. Original actions were brought to question the validity of the statute. The Voting Rights Act Amendments provide for three things: (1) the reduction of the minimum age of voters in both state and federal elections from twenty-one to eighteen, (2) prohibition of the use of literacy tests in all elections, state and federal, and (3) prohibition in disqualification of voters in presidential elections because of failure to meet state residency requirements.

OPINION BY MR. JUSTICE BLACK
(Vote: 5–4)

Question—Does this statute infringe on powers reserved to the states under the Constitution to control their own elections?

Decision—Yes when applied to state and local elections but not otherwise.

Reason—The Constitution reserved to the states the power to regulate the election of their own officials but Congress has ultimate supervisory power over congressional and presidential elections. Congress has the authority under the original Constitution to permit 18-year-old citizens to vote in national elections and to prohibit states disqualifying voters in presidential elections because of failure to meet residence requirements. This comes under Article I, Section 4 and Article II, Section 1 of the Constitution, the former dealing with congressional elections and the latter with presidential elections. Beyond the original Constitution the enforcement provisions of the Fourteenth and Fifteenth Amendments allow for the literacy test ban. (The Twenty-sixth Amendment has abrogated the practical effect of this case.)

Corollary cases

United States v. Classic, 313 U.S. 299 (1941)
Wesberry v. Sanders, 376 U.S. 1 (1964)
Smiley v. Holm, 285 U.S. 355 (1932)
Pope v. Williams, 193 U.S. 621 (1904)
American Party of Texas v. White, 415 U.S. 767 (1974)
Kusper v. Pontikes, 414 U.S. 51 (1973)
Harper v. Virginia State Board of Elections, 383 U.S. 663 (1966)
Katzenbach v. Morgan, 384 U.S. 641 (1966)
Minor v. Happersett, 21 Wallace 162 (1875)
Dunn v. Blumstein, 405 U.S. 330 (1972)

Dunn v. Blumstein, 405 U.S. 330; 92 S. Ct. 995; 31 L. Ed. 2d 274 (1972)

James Blumstein moved to Tennessee on June 12, 1970, to assume his duties as assistant professor of law at Vanderbilt University in Nashville. He attempted to register to vote on July 1, 1970. Tennessee law authorizes the registration only of persons who, at the time of the next election, will have been residents of the state for a year and of the county for three months. The county registrar therefore refused to register Blumstein.

OPINION BY MR. JUSTICE MARSHALL
(Vote: 6–1)

Question—Does a state durational residence law for voting violate the equal protection clause of the Fourteenth Amendment?

Decision—Yes.

Reason—Such laws must be measured by a strict equal protection test. They are unconstitutional unless the state can demonstrate that such laws are *"necessary* to promote a *compelling* governmental interest."* A preelection waiting period may aid in preventing fraud, but the Court felt that thirty days should be an ample period of time for the state to complete whatever administrative tasks are necessary to prevent fraud, while a year or three months would be too much. As to residence requirements limiting the franchise to voters who are minimally knowledgeable about the issues, such requirements exclude too many people who should not and need not be excluded. "They represent a requirement of knowledge unfairly imposed on only some citizens." The Court also noted that, in addition to depriving citizens of the right to vote, such laws also directly impinge on the exercise of the right to travel.

Corollary cases

Reynolds v. Sims, 377 U.S. 533 (1964)
Carrington v. Rash, 380 U.S. 89 (1965)
Evans v. Cornman, 398 U.S. 419 (1970)
Druedling v. Devlin, 380 U.S. 125 (1965)
Kramer v. Union Free School District No. 15, 395 U.S. 621 (1969)
Hill v. Stone, 421 U.S. 937 (1975)
Shapiro v. Thompson, 394 U.S. 618 (1969)
Oregon v. Mitchell, 400 U.S. 112 (1970)
Burns v. Fortson, 410 U.S. 686 (1973)
Marston v. Lewis, 410 U.S. 679 (1973)
American Party of Texas v. White, 415 U.S. 767 (1974)
Luhin v. Panish, 415 U.S. 709 (1974)
Storer v. Brown, 415 U.S. 724 (1974)
California v. Torres, 55 L. Ed. 2d 65 (1978)
Hoyt Civic Club v. Tuscaloosa, 439 U.S. 60 (1978)
Hicklin v. Orbeck, 437 U.S. 518 (1978)
Elkins v. Moreno, 55 L. Ed. 2d 614 (1978)
Baldwin v. Montana Fish and Game Commission, 56 L. Ed. 2d 354 (1978)

Note—Together with the Voting Rights Act Amendments and the Twenty-sixth Amendment, Congress has consistently enlarged voting rights. But contrast *Dunn* with *Oregon v. Mitchell,* 400 U.S. 112 (1970) for court limits.

Cousins v. Wigoda, 419 U.S. 477; 42 L. Ed. 2d 595; 95 S. Ct. 541 (1975)

In the election of 1972, the fifty-nine Wigoda delegates (pro-Mayor Richard Daley) had been elected from Chicago districts in the March 1972 Illinois Primary. The Illinois courts duly certified these delegates. The anti-Daley delegates, the Cousins delegates, privately caucused and sent a rival delegation to the national convention. It did so claiming the Wigoda delegates were elected in violation of party rules and regulations. The Democratic party Credentials Committee agreed and seated the Cousins delegates and not the Wigoda delegates.

OPINION BY MR. JUSTICE BRENNAN
(Vote: 9–0; 4 justices dissent in part)

Question—When a state duly certifies delegates elected under state law, are they to be given primacy over the national party's rules in the determination of the qualifications and eligibility of the delegates to the party's national convention?

Decision—No.

Reason—The national Democratic party and its adherents enjoy a constitutionally protected right of political association. There can be no doubt that the freedom to join with others in "the common advancement of political beliefs and ideas" is a form of orderly group activity protected by the First and Fourteenth Amendments. "The right to associate with the political party of one's choice is an integral part of this basic constitutional freedom." The Democratic National Convention was under no obligation to seat any delegation. An obvious intolerable result would occur if each state could determine the qualifications of its delegates to the national party conventions. "The convention serves the pervasive national interest in the selection of candidates for national office, and this national interest is greater than any interest of an individual state." Illinois's interest in protecting the integrity of its electoral process cannot be deemed compelling in the context of delegate selection. This is a case where the convention is the proper forum for determining intra-party disputes as to which delegates should be seated.

Corollary cases

Elrod v. Burns, 427 U.S. 347 (1976)
Kusper v. Pontikes, 414 U.S. 51 (1973)
Williams v. Rhodes, 393 U.S. 23 (1968)
NAACP v. Button, 371 U.S. 415 (1963)
Bates v. Little Rock, 361 U.S. 516 (1960)
Kramer v. Union School District, 395 U.S. 621 (1969)
Dunn v. Blumstein, 404 U.S. 330 (1972)
Ray v. Blair, 343 U.S. 214 (1952)
NAACP v. Alabama, 357 U.S. 449 (1958)
Newberry v. United States, 256 U.S. 232 (1921)
O'Brien v. Brown, 409 U.S. 1 (1972)
Smith v. Allwright, 321 U.S. 649 (1944)
Oregon v. Mitchell, 400 U.S. 112 (1970)
Illinois State Board of Elections v. Socialist Workers Party, 440 U.S. 173 (1979)
Democratic Party of the United States v. LaFollette, 67 L. Ed. 2d 82 (1981)
Branti v. Finkel, 445 U.S. 507 (1980)
Marchioro v. Chaney, 60 L. Ed. 2d 816 (1979)
McDaniel v. Paxy, 55 L. Ed. 2d 593 (1978)

Note—The *Wigoda* principle was strengthened most recently in *Democratic Party of the United States* v. *LaFollette* (1981).

Buckley v. Valeo, 424 U.S. 1; 46 L. Ed. 2d 659; 96 S. Ct. 612 (1976)

> Congress passed in 1971, and in 1974 amended, the Federal Election Campaign Act. This act broadly attempted to limit individual political contributions to $1000 to any single candidate with an overall annual limitation of $35,000 by any single contributor; contributions and expenditures above certain threshold levels must be reported and disclosed; a system of public financing of presidential campaigns is established in the Internal Revenue Code; and a Federal Election Commission is established.

Opinion Per Curiam

(No evidence from the report that the decision was not unanimous.)

Question—Is the Federal Election Campaign Act of 1974 (1) a violation of the First Amendment's freedom of communication and freedom of association? (2) Is its subsidy provisions a violation of the general welfare clause? (3) Is the commission as constituted a violation of the doctrine of the separation of powers?

Decision—1. No.
   2. No.
   3. Yes.

Reason—The Court held part of the Federal Election Campaign Act constitutional and part unconstitutional. Held constitutional under Congress's power to regulate elections and prevent corruption, is the part that allows Congress to set ceilings on political contributions as against the charge that the act violated the speech and associational provisions of the First Amendment and to provide public financing of presidential nominating conventions and primaries against the charge that it violated the general welfare clause (Article I, Section 8, clause 1). Held unconstitutional is the part that set limits to independent political expenditures by individuals and groups, as burdening the right of free speech as well as setting limits to the personal expenditures by the candidate himself. Also held void is the method of nominating the members of the commission as a violation of the doctrine of separation of powers. "The act's contributions and expenditure limitations," say the Court, "impinge on protected associational freedoms. Making a contribution, like joining a political party, serves to affiliate a person with a candidate." Although Congress can regulate elections it does not follow "it must have the power to appoint those who are to administer the regulatory statute" in violation of the appointing clause.

Corollary cases

New York Times v. Sullivan, 376 U.S. 254 (1964)
Kusper v. Pontikes, 414 U.S. 51 (1973)
United States Civil Service Commission v. National Association of Letter
   Carriers, 413 U.S. 548 (1973)
Harper v. Virginia Board of Elections, 383 U.S. 663 (1966)
Phoenix v. Kolozieiski, 339 U.S. 204 (1970)
Lubin v. Panish, 415 U.S. 709 (1974)

Red Lion Broadcasting Co. v. FCC, 395 U.S. 367 (1969)
Columbia Broadcasting System v. Democratic National Committee, 412 U.S.
   94 (1973)
Miami Herald Pub. Co. v. Tornillo, 418 U.S. 241 (1974)
Daugherty County Georgia Board of Education v. White, 58 L. Ed. 2d 269
   (1978)
California Medical Association v. Federal Election Commission, 69 L. Ed. 2d
   567 (1981)
Democratic Party of the United States v. LaFollette, 67 L. Ed. 2d 82 (1981)
First National Bank of Boston v. Bellotti, 435 U.S. 765 (1978)
Federal Election Commission v. Democratic Senatorial Campaign
   Committee, 70 L. Ed. 2d 23 (1981)

Democratic Party of the United States v. LaFollette, 450 U.S. 107; 67 L. Ed. 2d 82; 101 S. Ct. 101 (1981)

The Democratic party charter required that only those who would be willing to publicly affiliate with the Democratic party could participate in the process of selecting delegates to the party's national convention. Wisconsin's election laws permitted voters to participate in its Democratic presidential candidate preference primary without requiring a public declaration of party preference and without regard to party affiliation. Although Wisconsin's national convention delegates are selected separately after the primary, those delegates are bound to vote at the convention in accord with the result of the open primary. While Wisconsin's open primary does not in itself violate the national party's rules, the state's requirement that primary results at the national convention does. Suit was brought by the state when the national party refused to seat Wisconsin delegates at the 1980 national convention.

OPINION BY MR. JUSTICE STEWART
(Vote: 6–3)

Question—Can Wisconsin compel the national Democratic party to seat its delegates although they were chosen in a manner that violates the party's rules?

Decision—No.

Reason—". . . The national Democratic party and its adherents enjoy a constitutionally protected right of political association.

. . . This court has recognized that the inclusion of persons unaffiliated with a political party may seriously distort its collective decisions—thus impairing the party's essential functions—and that political parties may accordingly protect themselves 'from the intrusion by those with adverse political principles'. . . . A state or a court may not constitutionally substitute its own judgment for that of the party. A political party's choice among the various ways of determining the makeup of the state's delegation to the party's national convention is protected by the constitution. . . . The courts may not interfere on the ground that they view a particular expression as unwise or irrational.''

Corollary cases

Cousins v. Wigoda, 419 U.S. 477 (1975)
Kusper v. Pontikes, 414 U.S. 51 (1973)
Ray v. Blair, 343 U.S. 214 (1952)

SEPARATION OF POWERS

Morrison v. Olson, 487 U.S. _____; 101 L. Ed. 2d 569; 108 S. Ct. 2597 (1988)

The issue here is the constitutionality of the independent counsel provisions of the Ethics in Government Act of 1978. It began as a controversy between the House Judiciary Committee and the Environmental Protection Agency (EPA) with regard to producing certain documents. It was alleged that, along with two other officials, Edward Schmultz and Carol E. Dinkins, who withheld documents from the committee, Theodore B. Olson had given the judiciary committee false testimony. The special division (a special Court created by the act) appointed Alexia Morrison as independent counsel with respect to Olson and gave her jurisdiction to investigate Olson's testimony or any other matter involving a violation of federal law. The Federal District Court upheld the act's constitutionality and ordered the executive officials in contempt for ignoring the subpoenas. The Court of Appeals reversed holding that the act violated the Appointments Clause of the Constitution, the limitations of Article III, and the principle of separation of powers.

OPINION BY MR. CHIEF JUSTICE REHNQUIST
(Vote: 7–1)

Question—Is the Independent Counsel provision of the Ethics in Government Act constitutionally void as violating the constitution's Appointing Clause, Article III, or the doctrine of separation of powers.

Decision—No.

Reason—As to the tenure of the independent counsel she may be removed (other than by impeachment and conviction) only by the attorney general and only for good cause; and by the special division "acting either on its own or on the suggestion of the attorney general." Moreover, the act provides for congressional oversight of the activities of independent counsels. The distinction between "inferior" and "principal" is not easy to determine but in our view the independent counsel "falls on

455

the 'inferior officer' side of that line." She can be removed by the attorney general, has limited duties, can only operate within the scope of her jurisdiction, is a temporary appointment. The Court is aware that its judicial power is limited to "cases" or "controversies" and that, broadly stated, it will not assume non-judicial duties and is sufficiently isolated to resist any kind of encroachment. We do not think the act deprives the president of control of the independent counsel or truncates his power to faithfully execute the law. "Time and again we have reaffirmed the importance in our constitutional scheme of the separation of governmental powers into the three coordinate branches." Nor do we believe this case involves an attempt by Congress "to increase its own powers at the expense of the executive branch . . . nor think that the act works in any *judicial* usurpation of properly executive functions." The decision of the Court of Appeals is reversed.

Corollary cases

United States v. Germaine, 99 U.S. 508; 25 L. Ed. 482 (1879)

Buckley v. Valeo, 424 U.S. 1; 46 L. Ed. 2d 659, 96 S. Ct. 612 (1976)

United States v. Eaton, 109 U.S. 331; 42 L. Ed. 767, 18 S. Ct. 374 (1898)

Ex parte Siebold, 100 U.S. 371, 25 L. Ed. 717 (1880)

Gobart Importing Co. v. United States, 282 U.S. 344, 75 L. Ed. 374, 51 S. Ct. 153 (1931)

United States v. Nixon, 418 U.S. 683, 41 L. Ed. 2d 1039, 94 S. Ct. 3090 (1974)

Ex parte Hennen, 13 Pet. 230, 10 L. Ed. 138 (1839)

Muskrat, 219 U.S. 346, 56 L. Ed. 246, 31 S. Ct. 250 (1911)

United States Parole Comm'n v. Geraghty, 445 U.S. 388, 63 L. Ed. 2d 479, 100 S. Ct. 1202 (1980)

Commodity Futures Trading Comm'n v. Schor, 478 U.S. 833, 92 L. Ed. 2d 675, 106 S. Ct. 3245 (1986)

Bowsher v. Synar, 478 U.S. 714, 92 L. Ed. 2d 583, 106 S. Ct. 3181 (1986)

Myers v. United States, 272 U.S. 52, 71 L. Ed. 160, 47 S. Ct. 21 (1926)

Humphrey's Executor v. United States, 295 U.S. 602, 79 L. Ed. 1611, 55 S. Ct. 869 (1935)

Weiner v. United States, 357 U.S. 349, 2 L. Ed. 2d 1377, 78 S. Ct. 1275 (1958)

Youngstown Sheet & Tube v. Sawyer, 343 U.S. 579, 96 L. Ed. 1153, 72 S. Ct. 863 (1952)

Nixon v. Administrator of General Services, 433 U.S. 425, 53 L. Ed. 2d 867, 97 S. Ct. 2777 (1977)

McGrain v. Daugherty, 273 U.S. 135, 71 L. Ed. 580, 47 S. Ct. 319 (1927)

Note—Justice Oliver Wendell Holmes once spoke of hard cases making bad law. This appears to be one for, on the one hand, the Court's aloofness (or studied distance) from the political struggle between the president and Congress has been breached; and, on the other hand, this decision very much collides with on-going political-judicial disputes and might tilt to one side or the other. The decision is viewed as a major defeat for the presidency and one Congress welcomes, for in the arena of separation of powers Congress has not lately enjoyed Court support.

Bowsher v. Snyar, 478 U.S. _____; 92 L. Ed. 2d 583; 106 S. Ct. 3181 (1986)

The Balanced Budget and Emergency Deficit Control Act of 1985 (popularly known as the Gramm-Rudman-Hollings Act) put a cap on the amount of federal spending for the fiscal years 1986 through 1991. If in any fiscal year the budget rises beyond the prescribed maximum, by more than a specified sum, the act mandates across the board cuts in federal spending. The comptroller general has, as a consequence, the responsibility of preparing a report to the president indicating the projected revenues and reductions to reduce the deficit. The president will issue an order mandating these cuts. No sooner was the act signed when 12 congressmen filed a complaint contesting its constitutionality. The district court ruled, inter alia that the comptroller's role in the deficit reduction process was constitutionally infirm under the doctrine of separation of powers. It went to the Supreme Court on direct appeal.

OPINION BY MR. CHIEF JUSTICE BURGER
(Vote: 7–2)

Question—"The question . . . is whether the assignment by Congress to the comptroller general . . . of certain functions under the Balanced Budget and Emergency Deficit Control Act of 1985 violates the doctrine of separation of powers."

Decision—Yes.

Reason—"Even a cursory examination of the constitution reveals the influence of Montesquieu's thesis that checks and balances were the foundation of a structure of government that would protect liberty.'' No officer of the government can sit in Congress. The president is responsible not to the Congress, but to the people, subject only to inpudment proceedings and even here the chief justice presides if it involves the president. This system to be sure, produces, at times, conflicts, confusion, and discordance ''but it was deliberately so structured to assure full, vigorous and open debate.'' The fundamental necessity ''of maintaining each of the three general departments of government entirely free . . . is hardly open to serious question.'' In *INS* v. *Chadha* (1983), we struck down a one house ''legislative veto provision.'' To permit an officer (comptroller general) supervised by Congress to execute the laws would be, in essence, to permit a congressional veto. It is urged that the comptroller general performs his duties independently of Congress. This view ''does not bear close scrutiny.'' Although nominated by the president the comptroller general is removed not only by congressional impeachment but also by a joint resolution. The dissent is in error in believing the comptroller general is free of congressional influence. It is not enough to believe that judicial assessment turns on whether an officer exercising power is on good terms with Congress, for the fathers were dealing with structural protection against abuse of power.'' The judgment of the district court is affirmed.

Corollary cases

Burke v. Barnes, 475 U.S. _____, 89 L. Ed. 2d 569, 106 S. Ct. 1258 (1986)
Yakus v. United States, 321 U.S. 414, 88 L. Ed. 834, 64 S. Ct. 660 (1944)
Myers v. United States, 272 U.S. 52, 71 L. Ed. 160, 47 S. Ct. 21 (1926)
Humphrey's Executor v. United States, 295 U.S. 602, 79 L. Ed. 1611, 55 S. Ct. 869 (1935)
INS v. Chadha, 462 U.S. 919, 77 L. Ed. 2d 317, 103 S. Ct. 2664 (1983)
Youngstown Sheet & Tube Co. v. Sawyer, 343 U.S. 579, 96 L. Ed. 1153, 72 S. Ct. 863 (1952)
Weiner v. United States, 357 U.S. 349, 2 L. Ed. 2d 1377, 78 S. Ct. 1275 (1958)
Buckley v. Valeo, 424 U.S. 1, 46 L. Ed. 2d 659, 96 S. Ct. 612 (1976)
Shurtleff v. United States, 189 U.S. 311, 47 L. Ed. 828, 23 S. Ct. 535 (1903)
A.L.A. Schechter Poultry Corp. v. United States, 295 U.S. 495, 79 L. Ed. 1570, 55 S. Ct. 837 (1935)

Immigration and Naturalization Service v. Chadha, 462 U.S. 919; 77 L. Ed. 2d 317; 103 S. Ct. 2764 (1983)

Chadha, an alien, had been lawfully admitted to the United States. His visa expired and the INS—under the Immigration and Nationality Act which authorized either House of Congress by resolution to invalidate the decision of executive branch—ordered his expulsion, even though the attorney general, according to law, lifted the suspension. After the House vetoed the attorney general's decision, Chadha again appealed to the Board of Immigration Appeals. The board now agreed with Chadha. The Court of Appeals said that the House was exceeding constitutional authority in ordering Chadha's deportation and in essence violated the doctrine of separation of powers. The Supreme Court granted certiorari.

OPINION BY MR. CHIEF JUSTICE BURGER
(Vote: 7–2)

Question—Is a one House congressional veto constitutional?

Decision—No.

Reason—Despite Congress's view to the contrary, the Supreme Court has jurisdiction. Congress's view that if the one House veto provision were declared unconstitutional the whole act would fall. This is not so since the severability permission is clear. Congress can act on the valid portion when the objectional portion is severed as unlawful. We reject the view that Chadha lacks standing inasmuch that if the veto provision violates the constitution and is severable, the deportation order will be cancelled. Congress suggests alternative relief—other avenues that might be open but "at most these other avenues are speculative." Congress's authority over aliens is not contested. What is "challenged . . . is whether Congress has chosen a constitutionally permissible means of implementing that power." Congress has plenary authority "in all cases in which it has substantive legislative jurisdiction . . . so long as the exercise of that authority does not offend some other constitutional restriction." Eleven presidents from Mr. Wilson through Mr. Reagan "have gone on record at some point to challenge congressional vetoes as unconstitutional."

The fact that a given law or procedure is efficient, convenient, and useful in facilitating governmental functions will not save it if it offends the Constitution. Since the Constitutional Convention, the operative mandate is that legislation must, before becoming law, go first to the president. This power to veto legislation "was based on the profound conviction . . . . that the powers conferred on Congress were . . . to be most carefully circumscribed." Except for a narrow exception, not germane here, the Presentment Clauses serve the important purpose of assuring that a "national perspective is grafted on the legislative process." The Court of Appeals is affirmed.

Corollary cases

Duke Power Co. v. California Environment Study Group, 438 U.S. 59, 57 L. Ed. 2d 595, 98 S. Ct. 2620 (1978)

Parker v. Levy, 412 U.S. 733, 41 L. Ed. 2d 439, 94 S. Ct. 2547 (1974)

Deposit Guaranty National Bank v. Roper, 445 U.S. 326, 63 L. Ed. 2d 427, 100 S. Ct. 1166 (1980)

Buckley v. Valeo, 424 U.S. 1, 46 L. Ed. 2d 659, 96 S. Ct. 612 (1976)

Champlin Refining Co. v. Corporation Comm'n, 286 U.S. 210 76 L. Ed. 1062, 52 S. Ct. 559 (1932)

Electric Bond & Share Co. v. SEC, 303 U.S. 419, 82 L. Ed. 936, 58 S. Ct. 678 (1938)

Ashwander v. Tennessee Valley Authority, 297 U.S. 288, 80 L. Ed. 688, 56 S. Ct. 466 (1936)

Cheng Fan Kwok v. INS, 392 U.S. 206, 20 L. Ed. 2d 1037, 88 S. Ct. 1970 (1968)

McCulloch v. Maryland, 4 Wheat on 316, 4 L. Ed. 579 (1819)

Baker v. Carr, 369 U.S. 186, 7 L. Ed. 2d 663, 82 S. Ct. 691 (1962)

Marbury v. Madison, 1 Cranch 137, 2 L. Ed. 60 (1803)

National League of Cities v. Usury, 426 U.S. 833, 49 L. Ed. 2d 245, 96 S. Ct. 2465 (1976)

Myers v. United States, 272 U.S. 52, 71 L. Ed. 160, 47 S. Ct. 21 (1926)

Field v. Clark, 143 U.S. 649, 36 L. Ed. 294, 12 S. Ct. 495 (1892)

Cohens v. Virginia, 6 Wheat on 264, 5 L. Ed. 257 (1821)

The Pocket Veto Case, 279 U.S. 655, 73 L. Ed. 894, 49 S. Ct. 463 (1929)

Hollingsworth v. Virginia, 3 Dall 378, L. Ed. 644 (1798)

Youngstown Sheet & Tube Co. v. Sawyer, 343 U.S. 579, 96 L. Ed. 1153, 72 S. Ct. 863 (1952)

Note—*Chadha* is a biggie under the doctrine of separation of powers. Before attacking a thorny issue involving Congress, the Court—as it did in *Baker* v. *Carr* (1962) and *Powell* v. *McCormack* (1969)—quickly points out that this is a judicial and not a "political question."

MEMBERS OF THE SUPREME COURT OF THE UNITED STATES, 1789–1989

Chief Justices	State	Served	Appointed by	Born/Died
John Jay	N.Y.	1789–1795	Washington	1745–1829
John Rutledge	S.C.	1795	Washington	1739–1800
Oliver Ellsworth	Conn.	1796–1800	Washington	1745–1807
John Marshall	Va.	1801–1835	J. Adams	1755–1835
Roger B. Taney	Md.	1836–1864	Jackson	1777–1864
Salmon P. Chase	Ohio	1864–1873	Lincoln	1808–1873
Morrison R. Waite	Ohio	1874–1888	Grant	1816–1888
Mulville W. Fuller	Ill.	1888–1910	Cleveland	1833–1910
Edward D. White	La.	1910–1921	Taft	1845–1921
William H. Taft	Conn.	1921–1930	Harding	1857–1930
Charles E. Hughes	N.Y.	1930–1941	Hoover	1862–1948
Harlan F. Stone	N.Y.	1941–1946	F. D. Roosevelt	1872–1946
Fred M. Vinson	Ky.	1946–1953	Truman	1890–1953
Earl Warren	Calif.	1953–1969	Eisenhower	1891–1974
Warren Earl Burger	Va.	1969–1986	Nixon	1907–
William H. Rehnquist	Ariz.	1986–	Reagan	1924–

Associate Justices	State	Served	Appointed by	Born/Died
John Rutledge	S.C.	1789–1791	Washington	1739–1800
William Cushing	Mass.	1789–1810	Washington	1732–1810
James Wilson	Pa.	1789–1798	Washington	1742–1798
John Blair	Va.	1789–1796	Washington	1732–1800
James Iredell	N.C.	1790–1799	Washington	1751–1799
Thomas Johnson	Md.	1791–1793	Washington	1732–1819
William Paterson	N.J.	1793–1806	Washington	1745–1806
Samuel Chase	Md.	1796–1811	Washington	1741–1811
Bushrod Washington	Va.	1798–1829	J. Adams	1762–1829
Alfred Moore	N.C.	1799–1804	J. Adams	1755–1810
William Johnson	S.C.	1804–1834	Jefferson	1771–1834
Henry B. Livingston	N.Y.	1806–1823	Jefferson	1757–1823
Thomas Dodd	Ky.	1807–1826	Jefferson	1765–1826
Joseph Story	Mass.	1811–1845	Madison	1779–1845
Gabriel Duval	Md.	1812–1835	Madison	1752–1844
Smith Thompson	N.Y.	1823–1843	Monroe	1768–1843
Robert Trimble	Ky.	1826–1828	J. Q. Adams	1777–1828
John McLean	Ohio	1829–1861	Jackson	1785–1861
Henry Baldwin	Pa.	1830–1844	Jackson	1780–1844

Associate Justices	State	Served	Appointed by	Born/Died
James M. Wayne	Ga.	1835–1867	Jackson	1790–1867
Philip P. Barbour	Va.	1836–1841	Jackson	1783–1841
John Catron	Tenn.	1837–1865	Jackson	1786–1865
John McKinley	Ala.	1837–1852	Van Buren	1780–1852
Peter V. Daniel	Va.	1841–1860	Van Buren	1784–1860
Samuel Nelson	N.Y.	1845–1872	Tyler	1792–1873
Levi Woodbury	N.H.	1846–1851	Polk	1789–1851
Robert C. Grier	Pa.	1846–1870	Polk	1794–1870
Benjamin R. Curtis	Mass.	1851–1857	Fillmore	1809–1874
John A. Campbell	Ala.	1853–1861	Pierce	1811–1889
Nathan Clifford	Maine	1858–1881	Buchanan	1803–1881
Noah H. Swayne	Ohio	1862–1881	Lincoln	1804–1884
Samuel F. Miller	Iowa	1862–1890	Lincoln	1816–1890
David Davis	Ill.	1862–1877	Lincoln	1815–1886
Stephen J. Field	Calif.	1863–1897	Lincoln	1816–1899
William Strong	Pa.	1870–1880	Grant	1808–1895
Joseph P. Bradley	N.J.	1870–1892	Grant	1813–1892
Ward Hunt	N.Y.	1872–1882	Grant	1810–1886
Joseph M. Harlan	Ky.	1877–1911	Hayes	1833–1911
William B. Woods	Ga.	1880–1887	Hayes	1824–1887
Stanley Matthews	Ohio	1881–1889	Garfield	1824–1889
Horace Gray	Mass.	1881–1902	Arthur	1828–1902
Samuel Blatchford	N.Y.	1882–1893	Arthur	1820–1893
Lucius Q. C. Lamar	Miss.	1888–1893	Cleveland	1825–1893
David J. Brewer	Kans.	1889–1910	B. Harrison	1837–1910
Henry B. Brown	Mich.	1890–1906	B. Harrison	1836–1913
George Shiras, Jr.	Pa.	1892–1903	B. Harrison	1832–1924
Howell E. Jackson	Tenn.	1893–1895	B. Harrison	1832–1895
Edward D. White*	La.	1894–1910	Cleveland	1845–1921
Rufus W. Peckham	N.Y.	1895–1909	Cleveland	1838–1909
Joseph McKenna	Calif.	1898–1925	McKinley	1843–1926
Oliver W. Holmes	Mass.	1902–1932	T. Roosevelt	1841–1935
William R. Day	Ohio	1903–1922	T. Roosevelt	1849–1923
William H. Moody	Mass.	1906–1910	T. Roosevelt	1853–1917
Horace L. Lurton	Tenn.	1909–1914	Taft	1844–1914
Charles E. Hughes**	N.Y.	1910–1916	Taft	1862–1948
Willis Van Devanter	Wyo.	1910–1937	Taft	1859–1941
Joseph R. Lamar	Ga.	1910–1916	Taft	1857–1916
Mahlon Pitney	N.J.	1912–1922	Taft	1858–1924
James C. McReynolds	Tenn.	1914–1941	Wilson	1862–1946
Louis D. Brandeis	Mass.	1916–1939	Wilson	1856–1941
John H. Clarke	Ohio	1916–1922	Wilson	1857–1945
George Sutherland	Utah	1922–1938	Harding	1862–1942
Pierce Butler	Minn.	1922–1939	Harding	1866–1939
Edward Sanford	Tenn.	1923–1930	Harding	1865–1930

* After serving as Associate Justice was appointed Chief Justice.
** After resigning as Associate Justice was later appointed Chief Justice.

Associate Justices	State	Served	Appointed by	Born/Died
Harlan F. Stone***	N.Y.	1925–1941	Coolidge	1872–1946
Owen J. Roberts	Pa.	1930–1945	Hoover	1875–1955
Benjamin N. Cardozo	N.Y.	1932–1938	Hoover	1870–1938
Hugo L. Black	Ala.	1937–1971	F. D. Roosevelt	1886–1971
Stanley F. Reed	Ky.	1938–1957	F. D. Roosevelt	1884–1980
Felix Frankfurter	Mass.	1939–1962	F. D. Roosevelt	1882–1965
William O. Douglas	Conn.	1939–1975	F. D. Roosevelt	1898–1980
Frank Murphy	Mich.	1940–1949	F. D. Roosevelt	1890–1949
James F. Byrnes	S.C.	1941–1942	F. D. Roosevelt	1879–1972
Robert H. Jackson	N.Y.	1941–1954	F. D. Roosevelt	1892–1954
Wiley B. Rutledge	Iowa	1943–1949	F. D. Roosevelt	1894–1949
Harold H. Burton	Ohio	1945–1958	Truman	1888–1964
Tom C. Clark	Tex.	1949–1967	Truman	1890–1977
Sherman Minton	Ind.	1949–1956	Truman	1890–1965
John M. Harlan	N.Y.	1955–1971	Eisenhower	1899–1971
William J. Brennan	N.J.	1956–	Eisenhower	1906–
Charles E. Whittaker	Mo.	1957–1962	Eisenhower	1901–1972
Potter Stewart	Ohio	1958–1981	Eisenhower	1915–1985
Byron R. White	Colo.	1962–	Kennedy	1917–
Arthur J. Goldberg	Ill.	1962–1965	Kennedy	1908–
Abe Fortas	Tenn.	1965–1969	Johnson	1910–1982
Thurgood Marshall	Md.	1967–	Johnson	1908–
Harry A. Blackmun	Minn.	1970–	Nixon	1908–
Lewis F. Powell, Jr.	Va.	1972–1987	Nixon	1907–
William H. Rehnquist*	Ariz.	1972–1986	Nixon	1924–
John Paul Stevens	Ill.	1975–	Ford	1920–
Sandra Day O'Connor	Ariz.	1981–	Reagan	1930–
Antonin Scalia	Va.	1986–	Reagan	1936–
Anthony Kennedy	Calif.	1987–	Reagan	1936–

* After serving as Associate Justice was appointed Chief Justice.
*** After serving as Associate Justice was appointed Chief Justice.

THE CONSTITUTION OF THE UNITED STATES

Adopted September 17, 1787
Effective March 4, 1789

We the people of the United States, in order to form a more perfect union, establish justice, insure domestic tranquillity, provide for the common defense, promote the general welfare, and secure the blessings of liberty to ourselves and our posterity, do ordain and establish this Constitution for the United States of America.

ARTICLE I

Section 1. All legislative powers herein granted shall be vested in a Congress of the United States, which shall consist of a Senate and House of Representatives.

Section 2. 1. The House of Representatives shall be composed of members chosen every second year by the people of the several states, and the electors in each state shall have the qualifications requisite for electors of the most numerous branch of the state legislature.

2. No person shall be a representative who shall not have attained to the age of twenty-five years, and been seven years a citizen of the United States, and who shall not, when elected, be an inhabitant of that state in which he shall be chosen.

3. Representatives and direct taxes,[1] shall be apportioned among the several states which may be included within this union, according to their respective numbers, which shall be determined by adding to the whole number of free persons, including those bound to service for a term of years, and

---

1 See the 16th Amendment.

excluding Indians not taxed, *three fifths of all other persons.*[2] The actual enumeration shall be made within three years after the first meeting of the Congress of the United States, and within every subsequent term of ten years, in such manner as they shall by law direct. The number of representatives shall not exceed one for every thirty thousand, but each state shall have at least one representative; and until such enumeration shall be made, the state of New Hampshire shall be entitled to choose three, Massachusetts eight, Rhode Island and Providence plantations one, Connecticut five, New York six, New Jersey four, Pennsylvania eight, Delaware one, Maryland six, Virginia ten, North Carolina five, South Carolina five, and Georgia three.

4. When vacancies happen in the representation from any state, the executive authority thereof shall issue writs of election to fill such vacancies.

5. The House of Representatives shall choose their speaker and other officers; and shall have the sole power of impeachment.

Section 3.   1. The Senate of the United States shall be composed of two senators from each state, *chosen by the legislature thereof,*[3] for six years; and each senator shall have one vote.

2. Immediately after they shall be assembled in consequence of the first election, they shall be divided as equally as may be into three classes. The seats of the senators of the first class shall be vacated at the expiration of the second year, of the second class at the expiration of the fourth year, and of the third class at the expiration of the sixth year, so that one third may be chosen every second year; and if vacancies happen by resignation, or otherwise, during the recess of the legislature of any state, the executive thereof may make temporary appointments until the next meeting of the legislature, which shall then fill such vacancies.[4]

3. No person shall be a senator who shall not have attained

---

2 See the 14th Amendment.
3 See the 17th Amendment.
4 See the 17th Amendment.

to the age of thirty years, and been nine years a citizen of the United States, and who shall not, when elected, be an inhabitant of that state for which he shall be chosen.

4. The vice-president of the United States shall be president of the Senate, but shall have no vote, unless they be equally divided.

5. The Senate shall choose their other officers, and also a president *pro tempore,* in the absence of the vice-president, or when he shall exercise the office of the president of the United States.

6. The Senate shall have the sole power to try all impeachments. When sitting for that purpose, they shall be on oath or affirmation. When the president of the United States is tried, the chief justice shall preside: and no person shall be convicted without the concurrence of two thirds of the members present.

7. Judgment in cases of impeachment shall not extend further than to removal from office, and disqualifications to hold and enjoy any office of honor, trust or profit under the United States: but the party convicted shall nevertheless be liable and subject to indictment, trial, judgment and punishment, according to law.

Section 4. 1. The times, places, and manner of holding elections for senators and representatives, shall be prescribed in each state by the legislature thereof; but the Congress may at any time by law make or alter such regulations, except as to the places of choosing senators.

2. The Congress shall assemble at least once in every year, and such meeting shall be on the first Monday in December, unless they shall by law appoint a different day.

Section 5. 1. Each House shall be the judge of the elections, returns and qualifications of its own members, and a majority of each shall constitute a quorum to do business; but a smaller number may adjourn from day to day, and may be authorized to compel the attendance of absent members, in such manner, and under such penalties as each House may provide.

2. Each House may determine the rules of its proceedings, punish its members for disorderly behavior, and, with the concurrence of two thirds, expel a member.

3. Each House shall keep a journal of its proceedings, and from time to time publish the same, excepting such parts as may in their judgment require secrecy; and the yeas and nays of the members of either House on any question shall, at the desire of one fifth of those present, be entered on the journal.

4. Neither House, during the session of Congress, shall, without the consent of the other, adjourn for more than three days, nor to any other place than that in which the two Houses shall be sitting.

Section 6. 1. The senators and representatives shall receive a compensation for their services, to be ascertained by law, and paid out of the treasury of the United States. They shall in all cases, except treason, felony, and breach of the peace, be privileged from arrest during their attendance at the session of their respective Houses, and in going to and returning from the same; and for any speech or debate in either House, they shall not be questioned in any other place.

2. No senator or representative shall, during the time for which he was elected, be appointed to any civil office under the authority of the United States, which shall have been created, or the emoluments whereof shall have been increased during such time; and no person holding any office under the United States shall be a member of either House during his continuance in office.

Section 7. 1. All bills for raising revenue shall originate in the House of Representatives; but the Senate may propose or concur with amendments as on other bills.

2. Every bill which shall have passed the House of Representatives and the Senate, shall, before it becomes a law, be presented to the president of the United States; if he approves he shall sign it, but if not he shall return it, with his objections to that House in which it shall have originated, who shall enter the objections at large on their journal, and proceed to reconsider it. If after such reconsideration two thirds of that House shall agree to pass the bill, it shall be sent, together with the objections, to the other House, by which it shall likewise be reconsidered, and if approved by two thirds of that House, it shall become a law. But in all such cases the votes of both

Houses shall be determined by yeas and nays, and the names of the persons voting for and against the bill shall be entered on the journal of each House respectively. If any bill shall not be returned by the president within ten days (Sundays excepted) after it shall have been presented to him, the same shall be a law, in like manner as if he had signed it, unless the Congress by their adjournment prevent its return, in which case it shall not be a law.

3. Every order, resolution, or vote to which the concurrence of the Senate and the House of Representatives may be necessary (except on a question of adjournment) shall be presented to the president of the United States; and before the same shall take effect, shall be approved by him, or being disapproved by him, shall be repassed by two thirds of the Senate and House of Representatives, according to the rules and limitations prescribed in the case of a bill.

Section 8. The Congress shall have the power

1. To lay and collect taxes, duties, imposts, and excises, to pay the debts and provide for the common defense and general welfare of the United States; but all duties, imposts, and excises shall be uniform throughout the United States;

2. To borrow money on the credit of the United States;

3. To regulate commerce with foreign nations, and among the several States, and with the Indian tribes;

4. To establish a uniform rule of naturalization, and uniform laws on the subject of bankruptcies throughout the United States;

5. To coin money, regulate the value thereof, and of foreign coin, and fix the standard of weights and measures;

6. To provide for the punishment of counterfeiting the securities and current coin of the United States;

7. To establish post offices and post roads;

8. To promote the progress of science and useful arts, by securing for limited times to authors and inventors the exclusive right to their respective writings and discoveries;

9. To constitute tribunals inferior to the Supreme Court;

10. To define and punish piracies and felonies committed on the high seas, and offenses against the law of nations;

11. To declare war, grant letters of marque and reprisal, and make rules concerning captures on land and water;

12. To raise and support armies, but no appropriation of money to that use shall be for a longer term than two years;

13. To provide and maintain a navy;

14. To make rules for the government and regulation of the land and naval forces;

15. To provide for calling forth the militia to execute the laws of the Union, suppress insurrections and repel invasions;

16. To provide for organizing, arming, and disciplining the militia, and for governing such part of them as may be employed in the service of the United States, reserving to the States respectively, the appointment of the officers, and the authority of training the militia according to the discipline prescribed by Congress.

17. To exercise exclusive legislation in all cases whatsoever, over such district (not exceeding ten miles square) as may, by cession of particular states, and the acceptance of Congress, become the seat of the government of the United States, and to exercise like authority over all places purchased by the consent of the legislature of the state in which the same shall be, for the erection of forts, magazines, arsenals, dockyards, and other needful buildings; and

18. To make all laws which shall be necessary and proper for carrying into execution the foregoing powers, and all other powers vested by this Constitution in the government of the United States, or in any department or officer thereof.

Section 9. 1. The migration or importation of such persons as any of the states now existing shall think proper to admit, shall not be prohibited by the Congress prior to the year one thousand eight hundred and eight, but a tax or duty may be imposed on such importation, not exceeding ten dollars for each person.

2. The privilege of the writ of *habeas corpus* shall not be suspended, unless when in cases of rebellion or invasion the public safety may require it.

3. No bill of attainder or *ex post facto* law shall be passed.

4. No capitation, or other direct, tax shall be laid, unless in

proportion to the census or enumeration hereinbefore directed to be taken.[5]

5. No tax or duty shall be laid on articles exported from any State.

6. No preference shall be given by any regulation of commerce or revenue to the ports of one state over those of another: nor shall vessels bound to, or from, one state be obliged to enter, clear, or pay duties in another.

7. No money shall be drawn from the treasury, but in consequence of appropriations made by law; and a regular statement and account of the receipts and expenditures of all public money shall be published from time to time.

8. No title of nobility shall be granted by the United States: and no person holding any office of profit or trust under them, shall, without the consent of the Congress, accept of any present, emolument, office, or title, of any kind whatever, from any king, prince, or foreign state.

Section 10. 1. No state shall enter into any treaty, alliance, or confederation; grant letters of marque and reprisal; coin money; emit bills of credit; make anything but gold and silver coin a tender in payment of debts; pass any bill of attainder, *ex post facto* law, or law impairing the obligation of contracts, or grant any title of nobility.

2. No state shall, without the consent of the Congress, lay any imposts or duties on imports or exports, except what may be absolutely necessary for executing its inspection laws: and the net produce of all duties and imposts laid by any state on imports or exports, shall be for the use of the treasury of the United States; and all such laws shall be subject to the revision and control of the Congress.

3. No state shall, without the consent of the Congress, lay any duty of tonnage, keep troops, or ships of war in time of peace, enter into any agreement or compact with another state, or with a foreign power, or engage in war, unless actually invaded, or in such imminent danger as will not admit of delay.

---

5 See the 16th Amendment.

ARTICLE II

Section 1. 1. The executive power shall be vested in a president of the United States of America. He shall hold his office during the term of four years, and, together with the vice-president, chosen for the same term, be elected as follows:

2. Each state shall appoint, in such manner as the legislature thereof may direct, a number of electors, equal to the whole number of senators and representatives to which the state may be entitled in the Congress: but no senator or representative, or person holding an office of trust or profit under the United States, shall be appointed an elector.

The electors shall meet in their respective states, and vote by ballot for two persons, of whom one at least shall not be an inhabitant of the same state with themselves. And they shall make a list of all the persons voted for, and of the number of votes for each; which list they shall sign and certify, and transmit sealed to the seat of the government of the United States, directed to the president of the Senate. The president of the Senate shall, in the presence of the Senate and House of Representatives, open all the certificates, and the votes shall then be counted. The person having the greatest number of votes shall be the president, if such number be a majority of the whole number of electors appointed; and if there be more than one who have such majority, and have an equal number of votes, then the House of Representatives shall immediately choose by ballot one of them for president; and if no person have a majority, then from the five highest on the list the said House shall in like manner choose the president. But in choosing the president, the votes shall be taken by states, the representation from each state having one vote; a quorum for this purpose shall consist of a member or members from two thirds of the states, and a majority of all the states shall be necessary to a choice. In every case, after the choice of the president, the person having the greatest number of votes of the electors shall be the vice-president. But if there should remain two or more who have equal votes, the Senate shall choose from them by ballot the vice-president.[6]

3. The Congress may determine the time of choosing the electors, and the day on which they shall give their votes; which day shall be the same throughout the United States.

4. No person except a natural born citizen, or a citizen of the United States, at the time of the adoption of this Constitution, shall be eligible to the office of president; neither shall any person be eligible to that office who shall not have attained to the age of thirty-five years, and been fourteen years a resident within the United States.

5. In case of the removal of the president from office, or of his death, resignation, or inability to discharge the powers and duties of the said office, the same shall devolve on the vice-president, and the Congress may by law provide for the case of removal, death, resignation, or inability, both of the president and vice-president, declaring what officer shall then act as president, and such officer shall act accordingly, until the disability be removed, or a president shall be elected.

6. The president shall, at stated times, receive for his services a compensation, which shall neither be increased nor diminished during the period for which he shall have been elected, and he shall not receive within that period any other emolument from the United States, or any of them.

7. Before he enter on the execution of his office, he shall take the following oath or affirmation:—"I do solemnly swear (or affirm) that I will faithfully execute the office of president of the United States, and will to the best of my ability, preserve, protect and defend the Constitution of the United States."

Section 2. 1. The president shall be commander in chief of the army and navy of the United States, and of the militia of the several states, when called into the actual service of the United States; he may require the opinion, in writing, of the principal officer in each of the executive departments, upon any subject relating to the duties of their respective offices,

---

6 Superseded by the 12th Amendment.

and he shall have power to grant reprieves and pardons for offenses against the United States, except in cases of impeachment.

2. He shall have power, by and with the advice and consent of the Senate, to make treaties, provided two thirds of the senators present concur; and he shall nominate, and by and with the advice and consent of the Senate, shall appoint ambassadors, other public ministers and consuls, judges of the Supreme Court, and all other officers of the United States, whose appointments are not herein otherwise provided for, and which shall be established by law: but the Congress may by law vest the appointment of such inferior officers, as they think proper, in the president alone, in the courts of law, or in the heads of departments.

3. The president shall have power to fill up all vacancies that may happen during the recess of the Senate, by granting commissions which shall expire at the end of their next session.

Section 3.   He shall from time to time give to the Congress information of the state of the Union, and recommend to their consideration such measures as he shall judge necessary and expedient; he may, on extraordinary occasions, convene both Houses, or either of them, and in case of disagreement between them with respect to the time of adjournment, he may adjourn them to such time as he shall think proper; he shall receive ambassadors and other public ministers; he shall take care that the laws be faithfully executed, and shall commission all the officers of the United States.

Section 4.   The president, vice-president, and all civil officers of the United States, shall be removed from office on impeachment for, and conviction of, treason, bribery, or other high crimes and misdemeanors.

ARTICLE III

Section 1.   The judicial power of the United States shall be vested in one Supreme Court, and in such inferior courts as the Congress may from time to time ordain and establish. The judges, both of the Supreme and inferior courts, shall hold their offices during good behavior, and shall, at stated times, receive for their services, a compensation, which, shall not be diminished during their continuance in office.

Section 2. 1. The judicial power shall extend to all cases, in law and equity, arising under this Constitution, the laws of the United States, and treaties made, or which shall be made, under their authority;—to all cases affecting ambassadors, other public ministers and consuls;—to all cases of admiralty and maritime jurisdiction;—to controversies to which the United States shall be a party;—to controversies between two or more states; between a state and citizens of another state;⁷—between citizens of different states;—between citizens of the same state claiming lands under grants of different states, and between a state, or the citizens thereof, and foreign states citizens or subjects.

2. In all cases affecting ambassadors, other public ministers and consuls, and those in which a state shall be party, the Supreme Court shall have original jurisdiction. In all the other cases before mentioned, the Supreme Court shall have appellate jurisdiction, both as to law and to fact, with such exceptions, and under such regulations as the Congress shall make.

3. The trial of all crimes, except in cases of impeachment, shall be by jury; and such trial shall be held in the state where the said crimes shall have been committed; but when not committed within any state, the trial shall be at such place or places as the Congress may by law have directed.

Section 3. 1. Treason against the United States shall consist only in levying war against them, or in adhering to their enemies, giving them aid and comfort. No person shall be convicted of treason unless on the testimony of two witnesses to the same overt act, or on confession in open court.

2. The Congress shall have power to declare the punishment of treason, but no attainder of treason shall work corruption of blood, or forfeiture except during the life of the person attainted.

---

7 See the 11th Amendment.

ARTICLE IV

Section 1.   Full faith and credit shall be given in each state to the public acts, records, and judicial proceedings of every other state. And the Congress may by general laws prescribe the manner in which such acts, records and proceedings shall be proved, and the effect thereof.

Section 2.   1. The citizens of each state shall be entitled to all privileges and immunities of citizens in the several states.[8]

2. A person charged in any state with treason, felony, or other crime, who shall flee from justice, and be found in another state, shall on demand of the executive authority of the state having jurisdiction of the crime.

3. No person held to service or labor in one state under the laws thereof, escaping into another, shall in consequence of any law or regulation therein, be discharged from such service or labor, but shall be delivered up on claim of the party to whom such service or labor may be due.[9]

Section 3.   1. New states may be admitted by the Congress into this Union; but no new state shall be formed or erected within the jurisdiction of any other state, nor any state be formed by the junction of two or more states, or parts of states, without the consent of the legislatures of the states concerned as well as of the Congress.

2. The Congress shall have power to dispose of and make all needful rules and regulations respecting the territory or other property belonging to the United States; and nothing in this Constitution shall be so construed as to prejudice any claims of the United States, or of any particular state.

Section 4.   The United States shall guarantee to every state in this Union a republican form of government, and shall protect each of them against invasion; and on application of the legislature, or of the executive (when the legislature cannot be convened) against domestic violence.

---

8 See the 14th Amendment, Sec. 1.
9 See the 13th Amendment.

ARTICLE V

The Congress, whenever two thirds of both Houses shall deem it necessary, shall propose amendments to this Constitution, or, on the application of the legislature of two thirds of the several states, shall call a convention for proposing amendments, which in either case, shall be valid to all intents and purposes, as part of this Constitution when ratified by the legislatures of three fourths of the several states, or by conventions in three fourths thereof, as the one or the other mode of ratification may be proposed by the Congress; Provided that no amendment which may be made prior to the year one thousand eight hundred and eight shall in any manner affect the first and fourth clauses in the ninth section of the first article; and that no state, without its consent, shall be deprived of its equal suffrage in the Senate.

ARTICLE VI

1. All debts contracted and engagements entered into, before the adoption of this Constitution, shall be as valid against the United States under this Constitution, as under the Confederation.[10]

2. This Constitution, and the laws of the United States which shall be made in pursuance thereof; and all treaties made, or which shall be made, under the authority of the United States, shall be the supreme law of the land; and the Judges in every state shall be bound thereby, anything in the Constitution or laws of any state to the contrary notwithstanding.

3. The senators and representatives before mentioned, and the members of the several state legislatures, and all executive and judicial officers, both of the United States and of the several states, shall be bound by oath or affirmation to support this Constitution; but no religious test shall ever be required

---

10 See the 14th Amendment, Sec. 4.

as a qualification to any office or public trust under the United States.

ARTICLE VII

The ratification of the conventions of nine states shall be sufficient for the establishment of this Constitution between the states so ratifying the same.

Done in Convention by the unanimous consent of the States present the seventeenth day of September in the year of our Lord one thousand seven hundred and eighty-seven, and of the independence of the United States of America the twelfth. In witness whereof we have hereunto subscribed our names.   [Names omitted]
_____

Articles in addition to, and amendment of, the Constitution of the United States of America, proposed by Congress, and ratified by the legislatures of the several states pursuant to the fifth article of the original Constitution.

AMENDMENTS

First Ten Amendments passed by Congress Sept. 25, 1789.
Ratified by three-fourths of the States December 15, 1791.

ARTICLE I

Congress shall make no law respecting an establishment of religion, or prohibiting the free exercise thereof; or abridging the freedom of speech, or of the press; or the right of the people peaceably to assemble, and to petition the government for a redress of grievances.

ARTICLE II

A well regulated militia, being necessary to the security of a free state, the right of the people to keep and bear arms, shall not be infringed.

ARTICLE III

No soldier shall, in time of peace be quartered in any house, without the consent of the owner, nor in time of war, but in a manner to be prescribed by law.

ARTICLE IV

The right of the people to be secure in their persons, houses, papers, and effects, against unreasonable searches and seizures, shall not be violated, and no warrants shall issue, but upon probable cause, supported by oath or affirmation, and particularly describing the place to be searched, and the persons or things to be seized.

ARTICLE V

No person shall be held to answer for a capital, or otherwise infamous crime, unless on a presentment or indictment of a grand jury, except in cases arising in the land or naval forces, or in the militia, when in actual service in time of war or public danger; nor shall any person be subject for the same offense to be twice put in jeopardy of life or limb; nor shall be compelled in any criminal case to be a witness against himself, nor be deprived of life, liberty, or property, without due process of law: nor shall private property be taken for public use without just compensation.

ARTICLE VI

In all criminal prosecutions, the accused shall enjoy the right to a speedy and public trial, by an impartial jury of the state and district wherein the crime shall have been committed, which district shall have been previously ascertained by law, and to be informed of the nature and cause of the accusation; to be confronted with the witnesses against him; to have compulsory process for obtaining witnesses in his favor, and to have the assistance of counsel for his defense.

ARTICLE VII

In suits at common law, where the value in controversy shall exceed twenty dollars, the right of trial by jury shall be preserved, and no fact tried by a jury shall be otherwise reexamined in any court of the United States, than according to the rules of the common law.

ARTICLE VIII

Excessive bail shall not be required, nor excessive fines imposed, nor cruel and unusual punishments inflicted.

ARTICLE IX

The enumeration in the Constitution of certain rights shall not be construed to deny or disparage others retained by the people.

ARTICLE X

The powers not delegated to the United States by the Constitution, nor prohibited by it to the states, are reserved to the states respectively, or to the people.

ARTICLE XI

Passed by Congress March 5, 1794. Ratified January 8, 1798.

The judicial power of the United States shall not be construed to extend to any suit in law or equity, commenced or prosecuted against one of the United States by citizens of another state, or by citizens or subjects of any foreign state.

ARTICLE XII

Passed by Congress December 12, 1803. Ratified September 25, 1804.

The electors shall meet in their respective states, and vote by ballot for president and vice-president, one of whom, at least, shall not be an inhabitant of the same state with themselves; they shall name in their ballots the person voted for as president, and in distinct ballots, the person voted for as vice-president, and they shall make distinct lists of all persons voted for as president and of all persons voted for as vice-president, and of the number of votes for each, which lists they shall sign and certify, and transmit sealed to the seat of the government of the United States, directed to the president of the Senate;—The president of the Senate shall, in the presence of the Senate and House of Representatives, open all the certificates and the votes shall then be counted;—The person having the greatest number of votes for president, shall be the president, if such number be a majority of the whole number of electors appointed; and if no person have such majority, then from the persons having the highest numbers not exceeding three on the list of those voted for as president, the House of Representatives shall choose immediately, by ballot, the president. But in choosing the president, the votes shall be taken by states, the representation from each state having one vote; a quorum for this purpose shall consist of a member or members from two thirds of the states, and a majority of all the states shall be necessary to a choice. And if the House of Representatives shall not choose a president whenever the right of choice shall devolve upon them, before the fourth day of March next following, then the vice-president shall act as president, as in the case of the death or other constitutional disability of the president. The person having the greatest number of votes as vice-president shall be the vice-president, if such number be a majority of the whole number of electors appointed, and if no person have a majority, then from the two highest numbers on the list, the Senate shall choose the vice-president; a quorum for the purpose shall consist of two thirds of the whole number of Senators, and a majority of the whole number shall be necessary to a choice. But no person constitutionally ineligible to the office of president shall be eligible to that of vice-president of the United States.

ARTICLE XIII

Passed by Congress February 1, 1865. Ratified December 18, 1865.

Section 1.   Neither slavery nor involuntary servitude, except as punishment for crime whereof the party shall have been duly convicted, shall exist within the United States, or any place subject to their jurisdiction.

Section 2.   Congress shall have power to enforce this article by appropriate legislation.

ARTICLE XIV

Passed by Congress June 16, 1866. Ratified July 23, 1868.

Section 1.   All persons born or naturalized in the United States, and subject to the jurisdiction thereof, are citizens of the United States and of the state wherein they reside. No state shall make or enforce any law which shall abridge the privileges or immunities of citizens of the United States; nor shall any state deprive any person of life, liberty, or property, without due process of law; nor deny to any person within its jurisdiction the equal protection of the laws.

Section 2.   Representatives shall be apportioned among the several States according to their respective numbers, counting the whole number of persons in each state, excluding Indians not taxed. But when the right to vote at any election for the choice of electors for president and vice-president of the United States, representatives in Congress, the executive and judicial officers of a state, or the members of the legislature thereof, is denied to any of the male inhabitants of such state, being twenty-one years of age, and citizens of the United States, or in any way abridged, except for participation in rebellion, or other crime, the basis of representation therein shall be reduced in the proportion which the number of such male citizens shall bear to the whole number of male citizens twenty-one years of age in such state.

Section 3.   No person shall be a senator or representative in Congress, or elector of president and vice-president, or hold any office, civil or military, under the United States, or under any state, who having previously taken an oath, as a member of Congress, or as an officer of the United States, or as a member of any state legislature, or as an executive or judicial officer of any state, to support the Constitution of the United States, shall have engaged in insurrection or rebellion against the same, or given aid or comfort to the enemies thereof. But Congress may by a vote of two thirds of each House, remove such disability.

Section 4. The validity of the public debt of the United States, authorized by law, including debts incurred for payment of pensions and bounties for services in suppressing insurrection or rebellion, shall not be questioned. But neither the United States nor any state shall assume or pay any debt or obligation incurred in aid of insurrection or rebellion against the United States, or any claim for the loss or emancipation of any slave; but all such debts, obligations, and claims shall be held illegal and void.

Section 5. The Congress shall have power to enforce, by appropriate legislation, the provisions of this article.

ARTICLE XV

Passed by Congress February 27, 1869. Ratified March 30, 1870.

Section 1. The right of citizens of the United States to vote shall not be denied or abridged by the United States or by any state on account of race, color, or previous condition of servitude.

Section 2. The Congress shall have power to enforce this article by appropriate legislation.

ARTICLE XVI

Passed by Congress July 12, 1909. Ratified February 25, 1913.

The Congress shall have power to lay and collect taxes on incomes, from whatever source derived, without apportionment among the several states, and without regard to any census or enumeration.

ARTICLE XVII

Passed by Congress May 16, 1912. Ratified May 31, 1913.

The Senate of the United States shall be composed of two senators from each state, elected by the people thereof, for six years; and each senator shall have one vote. The electors in each state shall have the qualifications requisite for electors of the most numerous branch of the state legislature.

When vacancies happen in the representation of any state in the Senate, the executive authority of such state shall issue writs of election to fill such vacancies: *Provided,* That the legislature of any state may empower the executive thereof to make temporary appointments until the people fill the vacancies by election as the legislature may direct.

This amendment shall not be so construed as to affect the election or term of any senator chosen before it becomes valid as part of the Constitution.

ARTICLE XVIII

Passed by Congress December 17, 1917. Ratified January 29, 1919.

After one year from the ratification of this article, the manufacture, sale, or transportation of intoxicating liquors within, the importation thereof into, or the exportation thereof from the United States and all territory subject to the jurisdiction thereof for beverage purposes is hereby prohibited.

The Congress and the several states shall have concurrent power to enforce this article by appropriate legislation.

This article shall be inoperative unless it shall have been ratified as an amendment to the Constitution by the legislatures of the several states, as provided in the Constitution, within seven years from the date of the submission hereof to the states by Congress.

ARTICLE XIX

Passed by Congress June 5, 1919. Ratified August 26, 1920.

The right of citizens of the United States to vote shall not be denied or abridged by the United States or by any state on account of sex.

The Congress shall have power by appropriate legislation to enforce the provisions of this article.

ARTICLE XX

Passed by Congress March 3, 1932. Ratified January 23, 1933.

Section 1. The terms of the president and vice-president shall end at noon on the 20th day of January, and the terms of Senators and Representatives at noon on the 3d day of January, of the years in which such terms would have ended if this article had not been ratified; and the terms of their successors shall then begin.

Section 2. The Congress shall assemble at least once in every year, and such meeting shall begin at noon on the 3d day of January, unless they shall by law appoint a different day.

Section 3. If, at the time fixed for the beginning of the term of the president, the president-elect shall have died, the vice-president-elect shall become president. If a president shall not have been chosen before the time fixed for the beginning of his term, or if the president-elect shall have failed to qualify, then the vice-president-elect shall act as president until a president shall have qualified; and the Congress may by law provide for the case wherein neither a president-elect nor a vice-president-elect shall have qualified, declaring who shall then act as president, or the manner in which one who is to act shall be selected, and such person shall act accordingly until a president or vice-president shall have qualified.

Section 4. The Congress may by law provide for the case of the death of any of the persons from whom the House of Representatives may choose a president whenever the right of choice shall have devolved upon them, and for the case of the death of any of the persons from whom the Senate may choose a vice-president whenever the right of choice shall have devolved upon them.

Section 5. Sections 1 and 2 shall take effect on the 15th day of October following the ratification of this article.

Section 6. This article shall be inoperative unless it shall have been ratified as an amendment to the Constitution by the legislatures of three-fourths of the several states within seven years from the date of its submission.

ARTICLE XXI

Passed by Congress February 20, 1933. Ratified December 5, 1933.

Section 1. The Eighteenth Article of amendment to the Constitution of the United States is hereby repealed.

Section 2. The transportation or importation into any state, territory, or possession of the United States for delivery or use therein of intoxicating liquors in violation of the laws thereof, is hereby prohibited.

Section 3. This article shall be inoperative unless it shall have been ratified as an amendment to the Constitution by conventions in the several states, as provided in the Constitution, within seven years from the date of the submission thereof to the states by the Congress.

ARTICLE XXII

Passed by Congress March 24, 1947. Ratified February 26, 1951.

Section 1. No person shall be elected to the office of the president more than twice, and no person who has held the office of president, or acted as president, for more than two years of a term to which some other person was elected president shall be elected to the office of the president more than once. But this article shall not apply to any person holding the office of president when this article was proposed by the Congress, and shall not prevent any person who may be holding the office of president, or acting as president, during the term within which this article becomes operative from holding the office of president or acting as president during the remainder of such term.

Section 2. This article shall be inoperative unless it shall have been ratified as an amendment to the Constitution by the legislatures of three-fourths of the several states within seven years from the date of its submission to the states by the Congress.

ARTICLE XXIII

Passed by Congress June 16, 1960. Ratified Mar. 29, 1961.

Section 1. The district constituting the seat of government of the United States shall appoint such manner as the Congress may direct:

A number of electors of president and vice-president equal to the whole number of Senators and Representatives in Congress to which the district would be entitled if it were a state, but in no event more than the least populous state; they shall be in addition to those appointed by the states, but they shall be considered, for the purposes of election of president and vice-president, to be electors appointed by a state; and they shall meet in the district and perform such duties as provided by the twelfth article of amendment.

Section 2. The Congress shall have the power to enforce this article by appropriate legislation.

ARTICLE XXIV

Passed by Congress Aug. 27, 1962. Ratified Jan. 23, 1964.

Section 1. The right of citizens of the United States to vote in any primary or other election for president or vice-president, for electors for president or vice-president, or for Senator or Representative in Congress, shall not be denied or abridged by the United States or any state by failure to pay any poll tax or other tax.

Section 2. The Congress shall have the power to enforce this article by appropriate legislation.

ARTICLE XXV

Passed by Congress Jul. 6, 1965. Ratified Feb. 10, 1967.

Section 1. In case of the removal of the president from office or of his death or resignation, the vice-president shall become president.

Section 2. Whenever there is a vacancy in the office of the vice-president, the president shall nominate a vice-president who shall take office upon confirmation by a majority vote of both Houses of Congress.

Section 3.   Whenever the president transmits to the president pro tempore of the Senate and the Speaker of the House of Representatives his written declaration that he is unable to discharge the powers and duties of his office, and until he transmits to them a written declaration to the contrary, such powers and duties shall be discharged by the vice-president as acting president.

Section 4.   Whenever the vice-president and a majority of either the principal officers of the executive departments or of such other body as Congress may by law provide, transmit to the president pro tempore of the Senate and the Speaker of the House of Representatives their written declaration that the president is unable to discharge the powers and duties of his office, the vice-president shall immediately assume the powers and duties of the office as acting president.

Thereafter, when the president transmits to the president pro tempore of the Senate and the Speaker of the House of Representatives his written declaration that no inability exists, he shall resume the powers and duties of his office unless the vice-president and a majority of either the principal officers of the executive department or of such other body as Congress may by law provide, transmit within four days to the president pro tempore of the Senate and the Speaker of the House of Representatives their written declaration that the president is unable to discharge the powers and duties of his office. Thereupon Congress shall decide the issue, assembling within forty-eight hours for that purpose if not in session. If the Congress, within twenty-one days after receipt of the latter written declaration, or, if Congress is not in session, within twenty-one days after Congress is required to assemble, determines by two-thirds vote of both Houses that the president is unable to discharge the powers and duties of his office, the vice-president shall continue to discharge the same as acting president; otherwise, the president shall resume the powers and duties of his office.

ARTICLE XXVI

Passed by Congress March 23, 1971. Ratified June 30, 1971.

Section 1. The right of citizens of the United States, who are eighteen years of age or older, to vote shall not be denied or abridged by the United States or by any State on account of age.

Section 2. The Congress shall have power to enforce this article by appropriate legislation.

GLOSSARY

Legal Terms

Administrative law   Branch of law that creates administrative agencies, establishes their methods of procedure and the scope of judicial review of agency practices.

Adversary system   Legal proceeding with opposing parties who contest an issue or issues.

Amnesty   An act of "forgetfulness" by a sovereign state for a crime committed. A pardon is "forgiveness." Amnesty is usually granted for political offenses while pardon is for criminal acts. Amnesty is usually a group action whereas pardons are individual in their application.

Appellant   Party who appeals an adverse decision from one court or jurisdiction to another.

Appellee   Party in a suit against whom an appeal is taken. One who opposes an appellant.

Attainder   Legislative act directed against a specific person charged with a crime, pronouncing him guilty without a judicial trial. Usually without following recognized rules of procedure.

Bail   Freedom given accused person who posts an appearance bond.

Bankruptcy   Insolvency or the inability to pay one's debts. A legal process in which assets are sold to pay creditors and allow the debtor to start anew.

Beyond a reasonable doubt   Proof required for conviction in a criminal trial necessary to overcome a presumption of accused's innocence. Proof must be more than skepticism and less than absolutely no possibility of error.

Bill of Rights   First ten amendments to the U.S. Constitution and also those enumerated in state constitutions which list rights a person enjoys that cannot be infringed by governments.

Brief   Written notes citing issues, legal points, precedents, and arguments that constitute the essentials of a case.

Capital crime   One for which the death penalty may, but not necessarily, must be inflicted.

Case or controversy   Facts that furnish an occasion for the exercise of the jurisdiction of a court. Terms are distinguishable because multiple controversies may exist within a single case. Issues must be real and parties must be clearly identifiable and time for judicial determination "ripe."

Change of venue   Venue designates the place where a court of competent jurisdiction may hear and decide a case. A transfer to a different trial place may be permitted if unfairness or other difficulties make desirable a change of the situs of the trial at the request of the defendant.

Civil liberties   Immunities from governmental interference or limitations on governmental actions that reserve and preserve individual rights. This concept is negative in its nature.

Civil rights   A positive concept of rights possessed, defined, and circumscribed by laws for use and protection of citizens. Thus rights are claimed, asserted, and protected whereas liberties inhibit the actions of officials.

Closed shop   Labor bargaining unit whereby only union members may be employed. (See **Open shop** and **Union shop**.)

Code   Complete system of positive law, scientifically arranged, and promulgated by legislative authority. Compilation of existing laws into a logical and understandable whole relative to subjects to which they relate.

Collusion   Secret agreement between two or more persons with apparently conflicting interests to deceive a court and obtain an unlawful and unfair advantage over a third party.

Comity   Principle that one state or jurisdiction will give effect to the laws and judicial decisions of another as a matter of courtesy and deference. Also called "full faith and credit."

Common law   Body of law and theory, developed in England from custom and ancient usages that has provided a base for most states' judicial systems. This base is one that modifies or complements law created by legislative enactments termed statutory law. Also called "case law."

Commutation   An executive act that changes a punishment from greater to less. It differs from a pardon because there is no "forgiveness" of the crime. A reprieve is a "postponement" of the penalty.

Compact   Agreement or convention between two or more sovereign nations or states which creates obligations between their independent parts. Mutual consent resulting in binding law is the basis on which such relationship exists.

Contempt of court   Act calculated to embarrass or obstruct a court or lessen its authority or dignity.

Contract   Legally enforceable promise between two or more persons that creates or modifies a legal relationship. Legal consideration is necessary as a valid "offer" and "acceptance."

Court of record   Those whose proceedings are permanently recorded and which have authority to fine or imprison for contempt.

Declaratory judgment   Decision by a court to establish rights of the parties or express an opinion of the court on a question of law without ordering anything to be done. It stands by itself and no executory process follows.

Delegated powers   Powers granted to the national government under the Constitution. The first three articles enumerate them relative to the legislative, executive, and judicial branches. Such powers may be specific or implied. Power, which results from several read in combination, are termed "resulting powers."

Directed verdict   Jury verdict in either a civil or criminal case by order of the trial judge when opposing party fails to present a prima facie case or an adequate defense.

Domicile   Place where individual has permanent home and if absent has intention to return. Law presumes every person possesses one.

Double jeopardy   Provision in Fifth Amendment which prohibits double punishment and double prosecution in criminal suits for the same offense.

Due process   Consists of two types: procedural and substantive. Daniel Webster defined the first as that "which hears before it condemns, which proceeds upon inquiry, and renders judgment only after trial." Substantive due process is denied if any part of the trial or result "shocks the conscience of the court." (See **Fair trial**.)

Elastic clause   Final paragraph of Article I, Section 8 of the U.S. Constitution, which delegates powers to Congress authorizing all laws "necessary and proper" to carry out enumerated powers. Clause allows Congress to choose "means" by which it will execute its authority. It has enabled national government to adjust to needs of the times and reduce need for Amendments. (See **Necessary and proper clause**.)

Eminent domain   Right of sovereign to take private property for public use or public purpose on payment of just compensation.

Enabling act   Act of Congress authorizing people of a territory to take the necessary steps to prepare for statehood. Includes calling a convention to draft a constitution and preparing to conduct elections.

Equal protection   Requirement of Fourteenth Amendment that state laws not arbitrarily discriminate against persons. Identical treatment is not required nor is classification forbidden so long as either bears a reasonable relationship to the end sought. Three areas exist: (a) where any discrimination is clearly illegal, (b) suspect areas that will be carefully scrutinized by courts, and (c) no public involvement can be found and no protection will be afforded.

Establishment clause   Basic principle of American government set forth in First Amendment which forbids involvement of church and state. Position of neutrality must be maintained by state and it may neither advance nor retard religion. No public funds may be extended on behalf of any church, nor shall any public school be used for sectarian religious observances. Courts have attempted to distinguish between services that are primarily of benefit to pupils and those that advance religious tenets. (See **Separation of church and state.**)

Estoppel   Person's own act, which percludes him from making a contrary claim.

Exclusionary rule   Rule of law that otherwise admissible evidence may not be used in a criminal trial if it was obtained by police conduct that was illegal.

Fair trial   Hearing by an impartial court that usually utilizes a properly selected jury, an impartial judge, an atmosphere of calm, available witnesses testifying without fear or favor, a defendant represented by competent attorneys who assert their client's rights forcefully and fully, and all ascertainable, relevant truths sought to be considered. The test should not be observance only of proper rules of procedure, but the subjective question was "Was it fair?" (See **Due process.**)

Felony   Serious crime distinguished from those minor or lesser-termed misdemeanors. Usually, the distinction is based on whether or not the maximum penalty that *could be* imposed is one year or more imprisonment. If so, the crime is a felony.

Full faith and credit   Article 4, Section 1 requires that court judgments, records, public acts, and court decisions of one state be treated as equally binding in the courts of all the other states. (See **Comity.**)

General welfare   Article I, Section 8 of the U.S. Constitution authorizes Congress to lay and collect taxes, provide for the common defense and general welfare of the United States. Liberals and strict constructionists argue about whether this is an unlimited grant of power or whether it is a grant limited to only those authorized by other sections of the Constitution. A liberal view has prevailed and the spending power of Congress has not been successfully challenged.

Gerrymander Drawing of legislative district boundary lines in order to obtain a partisan or a factional advantage.

Government corporation Agency of government which administers a business enterprise. Activity is usually commercial, produces revenue and needs greater flexibility than regular departments. State level equivalents are normally called "Authorities."

Grand jury Investigative body which is part of court system whose duty it is to accuse persons (indict) when sufficient evidence has been presented or discovered to justify holding a person for trial.

Grandfather clause Exempting existing persons or businesses from restrictive provisions of a civil law which would be retroactive in application. Such a clause protects an already established business from meeting newly created criteria.

Guardian-ad-litem Person lawfully empowered and charged with the duty of prosecuting or defending a minor in any suit to which he is a party. Generally used when suit on behalf of a minor is termed by "next friend" of plaintiff.

Harmless error One not sufficiently prejudicial to an appellant or does not affect his substantive rights so as to justify a reviewing court from over-turning or modifying the lower court decision. (See **Reversible error.**)

Hatch acts Two corrupt practice acts passed in 1939 and 1940 which forbad civil service employees from being pressured to make political contributions or to participate actively in partisan political activities. The first act applied to federal employees and the second to state and local political appointees.

High crimes and misdemeanors   Term has never been precisely defined. Discretion is vested completely in Congress to define term. In practice the phrase is usually restricted to unethical conduct and criminal offenses; not incompetence or political disagreement.

Hung jury   Trial jury that is unable to reach any agreement on the guilt or innocence of the defendant.

Immunity   Legal exemption from a duty which would otherwise be imposed, such as testifying in a criminal trial. (See **Judicial immunity.**)

Impeach   To question the truthfulness of a witness's testimony or to charge a public official with a crime by a legislative body whom, if convicted, would cause his removal from office.

Implied powers   Inferred powers possessed by the national government from those specifically enumerated in the U.S. Constitution. Concept is derived from the "necessary and proper" clause in Article I, Section 8. (See **Necessary and proper,** and **Elastic clauses.**)

Indictment   Criminal accusation by a grand jury. Must be written and of sufficient clarity to inform the accused of the nature of his crime. (See **Information,** and **Grand jury.**)

Information   Criminal accusation by a competent public official and not by a grand jury. Must be written and sworn to before a proper magistrate. (See **Indictment.**)

Inherent powers   Authority vested in the national government, particularly in the area of foreign affairs, that does not depend on a specific grant of power. They are derived from the fact that the United States is a sovereign power.

Injunction   Order issued by a court in an equity proceeding to compel or restrain an act. Mandatory ones compel the performance of an act and prohibitory ones restrain.

Interlocutory   Order or court decree that is not final.

Interstate commerce   Buying and selling; transportation of goods and persons, navigable waters, commercial intercourse, electronic communication, and all the necessary facilities are subject to national regulation and control if they affect more than one state.

Intestate   Deceased who does not leave a will.

Involuntary servitude   Persons compelled by force, coercion, imprisonment, or against their will to labor for another. (See **Servitude**.)

Judicial activist   Person who believes the court system should determine desirable social policy when legislatures or Congress fail to do so.

Judicial immunity   Legal exception from duty to testify on a claim of self-incrimination whereupon court absolves witness from any criminal penalty, thereby coercing witness to testify.

Judicial notice   Court takes note of certain facts known to most people and thereby eliminating need for producing evidence necessary to prove their existence.

Judicial power   Authority exercised by that branch of government charged with declaring what law is and its construction or meaning.

Judicial review   Power of courts to declare invalid acts of legislatures and executive agencies, as well as subordinate courts.

Jurisdiction   Authority vested in a court to hear and decide a case.

Jury (grand)   See **Grand jury.**

Jury (trial)   Sometimes called petit jury. An impartial body that sits in judgment of facts in either civil or criminal cases. Under common law (frequently changed by statute) trial jury must consist of twelve persons and reach a unanimous verdict.

Justiciable question   Dispute that can be settled through exercise of judicial power. Controversy must actually exist, plantiff must have a substantial interest and standing to sue, case must be "ripe" for adjudication, other remedies have been exhausted, and court hearing case must possess jurisdiction. Question may be ruled "political" if court believes other branches of government could better handle the matter.

Kentucky and Virginia Resolutions (1799)   Concept which held that state may place itself between national government and one of its citizens. Each state was judge of constitutionality of actions of national government. Sometimes called "interposition" or "nullification." Theory was originally propounded by Thomas Jefferson and James Madison. Concept in contradiction to Article VI, Section 2 of the U.S. Constitution. (See **Nullification.**)

Libel   Defamatory written expression or oral expression on tape, radio, or TV which is untrue.

Malfeasance   Commission of an illegal act.

Mandamus Court order to official compelling performance of an act that is a legal duty. It is an emergency writ that is directed at ministerial duties rather than discretionary ones.

Mandate Judicial command usually directed by an appellate court to a lower court. Also means popular support for a political program.

Martial law Military government established over civilian population during emergency in which military decrees supersede civilian law and military tribunals replace civil courts.

Master-in-chancery Judicial officer appointed by courts of equity to hear testimony and make reports which, when approved by the presiding judge, become the decision of the court.

Military law Law enacted by Congress that governs the members of the armed forces and also established procedures for trial by courts-martial for alleged infractions. Authority: Article I, Section 8, Paragraph 14.

Ministerial act Act performed by explicit directions, usually by statute, by a subordinate official. Such acts must involve no discretion nor be quasi-judicial in character. Ministerial acts may be compelled to be performed through mandamus, while discretionary acts may not be so ordered unless a clear abuse of discretion can be demonstrated. (See **Mandamus.**)

Miranda rule Prior to any questioning in a criminal proceeding, the person must be warned that he has a right to remain silent, and that any statement he does make may be used against him, and that he has the right to the presence of an attorney, either one of his own or court appointed. If these rights are waived the act must be done "knowingly" and "intelligently."

Misfeasance Improper performance of a legal act.

Mitigation Does not constitute a justification or excuse of the offense, but facts which in fairness and mercy, may be considered as extenuating or decreasing the degree of moral culpability. Such circumstances may reduce or lessen the penalty imposed.

Moot case One not settled; undecided by judicial decisions.

Moratorium Suspension of all or certain legal remedies.

Naturalization Adoption by an alien of the rights and privileges of citizenship. Legal procedure whereby an alien becomes a citizen.

Navigable waters Encompasses all waters within the boundaries of the United States, which are, can be made to be, or contribute to the use as waterways for interstate or foreign commerce, such as rivers, streams, lakes, and inlets. The flow of any such waters cannot be impeded without the consent of the national government.

Necessary and Proper Clause Found in final paragraph of Article I, Section 8 of the U.S. Constitution. Congress being limited to its delegated powers is permitted to choose the means by which it executes its authority. Broad construction of this clause permits great flexibility of interpretation and reduces need for amendments. (See **Elastic clause,** and **Implied Powers.**)

Nullification Declaration by a state that a national law is null and void and therefore not binding on its citizens. Formulated by John C. Calhoun who argued our union was a compact between sovereign states, and the national government is not the final judge of its own powers. Thus, the right of secession was defended only to be finally determined by the Civil War. Rejection of concept based on Article VI, Section 2; the Supremacy Clause of the U.S. Constitution. (See **Kentucky and Virginia Resolutions (1799).**)

Obligation of contract Civil obligation to perform the terms of a legal contract but in the absence of specific performance as a remedy, then the party breaking the promise must pay damages.

Obscenity Conduct or material appealing to immoral tastes and lacking serious literary, artistic, political, or scientific value. Anything so found is not protected by the free speech guarantee of the First Amendment.

Omnibus bill Legislative act that incorporates various separate and distinct matters which necessitates the executive accepting some provision that he does not approve, or defeat the whole enactment; this because he does not have an "item" veto.

Open court One open to spectators who attend in an orderly and decent manner. This is in contra distinction to one closed to the public because of confidentiality as a recognized interest.

Open primary Direct voting system that permits a voter to choose the party primary in which he wishes to vote without disclosing his party affiliation, if any.

Open shop Industry which may or may not employ non-union workers. (See **Closed shop** and **Union Shop**.)

Opinion (advisory) Formal opinion by a court on question of law submitted by a legislative body or government official, but which has not yet become an actual case.

Opinion (concurring) Separate opinion in which one or more judges agree with the result reached by the majority, but disagree with the reasoning or arguments.

Opinion (court) Decision reached in a case by the court expounding the law and detailing the reasons upon which the decision is based.

Opinion (dissenting) Separate opinion in which particular members of court disagree with the majority position and expound their own view.

Opinion (per curiam) Concurred in by the entire court but without disclosing which judge was the author.

Original jurisdiction Authority of a court to hear a case for the first time. This jurisdiction is to be distinguished from "appellate," which hears cases on appeal from other courts or regulatory agencies.

Original package Legal doctrine that package prepared for interstate or foreign shipment becomes subject to state taxes and/or police power regulation after it is opened, divided, or has reached its final destination.

Pandering To pimp or cater to the lust of another or the promotion of obscenity.

Peonage Condition of enforced servitude. One condemned to labor for another against his will. (See **Servitude.**)

Perjury In criminal law the willful lying under oath or affirmation by a witness in a judicial proceeding.

Petit jury See **Jury (trial).**

Plea bargaining Process whereby the prosecutor and the accused in a criminal proceeding negotiate a settlement of the case by a plea of "guilty" by the accused to a lesser charge.

Plebiscite   Vote on an issue by the entire people entitled to franchise. Act is closely akin to a referendum.

Police power   Attribute of states and their subdivisions to impose restrictions upon private rights reasonably related to matters of health, safety, morals, and general welfare of the public.

Political question   Supreme Court doctrine that certain constitutional issues cannot be settled by the judicial branch. Generally invoked when question could be better resolved by either the executive or legislative branches.

Pre-emption   Federal doctrine relating to state legislation based upon the Supremacy Clause of the federal constitution, which deprives a state of jurisdiction where a federal act supersedes. (Article VI, Section 2).

Privileges and Immunities   U.S. Constitution uses this clause in Article IV, Section 2 and in the Fourteenth Amendment. The first refers to uniform non-political treatment of all citizens regardless of which state they are in; whereas the second use in the Fourteenth Amendment has not been completely defined. It is basically a limitation placed upon each state in matters of civil liberties in their relationship to U.S. citizens.

Probable cause   Necessary preliminary element in issuance of search, seizure, or arrest warrants that consists of existence of facts and circumstances within official's knowledge or trustworthy information that creates a reasonable belief that a crime is involved, to the satisfaction of an unbiased and objective magistrate, or later to be so determined by such a judge if the act has already occurred.

Procedural due process   Quoting Daniel Webster as procedure "which hears before it condemns, which proceeds upon inquiry, and renders judgment only after trial." Supreme Court considers that there has been a denial if any procedure is shocking to the conscience or that makes impossible a fair and enlightened system of justice. (See **Substantive due process**.)

Quartering of soldiers   Prohibition found in Third Amendment against housing soldiers in private homes during times of peace without the consent of the owner. In wartime quartering may be done under conditions prescribed by Law.

Rationale   Reasoning of the Court as the explanation for the decision it reached.

Reapportionment   New allocation of legislative seats based on census statistics. In the national House of Representatives there are 435 seats to be distributed among the fifty states. As population shifts so does individual state's allocation.

Recess   Temporary adjournment of a trial or a legislative session after it has started. If the delay is substantial, it is called a continuance. If a terminal time has been reached, it is termed an adjournment and if no date has been set for a re-opening, it is "sine die."

Recidivist   A habitual criminal or sometimes called an incorrigible criminal. One who is frequently occupied with crime.

Released time   The practice by which public school children can be dismissed from classes during the school day to attend some religious exercise.

Rendition   Return by a state of a fugitive from justice upon the demand of the executive authority of the state in which the crime was committed. This is an obligation imposed by Article IV of the U.S. Constitution and is enforceable only as a moral duty or comity. The term extradition is properly used when the return of the fugitive is sought between two nations pursuant to a treaty.

Resulting powers Powers of the national government derived from combination of delegated or implied powers; thus, powers that result from a number of other powers, rather than inferred from a single delegated or implied power.

Retroactive law Includes both retrospective and *ex post facto,* the former technically applying only to civil law and the latter to criminal or penal law. The former may be valid but the latter *(ex post facto)* is constitutionally prohibited under the U.S. Constitution.

Reversible error One substantially affecting appellant's legal rights and, if uncorrected, would result in an injustice occurring that justifies the reversing of a judgment handed down by a lower court. This term is synonymous with that of "prejudicial error" and is distinguishable from "harmless error."

Rider (bill) Provision which is unlikely to pass on its own merits is added to an important bill so that it will "ride" through the legislative process and become the law if the legislation to which it is attached passes. It should be noted that the President does not have "item" veto. (See **Omnibus bill.**)

Rule of reason Supreme Court holding (1910 in Standard Oil Case) that not every combination in restraint of trade is illegal but only those unreasonably so.

Scienter Guilty knowledge used in pleadings and signifies that a crime or tort was done knowingly, understandably, and designedly. Term is synonymous with criminal plea of premeditation.

Search and seizure   Must be reasonable and based on "probable cause." Usually based on warrant, but some exceptions may occur.

Search warrant   Order issued by a judge to law enforcement officers to conduct a search of specified places for specified things and bring them before the court. Issuance order is based upon "probable cause" supported by sworn allegations and things searched for and seized must be particularly described.

Sedition   Illegal action that tends to cause the disruption and overthrow of the government. An insurrectionary movement tending toward treason but lacking an overt act or direct and open violence.

Self-incrimination   Fifth Amendment provides that no person shall be compelled in any criminal case to be a witness against himself. This guarantee has been extended to legislative committees and executives agencies. It has not been extended to protect another person or to save oneself from shame or disgrace. Persons who are beyond criminal prosecution by reason of a grant of immunity or pardon may not refuse to testify.

Separate but equal doctrine   From 1896 to 1955 the Supreme Court upheld racial segregation if each race were provided with equal facilities. In the latter year the Court, after a series of weakening decisions, finally declared that "separate educational facilities are inherently unequal." For all practical purposes this separate but equal doctrine is now repudiated and constitutes a denial of "equal protection of the law" as guaranteed in the Fourteenth Amendment.

Separation of church and state   Basic principle set forth in the First Amendment declaring government must be neutral and neither advance nor retard religion. Two facets of this issue are involved: (a) no establishment of religion, and (b) no prohibition of the free exercise of religion. The permissible limitations of these issues are highly controversial and unresolved. (See **Establishment Clause**.)

Separation of powers Major principle of U.S. government in which power is divided into three branches: (a) legislative, (b) judicial, and (c) executive. Each is independent of the others but the separation is not complete. Legislative and executive are political, but the judicial is less so. Thus, no single branch can make, interpret, and enforce the law.

Servitude Peonage or slavery. The Thirteenth Amendment prohibits its existence in the U.S. except as punishment for a crime. Forcing the fulfillment of a contract, to support a child, military or jury service, or to pay alimony is not totally banned nor are laws that force service where public safety is jeopardized. Imprisonment or forced labor to pay a debt is, however. (See **Involuntary servitude,** and **Peonage**.)

Solicitor-general Official in the U.S. Department of Justice who conducts and argues cases on behalf of the government before the Supreme Court. His approval is required before any appeal may be taken on behalf of the federal government to any appellate court.

Standing to sue Legal rights of a person or group to challenge a judicial decision or conduct of another in a court, especially in regard to government conduct. Their status as litigants is essential to the necessary requirement that a controversy exists. Thus, standing-to-sue is dependent on the existence and the degree of the interest affected by the adverse relationships and the outcome of the trial.

Subpoena Two types: (a) to compel attendance at a judicial hearing, some administrative agency hearings, or legislative inquiry, and (b) *duces tecum,* to bring relevant papers to such a meeting. Failure to respond to such a command may result in a contempt charge being brought.

Substantive rights   Those essential for personal liberty. Generally includes those listed in First and Fourteenth Amendments to the U.S. Constitution. Those usually listed are freedoms of speech, press, religion, assembly, petition, and equal protection of the law. These rights are to be distinguished from procedural, which are protected by due process and fair trial concepts and are concerned with the manner by which the substantive rights are protected. (See **Procedural due process.**)

Suffrage   Right or privilege of casting a vote at public election—or participating meaningfully in the political process.

Summons   Writ directed to the sheriff or other proper officer requiring him to notify the person named that an action has been commenced against him in the court whence the writ issues, and that he is required to appear, on the day named, and answer the complaint in such an action.

Taft-Hartley   (Labor-Management Relations Act of 1947) Major revision of Wagner Act (1935), which places some limitations on internal union activities and enhances the power of individual workers. Passage of this law gave impetus to AFL-CIO merger in 1955.

Taxation (intergovernmental immunity)   Exemption of state and national governmental agencies and property from taxation by each other. This principle is subject to national supremacy, Article VI, Clause II.

Tort   Any private or civil wrong or injury, except for breach of contract, resulting from a failure to peform a legal duty, which causes an injury to another.

Trial May be either civil or criminal, held in accordance with the law of the land before a judge who has jurisdiction. Trial must be public, conducted fairly before an impartial magistrate and, in the case of criminal trials, started without an unreasonable delay.

True bill Accusation returned by a Grand Jury in which they indict (accuse) the individual investigated. Fifth Amendment of the U.S. Constitution requires that this be done for any capital or infamous crime. Many states have replaced this procedure by substituting an information that permits a prosecutor alone to bring charges.

Uniform Code of Military Justice Law enacted by Congress in 1950 that governs the conduct of enlisted men and officers of the U.S. armed forces.

Union shop Labor bargaining unit in which non-union members must join union within a prescribed period after employment. (See **Closed shop,** and **Open shop.**)

United States code Compilation of U.S. laws in force and classified by subject matter. Annual supplements are made and entire code is revised every six years. Resolutions adopted by Congress are not considered statutes and are therefore not included.

Waiver Intentional and voluntary giving up of some known right. It may be either express or inferred from circumstances but courts must use every reasonable presumption against the loss of any constitutional right. Abandonment of any right must be an intelligent one and a hearing should be held with explicit findings of fact supporting the waiver recorded.

War Powers Authority either expressly, impliedly, or inherently found in the national government to protect our nation from its enemies. Such power is vested in Congress and the President but the exercise by them is always subject to judicial scrutiny. Control over the domestic economy has now been accepted as a necessary part of these War Powers.

Warrants   Written order directing the arrest of a person involved in a crime or the search of specified property for either contraband or evidence. Both warrants are based upon a showing of probable cause before an impartial magistrate.

White primaries   Attempts by several states to exclude Negroes from voting by leaving determination of primary qualifications to political party acting as a private organization. This objective to be attained was based on the argument that political parties were private clubs and therefore discrimination was permissible. Such attempts have all been found to be unconstitutional.

Wire-tapping   Use of listening devices to intercept and record private messages electronically. Improper interception would involve the exclusionary rule in a criminal trial and a suit for the invasion of privacy in a civil suit. Federal law and state law are not in agreement and the entire area is highly controversial and in a state of flux. Permissible "wire-tapping" includes issuance of a warrant by a qualified judge.

Writs   Order issued by a court either ordering the performance of an act or prohibiting the act. Orderly progress of judicial functions is largely dependent on writs and essential to the enforcement of their decisions. (See **Injunctions.**)

FOREIGN PHRASES

A fortiori With stronger reason. Logical argument that because one fact exists, another that is included within it, must also exist.

Amicus curiae Friend of the court. Person or organization who has no right to appear in court and is not a party to the suit, but who is allowed to introduce arguments, authority, or evidence to protect their interest.

Certiorari To be informed of; to be made certain. Proceeding for reexamination of a lower tribunal's decision in order for an appellate court to ascertain whether an error has occurred in the original trial. Writ is directed at the lower tribunal to send a record of the proceedings to the appellate court.

De facto In fact; actually; in reality. Often used to qualify a legal term and is contrasted with "de jure." Office, position, and/or status exist under some color of right and are successfully maintained until over-turned by legal process.

De jure By right; by justice; lawful; legitimate. Term connotes "as a matter of law" while de facto connotes "as a matter of conduct or practice not founded upon law."

Duces tecum Bring with you. Writ (subpoena is most commonly used with this term) requiring party summoned to appear at hearing with certain documents or evidence.

En banc In the bench; (by full court). Many appellate courts sit with three or more judges from among a larger number, but sometimes either by their own motion or that of the litigant the court will consider the matter by the full court. A notation to this effect generally heads or precedes the opinion.

Ex parte On one side only; by or for one party. Name following this type of case if that of the party upon whose application the case is heard. Process is non-adversarial and usually deals with an injunction, bankruptcy, or other single party court orders. (As in Ex Parte Milligan, 4 Wall. 2, (1866).)

Ex post facto After the fact. Law passed after the occurrence of a fact or commission of an act which retrospectively changes the legal consequences of such a fact or deed. In the United States, the term is limited to those laws that may impose punishment, penalties, or forfeitures.

Habeas corpus You have the body. Object of writ is to bring a party in custody into open court before a judge; not to determine the person's guilt or innocence, but only to ascertain whether the prisoner is restrained of his liberty without due process.

In camera In the chambers. Judicial act performed by a judge who is not acting in an open court. If the court is not in session or the act occurs elsewhere, the term "in chambers" may be used to indicate the act was official but not public.

In loco parentis In the place of a parent. If used in a judicial proceeding the relationship is non-adversarial. If used to identify a personal or institutional relationship the claimant to the status may assume parental rights and must assume parental duties and responsibilities.

In re In the matter of; concerning. Proceeding in non-adversary matter in which there is some material thing involved.

It is sometimes used in manner similar to an ex parte proceeding where one party makes an application on his own behalf.

Jus sanguinis   Right of blood; law of the blood. Legal principle by which citizenship is determined by parentage rather than by place of birth.

Jus soli   Law of the soil. Basic rule under which American citizenship is determined by place of birth rather than by parentage.

Mandamus   We command. Writ issued by a court to compel performance of an act. It may be issued to an individual or corporation as well as to a public official if the act is to compel the performance of a ministerial duty which the official must perform. A discretionary act will not be mandated. Failure to obey the court order is contempt of court.

Nunc pro tunc   Now For Then. Acts allowed to be done after the time when they should have been with the same effect as if performed at the proper time. Purpose is not to supply omitted action but to supply omission in record of action really performed but omitted through inadvertence or mistake.

Obiter dictum   Otherwise said. Passing or incidental statements made in a judicial opinion which are unnecessary to the disposition of the case. Many are generalities with no actual bearing on issues involved. Equivalent in meaning to obiter dicta or dictum.

Per curiam   By the court. An opinion by the whole court as distinguished from one written by one judge. Sometimes it denotes an opinion written by the chief justice or presiding judge.

Posse comitatus   Power or force of the county. The population of a county which the sheriff may summon and mobilize to keep the peace or make an arrest for a felony. Mode is immaterial so long as the object is to require assistance.

Prima facie   At first sight; on the first appearance; on the face of it; so far as can be judged by the first disclosure; presumably; a fact presumed to be true unless disproved by some evidence to the contrary.

Quid pro quo   What for what. The giving or exchange of one valuable thing for another. In a contract the concept is essential for its enforceability; i.e. consideration.

Quo warranto   By what authority. Civil writ which tests the legal right of a company to operate a business or of a public official to discharge duties of the office which may or may not have been usurped.

Res judicata   A matter adjudged; a thing judicially decided; a matter settled by a court of competent jurisdiction; with adherence to due process and without error; finally decided. Term is synonymous with Res adjudicata.

Seriatim   In due order; successively; in order; in succession; individually; one by one; separately; severally. Court determination in which each judge or justice writes a separate opinion which may or may not agree in whole or in part with his brethren's opinions.

Stare decisis   To abide by, or adhere to, decided cases. A policy in which the court decides to stand by precedent and not to disturb a settled point of law. Doctrine that when a court has once laid down a principle of law as applicable to a certain state of facts, it will adhere to that principle and apply it to all future cases where facts are substantially the same.

Voir dire   To speak the truth. Prospective examination by the court or attorneys of prospective jurors to determine their qualification for jury service. Term also used where initial hearing on some issue of law or fact is held out of the presence and hearing of the jury.

ALPHABETICAL LIST OF CASES CITED

Abington v. Schempp, 374 U.S. 203 (1963)
Ableman v. Booth, 21 Howard 506 (1859)
Abrams v. United States, 250 U.S. 616 (1919)
Adamson v. California, 332 U.S. 46 (1947)
Adkins v. Children's Hospital, 261 U.S. 525 (1923)
Akron v. Adkins Ctr. for Reproductive Health, 462 U.S. 416 (1983)
American Communications Association v. Douds, 339 U.S. 382 (1950)
American Tobacco Co. v. Patterson, 71 L.Ed.2d 748 (1982)
Ashawanda v. Tennessee Valley Authority, 297 U.S. 288 (1936)

Bailey v. Drexel Furniture, 259 U.S. 20 (1922)
Baker v. Carr, 369 U.S. 186 (1962)
Baldrige v. Shapiro, 71 L.Ed.2d 199 (1982)
Baldwin v. G.A.F. Seelig, 294 U.S. 511 (1935)
Barron v. Baltimore, 7 Peters 243 (1833)
Board of Directors Rotary International v. Duarte, 95 L.Ed.2d 474 (1987)
Bowers v. Hardwick, 92 L.Ed.2d 140 (1986)
Bowsher v. Synar, 92 L.Ed.2d 583 (1986)
Branti v. Finkel, 445 U.S. 507 (1980)
Branzburg v. Hayes, 408 U.S. 205 (1972)
Bridges v. California, 314 U.S. 252 (1941)
Brown v. Board of Education of Topeka, 347 U.S. 483 (1954)
Brown v. Maryland, 12 Wheaton 419 (1827)
Buck v. Bell, 274 U.S. 200 (1927)
Buckley v. Valeo, 424 U.S. 1 (1976)
Bunting v. Oregon, 243 U.S. 426 (1917)
Burstyn v. Wilson, 343 U.S. 495 (1952)

Calder v. Bull, 3 Dallas 386 (1798)
California v. Ciraolo, 90 L.Ed.2d 210 (1986)
California v. Greenwood, 100 L.Ed.2d 30 (1988)

Cantwell v. Connecticut, 310 U.S. 296 (1940)

Carey v. Brown, 447 U.S. 455 (1980)

Chambers v. Florida, 309 U.S. 227 (1940)

Champion v. Ames, 188 U.S. 321 (1903)

Chandler & Granger v. Florida, 449 U.S. 560 (1981)

Charles River Bridge v. Warren Bridge, 11 Peter 420 (1837)

Child Labor Case (Hammer v. Dagenhart), 247 U.S. 251 (1918)
    (Hammer)

Chimel v. California, 395 U.S. 752 (1969)

City of Lakewood v. Plain Dealer Publishing, 100 L.Ed.2d 771 (1988)

Civil Rights Cases, 109 U.S. 3 (1883)

Cohens v. Virginia, 6 Wheaton 264 (1821)

Coleman v. Miller, 307 U.S. 433 (1939)

Collector v. Day, 11 Wallace 113 (1871)

Committee for Public Education and Religious Liberty v. Nyquist,
    413 U.S. 756 (1973)

Committee for Public Education and Religious Liberty v. Regan, 444
    U.S. 646 (1980)

Commonwealth of Massachusetts v. Mellon, 262 U.S. 447 (1923)

Cooley v. The Board of Wardens of the Port of Philadelphia, 12
    Howard 299 (1851)

Cousins v. Wigoda, 419 U.S. 477 (1975)

Cox v. New Hampshire, 312 U.S. 569 (1941)

Coyle v. Smith, 221 U.S. 559 (1911)

Dames and Moore v. Regan, 453 U.S. 654 (1981)

Dartmouth College v. Woodward, 4 Wheaton 518 (1819)

Davidson v. New Orleans, 96 U.S. 97 (1878)

In re Debs, 158 U.S. 564 (1895)

De Jonge v. Oregon, 299 U.S. 353 (1932)

Democratic Party of the United States v. La Follette, 450 U.S. 107
    (1981)

Dennis v. United States, 341 U.S. 494 (1951)

Dillon v. Gloss, 256 U.S. 368 (1921)

Duncan v. Kahanamoku, 327 U.S. 403 (1946)

Duncan v. Louisiana, 391 U.S. 145 (1968)

Dunn v. Blumstein, 405 U.S. 330 (1972)

Duren v. Missouri, 439 U.S. 357 (1979)

Hammer v. Dagenhart, 247 U.S. 251 (1918)
Hampton v. Mow Sun Wong, 426 U.S. 88 (1976)
J. W. Hampton, Jr. & Co. v. United States, 276 U.S. 394 (1928)
Harris v. McRae, 448 U.S. 297 (1980)
Hawke v. Smith, 253 U.S. 221 (1920)
Hazelwood School Dist. v. Kulmeier, 98 L.Ed.2d 592 (1988)
Heart of Atlanta Motel Inc. v. United States, 379 U.S. 241 (1964)
Head Money Cases, 112 U.S. 580; (1884)
Helvering v. Davis, 301 U.S. 619 (1937)
Herbert v. Lando, 441 U.S. 153 (1979)
Hicklin v. Orbeck, 437 U.S. 518 (1978)
Hishon v. King & Spaulding, 467 U.S. 69 (1984)
H.L. v. Matheson, 450 U.S. 398 (1981)
Holden v. Hardy, 169 U.S. 366 (1898)
Hollingsworth v. Virginia, 3 Dallas 378 (1798)
Home Building & Loan Association v. Blaidsell, 290 U.S. 398 (1934)
Houston, E. & W Texas Ry Co. v. United States, 234 U.S. 342 (1914)
Hurtado v. California, 110 U.S. 516 (1884)
Hustler Magazine v. Falwell, 99 L.Ed.2d 41 (1988)

Illinois v. Allen, 397 U.S. 337 (1970)
INS v. Chadha, 462 U.S. 919 (1983)

Jencks v. United States, 353 U.S. 657 (1957)
Jones v. Alfred H. Mayer Co., 392 U.S. 409 (1968)
Juilliard v. Greenman, 10 U.S. 421 (1884)

Katz v. United States, 389 U.S. 347 (1957)
Kentucky Whip and Collar Co. v. Illinois Central R.R. Co., 299 U.S.
    334 (1937)
Keyishian v. Board of Regents, 385 U.S. 589 (1967)
Korematsu v. United States, 323 U.S. 214 (1944)
Kovacs v. Cooper, 336 U.S. 77 (1949)

Legal Tender Cases, 121 Wallace 457 (1871)
Leisy v. Hardin, 1315 U.S. 100 (1890)
Ex Parte Albert Levitt, 302 U.S. 633 (1937)

Ybarra v. Illinois, 444 U.S. 85 (1979)
Youngstown Sheet & Tube Co. v. Sawyer, 343 U.S. 579 (1952)

Zablocki v. Redhail, 434 U.S. 374 (1978)
Ziffrin v. Reeves, 308 U.S. 132 (1939)
Zorach v. Clauson, 343 U.S. 306 (1952)
Zurcher v. Stanford Dailey, 436 U.S. 547 (1978)

INDEX